"As well as providing a well-informed and r[...]
debate over Islamic origins, *The Qur'an in Context* offers a substantial, theologically serious and at points provocative discussion on the Qur'an in its interface with the Bible and the core themes of the Christian faith. This lucid and thought-provoking study makes a significant contribution from an Evangelical and Reformed perspective to the wider field of Christian engagement with the scripture at the heart of Islam."
David Marshall, Duke Divinity School

"Demonstrating a familiarity with contemporary scholarship and respect for Muslim sensitivities, Mark Anderson describes the context in which the Qur'an arose and how it both reflected and challenged that world. While comparing and contrasting Qur'anic and biblical theology and the character of Jesus in the Qur'an and the Bible, he shows how close and how far apart they are. This study provides an excellent foundation for an informed and sensitive discussion with Muslims."
J. Dudley Woodberry, dean emeritus and senior professor of Islamic studies,
Fuller Theological Seminary

"Mark Anderson has produced an excellent, incisive, well-researched book highlighting similarities and distinctives between the Qur'an and the Bible. His research is impeccable and his conclusions will stand the test of scholarly investigation. Anderson avoids the pitfalls of inflammatory us-them polemics. He enters into the realities of the Muslim worldview by exploring the seventh-century context of the Qur'an, on which Muslim belief and behavior is built. Without reservation, I commend Anderson's work to all who desire to move beyond 'breaking news' and sensationalism and come to grips with the inside story of who Muslims really are."
Phil Parshall, SIM USA

The
Qur'an
in CONTEXT

A CHRISTIAN
EXPLORATION

Mark Robert Anderson

An imprint of InterVarsity Press
Downers Grove, Illinois

InterVarsity Press
P.O. Box 1400, Downers Grove, IL 60515-1426
ivpress.com
email@ivpress.com

InterVarsity Press® is the book-publishing division of InterVarsity Christian Fellowship/USA®, a movement of students and faculty active on campus at hundreds of universities, colleges and schools of nursing in the United States of America, and a member movement of the International Fellowship of Evangelical Students. For information about local and regional activities, visit intervarsity.org.

Scripture quotations, unless otherwise noted, are from the New Revised Standard Version of the Bible, copyright 1989 by the Division of Christian Education of the National Council of the Churches of Christ in the USA. Used by permission. All rights reserved.

Cover design: David Fassett
Interior design: Daniel van Loon
Images: FransDekkers/iStockphoto

ISBN 978-0-8308-5142-3 (print)
ISBN 978-0-8308-9343-0 (digital)

Printed in the United States of America ∞

Library of Congress Cataloging-in-Publication Data
A catalog record for this book is available from the Library of Congress.

P 25 24 23 22 21 20 19 18 17 16 15 14 13 12 11 10 9 8 7 6 5 4 3 2 1

Y 38 37 36 35 34 33 32 31 30 29 28 27 26 25 24 23 22 21 20 19 18 17 16

To the memory of

CHARLES J. ADAMS

1924–2011

and

HARVIE M. CONN

1933–1999

without whose inspiration and guidance
this book would not have been written

Truth has no special time of its own.
Its hour is now, always, and indeed then most truly
when it seems most unsuitable to actual circumstances.

ALBERT SCHWEITZER

Out beyond ideas of wrongdoing and rightdoing
there is a field. I'll meet you there.

JALAL AL-DIN RUMI

Contents

Preface   xi

Acknowledgments   xv

Maps: The Late Antique Middle East   xvii

Early Manuscript   xix

1 Approaching the Qur'an   1

PART I QUR'ANIC CONTEXT

2 Muhammad and the Origins of Islam   15

3 Coming to Terms with Muhammad's World   27

4 Reading the Qur'an in Its Muhammadan Context   35

PART II QUR'ANIC WORLDVIEW

5 God's Immanence and Transcendence   53

6 God's Justice and Mercy   71

7 Adam in Stereoscopic Vision   83

8 Measuring Adam's Fall   97

9 Divine Reprieve   113

10 Sin and Salvation in a World of Us Against Them   119

11 Prophets, Scriptures, Revelation   141

12 Qur'anic Spirituality's Devotional and Social Dimensions   163

13 Qur'anic Spirituality's Political Dimension   183

PART III QUR'ANIC JESUS

14 Jesus' Origins and Person   207

15 Jesus' Words and Works   223

16 Jesus' Death and Beyond   239

17 Jesus' Community and Scripture   257

PART IV CHRISTIAN RESPONSE

18 An Arabic Qur'an for the Arab People   281

19 Could the Qur'an Be the Bible's Sequel?   289

20 The Bible and the Qur'an: So Close, Yet So Far   305

Glossary   325

Author Index   329

Subject Index   331

Scripture Index   337

Preface

A book such as this—intended for both students and scholars as well as an interested lay public—demands writing that is thorough and precise while still being broadly accessible. To that end I have omitted all but essential diacritical marks in my transcriptions of Arabic. This should make things easier for non-Arabists without hindering Arabists. Like the Arabic they represent, my transcriptions have no uppercase letters except in the word *Allah* and in names of persons, places and so on. English loanwords from Arabic (hadith, jihad, sharia, sura, etc.) do not appear in italics, but they are listed in the glossary along with all the other Arabic terms used. The glossary and maps should assist readers unfamiliar with Muhammad's world. Translations from the Qur'an are my own unless otherwise noted. Full citations of Qur'an translations are given on the first occasion, after which I cite them simply by the translator's name. All quotations of the Bible are from the New Revised Standard Version unless otherwise noted. I abbreviate *Encyclopaedia of Islam* as *EI²* and *Encyclopaedia of the Qur'ān* as *EQ*.[1] Since I write specifically for non-Muslims, I give dates only according to the Western calendar.

---

[1]Their bibliographical data are as follows: *Encyclopaedia of Islam*, 2nd ed., ed. P. Bearman, Th. Bianquis, C. E. Bosworth, E. van Donzel and W. P. Heinrichs, 13 vols. (Leiden: J. Brill, 1960–2004); *Encyclopaedia of the Qur'ān*, ed. Jane Dammen McAuliffe, 6 vols. (Leiden: Brill, 2001–2006).

Regardless of the target audience, anyone writing about Islam must consider how Muslims will hear what is said. In that respect, I should explain my use of the term "the qur'anic author." Most Western scholars now limit themselves to personifications of the Muslim scripture, such as "the Qur'an says" or "in the mind of the Qur'an," in order to avoid offending Muslims, who believe the Qur'an is authored by God alone. Why, then, when I value courtesy and intend no offense, do I speak of the qur'anic author? My purpose is simply to connect the text of the Qur'an with its first hearers. Referring to the Muslim scripture as if it had no author makes it much harder to recognize the choices that made it speak so powerfully to its original audience. A scripture is best understood only when we consider those choices in relation to the full palette of possible options. This is vital to my analysis, since I view the Qur'an as authentic and effective communication.[2]

On hearing that I was writing this book, various individuals offered advice on how to approach my task. As it happened, some of the advice was diametrically opposite, with some people urging me to stress points of agreement between the Bible and Qur'an, and others to focus on points of difference. These contrary concerns puzzled and troubled me since they seemed equally partial, unbalanced and controlling. Our two scriptures bear both clear similarities and differences. What, I wondered, could possibly justify my editing either one out or even just downplaying one of them? Since the Qur'an has its own literary integrity as a scripture, does not faithful scholarship rather respect that integrity and allow it to speak for itself? Focusing on either similarity or difference without acknowledging the other seems subversive to me. Hence I have avoided both alternatives, viewing them as equally driven by fear—namely, the fear that a holistic approach to the Qur'an is simply unsuited to our current situation. With Schweitzer, I protest that Truth's hour is now, always.

Between us Christians and Muslims make up more than 50 percent of the world's population, with that number projected to exceed 60 percent by 2050.[3] I believe we will all pay an exorbitant toll if we do not put heart and soul into seeking a peaceable relationship. Since both our communities are founded

---

[2]Even an eternal scripture implies such choice: it would simply stand outside of time (see further 2n5 below).

[3]Pew Research Center, "The Future of World Religions: Population Growth Projections, 2010–2050," April 2, 2015, www.pewforum.org/2015/04/02/religious-projections-2010-2050.

on a sacred text, it is urgent that we listen carefully to each other's scripture. To be understood, we must seek first to understand. And that includes understanding points of disagreement, some of which are essential to who we are. But to hear our partners in dialogue truly, we must also meet them in Rumi's judgment-free field, as I have sought to do in this study. I leave it to you, my reader, to decide how well I have succeeded in that respect.

Acknowledgments

I picture my book like a river whose broad mouth gives no indication that it has been fed by innumerable streams and enriched by the earth across which it has so freely flowed. With its waters irretrievably intermingled, it appears self-sufficient. But in fact, a river is in one sense all debt. For though it clearly has a life of its own, it nevertheless carries nothing it did not receive. Likewise, this book would not be what it is without a host of people—scholars, family, friends and others. While I cannot possibly acknowledge them all, I must at least name a few.

Though I know only a handful of them personally, I am very conscious of the many scholars who have contributed to this book. My debt to Robert Hoyland—for his work on pre-Islamic Arabia, early non-Muslim sources and the Islamic origins narrative—will be abundantly evident to readers. Jean Bottéro, Patricia Crone, Reuven Firestone, Greg Fisher and Sidney Griffith are among the many others who have contributed vitally to my understanding of Muhammad's world. Mahmoud Ayoub, Rick Brown, Fred Donner, Yohanan Friedmann, William Graham, Toshihiko Izutsu, John Kaltner, Daniel Madigan, David Marshall, Angelika Neuwirth, Gordon Nickel, Iain Provan and Gabriel Reynolds are among those who have most strengthened my grasp of the Qur'an. For key biblical insights, I am also grateful to Andy Crouch, John Goldingay, Vern Poythress, Lamin Saneh, John Stackhouse and N. T. Wright. Some of these scholars are also among the many who graciously answered queries I put to them during the course of my writing.

Astute criticisms of the master's thesis from which this book grew were offered by Christopher Melchert and Andrew Rippin. My good friend Andy coupled his incisive criticism of every section of the book (scrutinizing multiple revisions of some parts!) with unfailing enthusiasm for my work, helping to energize it from start to finish. To say that his countless contributions have greatly improved the book is a huge understatement. My special thanks go to him and his family. Two other friends, Neil and Kevin, also read key parts of the manuscript and offered helpful suggestions. But despite all the help I have received, it goes without saying that I alone am responsible for any errors remaining.

I cannot begin to say how grateful I am to my dear wife, Cathy, for her steadfast love and support throughout this long process. This is her book no less than mine. Our four children offered continual encouragement, as did my four siblings. I am especially thankful to my mother, whose prayers, I believe, brought this book to completion, even though she unfortunately did not live to hold it in her hands. Jim Houston's friendship in the latter stages of this book has been a real inspiration and help. Also, I am grateful to Roger and Alayne, Joan and Keith, Sid and Lyn, and Sally for allowing me temporarily to turn their home or cottage into a writing den, without which I might never have found my way through the wilds of Muhammad's world (part one)! Friends Tom and Shirley, Marsha and Lane, Rick and Linda, the good folk at Rivendell and all my dear friends at L'Arche have generously supported this project in other ways. I am also grateful to the University of British Columbia and Regent College libraries and especially Vancouver Public Library's interlibrary loans department. I am especially indebted to Tom Wright for his invaluable help, affording me the chance to offer my book to IVP and giving me the courage to see it through to completion. Last but not least, my editor, Dan Reid, has been every writer's dream. For his wisdom, encouragement, gentleness (writers can be thin skinned!) and patience, I am deeply grateful. Neither do I take the rest of the team at IVP for granted: I have only praise for all of their dealings with me.

Maps

The Middle East in 602 CE. Before the War of 602–628, the boundary between the empires (as shown here) had remained fairly stable for centuries, with territory captured by one empire being recovered by its rival soon afterward. But owing to an ongoing civil war in the Byzantine realm, early military successes of Khusrau II seemingly raised the prospect of a Sasanian triumph that would end their centuries-old rivalry once and for all. Reports of this war's devastation preceded Muhammad's prophetic career and continued through most of its duration, thus providing the backdrop to most of the qur'anic recitations. (Please note: The absence of both a Byzantine border on Arabia's northwestern edge and a Sasanian border on Arabia's northeastern edge indicates that the boundaries were not clearly fixed there.)

The Middle East in 622 CE. Having already taken Armenia, Syria and Palestine, the Sasanians penetrated Anatolia to Chalcedon in 615, but most likely withdrew to Anatolia's eastern edge in 616. By 619 they had occupied Egypt, the Byzantines'"breadbasket." At the time of the *hijra* (622), Heraclius was raising an army for his counteroffensive. But the Persians would yet lay siege to Constantinople itself before Heraclius was finally able to defeat his Persian nemesis and restore equilibrium between the empires in 628. Four years later Muslim armies swept out of Arabia to conquer the Middle East. (Please note: The absence of a Sasanian border on both Arabia's north-western and northeastern edges indicates that the boundaries were not clearly fixed there.)

Early Manuscript

The world's oldest Qur'an Manuscript (Mingana 1572a). Written in an early form of Hijazi script, this manuscript's two parchment leaves contain parts of Suras 18 to 20. Radiocarbon analysis conducted at Oxford University has dated its parchment to the period between 568 and 645 CE with 95.4% accuracy. This means the manuscript was likely produced during Muhammad's lifetime or the first two decades after his death in 632. Till its discovery in the University of Birmingham's Mingana Collection in 2015, the manuscript had been misbound with leaves of a Hijazi script Qur'an from the late seventh century.

One

Approaching *the* Qur'an

*A*ny scripture with well over a billion believers on an increasingly small planet demands to be read by the rest of us. Even more, the Qur'an demands to be read by Christians, since it claims to complete our Bible and even improve on it. But most non-Muslims get no more than a few pages into the Qur'an before finding themselves hopelessly lost. In fact, Westerners who make it through all 286 verses of the Qur'an's second chapter, or *sura*, deserve a pat on the back, because it is anything but reader friendly to us a world away and well over a millennium removed in time.

Our first challenge then is simply to understand the Qur'an, which is not "a written, premeditated corpus of prophetical sayings," but rather "the transcript of an orally performed, open-ended drama."[1] The Qur'an's every word is centered in Muhammad's struggle for "God's Cause"[2] in his native Arabia. As Angelika Neuwirth says, we must read the Muslim scripture as a series of texts growing out of "lively scenes from the emergence of a community" under

---

[1] Angelika Neuwirth, "The 'Late Antique Qur'an': Jewish-Christian Liturgy, Hellenic Rhetoric and Arabic Language" (lecture, Institute for Advanced Studies, Princeton University, Princeton, NJ, June 3, 2009), www.yovisto.com/video/11805. Neuwirth uses *drama* here in the sense of a publicly recited monologue interacting with its audience.

[2] Literally "in God's path" (*fi sabil Allah*), this term refers to the God-ordained course of action for not just individuals but also God's community on earth within the context of the war of good against evil, faith against unbelief. The Qur'an calls humankind to join God in his cause.

its prophet.[3] Examples of her point abound. For example, Sura 93 urges Muhammad not to give up but to believe God will provide for him. By contrast, Q 8:67-71 speaks of the prophet's having enslaved captives taken in battle and addresses the issue of his followers' love of booty. We thus see that at one point Muhammad struggled to endure in faith, and at another he and his community, or *umma*, engaged in warfare and believed booty and slavery were regulated by divine command. In that sense the Qur'an represents an immense cache of historical data.

But despite the centrality of Muhammad's story to its recitations, they include only glimmers of it. For while the Qur'an pays considerable attention to narratives from the past, it is quite averse to supplying current narrative—and that despite the fact that Muhammad's recitations came to him in the midst of some very stormy events. Instead of recounting those events, the Qur'an "merely refers to them; and in doing so, it has a tendency not to name names."[4] The qur'anic author[5] often speaks as "I" or "we" or alternates between the two (e.g., Q 90:1-4) and addresses "you" in singular and plural (e.g., Q 94:1-4) but without identifying anyone. That leaves us piecing together the story behind the recitations as best we can from the mention of an unnamed town or other fragmentary details. For example, the Qur'an speaks of a "sacred precinct" (Q 5:1) and Christians (*nasara*). But which sacred precinct, and what kind of Christians?

These and a host of other questions find their answer only in the Qur'an's metahistory or narrative context. Being well known to those who first heard its recitations, however, most of that background information is left unstated, making the Qur'an singularly unhelpful as a historical source when

---

[3] Angelika Neuwirth, "Qur'an and History—A Disputed Relationship: Some Reflections on Qur'anic History and History in the Qur'an," *Journal of Qur'anic Studies* 5 (2003): 6.
[4] Michael Cook, *Muhammad* (Oxford: Oxford University Press, 1983), 69.
[5] Muslims emphatically consider the notion that Muhammad was the author of the Qur'an blasphemous. I do not equate the two here, leaving the qur'anic author unnamed instead. However, I fear even this may jar many Muslims. For deeming the Qur'an to be the word of God *alone*, they so exalt their scripture that they do not think of it in terms of authorship at all, which implies authorial choice. But supposing they are right to conceive of the Qur'an as uncreated, they must still acknowledge that its every word was chosen to meet the particular needs of its seventh-century audience, even if those choices were made by God in eternity past. In Christian theology, by contrast, human and divine authorship are not mutually exclusive categories. That is, for me to name David as the author of a psalm does not deny its divine inspiration, which is another matter entirely. Nevertheless, I do not address the question of qur'anic authorship here but rather leave readers to draw their own conclusions from the data presented.

taken on its own. Neither are its suras ordered chronologically.[6] All this makes the Qur'an "an extremely enigmatic and allusive document,"[7] one requiring readers to bring to the text some knowledge of Muhammad's historical context and prophetic career.

The Qur'an and Its Interpretation

According to the Qur'an, God, its implied speaker throughout, had revealed his Word in other languages for other peoples and was now putting it into Arabic for the Arabs (Q 12:1-2; 13:37; 20:11). The qur'anic monologues were delivered orally by Muhammad in the early seventh century CE and eventually collected and transcribed. The Qur'an denounced Arab polytheism and announced God's imminent judgment. As we will see, we can reasonably assume that Muhammad's pagan hearers had some awareness of biblical monotheism, since Christianity and Judaism offered the only other live options, religiously speaking. But, rejecting those options, the Qur'an called its hearers to its unique version of monotheism, for it clearly takes issue with both Christianity and Judaism on various points. Hence the Qur'an addressed a primarily pagan audience, but in a milieu that included Jews and Christians.

The Qur'an called the Muslim[8] community into being, established it in faith and empowered it to defeat its opponents. Its later (i.e., Medinan) suras often addressed Jews and Christians, though they did not constitute the core of its audience. Despite the obvious similarities between the Bible and the Qur'an, there are also major differences, most of which directly relate to the fact that the latter originated in a largely pagan milieu.

As is true of the Bible, the Qur'an is often interpreted by its adherents as a timeless book that speaks to current-day circumstances. This has allowed Muslims to contextualize it, whether in the eleventh or the twenty-first century. But however normal this may be, it becomes problematic when we detach the text from its original context. For any other meanings we see in a scripture must be grounded in its original and primary meaning—what its first audience understood when they heard or read it. As Paul Ricoeur put it, "If it is

---

[6]I follow the Weil-Nöldeke-Schwally chronological ordering of qur'anic suras. For a brief introduction to qur'anic chronology, see https://understandingislam.ink/the-chronology-of-the-quran.

[7]Patricia Crone, introduction to Neuwirth, "'Late Antique Qur'an.'"

[8]On my use of the terms *Muslim* and *Islam*, see 16n3 below.

true that there is always more than one way of construing a text, it is not true that all interpretations are equal."[9] Otherwise, we can make a scripture mean whatever we want and thus render it meaningless.[10] The Qur'an's primary meaning does not "reside" in the mind of the author, nor in that of the audience, nor yet in the text itself, but rather emerges in the complex relationship between the text and its first hearers in their particular context. A scripture's original meaning acts as arbiter, then, either grounding or calling into question other meanings later readers find in it. This underscores the vital importance of rightly appreciating the Qur'an's historical setting, since, as interpreters, we do not create but rather discover the text's original meaning.

Historically, polemical reasons kept Western scholars from appreciating the Qur'an's very distinctive character and originality. Until well into the twentieth century, in fact, the obvious but unstated goal of many was to lampoon the Qur'an as a very bad copy of the biblical original and Muhammad as a buffoon for making it.[11] That approach has since given way to a stress by many on the sameness of the Bible and Qur'an, often to validate Islam as another "Abrahamic" pathway to God. Sometimes this includes Christianizing the Qur'an to the point of seeing the Trinity in it and making its portrait of Jesus reminiscent of that of the Gospels.

I strive to avoid both traps here. As a Christian seeking peace with my Muslim brothers and sisters, I take their scripture seriously and have no interest whatsoever in mocking it. I aim to highlight the Qur'an's uniqueness and do not wish to belittle the Muslim prophet or present the Qur'an as a "copy" of anything. I do consider it vital, however, that we acknowledge the many historical factors influencing its origins. And since the Qur'an implicitly calls for a response from us, my goal is to respond "Christianly," with both grace and truth (Jn 1:17).

---

[9]Paul Ricoeur, *Interpretation Theory: Discourse and the Surplus of Meaning* (Fort Worth, TX: Texas Christian University Press, 1976), 79.

[10]Wilfred Cantwell Smith says the Qur'an's meaning is the "history of its meanings," explaining that "the meaning of the Qur'an as scripture lies not in the text, but in the minds and hearts of Muslims"; see "The True Meaning of Scripture: An Empirical Historian's Nonreductionist Interpretation of the Qur'ān," *International Journal of Middle East Studies* 11 (1980): 504-5. Smith's statement is undeniably true insofar as it relates to the history of religion. But his implicit refusal to decide between interpretations is unhelpful in its minimization of original meaning and its detachment of text from original context. However broadminded and fair that seems, it potentially makes the Qur'an's meaning infinitely broad and hence utterly empty.

[11]W. Paul MacLean, "Jesus in the Qur'an and Hadith Literature, His Roles in the Eschatology of Early Islam" (master's thesis, McGill University, 1970), 23.

Qur'anic Context and Interpretation

As we understand most of the texts we encounter daily almost automatically, as easily as we speak, we sometimes forget that "there is no meaning without context."[12] But the more complex or emotionally loaded the topic, or the more a writer's language, history and culture diverge from ours, the harder we must work at keeping the text grounded in its context. That is precisely the situation when we interpret a sacred scripture from a remote time, place and culture. And if we must work hard to understand any ancient scripture, we must work harder still to comprehend one with as few contextual markers as the Qur'an has. Its allusiveness made it essential for the Muslim community to keep alive traditions explaining its context. But for political, polemical and legal reasons, those traditions became corrupted and embellished long before they were recorded in writing, greatly complicating matters for Qur'an interpreters ever since.

In response, some twentieth-century scholars in the West rejected the traditional Islamic origins narrative, at least on the matter of the Qur'an's milieu. Besides challenging tradition, most of them also denied the authenticity of pre-Islamic poetry, those being the two great pillars on which qur'anic interpretation had been built. While the revisionists never set out to deny the importance of context in qur'anic interpretation, the level of uncertainty their challenges produced made context of little use. Indeed, so widely varied are their answers to the question of milieu that Patricia Crone likens the situation to one in which we encounter Jesus' quotations from the Jewish scriptures in the Gospels but do not know whether he was Jewish, or whether the Tanakh was native to his tradition or imported from outside. Also, suppose the Gospels' geographical markers were so few and so vague that scholars disputed whether Jesus lived in Palestine, Mesopotamia or Greece. Such uncertainty would render the Gospels' meaning exceedingly elusive, which is precisely the situation we now face in qur'anic studies.[13]

To understand the Muslim scripture truly, we must hear it as the uniquely speech-centered, event-birthed communication it was. Attempting to do so without reference to its original context is actually rather comical, unless we think Muhammad's first hearers were somehow able to do that. Even those

---

[12]N. T. Wright, personal interview, McGill University, November 1983.
[13]Crone, introduction to Neuwirth, "'Late Antique Qur'an.'"

who dismiss its original context as irretrievable cannot help but approach the Qur'an with some working hypothesis of what it was—whether or not they are conscious of doing so—because every interpretation of the Qur'an goes back to a particular reading of its context. And since we agree on how to interpret the Qur'an only to the extent that we agree on the story behind it, the debate over qur'anic milieu and narrative is vital to our hermeneutic.[14]

The Goals of This Book

With all this in mind, I aim to do three things in this book:

- Establish the Qur'an's original context as the key to its original meaning

- Inform readers unfamiliar with the Qur'an of its teachings and show how they relate to those of the Bible, giving special emphasis to Jesus' place in the Qur'an

- Offer an initial response to the Qur'an's truth claims and encourage open dialogue between Christians and Muslims on our respective faiths

Because everything about a scripture answers to its narrative, cultural and historical context, part one focuses on that external context.[15] To begin, we must decide who Muhammad was, who his first hearers were and what aspects of their situation significantly shaped their understanding of the Qur'an. Chapter two briefly recounts the traditional Islamic origins narrative and considers the Western debate surrounding it as well as the scholarly consensus that seems to be forming on it. Chapter three zooms out to look at key aspects of the larger world in which Muhammad lived, while chapter four zooms in to consider key qur'anic characteristics that, rightly understood, corroborate the traditional view of Muhammad's pagan Hijazi origins. All these issues are vital to a sound understanding of the Qur'an.

Most Christians want to start with what the Qur'an says about Jesus, who naturally stands at the heart of Christian-Muslim dialogue. But that is not the right place to begin, for doing so assumes that all of the Qur'an's other theological components are equivalent to those of the Bible, which is not at all the

---

[14]Misinterpretations so often relate to an interpreter's giving priority to a hermeneutical precommitment, recognized or not, over truly taking the text in context. Cf. 9n21 below.

[15]Relying on Umberto Eco, Stefan Alkier calls this the text's "encyclopedia"; Alkier, "Intertextuality and the Semiotics of Biblical Texts," in *Reading the Bible Intertextually*, ed. Richard B. Hays, Stefan Alkier and Leroy A. Huizenga (Waco, TX: Baylor University Press, 2009), 8.

case. We must begin with the qur'anic worldview, the conceptual framework within which all of its ideas find their place, for a scripture is not a catalog of isolated theological components, and we cannot accurately compare and contrast Jesus in the two scriptures without seeing his place in the integrated whole of each scripture's theology and spirituality.

Part two then focuses on the qur'anic worldview.[16] The topics covered here include God's ontological and ethical being, in chapters five and six; humankind's creation, fall and reprieve, in chapters seven through nine; sin and salvation, in chapter ten; and prophethood, scripture and revelation, in chapter eleven. Chapters twelve and thirteen focus on qur'anic spirituality, respectively its devotional and social aspects and its political aspect. And with all these topics, the depth of my coverage varies primarily in relation to a topic's relevance to Jesus. I seek to approach the Qur'an in a way that is appreciative of widely held Muslim interpretations of it but yet is not limited to them when they seem anachronistic, the product of later theological concerns. I also show where the teachings of the Qur'an and Bible are similar and where different. This is vital because the Qur'an often suggests more agreement with the Bible than actually exists, and when doctrines seem more similar than they actually are, such similarity obstructs understanding.[17] The Qur'an's worldview provides the frame within which to view its portrayal of Jesus, while comparing it to the biblical worldview ensures our accuracy on the dimensions of that frame.

Part three focuses on the qur'anic portrait of Jesus, again showing how the qur'anic author's presentation is like and unlike that of the biblical writers. Chapter fourteen considers Jesus' origins and person, and chapter fifteen his words and works. Both of these topics are vital to a true appraisal of how the qur'anic author simultaneously honors and marginalizes Jesus. Although most

---

[16]Stefan Alkier, in reliance on Charles Sanders Peirce, calls this the text's "universe of discourse"; ibid., 8.

[17]Charles J. Adams, "Islam and Christianity: The Opposition of Similarities," in *Logos Islamikos: Studia Islamica in Honorem Georgii Michaelis Wickens*, ed. Roger H. Savory and Dionisius A. Agius (Toronto: Pontifical Institute of Mediaeval Studies, 1984), 306. As we will see, such "obstructive similarity" is especially problematic in the Qur'an's presentation of Jesus, which uses a number of key words and titles of Jesus very differently from the Bible's use of them. Also, a number of theological concepts directly related to Jesus are similar enough to their biblical counterparts to obscure their vital differences. These things increase the Christian reader's confusion until discovering the qur'anic Jesus is like walking through a house of mirrors.

Muslims believe the Qur'an denies Jesus' crucifixion, they also acknowledge that the Qur'an speaks plainly of his death and resurrection in Q 19:33. Hence, chapter sixteen assesses how best to make sense of the qur'anic data on Jesus' death, resurrection and place in the future, focusing especially on Q 4:157-58. Chapter seventeen concludes this part of our study with an examination of the Qur'an's presentation of Jesus' community and scripture, also addressing the common Muslim claim that the biblical text has been corrupted.

Finally, part four takes into account the overall meaning of the Qur'an presented in parts two and three, offers an initial Christian response to the Qur'an's truth claims and hopefully makes a positive contribution to the ongoing dialogue between Christians and Muslims. I include this out of a concern to take the Qur'an seriously, especially its most urgent claims.[18] Chapter eighteen considers the Qur'an's uniqueness as an Arab scripture. And since every sequel is read in relation to its precursors, chapter nineteen assesses the Qur'an's claim to be the Bible's sequel by briefly surveying three central biblical motifs diachronically and looking for them in the Qur'an. Chapter twenty then summarizes the comparative and contrastive points on worldview and the portrait of Jesus, from parts two and three, and concludes by raising three vital issues I see as particularly relevant to Christian-Muslim dialogue.

Three Provisos

Three points are important to note about my approach in parts two and three. First, I mainly leave Muslim interpretations of the Qur'an to other studies. Readers seeking a "standard" Muslim reading of the text must look elsewhere for that. I engage with the text of the Qur'an itself, touching on Muslim interpretations primarily where they differ sharply from mine. I aspire to biblical scholar N. T. Wright's approach to textual study. Avoiding both the objectivity of the positivist and the subjectivity of the phenomenalist, Wright advocates a form of "critical realism" by which we access a text's meaning "along the spiraling path of *appropriate dialogue or conversation*" between student and text.[19]

---

[18]Most Western scholars now equate taking the Qur'an's truth claims seriously with the hostility so typical of medieval Christian-Muslim polemics and choose rather to study the Qur'an as a mere cultural or historical artifact. But that hardly does it justice, since it purports to be so much more than that. And it is possible to offer a gracious assessment of the Qur'an's truth claims.

[19]N. T. Wright, *The New Testament and the People of God* (London: SPCK, 1992), 35, italics original.

With that in mind, I ask my readers simply to come explore the Qur'an with me and see whether my interpretation of it makes sense.[20]

Second, my basic criterion for asking the questions of the Qur'an that I do is how vital an issue appears to have been to the qur'anic author. I avoid assuming that the concerns of the Bible and Qur'an are the same, making issues central that are of only peripheral qur'anic concern.[21] But since many of the questions I put to the Qur'an are not questions Muslims typically ask of their scripture, many of my conclusions will also be new to them.

Third, to avoid making my treatment of biblical theology either too unwieldy or too nebulous to nonspecialists, I approach it from a single Christian perspective, one that is evangelical and Reformed. While I recognize that Reformed Christianity has much to learn from other Christian traditions, I find its theological framework most helpful. And I think most of what I say about the Bible will be accepted by a majority of Christians from all quarters.[22]

Truth and Grace in Dialogue

My goal of encouraging dialogue should need little justification from a Christian perspective. The psalmist says how pleased God is when brothers and sisters live together peaceably, and the New Testament calls us to do all we can to be at peace with everyone (Ps 133:1-3; Rom 12:18; Heb 12:14). In our global village, that demands dialogue.

But true dialogue does not deny or minimize difference. Rather, it begins with an honest acknowledgment of difference no less than similarity. Without that, we cannot be truly heard and understood. Using the term *neighbor* in its broadest sense, Jesus commands us to treat our neighbor as

---

[20]I reject the postmodern hermeneutic theory that philosophically imprisons the reader in the circle of her meanings by making the gulf between her and the ancient text impassable. As David Marshall argues, bridging that gap as best we can is precisely the work of scholars. If the gap makes it impossible to seek the Qur'an's "original meaning," then the very same thing applies to our interpretation of the classical Muslim commentaries; David Marshall, *God, Muhammad and the Unbelievers: A Qur'anic Study* (London: RoutledgeCurzon, 1999), 9-15.

[21]For example, the biblical question of the means of salvation.

[22]I inevitably bring my Christian presuppositions to my study of the Qur'an, just as Muslims and secularists bring their presuppositions to it. But while none of us has a God's-eye view of things, this need not keep us from pursuing scholarly excellence and truth. Indeed, recognizing our presuppositions is arguably the best starting point for just such a pursuit: the more aware we are of our own limitations, the more open we may be to correction from whatever quarter. Blindness to our presuppositions has greater potential to distort our scholarship and lead to findings that reflect what we bring to the text more than what is actually there.

we want her to treat us (Mt 7:12; cf. Lk 10:25-37). Paul also counsels us to do good to everyone, Christian or not (Gal 6:10). So we lovingly speak what we hold to be true and graciously listen as our Muslim brother or sister does likewise. And we remain ready, as Peter charges us, to offer a defense to anyone who seeks the reason for our hope, doing so with gentleness and reverence (1 Pet 3:15-16). So our truth telling is to be marked always by kindness and honor for our partner in dialogue—as a *Thou*, not an *It*, in Martin Buber's terms.

While the Qur'an's attitude to Christians is somewhat mixed,[23] it sometimes calls for open, irenic discussion with them. Q 29:46, for example, counsels Muslims: "Do not dispute with the People of the Book except in the best manner—apart from those of them who have done wrong. Say, 'We believe in what has been sent down to us and in what has been sent down to you. Our God and your God are one and we have submitted to him.'"

And Q 3:64 tells Muslims to say to Christians and Jews, "O people of the Scripture, come to a word that is common between you and us: 'We serve only God, and we associate nothing with Him.'" The verse continues, "If they turn away, say, 'Bear witness that we surrender.'"[24] Even of the Muslim community's enemies, whoever they are, Q 8:61-62 tells Muslims, "If they incline to peace, you should incline to it and trust God. He is the Hearer and the Knower. And if they wish to deceive you, God is sufficient for you."

Sadly, neither side has lived up to the standards our scriptures have set for us here. From early on, our shared history has been marked by hostility and misunderstanding. This raises the question, If we in the world's two largest faith communities cannot dialogue amicably about our respective understandings of Jesus, for example, how can we realistically hope to have the kind of relationship that sets us on the path to peace?

While most Muslims reject the West's religious pluralism, some go so far as to oppose any public discussion of the Qur'an's truth claims by non-Muslims and seem to make conversion to Islam a prerequisite to that. This is ultimately counterproductive. For how can anyone's beliefs be promoted by so sheltering them from objections? Surely truth is strong enough to withstand unjustified criticism. This makes non-Muslims wonder whether such

---

[23]For more on this, see chapter seventeen below.

[24]Alan Jones, trans., *The Qur'ān* (Cambridge: Gibb Memorial Trust, 2007).

rigor in controlling public discussion masks an underlying fear that their truth is not in fact true but only communally constituted as such.

Thus I seek a middle way between secular pluralism and Muslim protectionism, making every effort to take seriously the Qur'an's truth claims while still being respectful of my Muslim brothers and sisters. This approach will doubtless yield more questions than answers, but it seeks to foster dialogue in an atmosphere of honesty, humility and sympathetic understanding—that is, of friendship. And what could be more urgently needed between Christians and Muslims now than that friendship that lovingly speaks the truth?

Part I

Qur'anic
Context

Two

Muhammad and the Origins *of* Islam

Muslims implicitly accept the traditional narrative of Islamic origins by which an Arab trader-turned-prophet named Muhammad preached reformed monotheism to his people in Mecca (*Makka*) and Medina (*Madina*) during the early seventh century CE. For centuries Western scholars generally accepted the traditional narrative also. In the modern period, however, some have elected to dispense with all or much of it because it is largely based on conflicting Muslim traditions dated some two centuries after the events recounted. Though variously motivated, all such revisionism has rendered the Qur'an's milieu an open question and thus made its meaning exceedingly flexible depending on the milieu and narrative ascribed to it. Yet the early non-Muslim evidence for the emergence of Islam confirms the traditional Muslim account in broad outline. Hence a consensus seems to be forming around the view that Islam emerged in Arabia by a process initiated by Muhammad and the recitations found in the Qur'an, but a process within the world of Late Antiquity more protracted and uneven than the traditional view allows. While there is clear textual evidence that the Qur'an underwent sustained editing during the seventh century, that evidence in no way undermines the traditional understanding that Islam began as a reformation of pagan polytheism and existing monotheism.

The Traditional Origins Narrative

Muslims implicitly accept the traditional Islamic origins narrative, forming the backdrop against which they read the Qur'an.[1] Putting all questions of historical accuracy aside for now, we note that that narrative begins with Muhammad's birth in 570 CE in Mecca (*Makka*),[2] a town with two claims to fame: it was a key player in Western Arabia's overland trade route and was home to a then-pagan shrine, the Ka'ba, making it rival a Christian pilgrimage site in Sana'a. Orphaned as a child, Muhammad grew up to accompany his uncle on trading expeditions to Syria and earn a reputation for intelligence, character and diplomacy. After managing a wealthy widow's trading operations, Muhammad married her. And besides a business partnership and a son who died in infancy, Khadija eventually gave him four daughters as well as the moral support he so needed as a fledgling prophet.

Muhammad received his prophetic call in 610. In an experience that straddled dreaming and wakefulness, the Seen and Unseen, earth and sky, the angel Gabriel appeared, commanding him to "Recite!" (*iqra*). When Muhammad submitted, Gabriel inscribed the first recitation on his heart. Thus began the Qur'an, or "Recitation," a series of divine revelations presented as the sequel to the biblical scriptures. Though Muhammad initially questioned his sanity and feared people would label him possessed, he eventually went public, calling his fellow Meccans to forsake their idolatry for the God of Abraham. Besides denouncing their religion, Muhammad warned of imminent judgment if they did not forsake their immorality and submit to God and his prophet, the meaning of the Arabic word *islam* being "submission." Being rightly related to God in this dual sense made one a *muslim*, or "submitter."[3]

Though some believed, Muhammad's fears proved well founded, as most people rejected his prophetic claims, accusing him of being a mere poet and possessed. As Muhammad's band of followers grew, the Meccans increasingly persecuted them. So he sent some of them to seek refuge in Ethiopia. During this period God favored Muhammad with his famed Night Journey to heaven.

---

[1] Ibn Ishaq, *The Life of Muhammad*, trans. Alfred Guillaume (Oxford: Oxford University Press, 1995).
[2] See map one which illustrates the Middle East in 600 CE, ten years before Muhammad began his prophetic career.
[3] The first records we have of Muslims calling themselves "Muslim" and their faith "Islam" are from some sixty years after Muhammad. But since their adoption of these terms signals no abrupt change in their self-understanding, for simplicity's sake I use both to refer to them from the first.

But relocating his entire community took on new urgency when a powerful and supportive uncle and Khadija both died. About a year later he married the young ʿAisha, who would become his favorite wife. (In all he is said to have had twelve wives.) A year or so later, in 622, the leaders of Yathrib—later called Medina (*Madina*)—a few hundred miles north of Mecca, welcomed him as their arbiter and ruler, as the town was divided between its constituent tribes, some of which were Jewish. The *hijra*, Muhammad's emigration to Yathrib with some seventy followers, signaled the birth of his community, or *umma*, as a sovereign geopolitical entity.

The constitution Muhammad drew up as the basis for his rule of Yathrib referred to its Jewish signatories as "believers," signifying that they could remain Jews. But even so, it required them to submit to Muhammad's theocratic rule. When the revelation came declaring war on Mecca and conscripting all able-bodied "believers" to take up arms (Q 22:39-40), the Jews resisted, in violation of their agreement. Then revelations came that changed the direction of prayer from Jerusalem to Mecca and urged the Muslims to be wary of the Jews, ultimately calling for their exile or slaughter. While the war relieved tensions between Yathrib's natives and its Meccan immigrants by enabling the latter to live off their battle spoils, the Jews were not the only ones who hated it. The revelations also decried as "hypocrites" or "imposters" others who accepted Muhammad's prophethood but were reluctant to support his war effort for "God's Cause." Such revelations helped ensure that most of his followers gave him their loyal support.

Muhammad's war against Mecca continued through much of his Medinan period. Muslim attacks on Mecca's caravans undermined confidence in its trade and ate into its profits. Each successful raid increased not only the Muslims' booty but also their prestige and power in the eyes of surrounding tribes. Whenever the Muslims won battles in which the odds were against them, they took it as proof of God's favor on them. Whenever they lost to the Meccans, a revelation came fingering traitorous Jews or hypocrites. And Muhammad's wisdom and generosity in handling prisoners and booty earned him the respect of followers, both actual and potential.

Despite his many challenges, Muhammad proved as able a politician and a military strategist as he was a religious leader. He built a powerful tribal coalition and used it to secure a peace treaty with the Meccans in 628, one that included permission for his followers to perform a pilgrimage to the Kaʿba the following year. That event proved a great moral victory, boosting Muhammad's support among the tribes and prompting him to summon emperors and kings far and wide to submit to his rule. When the Meccans breached the peace treaty's terms in 630, he advanced on the city, capturing it with little resistance. On entering Mecca, his followers cleansed the Kaʿba of its idols and executed Muhammad's most vocal Meccan foes.

Muhammad spent his final years consolidating his power until he ruled the entire peninsula, including Sasanian-allied Yemen. He also led or sent his armies north to begin the conquest of Byzantine Palestine. Muhammad died in Medina in 632, after making a pilgrimage to Mecca during which he recited his final qur'anic message. It proclaimed, "Today I have perfected your religion for you and completed my blessing upon you and chosen for your religion submission (*islam*)" (Q 5:3). His farewell sermon also assured his followers that no prophet would come after him and that, together with the Qur'an, his example would be sufficient to keep them from going astray.

With respect to his example, the hadith present Muhammad as observing or exceeding the Arabs' ethical norms, the only exceptions being those cases where a special revelation allowed him to break the rule. For example, Q 33:50 is understood to have permitted him to exceed the normal limit of four wives. In the strangest case of all, the Qur'an authorized Muhammad's marriage to his adopted son Zayd's wife by prohibiting adoption wholesale (Q 33:4-5, 37). Rescinding Zayd's adoption precluded the charge of incest in Muhammad's marrying the wife Zayd would divorce for him. As the hadith evidence, this deeply disturbed many of Muhammad's followers at the time. But whatever ethical struggles they had with it, they ultimately accepted God's right to do as he pleases and Muhammad's being "a good example for those who hope for God and the Last Day" (Q 33:21 Jones).

The Islamic Origins Debate

For well over a millennium Western scholars interpreted the Qur'an with this traditional origins narrative in mind, rejecting only the latter's miraculous and blatantly polemical elements. Beyond that they were largely uncritical, thus making the Islamic origins narrative seem solidly founded. But as qur'anic studies began catching up to biblical criticism in the late nineteenth century, scholars came to view the traditional origins narrative more critically, resulting in a growing divide between tradition-guided and more skeptical scholars. Everyone agreed on the hadith's historical unreliability—just not its extent or how to deal with it.[4]

Although united in their rejection of Muhammad's collective legacy or some key part of it,[5] revisionists are variously motivated by polemics, ecumenism, evangelism or secular rationalism. Some skeptics argue that we know almost nothing about Islam's origins, dismissing the traditional sources as so polluted that the origins narrative they gave rise to tells us nothing true, only what later generations wanted to believe about Islam's origins. Others are happy to co-opt the traditional narrative while reversing key elements to establish their own distinct vision of Islamic origins. Until the present, however, no revisionist has been able to construct a compelling new origins narrative.

The best-known polemicist-revisionist, the pseudonymous Christoph Luxenberg, argues the Qur'an originated as a Syro-Aramaic lectionary.[6] Some of Luxenberg's colleagues even question Muhammad's existence.[7] By contrast, ecumenically minded revisionists like Geoffrey Parrinder (d. 2005) and Giulio Basetti-Sani (d. 2001) view the Bible and Qur'an as complementary, attacking only a heretical, tritheistic version of Christianity, which they claim was present in Muhammad's Arabia. They thus transform the Muslim prophet from a "heretic" into a champion of Christian orthodoxy and discover an underlying unity between Christianity and Islam.[8] And some Christians put this to evangelistic use.

Best represented by John Wansbrough (d. 2002), secular revisionists usually work with a linear model of religious development, hypothesizing that

---

[4]The hadith, which give rise to the traditional origins narrative, are replete with discrepancies and contradictions. Recognizing this problem, classical Muslim scholars sought to judge each hadith's authenticity primarily by scrutinizing the links in its *isnad*, or chain of oral sources (*A* told *B*, who told *C*, who told *D*, etc.). But a hadith's *isnad* can be forged just as easily as its text, and conflicts and discrepancies aplenty remain between even the most highly credentialed hadith.

[5]Aziz Al-Azmeh, *The Arabs and Islam in Late Antiquity: A Critique of Approaches to Arabic Sources* (Berlin: Gerlach Press, 2014), 9n23.

[6]Christoph Luxenberg, *The Syro-Aramaic Reading of the Koran: A Contribution to the Decoding of the Language of the Koran* (Berlin: Verlag Hans Schiler, 2007).

[7]Karl-Heinz Ohlig and Volker Popp, in Karl-Heinz Ohlig, ed., *Early Islam: A Critical Reconstruction Based on Contemporary Sources* (Amherst, NY: Prometheus Books, 2013).

[8]Geoffrey Parrinder, *Jesus in the Qur'an* (Oxford: Oneworld, 1995); and Giulio Basetti-Sani, *The Koran in the Light of Christ: An Essay Towards a Christian Interpretation of the Sacred Book of Islam* (Chicago: Franciscan Herald Press, 1977); see also the discussion on 44-46 below.

the Qur'an is the product of a lengthy evolutionary process that occurred among monotheists in the Fertile Crescent, not pagans in remote Arabia.[9] In keeping with this, G. R. Hawting postulates that the Qur'an uses "idolatry" only figuratively, to attack not actual polytheism—as the hadith maintain—but rather just retrograde Iraqi monotheism.[10] By the 1980s a sharp division had developed between such radical revisionists and those unprepared to radically revise the traditional origins narrative, with each side vehemently accusing the other of ignoring the obvious.

One problem with most revisionism is that, in its criticism of tradition, it is remarkably uncritical of its own underlying rationalistic hostility to tradition. Inherent in the historical method is the premise that tradition does not mediate history, making the historian duty-bound "if possible, to see through tradition to the history that might (or indeed might not) exist behind it."[11] Evangelical revisionists often stress how much wider the time gap is between Jesus and the New Testament documents, on the one hand, and Muhammad and the hadith, on the other. What they fail to mention is that a far larger gap exists between the earliest Old Testament texts and the events they recount. So if we reject the Muslim tradition's authenticity wholesale on that ground, we must reject the Old Testament's historicity too. Rather than take so uncritical an approach, we need to remain open to testimony of all kinds—including that of tradition.

Despite their inability to construct a compelling alternative origins narrative, however, the revisionists have done us all a great service especially in two respects:

- They have reminded us that Islam emerged by a process that was protracted and uneven, and occurred within the world of Late Antiquity.

- They have driven us to more rigorous scrutiny of historical sources, a broader search for data and more honesty about the remaining holes in our knowledge.

---

[9]John Wansbrough, *Quranic Studies: Sources and Methods of Scriptural Interpretation* (Oxford: Oxford University Press, 1977); and John Wansbrough, *The Sectarian Milieu: Content and Composition of Islamic Salvation History* (Oxford: Oxford University Press, 1978).

[10]G. R. Hawting, *The Idea of Idolatry and the Emergence of Islam: From Polemic to History* (New York: Cambridge University Press, 1999). See also 24n29 below.

[11]Iain Provan, V. Philips Long and Tremper Longman III, *A Biblical History of Israel* (Louisville, KY: Westminster John Knox, 2003), 24.

Toward a More Critical Approach

While some fine scholars still position themselves on the revisionist side of the origins debate, a scholarly consensus seems gradually to be forming on the other side, as scholars increasingly realize that such broad criticism of the Muslim tradition is unwarranted.[12] These scholars refuse that "empirical fundamentalism"[13] that summarily damns all of the hadith simply due to either their oral and relatively late origins or their Muslim bias—as if other sources are unbiased.[14] Instead, they scrutinize all the available data—the qur'anic data included[15]—to determine which elements in the traditional narrative best accord with early non-Muslim and Muslim sources, including the Qur'an. They also refuse to pronounce on what did not exist based on missing evidence. They thus base their historical verdict on the preponderance of the evidence, believing that they have much to lose by embracing radical revisionism, regardless of the apparent freedom it offers.

Despite numerous hadith discrepancies, Muslims agree on Muhammad's pagan origins, the location of the two cities in which he lived, all the major challenges he faced, the milestones that marked his prophetic career, the scripture he was given, the kind of community he founded and its relations to the other two monotheistic communities. Given the major divisions that occurred within the *umma* early on, this unanimity is not to be taken lightly. Muslims disagree on such things as who Muhammad's first male convert was and when various battles—such as the Battle of Badr—occurred. But as Maxime Rodinson says, "Such disputes can only take place because everyone agrees the battle did take place."[16] "In broad outline," Andrew Rippin concurs, "all these sources present the same story, but matters of chronology and detail are always problematic."[17] And Gregor Schoeler writes that, when carefully

---

[12]It is precisely the craft of the historian critically to bring order to the "messiness" of the extant historical sources. Cf. Al-Azmeh, *Arabs and Islam in Late Antiquity*, 3-6, 37-38.

[13]Robert G. Hoyland, *Seeing Islam as Others Saw It: A Survey and Evaluation of Christian, Jewish and Zoroastrian Writings on Early Islam* (Princeton, NJ: Darwin Press, 1997), 546.

[14]This stems from a realistic appreciation of the challenges inherent in reconstructing history—especially ancient history. Since the past cannot be reproduced in a test tube, historical certainty refers to the integrity of our historical evidence and reasoning. Demanding absolute proof here is fruitless, for one can always come up with a conspiracy theory to dismiss the evidence. But as in a law court, such second-guessing takes us well beyond the realm of reasonable doubt.

[15]Patricia Crone, "The First Century Concept of the HIǦRA," *Arabica* 41 (1994): 354.

[16]Maxime Rodinson, *Muḥammad*, trans. Anne Carter (London: Penguin Books, 1996), xii.

[17]Andrew Rippin, *Muslims, Their Religious Beliefs and Practices*, vol. 1, *The Formative Period*, 4th ed. (New

analyzed, the traditions "sometimes confirm the outlines of what Muslim believers had accepted as fact all along." And when they do, "scholarly honesty requires us to declare that Muslim tradition is not always as unreliable as many Western scholars have assumed."[18]

What early non-Muslim evidence supports the general contours of the traditional origins narrative? Since Muhammad was unknown outside the Arabian Peninsula before the Muslim conquest, the earliest non-Muslim evidence we have for Islam dates to that time.[19] The limits of the present study allow me to mention only a few sources. As early as 633 Jerusalem's patriarch Sophronius (d. ca. 639) wrote of the Arabs' unprovoked military aggression, their hostility to the cross (i.e., Christianity), their destruction of churches and their capture of Bethlehem.[20] On their conquest of Jerusalem in 637, he said the Arabs were preparing to build a mosque on the temple site. Muslim sources likewise tell of a mosque built there by ʿUmar in 638.[21] Another document from the same time refers to a "people of the desert overrunning another's lands as though they were their own."[22] These witnesses confirm the unprovoked advance of the Arab armies in Palestine at the very time when Muslim tradition says it happened. Two early Coptic documents describe the Arabs' conquest of Egypt in mixed terms, telling of their massacres, plunder and enslavement of prisoners, alongside their fasting, prayer and respect for church property.[23] Ishoʿyahb III of Adiabene (d. 659), an Assyrian church leader, says of the conquest that Christians were required "to give up half of

---

York: Routledge, 2012), 43. It is one thing to question or dismiss details of the Muslim tradition, including details about Mecca. It is another to reject something as integral as Islam's Meccan origins outright. The map Herodotus drew of the region in the second century BCE positioned both Yathrib and Mecca—"Yathrippa" and "Macoraba"—correctly, given his level of cartographic accuracy; Neal Robinson, *Discovering the Qur'an: A Contemporary Approach to a Veiled Text* (Washington, DC: Georgetown University Press, 2004), 32-33. As we will see in chapter three, Arabia's religio-political situation was far more nuanced in the early seventh century than the Muslim tradition suggests. It is easy to see why the early Muslims oversimplified the situation the Qur'an addressed and sacralized both Muhammad and Mecca. But to suggest that Islam originated outside the Hijaz is signally unhelpful.

[18]Gregor Schoeler, *The Biography of Muhammad: Nature and Authenticity*, trans. Uwe Vagelpohl (New York: Routledge, 2011), 122.

[19]This is to be expected, given that nothing on Islam's origins from Arabia's Jewish and Christian communities has survived.

[20]Hoyland, *Seeing Islam as Others Saw It*, 69-73, 549.

[21]Ibid., 63-65.

[22]Ibid., 77-78.

[23]Ibid., 120-21, 154-55.

their possessions to keep their faith" and laments the loss of those who chose to sacrifice their faith to keep their worldly wealth.[24]

An Armenian chronicle believed to be from the 660s says a merchant named Muhammad—together with some Jewish refugees—had awakened the Arabs to the reality of Abraham's God. It depicts Muhammad as a military leader who urged the Arabs to take possession of Palestine since God had given it to them as Abraham's descendants through Ishmael. It says that, having led his followers to attack Palestine, Muhammad "had not fallen short of his promise to them" when they returned home rich in slaves and other booty.[25] In the 680s a Mesopotamian monk wrote that the Saracens (Arabs) follow Muhammad's "tradition" strictly,[26] while another said that anyone in their community who publicly opposed his commandments risked execution.[27] We thus have every reason to believe that "Muhammad's commandments" were central to their religious piety, centered in such practices as prayer, fasting and territorial expansion by military conquest in God's name—especially when the Qur'an and hadith so abundantly confirm it. Further, Jacob, bishop of Edessa (d. 708), attests that the Muslims in Alexandria prayed toward the Ka'ba just as Jews prayed toward Jerusalem.[28]

There is then sufficient early non-Muslim evidence for us to accept that a trader named Muhammad presented himself as a prophet in early seventh-century

---

[24]Ibid., 181 (cf. 179). Ignoring this evidence, as well as that given below, C. Jonn Block makes a seemingly ecumenical quotation of Isho'yahb foundational to his revision of the Islamic origins narrative. But as we will see (48-49 below), we cannot take that particular quotation at face value. C. Jonn Block, *The Qur'an in Christian-Muslim Dialogue: Historical and Modern Interpretations* (New York: Routledge, 2014), 154.

[25]Hoyland, *Seeing Islam as Others Saw It*, 128-31. We should not be misled by this inclusion of Jews: Christians during this period typically blamed most of the world's ills on the Jews.

Lest we dismiss as fabrication Muhammad's having promised the Arabs Palestine, Q 33:27 makes a similar point. Some early Arab generals likewise spoke of their possession of other conquered lands as their divinely appointed destiny, according to al-Tabari; quoted in Hoyland, *Seeing Islam as Others Saw It*; and Robert G. Hoyland, "Writing the Biography of the Prophet Muhammad: Problems and Solutions," *History Compass* 5, no. 2 (2007): 581-602.

[26]Hoyland, "Writing the Biography of the Prophet," 590.

[27]Robert G. Hoyland, "The Earliest Christian Writings on Muḥammad: An Appraisal," in *The Biography of Muḥammad: The Issue of the Sources*, ed. Harald Motzki (Leiden: Brill, 2000), 284.

[28]Hoyland, *Seeing Islam as Others Saw It*, 565-66. That Samarkand's early Muslims, for example, were divided over which direction to orient their city's mosque points to differences over scientific understanding, not alternative shrines. "From the late eighth century onwards," writes Hoyland, "we find Muslim astronomers busily devising trigonometric and geometric solutions to the problem of determining the *qibla* for any given locality." Given that these mathematical advances occurred more than 130 years after the Muslim conquest began, that there was little consistency in the first century and a third proves nothing about the Ka'ba's location; Hoyland, *Seeing Islam as Others Saw It*, 568-69. For more on Mecca see 21n17 above.

Arabia, calling his people to abandon their polytheism and embrace his version of monotheism. On moving from Mecca to Medina, he assumed theocratic rule and led his followers to conquer in God's name. We have no reason to doubt that Muhammad's background was pagan, a fact the Qur'an and hadith substantiate in numerous ways.[29] At least this much of the traditional origins narrative we should accept.[30] Most scholars also accept that a large cache of ancient Qur'an manuscripts discovered in Sana'a in the early 1970s and the Tübingen Qur'an establish that the Qur'an's written text was undergoing editing during the late seventh century, which also accords with Muslim tradition.[31]

However, with abundant evidence for the development of Islamic thought and practice since the ninth century, when written records became normative, we have no reason to doubt that similar development took place in Islam's first two centuries, before a more literate Arab culture documented it. This means that early Islam was more fluid then than once thought, which is another reason why we must assess the hadith critically. Hence we are rightly skeptical about such things as the glorification of Muhammad, Mecca and the early *umma* (in Islam's supposed golden age), and the vilification of Medina's Jews as presented by the *sira*, or biographical literature on Muhammad.[32] We should also reject the Muslim tradition's polemical material on Christianity as well as its claim

---

[29]While the Qur'an sometimes accuses Christians and Jews of being polytheists, Hawting's thesis that the idolatry it confronts is only that of errant monotheism is unconvincing; see *Idea of Idolatry and the Emergence of Islam*. Indicting pagan idolaters as well as Jews and Christians, whose religion it roundly condemns as polytheistic also, the qur'anic offensive against polytheism is one of both-and rather than either-or. On this see chapter four below.

[30]The rule of thumb is that we are open to historical elements that the hadith broadly support, the primary exceptions being elements that are obviously polemical, hagiographical or otherwise anachronistic in nature. Thus, while we accept the historicity of both the pagan Meccans' persecution of Muhammad and the Medinan Jews' opposition to his war against the Meccans, we reject Muhammad's purported interactions with world political leaders.

[31]Sixty pages of the Sana'a manuscripts are palimpsests, the overtext (likely from the 670s to 690s) being quite similar to the current-day Qur'an, the undertext (from the 640s to 650s) being rather different; Keith E. Small, "Qur'an Manuscripts: Thoughts on How the Text Was Preserved and Passed On" (lecture, Al-Maktoum College of Higher Education, Dundee, Scotland, February 20, 2013), www.youtube.com/watch?v=Hou4JcHo67o. Also, two leaves from an early Qur'an manuscript (found in Birmingham) have been radiocarbon-dated between 568 and 645. Though disputed on graphical grounds, that dating—if accurate—may mean the manuscript was written during Muhammad's lifetime or the decades following.

[32]Strongly resembling Mazdean and Manichaean precursors, the Night Journey is clearly a post-Muhammadan embellishment. The qur'anic "hook" on which Muslims hang this event (Q 17:1) likely refers not to a supernatural cosmic adventure but rather to the *hijra*, which suggests that the verse's Middle Meccan placement in the Weil-Nöldeke-Schwally chronology may be mistaken.

that the whole of Arabia converted to Islam during Muhammad's lifetime. And since the Qur'an gives ample evidence of Muhammad's never having done any miracles, we are fully justified in discounting that entire hadith element as a later accretion designed to strengthen Muslim piety and polemics.[33]

Recent studies have also discovered a number of key points about both the composition and the transmission of the qur'anic text. Computerized analysis has revealed that a very high 52 percent of the qur'anic text consists of re-peated, oral-formulaic material, demonstrating its use of folklorist oral tech-niques.[34] Keith E. Small also marshals evidence from the manuscript record for the Muslim authorities' deliberate and sustained efforts to standardize the text, which fits well with the traditional accounts, though Muslims have ever since downplayed the effects of that program.[35] Critical study of the text of the Qur'an is still in its early stages, with nothing remotely resembling the evidence for the New Testament's demonstrable families of texts. But one thing is clear: no single version of the Qur'an goes right back to Muhammad, though nearly all Muslims believe their Qur'an does.[36] While there was an early form of *textus receptus*, that text has never corresponded to one single, identifiable manuscript universally accepted by Muslims.[37]

To sum up, we have good reason to accept any elements in the traditional origins narrative that early non-Muslim evidence confirms or that are both universally accepted by Muslims and not patently polemical, hagiographical or otherwise anachronistic in nature. The Qur'an thus appears to constitute a largely authentic collection of the recitations given by Muhammad, an early seventh-century Arab trader-turned-prophet who originated in a polytheistic Arab milieu influenced by both Judaism and Christianity. As we shall see, the

[33]By contrast, not only do the Gospels detail Jesus' miracles, but early Jewish and pagan sources also refer to Jesus' having been either a magician, sorcerer or alleged miracle worker. While their wit-ness does not prove that Jesus did miracles, it does verify that he did crowd-mesmerizing feats of some kind or other, making the Gospel accounts worthy of historical consideration.

[34]Andrew G. Bannister, *An Oral-formulaic Study of the Qur'an* (Lanham, MD: Lexington Books, 2014), 274-75; Alan Dundes, *Fables of the Ancients? Fables in the Qur'an* (Lanham, MD: Rowman & Little-field, 2003), 65.

[35]Keith E. Small, *Textual Criticism and Qur'an Manuscripts* (Lanham, MD: Lexington Books, 2011), 175.

[36]Fred M. Donner, "The Qur'an in Recent Scholarship—Challenges and Desiderata," in *The Qur'an in Its Historical Context*, ed. Gabriel Said Reynolds (New York: Routledge, 2008), 78; Small, *Textual Criticism*, 179.

[37]Donner, "Qur'an in Recent Scholarship," 74. Doubtless, considerable editing was done to the text promulgated by ʿUthman (d. 653) and al-Hajjaj (d. 705); Small, *Textual Criticism*, 179.

Qur'an itself amply demonstrates what William A. Graham has termed Islam's "avowed reformation of previous monotheism and pagan polytheism," that reformational spirit it has cultivated at a very fundamental level from its first beginnings right down to the present day.[38]

[38]William A. Graham, "Islam in the Mirror of Ritual," in *Islam's Understanding of Itself*, ed. Richard G. Hovannisian and Speros Vryonis Jr. (Malibu, CA: Undena Publications, 1983), 66.

Three

Coming to Terms *with* Muhammad's World

The Qur'an is truly understood only against the backdrop of early seventh-century Arabia. Though geographically isolated, Arabia was not insulated from major trends or events in the wider Middle East. The Byzantine and Sasanian empires used religion variously to legitimize their rule. The Byzantines also used it to pull neighboring peoples into their orbit, and their defense of orthodoxy and attacks on heterodoxy both within and without their realms could take on the character of a "holy war." A number of times in the fifth and sixth centuries there had been considerable violence between Christians and Jews in Palestine and Yemen, at either end of the Incense Road. In Arabia's highly politicized environment, its indigenous animistic polytheism gradually lost adherents to Christianity and Judaism but still held out in central Arabia and the Hijaz, in western Arabia. For some decades the superpowers divided most of Arabia's northern tribes into two tribal confederations aligned with them. While this division highlighted the weaknesses inherent in their tribalism, Arabia's a-religious poetry became a culturally uniting factor. Both natural and manmade catastrophes—one of which was a war of epic proportions that raged for over a quarter of a century—put the Arabs, no less than others in the wider Middle East, in a decidedly apocalyptic mood. This interested the Arabs in the early Meccan recitations, even if very few believed at first. In fact, a multiplicity of localized apocalyptic prophets in western and central Arabia—Muhammad being the most successful of them—precipitated a veritable "sea change" from paganism to monotheism there too.

The Qur'an is understood truly only against the backdrop of early seventh-century Arabia. Hence we must understand something of Muhammad's world. In particular we must grasp five aspects of Arabia that significantly shaped the thinking of his audience:

- its location between the empires

- its indigenous spiritual tradition and values

- its place in the religious contest of the day

- its apocalyptic-prophetic mood

- its tribalism

Surviving the Region's Religio-political Firestorms

Arabia's massive size—nearly that of India—and unyielding physical char-acter were largely determinative of its inhabitants' lives and economic pros-pects, an endless mix of daunting challenge and shimmering possibility. But located between the Sasanian and Byzantine empires and the latter's ally, Ethiopia, Arabia's tribes could hardly have escaped the superpowers' designs and impact.[1] While the rest of the peninsula's extreme climate and sparse population made annexing it impracticable, Yemen's fertility made it exceptional in that respect. Already in the fourth century the Arab tribes had begun abandoning their indigenous religion in favor of Judaism and Christianity. That movement accelerated as the empires' involvement swept Yemen onto the world stage in the early sixth century and drew most of the peninsula's northern tribes into one of two tribal confederations, respectively clients of Constantinople or Ctesiphon. Thus the empires sought to extend their influence across the peninsula. While the conflict in Yemen was resolved and the northern Arabs ceased to function as imperial clients before Muhammad began his prophetic career, the sixth century strongly imbued religion in Arabia with the geopolitical understanding of it characteristic of the surrounding empires.

---

[1]For a survey of the archaeological evidence documenting this, see Barbara Finster, "Arabia in Late Antiquity: An Outline of the Cultural Situation in the Peninsula at the Time of Muhammad," in *The Qur'ān in Context: Historical and Literary Investigations into the Qur'ānic Milieu*, ed. Angelika Neuwirth, Nicolai Sinai and Michael Marx (Leiden: Brill, 2010), 31-114.

It had always been normative for the political and religious spheres to overlap largely. But while ancient Rome, for example, never excluded religion from government, Roman religion was neither universal in scope nor missional in practice. By contrast, Christianity and Judaism—the two monotheistic faiths married to the governments in Palestine and Yemen in the sixth century—were both.[2] This resulted in escalating Jewish-Christian hostility issuing in tragic violence in both regions. Byzantine suppression and persecution of Jews and Samaritans increased dramatically in Palestine during the century or so before Muhammad. In response to one uprising, for example, the Byzantines mounted genocidal attacks on Palestine's Samaritans, and the Arabs bound to Byzantium actively participated in the religious violence of their imperial overlord. During the same period, the Byzantines (Ethiopia's allies) and Sasanians both tried to pull strategic Yemen into their orbits. And partly in response to Byzantine violence in Palestine, an early sixth-century Jewish king in Yemen massacred Christians in Najran, the Yemeni city closest to Mecca. That event, to which Q 85:4-8 most likely refers, precipitated the direct intervention of the Ethiopians, followed by the Sasanians. And long afterward, the story of that massacre served as a powerful propaganda tool rallying support for the Christian cause in the Byzantine world. The key point though is that religious communities were massacred in God's name at both ends of western Arabia's Incense Road.

By officially subscribing to a given religion, a government embraced the notion that its supreme ruler was ordained by God to establish his rule on earth and, conversely, to defend his cause against all threats, theological ones included. Implicit also was the notion that his cause must triumph and, for the Byzantines, must also *appear* to triumph by ensuring that any religious minorities allowed to survive could not thrive and must endure a measure of visible humiliation. Whenever the empires saw their minorities as a threat, they persecuted them. The Byzantines also drew on the Old Testament model of a God-ordained "holy war" in their defense of orthodoxy and their struggle against heterodoxy, both inside and outside the empire. Doubtless out of sheer desperation, Heraclius (r. 610–641) took that motif

---

[2] For more on this, see Garth Fowden, "Varieties of Religious Community," in *Interpreting Late Antiquity: Essays on the Postclassical World*, ed. G. W. Bowersock, Peter Brown and Oleg Grabar (Cambridge, MA: Belknap Press, 2001), 82-106. Aside from the Byzantine empire, Ethiopia was Christian, while Yemen swung back and forth between Judaism and Christianity. By contrast, the Sasanians' Mazdaism was universal, but seldom missional.

farther than any emperor before him, promising anyone who died fighting the Sasanian "infidels" the honor of a martyr's entrance into heaven.[3] That war between the empires, beginning in 602 and overlapping most of Muhammad's prophetic career, engulfed the entire eastern end of the Mediterranean, as well as Iraq and Iran. So devastating was it that when Heraclius finally crushed his archrival in 628, both empires were thoroughly spent, a fact of which Muhammad's armies took full advantage beginning in 630.[4]

Though Arabia's tribes were divided by dialect, religion, politics and unending blood feuds, a kind of "secular" poetry emerged as the great unifying force between them and became their greatest cultural achievement. That the formalized language of poetry overcame such fragmentation to forge a common identity and "provide the basis for a homogeneous memory"[5] is simply spectacular. And the existence of so large a body of literature from Muhammad's Arabia is immensely important to qur'anic interpretation, despite its a-religious character. For putting the tribe's life, ethos and solidarity into words—conveying everything from individual and tribal panegyric to gossip and lampoon—early Arabic poetry serves Qur'an interpreters as a virtual "archeological site, with . . . a palpable stratigraphy."[6] Such poetry was as vital to the average Arab in Muhammad's day as poetry is negligible to the average American today. Though some scholars doubt its authenticity, a growing body of evidence—epigraphic, narrative and linguistic—makes the issue one of "minor contamination rather than . . . major fabrication."[7]

Yemen's alternate embrace of the two great rival religions made for an incendiary contest there, one that sent sparks flying all across the peninsula. For

---

[3]J. D. Howard-Johnston, "Heraclius' Persian Campaigns and the Revival of the Eastern Roman Empire," History 6 (1999): 40, cited in Peter Sarris, Empires of Faith: The Fall of Rome to the Rise of Islam, 500–700 (Oxford: Oxford University Press, 2011), 250.

[4]See maps two and three, which show the Middle East during and after the war of 602–628. While not directly involving the Arabian Peninsula, the war would have affected regional trade profoundly.

[5]Navid Kermani, "Poetry and Language," in The Blackwell Companion to the Qur'an, ed. Andrew Rippin (Oxford: Blackwell, 2006), 108.

[6]The statement is taken from James Porter's description of the Homeric corpus; James Porter, "Homer: The History of an Idea," The Cambridge Companion to Homer, ed. Robert Fowler (Cambridge: Cambridge University Press, 2004), 336.

[7]Robert G. Hoyland, Arabia and the Arabs: From the Bronze Age to the Coming of Islam (London: Routledge, 2001), 212; Thomas Bauer, "Relevance of Early Arabic Poetry for Qur'anic Studies," in Neuwirth, Sinai and Marx, eds., Qur'ān in Context, 702. On this poetry's development and place in pre-Islamic culture, see Greg Fisher, Between Empires: Arabs, Romans and Sasanians in Late Antiquity (New York: Oxford University Press, 2011), 153-62.

a time in the sixth century, Ethiopian-allied Yemen controlled the Hijaz as far north as Yathrib. But by the time Muhammad took up his prophetic mantle, the Hijaz had already enjoyed decades of independence from (by then Sasanian-allied) Yemen. Since religious conversion involved political alignment, the polytheistic tribes in central Arabia and the Hijaz—Muhammad's tribe, the Quraysh, among them—likely represented fiercely independent holdouts against monotheism's steady advance. Resistant to outside interference of all kinds, they were not about to be swallowed up by either foreign religious alternative, Judaism or Christianity. This gave Mecca, Ta'if and other regional cultic centers a base from which to draw pagan pilgrims.

Spirituality and Hedonism at the End of Time

Arabia's indigenous religion is more accurately described as animistic polytheism, since it did not separate the material from the spiritual realm—qur'anically, "the Seen and the Unseen"—believing that everything existed in both. They thus considered animals, rocks, rivers and stars, no less than humans, to have spirits. They also believed the world was inhabited by various other spirit beings, including angels, demons, *jinn*—somewhere between angels and demons—and others, ranging from the benign and playful to the treacherously evil.

As primary expressions of communal activity and will, the patron god cults formed the focus of tribal loyalty and cohesion, acting like "a sort of social glue" that enabled communities to operate as coherent entities "as opposed to a mass of discrete localized kinship groups."[8] Since Arab society lacked many other social institutions, we should not underestimate the sociopolitical importance of this to its polytheistic tribes. Tribal solidarity was also integral to a tribe's self-perception since, as Toshihiko Izutsu says, "All the noble qualities were considered to reside not so much in the individual members of the tribe as in the tribe itself." Again, "moral virtues were rather a precious communal possession inherited from fathers and forefathers."[9] All this was bound together with a firm belief in the need to honor one's ancestors, something that translated into an unshakable conviction that tribal tradition was binding.

Indigenous Arab religion evidenced considerable similarity to the early Middle Eastern religious traditions in many respects. Besides ritual purity, formal

[8]Hoyland, *Arabia and the Arabs*, 141.
[9]Toshihiko Izutsu, *Ethico-Religious Concepts in the Qur'ān* (Montreal: McGill University Press, 1966), 62.

prayers, incense offerings and blood sacrifice, pre-Islamic religion featured regular pilgrimage to sacred enclaves with circumambulation around a sacred object, such as the Black Stone, embedded in the Kaʿba. Tradition tells us these pilgrimages coincided with market fairs, enabling the host tribe to derive economic benefit from them. While the Arabs had formerly worshiped sacred stones, by Muhammad's day many of the gods had been personalized. Though traditional sources name Hubal and many other Arabian gods, the Meccans considered Allat, al-ʿUzza and Manat—who they counted the daughters of *Allah*, the High God— their tribal patrons. With Allat and al-ʿUzza representing different phases of the Morning Star, their sister was a goddess of Fate.[10]

With regard to such divine procreation, two points are key. First, the pre-Islamic Arabs viewed God's fathering of other divinities as neither ethereal nor delicate: it involved his sexual lust, leading to coitus with a partner, divine or human. Second, tradition says the Kaʿba had 360 gods—one for each day of their lunar calendar—among which were icons of Mary and Jesus. While this elaboration may exaggerate the situation somewhat, its inclusiveness is entirely plausible, since polytheism typically accommodates other religions. As an old Arab proverb puts it, "When you enter a village, swear by its god."[11] Swearing by one god never kept you from swearing by another. In any case, tradition suggests that the biggest differences between Jesus and his mother and the other representatives of the "family of the gods" would have been that of exclusivity, since monotheism allows no lesser deities, and locality, since the Meccans would have viewed Jesus and Mary as imported deities (cf. Q 43:57-58).

While the Qur'an gives us no sense that the Meccans disputed God's existence, the Muslim tradition is likely anachronistic in saying that they called him the "Lord of the Kaʿba." And even if that were true, they had clearly reduced him to a ringmaster of sorts, with all the attention going to the show's stars instead of him. The Qur'an makes it clear that the Quraysh saw God as irrelevant to their lives: like an absentee landlord, he maybe owned the place, but he never bothered to come around. Governed by the haphazardness of Fate (*dahr*), life was meaningless, and there was no resurrection or final

---

[10]See the articles on Manat, al-ʿUzza, Hubal and Kaʿba in *EI²*. Cf. 54n1 below on Hubal.

[11]Hoyland, *Arabia and the Arabs*, 139. For more on this, see Robert G. Hoyland, "The Jews of the Hijaz in the Qur'an and in Their Inscriptions," in *New Perspectives on the Qur'ān: The Qur'ān in Its Historical Context 2*, ed. Gabriel Said Reynolds (New York: Routledge, 2011), 91-116.

judgment for which to prepare.[12] Death was the final end of the individual's evanescent existence, since they deemed belief in a hereafter unthinkable.

This worldly-mindedness issued in that desperate hedonism so abhorred by the Qur'an: since human existence was essentially futile, voluptuous indulgence—wine, women and song—afforded the illusion of transcending one's ephemerality by dulling the pain, as it were.[13] Belief in the vanity of human existence also showed itself in a general contempt for human life, as in the callous disposal of unwanted infant daughters and the abuse of orphans and others in society's margins. Later Muslims referred to this entire package of pre-Islamic belief and practice as the *jahiliyya*, which we can translate as the "Age of Moral Abandon," or "Hedonism."[14]

One other important aspect of Muhammad's world was that successive catastrophes had put the Arabs—no less than others in the wider Middle East—in a decidedly apocalyptic mood. Beginning in the 540s and recurring each decade or so until well beyond Muhammad's day, the bubonic plague devastated many towns and cities. The recurrence of this pandemic is widely thought to have reduced the survivors' ability to recover from the more "normal" ravages of war, which by itself led to serious economic depression. In 536 and 537 massive volcanic ash clouds appear to have reduced sunlight and temperatures globally, substantially decreasing agricultural production. Major earthquakes shook the Middle East during the sixth century also. Such cataclysms—both natural and manmade—led to the rampant spread of apocalypticism in the century before Muhammad began to preach. For how could such dark days precede anything but the end of the world?

Though such thinking was by no means new, early sources show that the start of the seventh century was characterized by a virtual apocalyptic fever

---

[12]Creation's order was thus external to God in Fate's mechanistic inevitability. In early Arabic poetry, *dahr* usually appears in connection with life's essential unpredictability and vindictiveness, humankind's smallness and futility, and the certainty of each individual's appointment with death. Though *dahr* looms large in early Arabic poetry, the Qur'an addresses it specifically only once (Q 45:24-29). Instead the Qur'an addresses Fate's associates—idolatry's absentee *Allah* and the irresponsibility deriving from life's futility—which supports that poetry's general authenticity.

[13]Izutsu, *Ethico-Religious Concepts in the Qur'ān*, 53; cf. 45-54.

[14]Most Muslims understand *jahiliyya* as the "Age of Ignorance," the Qur'an being the antidote to the Arabs' great lack. But, as Goldziher has shown, the Arabic root *j-h-l* opposes not *ʿ-l-m* (knowledge), but rather *h-l-m* (restraint or self-control), qur'anically speaking. Hence *jahiliyya* relates to the period's moral deficiencies, not its lack of culture; Ignác Goldziher, *Muslim Studies*, ed. S. M. Stern, trans. C. R. Barber and S. M. Stern (London: Allen & Unwin, 1967–1971), 1:219-28.

among Christians and Jews. Nor were pagan Arabs immune to this end-times delirium, which explains the appeal of the Meccan suras with their strong focus on the imminence of the Last Day. In fact, traditional Muslim sources document the existence in the 620s and 630s of some seven or eight native Arab prophets preaching apocalyptic messages in different locales in the Hijaz and central Arabia.[15] Each prophet's revelations made him or her the leader of an autonomous polity under God, most likely viewed syncretistically. Though conflicted in detail—as is typical of such traditional Arab sources—these accounts clearly document a real historical phenomenon, representing the final moments of a religious "sea change" in Western and Central Arabia, from polytheism to monotheism. By executing all of Muhammad's competitors and crushing their prophetic movements one by one, his armies made Islam the sole surviving manifestation of the phenomenon.

To sum up, while many Arabian tribes were Jewish and most were Christian at the start of seventh century, some still clung to their traditional polytheism. The union of polity and religion was as much a part of people's thinking in Muhammad's day as it is foreign to our Western mindset today. The Arabs' previous involvement with the superpowers had shown them monotheism's modus operandi and that the world beyond their peninsula was ripe for the taking. In their world, poetry proved able to unite disparate tribes, but divinely revealed scripture and symbols served as a ruler's trump card. Both Christians and Jews had proven themselves very amenable to violence in God's name, with such violence reaching an all-time high in the century before the Muslim conquest. In the aftermath of a devastating world war, plagues and other cataclysms, the peoples of the Middle East were wracked by apocalyptic fever. Among western and central Arabia's pagans this trend gave rise to a multiplicity of indigenous prophets of doom leading localized theocratic movements. Muhammad's movement was the only one to survive.

---

[15]Musaylima and Sajah are examples, while Tulayha, Muhammad's Yemeni-based competitor, seems not to have claimed to be a prophet; Aziz Al-Azmeh, *The Emergence of Islam in Late Antiquity: Allāh and His People* (Cambridge: Cambridge University Press, 2014), 394-96.

Four

Reading *the* Qur'an in Its Muhammadan Context

While some aspects of the Qur'an seem to suggest that it had Judeo-Christian origins, the weight of evidence supports the traditional Muslim view that it was directed to a primarily pagan audience. The relative infrequency of its overt references to pagans can easily be reconciled with that fact. The Qur'an distinctly echoes the Middle East's early seventh-century religious discourse, so rich in Jewish and Christian texts. But most of the Judeo-Christian material it echoes is noncanonical, suggesting that the qur'anic author was strongly inclined toward a spirituality without confining dogmas. While he often challenges the beliefs of Jews and Christians, in the manner of an in-house discussion, he nowhere actually reinterprets their scriptures. Likewise, the elliptical style of the Qur'an's prophetic narratives point not to its originating in a monotheistic milieu but rather to Muhammad's brand of messianic leadership. The Qur'an's stock of foreign loanwords tells us only that its author employed terminology being used by other Middle Eastern monotheists, while its form and worldview undercut any notion of its direct continuity with either the Jewish or Christian community. Its polemics against Christians and Jews, so often marked by lampoon, do not support the idea of the Qur'an's Judeo-Christian origins either. Further, the presence of Christian materials in the hadith, as well as the ideas that the "Hanifs" were Muhammad's precursors and that early Christian testimony connects Islam with Christianity, are red herrings in the sea of Islamic origins. This means that the Qur'an's anti-polytheistic polemic was primarily directed against pagans. Reflecting the culture's popular interest in biblical narratives, the qur'anic author simply repurposed those narratives to support Muhammad's prophetic claim. Hence we must not superimpose onto the Muslim scripture Jewish or Christian concerns that were never in the mind of its author.

*H*aving seen that both the early non-Muslim evidence and the shape of Muhammad's broader context support the general plausibility of the traditional origins narrative, we need to recognize that these witnesses also align with the incontrovertible fact of the Muslim conquest. The main objection to this, made by defenders of moderate Islam, is that the early conquest was entirely preemptive. To uphold that claim, they make the Qur'an endorse defensive violence only. But that interpretation of the Qur'an flies in the face both of tradition and of Late Antique history, for the two great empires the Muslims either fully or significantly overran in just decades had just barely ended a devastating war and were in neither the mood nor the condition to attack anyone. Indeed, their exhaustion at least partly explains why the Muslim advance was so swift and decisive.[1] The moderate Muslim claim that the early umma's huge territorial expansion came from defensive warfare alone is purely fictitious.

Another major disputed element in the traditional origins narrative is its presentation of Muhammad as a prophet who sought to restore the biblical tradition to its original purity but from outside either biblical community. Virtually all revisionists claim that the Qur'an is rather "a continuation of the Christian [or the Jewish] tradition"[2] and that later Muslims ascribed pagan origins to Muhammad in order to stress the Qur'an's supernatural origins and deliberately hide its derived nature, Christian or Jewish.

To address this claim, we must consider the following seven aspects of the Qur'an:

1. The relative infrequency of its references to pagans

2. Qur'anic intertextuality in general

3. The frequency and style of the Qur'an's biblical narratives

4. Loanwords in the Qur'an

5. The Qur'an's form

---

[1] The Muslim advance in every direction other than across the Red Sea seems to corroborate this: they did not attack Ethiopia due to its relative strength, since it was not involved in the Sasanian-Byzantine War of 602–628. For an account of the early Muslim conquest, see Robert G. Hoyland, *In God's Path: The Arab Conquests and the Creation of an Islamic Empire* (New York: Oxford University Press, 2015), chaps. 2-3.

[2] C. Jonn Block, *The Qur'an in Christian-Muslim Dialogue: Historical and Modern Interpretations* (New York: Routledge, 2014), 6.

6. The qur'anic worldview

7. The Qur'an's approach to Jews and Christians

Taken on its own, any of these aspects may seem to suggest the Qur'an's Judeo-Christian origins. But taken together, they point in the opposite direction. That is, they better fit the idea that the Qur'an addressed the Arabs from outside both biblical communities.

The Relative Infrequency of Qur'anic References to Pagans

One aspect of the Qur'an that seems to support the theory of its Jewish or Christian origins is that it explicitly refers to Jews and Christians more often than polytheists. But this is misleading for a number of reasons. First, since pagans comprise Muhammad's homogeneous audience in Mecca, they are his default addressees there and so do not need to be singled out. Second, the qur'anic offensive against polytheism ramps up only partway through the Meccan period. As Muslim numbers in Mecca peak and the intransigence of Muhammad's Meccan opposition increases, the Qur'an critiques polytheism more stridently.[3]

Third, once the Muslim *umma* is born in Medina, pagans are external to it and are targeted mainly for military, not verbal, attack. The Medinan suras primarily attack Medina's Jews and (Muslim) "hypocrites." Then, as the Muslim conquest takes in more and more Christian tribes after Mecca's surrender, the Qur'an turns its attention more to Christians. Hence the relative infrequency of explicit qur'anic references to pagans does not point to the Qur'an's Judeo-Christian origins as it first appears.

Qur'anic Intertextuality in General

The Qur'an's intertextuality is also taken as proof that it originated within a Jewish or Christian milieu. Admittedly, its echoing of Jewish and Christian texts does show that the Qur'an and its *umma* were in some way or other related to the other monotheistic communities. But it does not point to anything as simple as direct derivation. Rather, this qur'anic aspect is easily reconciled to the traditional claim that the Qur'an first addressed polytheists in a mixed religious milieu.

---

[3]Sura 112, which appropriates and universalizes the *Shema* near the end of the Early Meccan period, attacks polytheism very clearly.

A great deal of lore of various kinds and numerous motifs echoed by the Qur'an attest to the influence of the region's Jewish and Christian communities on its author. That lore included such tales as the Seven Sleepers and the Alexander legend.[4] It also included stories of the biblical prophets and Jesus, often as given by the Jews or Christians' "interpreted Bible," for many extrabiblical texts and traditions circulating in the Middle East were interpreted biblical texts, embellished or adjusted to "better fit" the Jewish or Christian community's needs. Stories were normally traded along with goods,[5] and a great many of those stories were religious in this consummately religious age. Their traces appear in homiletic, midrashic and targumic texts in all the Jewish and Christian communities' major languages. As Sidney Griffith notes, more than the Bible itself, it is this interpreted Bible that the Qur'an so often resembles in presenting the biblical prophets.[6] It is thus within the Middle East's religious discourse, so rich with Jewish and Christian texts at the start of the seventh century, that the Qur'an appears. Its clear echoes of this rich and varied, mainly noncanonical Judeo-Christian literature suggest that the qur'anic author was strongly inclined toward a spirituality without set borders or confining dogmas. But they do not decisively tell us whether Muhammad initially approached that spirituality as a Jew or Christian or, as the *sira* asserts, as a polytheist.

The qur'anic use of biblical and other monotheistic materials, however, recombines their elements in such a way that it redefines the entire divine-human relationship: the basic human problem is no longer sin (i.e., moral deficiency), requiring salvation, but rather a simple lack of guidance calling for revelation. Some may argue that this still falls within the general parameters of a biblical-type religion. However, it much more likely points to the Qur'an's free use of the biblical repertoire of stories—which the day's apocalyptic mood made broadly appealing—from outside either monotheistic tradition. That would mean that the Qur'an's connection with the Judeo-Christian

[4]Respectively, these correspond to the Companions of the Cave and the Two-horned One, Q 18:9-26, 83-102. The qur'anic version is most closely related to the Syriac version of the Alexander legend.
[5]Reuven Firestone, *Journeys in Holy Lands: The Evolution of the Abraham-Ishmael Legends in Islamic Exegesis* (Albany: State University of New York Press, 1990), 6.
[6]Sidney H. Griffith, *The Bible in Arabic: The Scriptures of the "People of the Book" in the Language of Islam* (Princeton, NJ: Princeton University Press, 2013), 91-94. For example, we see the Talmudic interpretation of Ex 19:17 in the Qur'an's oft-mentioned "biblical" story in which God held the mountain (Sinai) over the Israelites to force his law on them (e.g., Q 2:93); Michael E. Lodahl, *Claiming Abraham: Reading the Bible and the Qur'an Side by Side* (Grand Rapids: Brazos, 2010), 18-20.

tradition represents not organic outgrowth, but rather merely contiguous influence within a very mixed religious milieu.[7]

Furthermore, had Muhammad been a Jew or Christian, we might expect the Qur'an to approach the earlier scriptures as the New Testament writers do, quoting or referring to the Jewish scriptures and freely crediting its writers when they do (e.g., Gal 3:6, 8, 11-13; Jas 4:6; 1 Pet 1:24). In that, they follow Jesus' example (e.g., Mt 5:27, 31), for having grown up in the Jewish tradition, these men also swim in a veritable sea of biblical concepts, images and narratives.

By contrast, while the Qur'an mentions the biblical scriptures often, it rarely quotes or explicitly interacts with specific known texts. It sometimes quotes a biblical text without giving credit—as in Q 112:1—or indistinctly, such that we are unsure of which text it quotes. Q 61:6, where Jesus is quoted as predicting Muhammad's coming, is a prime example of the latter.[8] Q 48:29, likewise, says the Torah and Injil both describe faith in terms of a growing plant, which relates very generally to a multitude of biblical passages. Thus we typically find very general references, allusions and indiscernibly specific references. Quoting Psalm 37:29 as "My righteous servants will inherit the earth," Q 21:105 gives one of the Qur'an's few explicit references to a known biblical text.[9] But while the Qur'an frequently challenges Jewish and Christian interpretations of their scriptures implicitly, it never does so directly in the manner of an in-house discussion, where a writer uses a specific biblical text to recover a lost or misunderstood truth.[10] What we find, rather, is the qur'anic author's approaching the Bible from outside the biblical tradition and claiming its authority, but in such a way as to marginalize it.[11]

---

[7]It is remarkable the degree to which Jewish and Christian scholars alike see Muhammad as originating from within their own communities. The exceptions are those who hypothesize a hybrid Jewish-Christian sect. The mistake in each case seems to be the assumption that biblical narratives would interest only people from Bible-based communities. But that was as untrue of early seventh-century Arabia as it is generally true of the West today, for while religion was far from waning in Muhammad's day, every ambitious Arab knew that polytheism was in decline. Hence the universal attraction of biblical religion in Muhammad's Arabia.

[8]On this see 226-27 below.

[9]On this see 195 below.

[10]Clearly, the qur'anic author had a very different relationship to the biblical texts as compared with the relationship of Jesus and the New Testament writers to the Old Testament.

[11]Hence, while the Qur'an is plainly "in dialogue" with the biblical texts in the sense that it jostles for position within the field of texts in which they are located, we must not take that to mean that it often engages with those texts explicitly, for it does not, even though it echoes and implicitly challenges them in numerous respects. For examples of how its early Meccan suras echo the biblical

The Style of the Qur'an's Prophetic Narratives

The decline of polytheism amid Arabia's religious fervor in the first decades of the seventh century explains the broad appeal of the Qur'an's echoes of biblical narratives. However, some scholars believe the elliptical style of the Qur'an's prophetic narratives points to its Christian or quasi-Christian origins, reasoning that such a style would otherwise have confused their hearers. But the Qur'an's prophetic narratives do not necessarily support the Christian milieu hypothesis for a number of reasons. To begin, we can reasonably expect all of Muhammad's hearers, Arab pagans included, to have had some basic interest in and familiarity with biblical narratives. Together with poetry, storytelling was the primary mode of entertainment, and narratives form that part of a religion's repertoire most accessible to outsiders. Religion's geopolitical aspect made it a very hot topic in early seventh-century Arabia, and the biblical religions offered the only real counterstories to paganism. Divorced from the Bible's grand narrative—as they are in the Qur'an—the biblical narratives are very plastic, taking on whatever form or meaning they are given. That is, they are easily repurposed in the service of another form of monotheism.

Admittedly, we lack irrefutable evidence for the average pagan Arab's knowledge of biblical narrative. But even if my estimate of it were shown to be inflated, the point is moot, for Muhammad's style of prophetic leadership put all of the unknown at his disposal. Whether or not a biblical story was familiar or altogether foreign to the Qur'an's hearers was never the point, for most basically, submission (*islam*) to God required obedience to the revelations, with or without understanding. Since Muhammad purportedly had no control over the messages he received, the qur'anic style of prophecy professed to be clear but was explained only gradually (Q 6:50). The recitations repeatedly assured his hearers that though they did not yet understand all, all would eventually be made clear (e.g., Q 5:48; 6:164). So any questions their narratives raised simply increased their hearers' dependence on their prophet in the hopes that the next revelation—or if not, perhaps the one after it—might bring the missing clarity. Hence this has as much to do with Muhammad's particular style of messianic leadership as with his audience's knowledge: the

psalms, see Angelika Neuwirth, "Qur'ānic Reading of the Psalms," in *The Qur'an in Context: Historical and Literary Investigations into the Qur'ānic Milieu*, ed. Angelika Neuwirth, Nicolai Sinai and Michael Marx (Leiden: Brill, 2010), 733-78.

prophetic narratives' omission of key details binds Muhammad's hearers to him due to their need for certainty in desperate times.

Further, we must not let the prophetic narratives' frequency obscure the key point here: the Qur'an never approaches any biblical story it tells with reference to the Bible's version of it. Rather, it always does so independently, with the assumption that its own version is true and hence final.[12] This represents an implicit assertion of the Qur'an's independence of the Bible. Along with the Qur'an's claim to be the Word of God, its assumption of its finality also obviates any need to reference biblical sources. Hence its frequent references to biblical prophets—including Abraham, Moses and Jesus—clearly reveal the tightrope it sets up for itself by claiming to be the sequel to the Jewish and Christian scriptures. Its insistence that Muhammad is a prophet in the biblical tradition anchors the rope on one end, while its refusal to be bound by Jewish or Christian interpretations of that tradition anchors the other end. The challenge then is for the Qur'an to incorporate characters and narratives from the Jewish and Christian traditions without allowing those traditions to judge its use of them within the context of its own account of God's dealings with humankind.

Loanwords in the Qur'an

The Qur'an's linguistic stock underscores what we have just seen—namely, that Muhammad's milieu was strongly influenced by Aramaic- and Syriac-speaking Christians in adjacent lands.[13] That qur'anic stories like the Companions of the Cave and the Two-horned One (Q 18:9-26, 83-102) evidence a greater Syriac residue than most other qur'anic texts points to their Christian origins.[14] Some of the Aramaic influence could have come from Arabia's Jews also, for even Yemen's Jews were taught by rabbis from Palestine, suggesting that their Judaism had a marked Aramaic flavor. In the case of the Jewish credo (Deut 6:4) found in Q 112:1, the Hebrew "remains audible" in the awkwardness of the verse's

---

[12]Thus Muslims very reasonably—that is, from their perspective—assume that the qur'anic narrative's biblical antecedent should conform to the qur'anic version and not vice versa.

[13]Griffith, *Bible in Arabic*, 20.

[14]Sidney Griffith, "Christian Lore and the Arabic Qur'ān: The 'Companions of the Cave' in Surat al-Kahf and in Syriac Christian tradition," in *The Qur'ān in Its Historical Context*, ed. Gabriel Said Reynolds (New York: Routledge, 2008), 116-34; and Kevin Van Bladel, "Alexander Legend in the Qur'ān 18:83-102," in Reynolds, *Qur'ān in Its Historical Context*, 175-203; cf. Gabriel Said Reynolds, *The Qur'ān and Its Biblical Subtext* (New York: Routledge, 2010), 167-85.

ungrammatical *ahad*.[15] The Medinan suras' introduction of Hebrew words—for example, *nabî'* and *ṣədaqâ*, supplementing the synonymous Arabic *rasul* and *zakat* of the Meccan suras[16]—implies what the text states, namely that the Qur'an appeals to the Jews in its Medinan audience. A lesser but still significant Ethiopic influence is evident in the Qur'an also, pointing to Mecca and Medina's location on the Red Sea corridor. It was only natural then that the qur'anic author found religious language readily available among monotheists living in and adjacent to Arabia. So while the Qur'an is written in "clear Arabic," that Arabic evidences the sort of normal linguistic borrowing that occurs in a polyglot society like Arabia then was.[17] And the very mixed nature of the Qur'an's stock of foreign loanwords suggests that the qur'anic author did not himself identify with a single established monotheistic sect.

The Qur'an's Form and Worldview

In terms of scriptural form, the Qur'an is profoundly unlike the biblical scriptures in that its author excludes even the briefest of introductory notes to help mediate his message to a wider audience. By contrast, for example, even single verses in the biblical books—such as Amos 1:1—briefly introduce the human speaker and the situation he addresses, for implicit in the biblical scriptures is the recognition that they cannot be understood in isolation from the historical situation they address. Like the biblical texts, the qur'anic text clearly presupposes a historical situation also, but it has no interest whatsoever in specifying what it is. The primary reason for this is that the Qur'an's *in situ* recitations are said to be authored exclusively by God, with no human input whatsoever, and hence are exclusive of all editorial comments.[18]

---

[15]Angelika Neuwirth, "The 'Late Antique Qur'an': Jewish-Christian Liturgy, Hellenic Rhetoric and Arabic Language" (lecture, Institute for Advanced Studies, Princeton University, June 3, 2009), www.yovisto.com/video/11805.

[16]Later Muslim scholarship assigned different meanings to these words, but their distinctions seem patently contrived. On *nabi*, see 144n7 below.

[17]Hence the Qur'an's linguistic stock does not negate the traditional claim that Muhammad and most of his early followers had polytheistic Hijazi backgrounds. It challenges only the later theologians' assumption that its Arabic exhibited a level of purity unlike that of any normal language. See Manfred Kropp, "Mechanisms of Transmission into the Ethiopic (Ga'az) Bible and the Qur'anic Text," in Reynolds, *Qur'ān in Its Historical Context*, 204-16; Griffith, *Bible in Arabic*, 18-20; Arthur Jeffery, *The Foreign Vocabulary of the Qur'an* (Baroda, India: Oriental Institute, 1938).

[18]In its living encounter with Muhammad, his audience had no need of contextual description. But the absence of such contextual markers has been the bane of every interpreter's existence since and has bound every generation of Muslims to the hadith, which grew up partly to remedy it.

This points beyond the Qur'an's form to its theology. Since part two of our study compares the biblical and qur'anic worldviews in detail, here we may simply note that, despite numerous surface similarities, the two worldviews are profoundly different. All monotheism is bound to include such features as God's unity, revealed scripture, and the call to faith and obedience to escape divine judgment. But the specific content of all such theological entries is the key factor. In contradistinction to the Qur'an, the Bible presents scriptural revelation as exclusive of human authorship very rarely. Likewise, the biblical call to faith comes to us amid great doubts and unanswered questions (e.g., the book of Job), whereas the Qur'an's call to faith leaves no room whatever for doubt, since it purportedly makes everything clear (e.g., Q 11:1; 16:89). Also, the biblical concept of prayer as intimate, honest conversation with God is radically different from that of the Qur'an, which only exceptionally allows for direct communication with God. As we will see, all these contrasts derive from more fundamental differences in the two scriptures' views of God, humankind and their relationship.

The Qur'anic Approach to Christians and Jews

Though we will return to this topic in chapter seventeen, we must briefly consider the qur'anic view of Christianity and Judaism in relation to the question of the qur'anic milieu. In Late Antiquity the Byzantines tied their political alliances to the spread of Christianity. As a result, Byzantine-leaning Christianity was well represented in northwestern Arabia and Yemen.[19] The Sasanians favored Judaism and Assyrian (Nestorian) Christianity instead, although we do not know that they actively fostered them. In any case, Judaism was also well represented in the Hijaz and other parts of Arabia, especially Yemen. But the Muslim tradition says neither religion was predominant in Mecca or environs, a point the Meccan suras support.

Given that the qur'anic vision materialized geopolitically in Medina, we must understand the qur'anic approach to Christianity and Judaism in

---

[19]The Byzantines were represented by Eastern Orthodox (Melkite), Syrian Orthodox (Jacobite) and Ethiopian Orthodox (Tewahedo) Christianity. Sidney H. Griffith, s.v. "Christians and Christianity," in *EQ*; Rick Brown, "Who was 'Allah' Before Islam? Evidence that the Term 'Allah' Originated with Jewish and Christian Arabs," in *Toward Respectful Understanding and Witness Among Muslims: Essays in Honor of J. Dudley Woodberry*, ed. Evelyne A. Reisacher (Pasadena, CA: William Carey Library, 2012), 157-59.

geopolitical terms. That is not to say the qur'anic author is not at all interested in Christian theology, for he is deeply disturbed by its Trinity. But the
finer points of theological difference between competing Christian confes-
sions are of no import to him or his primarily pagan audience.[20] The Jewish-
Christian conflict, however, is different, since it dominates both Palestine
and Western Arabia, and the mere presence of Jewish and Christian tribes
spells mutual hostility. By highlighting the Jewish-Christian division but
barely mentioning Christian infighting, the Qur'an reflects this situation
well and implies that its origins are not Christian. Given the scale and intensity of Jewish-Christian hostility, Muhammad could hardly have expected to end it conclusively, though he doubtless sought to win both
Jewish and Christian tribes to his cause. The Qur'an says its revelations
clarify what Jews and Christians differ over (Q 27:76), and those differences clearly pertain to what it considers the Jews' shocking devaluation
of and the Christians' gross overestimation of Jesus. Muhammad clearly
seeks to create his own separate community as the "golden mean" between
those extremes.

One point we absolutely must see is that the Qur'an's anti-Jewish and anti-
Christian polemics alternate between serious rebuttal and biting caricature.
Q 9:30-31, for example, accuses Jews and Christians respectively of calling
Ezra ('Uzayr) and Christ (al-masih) God's Son and of taking their rabbis and
monks as lords besides God. Not recognizing the verse's initial polytheistic
charge as lampoon, Moshe Sharon postulates some sort of Jewish messianic
sect in Yathrib to explain it[21] in the very same way that Geoffrey Parrinder,
C. Jonn Block and others hypothesize various Christian sects to explain similar
qur'anic caricature of the Christian Trinity. All such hypotheses mistake
qur'anic lampoon for direct censure, the former being aimed at reducing all of
Muhammad's opponents to one common enemy: polytheists, whether or not
anyone else would call them that.[22] Rather than postulating a multiplicity of
idiosyncratic sects to make sense of our mistakenly literal interpretations of
such qur'anic lampoon, we must simply see the latter for what it is.

[20]Unlike the Jewish-Christian split, Christian sectarian division is rarely mentioned (Q 5:14).
[21]Moshe Sharon, s.v. "People of the Book," in *EQ*.
[22]As previously noted, the passage renders Jews no less than Christians polytheists. Contrary to
Yusuf Ali's unhelpful comment on Q 9:30, the Hebrew Bible's use of the expression "son of God"
in the singular is very different from that of the plural: Jews would not have confused them.

Not all qur'anic criticism is caricature, however. Q 9:30, for example, also calls on God to attack Christians for perverting the truth in saying, "The Messiah is the Son of God." This mixture of straightforward denunciation of Christianity with parody confuses many. The Qur'an, for example, often rebuts belief in Jesus' deity by twisting the words of Christians, turning "one God in three persons" into "God is the third of three" and "The Messiah is God" into "God is the Messiah" (Q 5:72-73).[23] Such alterations distort Christian teaching enough to make it appear polytheistic, simultaneously aggravating Christian and entertaining non-Christian hearers.

The key point is that the Qur'an has no real interest in presenting Christian (or Jewish) belief on its own terms but seeks rather to make it look as bad as possible after the manner of early Arabic poetry's lampoon. In Sura 5, God grills Jesus over whether he had told his followers to take himself and his mother "as gods beside God" (Q 5:116), as if Christians believe in three gods and make Mary part of their Trinity. The words "gods beside God" would have horrified Christians then no less than now. Q 4:171, "Do not say 'Three!' . . . God is one God." Another verse that casts Christian belief in terms of the pagan notion of God's having carnally conceived "offspring" exclaims that God is far above having a son.[24]

Taking such invective literally, Parrinder says the Qur'an rejects not the Christian Trinity but rather tritheism. Technically he is right, but he misses the point entirely in suggesting the Qur'an is attacking Collyridianism, a syncretistic Marian heresy that may have existed in Arabia three centuries earlier.[25] François de Blois identifies the object of the attack with Nazoreans and Block with Philoponian Tritheists.[26] Others claim the Qur'an was the product of

---

[23]While a Syrian Christian sect may have spoken of God's being the third of three (Griffith, "Christians and Christianity"), the Qur'an does not target that sect. It simply ridicules mainstream miaphysite (monophysite) Christians, whose presence in Muhammad's Arabia is amply attested; cf. 43n19 above.

[24]Although the text uses the word *walad* for "son," we can be sure the Christian Trinity is meant (on *walad* see below). But Muslim translators who substitute "Trinity" for the Arabic text's "Three" wrongly flatten qur'anic diatribe in an effort to lessen its dissonance.

[25]Geoffrey Parrinder, *Jesus in the Qur'an*, (Oxford: Oneworld, 1995) 133-37. Averil Cameron doubts that such a sect ever existed. See Cameron, "The Cult of the Virgin in Late Antiquity: Religious Development and Myth-Making," *Studies in Church History* 39 (2004): 6-7.

[26]Block, *Qur'an in Christian-Muslim Dialogue*, 40-43; François de Blois, "*Naṣrānī* (*Nadzoraios*) and *ḥanīf* (*ethnikos*): Studies on the Religious Vocabulary of Christianity and of Islam," *Bulletin of the School of Oriental and African Studies* 65 (2002): 1-30. These approaches are all based on woodenly literal readings of the qur'anic passages on *al-nasara*. But while the presence of Syrian Orthodox, Ethiopian

heterodox Christians who denied the Trinity. All such hypotheses produce a major disconnect between a hypothetical proto-Islam and the later Muslim community when written Islamic documentation makes such historical free-wheeling impossible.[27]

It would be far tidier if all qur'anic critique were either ridicule or straight attack, but lampoon works best with just such a mix as we find in the Qur'an. Q 5:17 follows the preceding verse's ridicule with straight argumentation when it says no one could possibly restrain God if he chose to destroy the Messiah and his mother along with everyone else on earth. As the context indicates, Jesus' sheer expendability relates to his being a mere creature and so entirely at God's disposal. Thus the Qur'an attacks not Christian heterodoxy but rather orthodoxy, driving home what it considers Christian folly through both straight criticism and biting parody.[28] This also points to the Qur'an's having originated outside the Christian tradition, since it aims to dismantle both the Christian and Jewish worldviews and polities in favor of its own.

The Qur'an reflects other details concerning Jews and Christians that the hadith corroborate. For example, the rarity of the Meccan suras' direct address of Jews and Christians agrees with the traditional view that Mecca had only a few Christian residents. Tradition also puts a number of Jewish tribes in Medina and further north as well as Christian tribes in Yemen and northern Arabia, which accords with what the early evidence tells us of the strong presence of Christians in most of Arabia and of Jews in Yemen, as well as scattered across northwestern Arabia. The Medinan suras reflect this in their frequent address of Jews and Christians as the expanding Muslim *umma* runs into increasing contact with them.[29]

---

and Assyrian (Nestorian) Christians in Arabia is well attested, there is no evidence for Nazoreans or Ebionites there for at least two centuries before Muhammad. Further, taking this term to refer to a minor sect agrees with neither Muslim tradition nor early Qur'an interpretation. And we should expect the Qur'an to engage with standard forms of Christianity unless Muhammad had no interest in expanding beyond the Hijaz, which was clearly not the case.

[27]The multiplicity of sects proposed points to a total lack of compelling evidence. Block argues that the use of "Trinity" (*al-thaluth*) in Arabic more than a century before Muhammad shows that the Qur'an intentionally chose to use "three" (*thalatha*) in Q 4:171 and 5:73 because "the word 'trinity' did not express the meaning intended." Block is correct to argue that the choice of "three" instead of "Trinity" was deliberate. But he totally overlooks the explanation that the qur'anic author's aim here was dysphemistic; *Qur'an in Christian-Muslim Dialogue*, 40-43.

[28]Most Muslims approach the Trinity in this same way, moving seamlessly from parody to straight criticism and back again, the difference being that they are unaware of doing so.

[29]Robert G. Hoyland, *Arabia and the Arabs: From the Bronze Age to the Coming of Islam* (London: Routledge,

Thus, rightly appreciated, none of the seven features of the Qur'an we have considered contradicts the traditional view that Muhammad and his first followers had a pagan background. Rather, all seven are very compatible with that aspect of the traditional origins narrative. Hence Western scholarship's recent emphasis on the Qur'an's connection with the Bible has real merit: there is indeed a major connection between the two scriptures, one that classical Muslim scholars seriously downplayed in their emphasis on the Qur'an's supernatural origins. But to say the Qur'an is more interested in the Bible than in paganism equally distorts the issue. Such Christianization of the Qur'an represents a pendulum swing, correcting one excess with another. Many biblical narratives retold by the Qur'an, for example, form an integral part of its anti-pagan polemic.

Red Herrings in the Islamic Origins Sea

In seeking the origins of Islam, three other red herrings can lead us falsely to conclude that Islam's origins were Christian or quasi-Christian, not pagan:

1. The idea that the "Hanifs" of the Qur'an and hadith were Muhammad's precursors

2. The presence of clearly Christian materials in the hadith

3. Early Christian testimony appearing to connect Islam with Christianity

To begin, Muslim tradition takes the Qur'an's so-called Hanifs to be indigenous pre-Islamic monotheists who lived moral lives in anticipation of the judgment but who identified with neither Jews nor Christians. Many Western scholars thus view the Hanifs as Muhammad's precursors, while some mistakenly identify him with the generic monotheistic cult associated with the *Rahmanan* inscriptions in Yemen.[30] Furthermore, the qur'anic data support Andrew

---

2001), 146, 235-36. Our earliest source on Medina's Jewish tribes is the Qur'an. The Muslim tradition expands on it, but some of what it says appears to be conjecture; Robert G. Hoyland, "The Jews of the Hijaz in the Qur'an and in Their Inscriptions," in *New Perspectives on the Qur'an: The Qur'ān in Its Historical Context 2*, ed. Gabriel Said Reynolds (New York: Routledge, 2011), 91, 111, 113-15.

[30] As Norbert Nebes has shown, the so-called *Rahmanan* cult was actually just Jewish. See Norbert Nebes, "Martyrs of Najran and the End of the Himyar," in Neuwirth, Sinai and Marx, eds., *Qur'ān in Context*, 35-40. The Himyarites likely toned down their Judaism for political reasons, publically inscribing nothing Ethiopia could take as a pretext for interfering on behalf of Himyar's Christians. This made it possible for Himyar to resist Ethiopia's claims on it without risking war with Ethiopia, something Himyar's earlier rulers were not prepared to do.

Rippin's claim that, unlike the later hadith, the Qur'an uses *hanif* to identify not a religious group but rather just the specific moral character "embodied in the myth of Abraham and captured in the word *muslim*."[31] Though the Qur'an makes repeated use of the word *hanif*, it never addresses Hanifs as it does Jews and Christians, and this suggests that Hanifs refers to no sect at all.

Second, one might think the presence of such quintessentially Christian materials as the Lord's Prayer in well-authenticated hadith points to Muhammad's Christian, as opposed to polytheistic, origins. But in its first centuries after Muhammad, "whatever Islam produced on its own or borrowed from the outside was dressed up as hadith." Biblical passages, rabbinic sayings, quotations from apocryphal gospels and wisdom from the Greeks, Persians and Indians "all gained entrance into Islam disguised as utterances of the Prophet."[32] This evidences not Muhammad's actual affinity to Christianity (or Hinduism!) but only the later *umma*'s urge to correct what it perceived as qur'anic lacunae by borrowing from many diverse sources.

Finally, we must beware of misinterpreting early Christian testimony concerning Islam. Donner points out that John of Damascus (d. 749) categorizes Islam as a "Christian heresy" as if he thus asserts its Christian origins.[33] But John is, instead, simply categorizing Islam as a heresy that includes belief in Jesus as Messiah.[34] Likewise, we cannot take at face value Isho'yahb's statement that the Arabs did not oppose the Christians but rather encouraged and aided them.[35] He was merely ingratiating himself with the Muslim authorities in a

---

[31]Andrew Rippin, "RHMNN and the Hanifs," in *Islamic Studies Presented to Charles J. Adams*, ed. Wael B. Hallaq and Donald P. Little (Leiden: Brill, 1991), 161; cf. 158-60. For example, see Q 2:135; 3:67, 95; 16:120, 123. In qur'anic usage even the word *muslim* refers not to members of a reified religion—namely Islam—but rather to those who had rightfully submitted to God by following Muhammad. As noted above, Muslims only began calling themselves by that name in the 690s. The Muslim tendency to read the qur'anic *hanif* as a sect is similarly anachronistic.

[32]Ignác Goldziher, *Introduction to Islamic Theology and Law*, trans. Andras Hamori and Ruth Hamori (Princeton, NJ: Princeton University Press, 1981), 40.

[33]Fred M. Donner, *Muhammad and the Believers: At the Origins of Islam* (Cambridge, MA: Belknap Press, 2010), 223.

[34]John's schema has just two categories of heresy: "non-Christian" and "Christian" heresies, the former rejecting Jesus' messiahship outright, the latter professing it in some garbled form.

[35]Block supports his ecumenical interpretation of Isho'yahb's statement by attributing to Hoyland the view that Isho'yahb never considered Islam "a 'separate phenomenon' from Christianity"; Block, *Qur'an in Christian-Muslim Dialogue*, 154. But taken in context, Hoyland is not saying that at all (Robert G. Hoyland, *Seeing Islam as Others Saw It: A Survey and Evaluation of Christian, Jewish and Zoroastrian Writings on Early Islam* [Princeton, NJ: Darwin Press, 1997], 179), as Hoyland himself confirms; Robert G. Hoyland, personal communication, July 12, 2015. Seventh-century Christians

futile effort to avoid paying taxes. After the Muslims had caught onto his scheme, imprisoned and tortured him, and ransacked some of his churches, Isho'yahb spoke about Islam with far more candor.[36]

To sum up, the early non-Muslim evidence, the Qur'an and the hadith combine to tell us that

- the first Muslims came out of a polytheistic tribe—not a preexisting monotheistic group—in a Hijazi milieu in which some familiarity with the biblical religion was normative;

- Muhammad was a messianic-type leader who was far more urgent that his followers be dependent on him for further clarity than that they understand everything in his recitations; and

- the Qur'an's polemic against actual polytheism is primary in the Meccan suras; only in the Medinan period does its polemics against Judaism and Christianity come to the fore.

Hence tradition's claim that Muhammad's milieu was pagan is solidly founded—compatible with both the qur'anic and the early non-Muslim data. What remains for us to consider in more depth is how well the qur'anic worldview supports the traditional claim, and to that we now turn.

---

commonly recognized that God had sent the Arabs to punish them for their sins. Block seems to equate that admission with their acceptance of the Arabs' religion (Islam) as being from God, which is an entirely different matter. And to do so he must totally disregard the many other early Christian witnesses who point to a great gulf between the two faiths (for examples, see 22-23 above). What Hoyland says of Donner's ecumenical approach is equally relevant here: though it is a worthy aim harmoniously to combine Muslims in Islam's early period with their fellow monotheists, "it is concerned more with our modern world than with that of Muhammad and his followers"; Robert G. Hoyland, review of *Muhammad and the Believers: At the Origins of Islam* by Fred M. Donner, *International Journal of Middle East Studies* 44, no. 3 (August 2012): 576.

[36]Hoyland, personal communication, July 12, 2015.

Part II

Qur'anic Worldview

Five

God's Immanence *and* Transcendence

The complexity of the question of whether the God of the Qur'an is the God of the Bible means that it cannot be answered with a simple *yes* or *no* and demands a more nuanced and holistic approach. We should, however, graciously allow that Muslims too seek the God of Abraham. The Qur'an challenges the *jahili*, or pre-Islamic pagan, notion of God's being unconcerned about humanity's moral choices. It thus presents God as the Lord and master of all and furthermore as a judge who is ready to strike the arrogant down. It also shows him to be our creator, king, guide and deliverer. Much about the qur'anic treatment of God derives from the *jahili* Arab concept of nobility, the chief characteristics of which are independence and the refusal to bow to anyone. Hence, while the Qur'an challenges *jahili* theology in some regards, it reflects it in others—for example, downplaying anything that might be thought to put him in a serving role. It challenges *jahili* thinking on divine immanence, yet in true *jahili* fashion makes him so transcendent that he is not truly approachable. By comparison to biblical theology, God's immanence seems overpowered by his transcendence in the Qur'an. For that reason, the Qur'an implicitly rejects the biblical metaphors pointing to our being able to know God intimately. Rather, the primary qur'anic metaphor for God is that of master—one who, in fact, has no obligations whatsoever to any of his creatures. For while God certainly reveals himself to us in various ways in the Qur'an, such knowledge seems almost illegitimate, since his transcendence takes precedence over everything else. And that signals a major difference between the Qur'an and the Bible.

God is not merely one of many topics in the Muslim scripture. He is before, behind and in every topic found there. He is the speaker and, implicitly at least, the subject throughout. The Qur'an says a great deal about God explicitly also, raising the question, How does its presentation of God differ from that of the Bible, and what accounts for the difference? In this chapter and the next, we will consider that question in ontological and ethical terms. Before we move into those discussions, however, we must pause briefly to consider a critical question of general import: Do Christians and Muslims believe in the same God?

Is It the Same God?

The question of whether or not *Allah* is the God of the Bible is straightforward enough. Arabia's Jews and Christians used the word *Allah* long before Muhammad did, since it is simply the Arabic word for "God."[1] Accordingly, *Allah* is equally Jewish, Christian and Muslim.

If we mean rather to ask if the God of the Qur'an is the same as the God of the Bible, however, then the answer is a resounding yes-and-no. Both the Bible and Qur'an proclaim monotheistic messages. In both, God is personal, transcendent and unique. In both, he has sent prophets—Abraham, Moses, David and Jesus among others—to reveal his truth, and each individual's eternal destiny depends on her response to his revelation. And the Qur'an understands the earlier God-given scriptures to include the Torah, the Psalms and the Injil[2] (Q 4:163; 5:49). In all these respects, the answer is, *Yes, we are talking about the same God.* However, the Qur'an and Bible predicate many other things of God

---

[1]Robert Morey, Pat Robertson and other Christian apologists have popularized the early twentieth-century notion that the word *Allah* can be traced to *Ilah*, a South Arabian title of the moon god, who was purportedly called Hubal in Mecca; Robert Morey, *The Moon-God Allah in the Archeology of the Middle East* (Newport, PA: Research and Education Foundation, 1994). Aside from its obvious polemical value, this claim is no more learned than the nineteenth-century claim that the word *God* derives from the Buddha's patriarchal name of Gotama/Gautama. It is indisputably clear from inscriptions in Nabatea and elsewhere that *Allah* meant "the God"; Alfred Guillaume, *Islam* (Harmondsworth, UK: Penguin Books, 1956), 7. And the Muslim tradition confirms this. Furthermore, Hubal is not to be identified with a moon god at all, but rather with a warrior god and a god of rain; David Adams Leeming, *Jealous Gods and Chosen People: The Mythology of the Middle East* (Oxford: Oxford University Press, 2004), 121. As Rick Brown says, outside of the Hijaz, Arabia's tribes were nearly all either Christian or Jewish and both communities referred to God as Allah, which made Allah the natural choice for the qur'anic author; Rick Brown, "Who was 'Allah' Before Islam? Evidence that the Term 'Allah' Originated with Jewish and Christian Arabs," in *Toward Respectful Understanding and Witness Among Muslims: Essays in Honor of J. Dudley Woodberry*, ed. Evelyne A. Reisacher (Pasadena, CA: William Carey Library, 2012), 147-78.
[2]On the meaning of *al-injil*, often unhelpfully translated "Gospel," see chapter seventeen below.

that are profoundly different. The Qur'an presents God as neither a unity-in-trinity nor remotely open to incarnation. It differs dramatically from the Bible on God's character also. For example, the Qur'an nowhere describes God as being in his very nature love and hence interested in a love relationship with human beings. In these respects, the answer is, *No, this is not the same God.*

How then do we call it? Do we come down on the side of our theological similarities or differences? There may be as many differences as similarities, and it is only right that we point those differences out in a spirit of mutual respect and honor, as I do in this book. But despite the differences, the Qur'an affirms that Muslims, Christians and Jews together believe in the God of Abraham, a point vital to its polemical approach. And I believe Christians should graciously reciprocate, acknowledging the theological beliefs we have in common.

Fearing syncretism, some Christians disagree with me here. But showing such grace to Muslims does not have to mean glossing over deep theological disruptions as if they do not exist. My point is that the question *Is it the same God?* cannot be answered either affirmatively or negatively because both answers represent a case of theological overreach. As we will see, the Qur'an often plugs biblical words, concepts and narratives into its own very different theological grid, giving them very different meanings. However, simply affirming that my Muslim friend and I both believe in the one Creator God says nothing about the sufficiency or deficiency of our respective theologies. I accept our need to draw a line in the sand, as it were, but this is not the place for us to draw that line. The question is the wrong question and leads to an either-or dilemma. Instead, I would argue for a more nuanced, holistic and relationally grounded approach.

Up close, the simple question "Do we believe in the same God?" turns out to be rather complex, because everyone's knowledge of God is inherently personal and multidimensional.[3] It is never just a question of competing belief systems. Rather, it relates to our knowledge of God as individuals, and that knowledge has normative, situational and existential dimensions.[4] And we must keep all three in mind to do theology well.

---

[3]Biblically, God encounters everyone—those who reject him included. In that sense, despite his loud denials, even Pharaoh "knew" God (Ex 5:2; cf. Jas 2:19).

[4]I borrow these dimensions from John M. Frame, who refers to them as "perspectives," in *The Doctrine of the Knowledge of God: A Theology of Lordship* (Phillipsburg, NJ: Presbyterian and Reformed, 1987), 169-346.

As Christians, we rightly view the Bible as normative for our under-standing of God. Where the Qur'an differs from the Bible, we judge the former by the latter. However, as fallen human beings, our capacity to em-brace biblical truths about God is imperfect, and this situation affects everyone irrespective of creed. Many Christians misunderstand the Trinity and other vital truths about God. And we have all at times lapsed into that practical deism where we view God as distant and implicitly deny his goodness and love, two core attributes. Yet despite our sub-Christian under-standings, we stand together in worship and simply pray that God will help us all understand him better. We accuse no one of worshiping a different God. Why then should we do so with Muslims? After all, we should judge ourselves more strictly than outsiders (Lk 12:48; 1 Pet 4:17). The apostles could have told those Jews who persisted in rejecting Jesus that they worshiped a dif-ferent God, but they very wisely refrained from doing so.[5] We do well to learn the humility that kept them from that mistake.

This brings us to the existential dimension of our knowledge of God. Here I refer to the fact that every human being is directly encountered by God, who works as he will to draw us into a love relationship with himself. Thankfully, he hears our prayers, even though we perceive him imperfectly. The reality is that he hears Muslim prayers too and speaks to Muslim hearts. In that sense, despite the New Testament's clear teaching that Jesus is the only way to God, we Christians have no monopoly on God. If our theology does not allow God to be God, then we have missed the whole point of it. Further, when we do not even know our own hearts, how can we claim to know where our Muslim friends are in their spiritual journeys? For pronouncing on the "Muslim God" speaks to that too. Doing theology without a keen awareness of our limitations, we flirt with that rationalism that does not defer to the only Searcher of hearts.

---

[5]John Piper seemingly fails to see the irony in his statement that since Muslims do not believe in the Trinity or that God sent Jesus to die for our sins, they do not believe in the God of the Bible. See John Piper, "A Common Word Between Us?," *Desiring God*, January 23, 2008, www.desiringgod.org/articles /a-common-word-between-us. The very same things are true of Jews who believe in the God of the Bible—that is, of its First Testament. Admittedly, Jews and Muslims are not in the same situation with respect to biblical truth, and I too have problems with the Yale response to "A Common Word Between Us and You" (November 18, 2007), which Piper laments. See "Christian Responses," A Common Word, accessed October 4, 2015, www.acommonword.com/category/site/christian-responses. For more on the ACW letter see 180 below. But the fact remains that isolating the normative from the other two dimensions of our knowledge of God leads us to draw unhelpful lines.

As important as theological clarity is, it must never be allowed to trump our needful humility: we who are but dust must not play God.

So again, biblically, we must keep the normative, situational and existential together. Isolating any one dimension from the other two invariably leads to theological overreach. That is why Jesus' teaching on the radical hospitality of God (Lk 15:11-32) is not only music to a sinner's ears but also wisdom from above. Since God welcomes us home long before we can dot our theological i's and cross our theological t's, we must not withhold from our Muslim friends the grace he has so lavished on us. Paul modeled this generosity toward pagans in Athens by both affirming their worship of God—even though they worshiped him in ignorance—and then correcting their false view of him (Acts 17:23-31). If such grace was warranted to pagans, how can we possibly withhold it from Muslims, who share our belief in one God?

Master and Judge

What then can we say of the qur'anic view of God?[6] The Qur'an presents him in terms of six interrelated images:

- master
- judge
- creator
- king
- guide
- deliverer

As previously noted, the *jahili* Arab conceived of God as remote and indifferent to humankind. Against that backdrop, the Qur'an presents him as a judge who is poised and ready to strike. There is a real blurring of lines between temporal and eschatological here as the Qur'an warns that the eschaton may at any point break through into the here and now to obliterate the heedless (e.g., Suras 74, 82, 96, 102, 111). Emphasizing the terrors

---

[6]The Qur'an arguably begins with the worship of one god among many (henotheism) and then gradually shifts to a rejection of all but God. For a presentation of this perspective, see Aziz Al-Azmeh, *The Emergence of Islam in Late Antiquity: Allāh and His People* (Cambridge: Cambridge University Press, 2014), 279-357.

awaiting the rebellious, the Qur'an insists that God commands everyone to fear him and repent while they can. Since he is all-seeing and everywhere present, he knows full well what each person has coming to her (Q 6:3). In addition, he is utterly exacting in his punishment of the careless and un-believing and can rain down swift judgment on them whenever he chooses. And while such dramatic interventions may be exceptional, the Qur'an's mention of them definitely is not.

Inherent in God's being our final judge is the idea of his being our master, the one who makes covenants (singular *mithaq*) with humankind. The ancient Middle Eastern covenant concept centers in the idea of mutual responsibility. Since God provides bountifully for us (e.g., Suras 93, 94, 106), we must grate-fully submit and obey his covenant, the basis on which he rewards or punishes. Human responsibility is thus the pivotal point of the Qur'an's great emphasis on the hereafter, its insistent call for faith in "God and the Last Day."

This is in sharp contrast to the *jahili* package of polytheism-pessimism-hedonism it addresses. Such polytheism made God remote—indifferent to us and our behavior—and yet humanized him in that it made him compete with others for rank and glory. The Qur'an is utterly intolerant of both beliefs. Thus it damns polytheism for its "association" (*shirk*) of rivals with God. But this is better put the other way around: the qur'anic author perceives as polytheism anything he views as in any way reducing God to our level. This is vital for us to understand what he finds so disturbing about not just the Christian worship of Jesus but so many other aspects of biblical religion also—although he only hints at this.[7] The Qur'an is thus equally concerned that we not reduce God to our level or shrug him off as indifferent to how we live.

Against a concept of God as remote, indifferent, uninvolved in the affairs of humankind, the Qur'an is at great pains to present him as very near—sometimes startlingly so. In that regard, God tests everyone, rich and poor, through the circumstances of our lives and holds the power of life and death over us. When Q 50:16 says that God is nearer to a man "than his jugular vein," the context makes clear that it refers to the ease with which he can cut off the life of the arrogant. Likewise, the context of Q 56:83-87 shows it to be about the terror of God's nearness in death, and that of Q 2:115 about our

---

[7]For examples see chapter nineteen below.

inability to escape his scrutiny, no matter where we turn. Contrary to Sufi assertions, these verses do not point to humankind's essential oneness with God. Rather, the emphasis is on the divine immanence as a fear-striking intensity of presence, a threatening all-inclusiveness of knowledge, and this motif is one we find repeated throughout the Qur'an (e.g., Q 3:29; 17:60; 34:50-51; 58:7). The one clear exception is found in Q 2:186, where God is seen as responsively present to the believer who calls (*da'a*) on him. But the context there gives us reason to expect such responsiveness only in the direst of situations.[8]

Creator and King

Besides depicting God as our final judge, the Qur'an presents him as the creator and sovereign ruler of all, the one who embraces all things in his will. Hence nothing happens in all of creation without his willing it to happen, and human actions never determine the course of events.[9] With a simple word of command, he brought the universe into being (Q 6:73; 16:40; 36:81-83). He then created the world in a single week,[10] and by his word he rules and sustains everything (Q 10:3; 23:17-20; 30:25-26; 35:41; 41:9-12; 50:38; 67:19; cf. Q 79:29-33). Everything then, evidences God's immediate presence and involvement in his creation, and that is why the Qur'an insists the created order is replete with "signs" (*ayat*) of God's involvement in our world (e.g., Q 2:164; 3:190; 10:5-6; 17:12; 56:63-73; 88:17-20). Just as the Qur'an speaks of God's providentially blessing us, it also refers to his wisely meting affliction out to us in this life. And since God is the giver of all we receive of good or ill, we should equally receive life's prosperity and adversity with gratitude, reverence and faith in his wisdom. Indeed, it is the lack of these things that spells the unbeliever's downfall.

Accordingly, God chooses everyone's destiny, whether believer or unbeliever (Q 7:156), though the qur'anic stress on human responsibility suggests that this happens with each individual's full involvement. On one hand, the Qur'an repeatedly describes God as merciful, but on the other, it says he leads some

---

[8]See Toshikiho Izutsu, *God and Man in the Koran: Semantics of the Koranic Weltanschauung* (Tokyo: Keio Institute of Cultural and Linguistic Studies, 1964), 193-97.

[9]John Kaltner, *Ishmael Instructs Isaac: An Introduction to the Qur'an for Bible Readers* (Collegeville, MN: Liturgical Press, 1999), 105.

[10]While Q 41:9-12 speaks of eight days, most Muslim interpreters take it to mean seven days.

people astray and created some specifically to populate hell (Q 7:179; 14:4). He thus superintends every human choice we make, both good and evil.[11]

Though the Bible speaks somewhat similarly of divine sovereignty and election (e.g., Ex 7:3; Rom 9:17-18; Eph 1:4-5), it differs from the Qur'an in three key respects. First, it balances its emphasis on divine sovereignty with not just human responsibility but also a strong emphasis on God's self-revelation and his utter separation from evil (e.g., Lev 19:2; Jas 1:13), two emphases notably lacking in the Qur'an. Second, these biblical emphases create a marked tension between God's ontological and his ethical greatness, prompting the question, How can a merciful, good and sovereign God permit evil? By contrast, the *jahili* Arab saw *Allah* as not remotely answerable to anyone and, taking the same view, the Qur'an treats the problem of theodicy like the nonissue it was to Muhammad's *jahili* hearers. The Qur'an never so much as raises the question of the book of Job.[12] Last, in connection with Christ's redemptive death, the element of antinomy stands in far bolder relief in the Bible. There the evil God ordains is not only the moral cancer to which he is unalterably opposed but also the very means he uses to undo evil in our world (Acts 2:23-24; 3:18). Biblically speaking, this makes Jesus' death the enigma explaining all, since the full expression of good and evil that brought it about perfectly accomplished God's will. And being paradigmatic of the meaning of history, it thus lessens theodicy's tension somewhat.[13]

Guide and Deliverer

The Qur'an evidences two more metaphors for God: that of guide and protector or deliverer. To begin, God guides humankind by constantly

---

[11]Daud Rahbar is mistaken to say the entire notion of foreordination represents a post-qur'anic innovation in Muslim theologizing; see *God of Justice: A Study in the Ethical Doctrine of the Qur'ān* (Leiden: Brill, 1960), chaps. 9-10. As Izutsu points out, belief in foreordination was already common among religiously minded Arabs in pre-Islamic times; Izutsu, *God and Man in the Koran*, 131-32.

[12]This was highly problematic to many Hellenized converts to Islam, whose rationalism led them to isolate divine sovereignty from human responsibility and conclude that if God's sovereignty is absolute, it must also be arbitrary. Sunni theologians reacted by embracing a virtual agnosticism relative to ethical—and ultimately all—descriptives of God. Fazlur Rahman's reaction to such obscurantism revived much of the old debate in the modern era in *Islam*, 2nd ed. (Chicago: University of Chicago Press, 1979).

[13]That tension may call for some logical qualification of God's ordaining evil as "permissive" in contrast to the "prescriptive" or "perfect" will of God. But this goes beyond the Bible, which apparently views such tension holistically, as inherent in the nature of reality.

presenting us with signs of his existence as mentioned above. The Qur'an points to such signs mainly to orient its audience to God so they might listen to his verbal revelation to them. In that regard, God sends prophets to guide humankind in the "straight path," which the Qur'an uses as a technical term for the path of submission it marks out for believers (Q 4:163; 6:19; 18:27; 42:7). That God guides his prophets and their communities is the concept most basic to the Qur'an (Q 2:143; 7:155; 25:31; 37:114-22; 93:7), even though God is seldom given the specific title of "guide" (Q 22:54; 25:31).

Because God's prophet and *umma* represent him on earth, God sustains them and leads them to victory (Q 2:257; 41:30-31). He is described as "the best of helpers" and named "deliverer" and "guardian" also (Q 3:150; 4:45; 7:196; 13:11; 34:26; 42:28; 45:19; 59:23). Most of the Meccan punishment narratives imply this, since the punishment of a prophet's enemies represents a kind of victory, even if he simply stands by and observes. The Medinan suras make this point explicit (e.g., Q 3:110-12; 8:45-48, 65-66), since Medina was where Muhammad and his followers regained their honor by triumphing over the Meccans. The Qur'an also speaks of God's deliverance in relation to life's crises (Q 6:63-64), to divine judgment—e.g., Noah from the flood (Q 2:49; 7:64; 21:71)—and apparently to the Battle of Badr (Q 3:13, 123-25). Further, the Qur'an speaks of God's ransoming Abraham's nearly sacrificed son (Q 37:107). But the Qur'an never refers to divine deliverance (or redemption) from sin itself, that is, from sin's grip on the human soul, for in its view none is needed.

We might say that Muhammad's entire mission to his people—like that of all the prophets before him—is to save them from the coming wrath (Q 1:7; 3:103; 40:41). And in that regard, the Qur'an repeatedly refers to God as "the All-forgiving" (*al-ghafur* and *al-ʿafuw*) and "the One who turns" in forgiveness (*al-tawwab*) and grants "salvation" (*al-furqan*) (Q 4:16, 64, 110, 149; 8:29).[14] God is also described as "the best of forgivers" (*khayru-l-ghafir*), forgiveness being vital to his rescuing believers from hellfire (Q 7:155). But compared to the biblical emphasis on salvation, the Qur'an dramatically de-emphasizes the theme of divine deliverance.

---

[14]Variously translated, *al-furqan* seemingly refers to the qur'anic revelation.

Immanence in the Two Scriptures

Though the qur'anic treatment of divine immanence resembles its biblical counterpart in many respects, the two are very different also. As we have seen, the Qur'an embraces six of the Bible's central metaphors of God's relationship to us, depicting him as master, judge, creator, king, guide and deliverer, though its treatment of the latter two themes is comparatively slight. This raises the question of why the Muslim scripture fails to emphasize things so obviously intrinsic to it. The answer may partly relate to the intimacy of this metaphor in the Bible. There God not only verbally guides us through his prophets but also reveals himself to us. And with respect to our salvation, he bares "his holy arm" to save us and even sacrifices himself for us (Is 52:10; Jn 10:11). Thus the answer seems to lie in the Qur'an's presentation of God in terms of the *jahili* notion of nobility. For the *jahili* master does not reveal himself to his servants, and the idea of God's being savior may be minimized because it implicitly reduces him to a servant.

Three more images combine to make God's intimacy with his people yet more central to the Bible, and they are either altogether omitted from the Qur'an or else virtually so. They are of God as father, husband and friend to his people.[15] Though the ancient Middle Eastern concept of king included the notion of his being a "father" to his people, the Qur'an never reflects that metaphor. Such a description is apparently too close to the careless woman-izing of the *jahili* God and at the same time too evocative of mutual intimacy for him. The same holds true of the biblical description of God as the husband to his people, even though the fact that God's partner in the relationship is a corporate entity clearly excludes all thought of either God's physicality or sensuality. Qur'anically speaking, however, such metaphors are too close to the sensual for comfort. The Qur'an does actually refer once to Abraham as God's "friend" (*khalil*, Q 4:125), but that being the Muslim scripture's sole reference to intimacy with God, the concept of divine friendship there seems like a bit of flotsam from another conceptual world.[16] It is their intimacy that excludes

---

[15]Five of my metaphors here—those of judge, master, king, father and husband—come from G. B. Caird, cited in Andrew Rippin, "God," in *The Blackwell Companion to the Qur'an*, ed. Andrew Rippin (Oxford: Blackwell, 2006), 226-27.

[16]The Qur'an describes the believer as God's "friend" (*waliy*) elsewhere (Q 10:62; 45:19). But *waliy* carries the sense of political alliance, not of intimate companionship. Hence this sole qur'anic mention of intimate friendship with God suggests that it involved Abraham's elevation, since the Qur'an simply cannot conceive of God's condescension.

these three metaphors from the Qur'an—or virtually so in the latter case. And the net effect of this restriction of qur'anic imagery to the formal and non-intimate is that God's transcendence vastly outweighs his immanence. Perhaps the qur'anic author's insertion of an affirmation of God's being "the Merciful and Compassionate" at the head of virtually every sura was intended to balance things out here, but if so, it is only marginally effective.[17]

Transcendent God

Despite the place it gives to his immanence, the Qur'an is at far greater pains to portray God as unapproachably transcendent. It reveals him as forever peerless in his omnipresence, omniscience and omnipotence. It presents his authority as ultimate and asserts that he is dependent on none and needs nothing. As we have seen, the theology of *jahiliyya* reduced *Allah* to merely the most elevated of a multitude of gods and the immediate father of a number of them. Against so shocking a humiliation of God, the Qur'an asserts his untrammelled glory and utter inapproachability, making its creator-creature distinction as sharp as possible.

Thus far the Qur'an and Bible seem to agree. However, two major points of disagreement between them lie in their respective positions on the topics of God's having come down to us who are by nature unable to approach him and of God's having a Son. With regard to God's choosing to approach us, this is what so sets biblical monotheism apart from polytheism: from Genesis to Revelation, the unapproachable God comes down to us where we are. Not to satisfy some fleeting whim, but—astonishingly—to seek an enduring relationship with us. The prime example is that "when moral evil enters God's good creation, he does not abandon his creatures but comes closer, accommodates himself further, and helps them" deal with evil's consequences.[18] And

---

[17]Ismail Ragi al-Faruqi claims that "Islam . . . repudiates all forms of immanentism," distinguishing itself "among the world's religions precisely by insisting on an absolute metaphysical separation of the transcendent from the spatiotemporal"; "Islam," in *The Great Asian Religions: An Anthology*, compiled by Wing-tsit Chan et al. (New York: Macmillan, 1969), 309. While al-Faruqi is right to view divine immanence as problematic in the Qur'an, his claim is at the same time impossible, for monotheism—qur'anic monotheism included—is inherently a declaration of divine immanence.

[18]Iain Provan, *Seriously Dangerous Religion: What the Old Testament Really Says and Why It Matters* (Waco, TX: Baylor University Press, 2014), 254. Provan refers here to God's provision of clothing to address the problem of Adam and Eve's newfound shame, provision which involved animal sacrifice. And the same is true of us when we do wrong individually: God does not say, "Let me know when you get yourself out of your mess, so we can move on from there." Instead, he meets us right where we are and, metaphorically, gets his hands dirty, helping us find our way out.

we see this time and again in Scripture: for example, when God meets Jacob both escaping from the brother he has cheated and returning to face the music years later (Gen 28:10-22; 32:22-32).[19]

We find no such picture of God in the Qur'an. As Iain Provan points out, ironically, the qur'anic view of God's unapproachability is the very stuff of which polytheistic gods are made.[20] In Jean Bottéro's description of ancient Middle Eastern religion, the gods are

> above all considered to be something grandiose, inaccessible, dominating, and to be feared . . . distant and haughty "bosses," masters and rulers, and above all not friends! One submitted to them, one feared them, one bowed down and trembled before them; one did not "love" them or "like" them. . . . [The gods'] powers, like their nature, were much too far beyond the human grasp, much too crushing and formidable to unleash in human hearts anything other than a fearful reverence, an admiring respect and a humble submission.

Though words for "like"/"love" were sometimes used with reference to submission to the gods of ancient Mesopotamia, they never actually signified the intimacy of love, "but only the inclination that a modest and self-effacing servant might feel toward an omnipotent and sublime 'lord and master.'"[21] The same is true of the Qur'an's use of love. Lacking the voluntary condescension of divine approach so intrinsic to biblical theology, God's inaccessibility in the Qur'an leads us not actually to love but only to fear him.[22] If anything in all of the Qur'an argues for its pagan background, its view of God's remoteness surely does.[23]

Likewise, the qur'anic concept of divine "begetting" is to be understood in terms of the sensual appetites and indiscretions of the *jahili* God. The Qur'an denies that God could ever lack anything (Q 31:26; 35:15), making the very idea of corporeality—with its ever-changing needs of eating, eliminating, sleeping, procreating, etc.—utterly beneath him.[24] By contrast, the biblical concept of divine begetting does not inhere in physical appetites. Rather, it represents

---

[19]See 196 below.

[20]Provan, *Seriously Dangerous Religion*, 74n62.

[21]Jean Bottéro, *Religion in Ancient Mesopotamia* (Chicago: University of Chicago Press, 2001), 37-38.

[22]Provan, *Seriously Dangerous Religion*, 78; cf. 319-22.

[23]It also makes it easy to understand why the qur'anic author may have lapsed from such a version of monotheism into henotheism in the matter of the Satanic verses.

[24]See 32 above and 219-20 below.

God's very being, since he always was and always will be Father, Son and Holy Spirit. Neither does the incarnation have anything to do with impulsiveness on the Father's part. Rather, it represents something God willed from before his foundation of the world: the ultimate exercise of God's transcendence in the ultimate expression of his immanence: his exercising his divine prerogative uniquely to transcend the bounds of the Creator-creature distinction in becoming a man. That is, it represents God's being utterly and uniquely God.

Relative to authority, the Qur'an deals with our creaturehood in terms of an absolute master-servant distinction. The point is not that no authority is given to humankind, but rather that only of God can it be said that he is *not* a servant. For he does the bidding of none and answers to none (Q 18:26-27; 85:15-16). Winfried Corduan likens the qur'anic relationship between God and his creation to a child who has total control over a sandcastle she has built: "She may decorate it with seashells, protect it from the water, add to it, or she may trample it. . . . The decision is entirely hers, and she owes nothing to the sandcastle, but the structure owes everything to her. Insofar as she does take care of it, it is purely a matter of her good nature, which she is not obligated to maintain."[25] By contrast, God's creatures do everything "by God's permission" and nothing at all apart from it (Q 18:23-24; 76:30, cf. Q 8:17).

This basic ontological distinction is biblical also, but the biblical position is significantly qualified in that the God to whom all authority belongs has always demonstrated his love in two ways. First, biblically, God pours himself out freely in service. That is, each person of the Trinity—Father, Son and Spirit—has always freely served the others in love. Second, God's absolute control over his creation is balanced with covenant commitments by which he obligates himself to us.[26] Accordingly, God is not only master but eternally servant also. This is the most striking dissimilarity between the biblical and qur'anic concepts of God. But the Bible presents God as emphatically one, despite its teaching the incarnation and pointing to the Trinity.[27]

Ironically, the doctrines of divine immanence and transcendence stand in far more tension in the Qur'an than in the Bible. The reason is that, by so

---

[25]Winfried Corduan, "A View from the Middle East: Islamic Theism," in James W. Sire, *The Universe Next Door: A Basic Worldview Catalog*, 5th ed. (Downers Grove, IL: InterVarsity Press, 2009), 255.

[26]For example, he promises humankind never to repeat the flood (Gen 9:9-16).

[27]While its data on God is sufficient clearly to point readers to the Trinity, the biblical writers left the later church the task of spelling that doctrine out in detail.

stressing transcendence, the Qur'an gives it the run of the place, so to speak, while immanence, like an unruly family member, is carefully constrained and controlled. By contrast, as we have just seen, the biblical doctrine of Christ's incarnation pushes both divine transcendence and immanence to their very limits—far beyond anything found in the Qur'an. While one might expect this to increase the tension between them, the very opposite is true. For in refusing to make either divine attribute secondary to the other, the Bible balances the tension between them. And in that it represents the ultimate expression of both attributes, the incarnation thus reveals the real oneness of the divine being. As Kenneth Cragg observes, "Belief in the Trinity does not make God less one but rather more one." For in Christ, God demonstrates that he alone is God.[28] By excluding the incarnation, the Qur'an offers no resolution of the inherent tension in these polar attributes.

The Inevitability of Divine-Human Analogy

As we will see, the Qur'an's maximization of divine transcendence at the expense of divine immanence is seen in its omission of Adam's being created in the image of God. This is ironic when we consider that humankind's imaging of God is the only thing that makes monotheism—with its insistence on both divine transcendence and immanence—bearable, for the numinous is comprehensible only to the degree that he is truly like us. Hence there is no theism without an acceptance—implicit, at least—of divine-human analogy.

Three things make divine-human likeness inherent in all theism:

1. The central doctrine of verbal revelation assumes it.

2. The emphasis on moral responsibility requires it.

3. The prophet's representation of God on earth implies it.

In terms of the first point, real communication requires real likeness. And the corollary of this is that God is everywhere described by recourse to the same linguistic stock as is used of humans. For example, nearly every qur'anic verb predicated of God (*create, judge, rule, punish*, etc.) is also predicable of humans, making our God-likeness impossible to miss. Far from being inaccessible in meaning—like accessories of magical or mystical value only—

---

[28]Kenneth Cragg, *The Call of the Minaret* (Oxford: Oxford University Press, 1985), 264, 283.

qur'anic descriptions of God make explicit what the very fact of revelation implies. When the Qur'an calls God "the most merciful of the merciful," "the best of forgivers" and "the justest of judges" (Q 7:151, 155; 12:64, 92; 95:8), it means just that. Language may here be stretched to its limits, but regular user meaning is intended. Analogy is not denied but only qualified in that to God belongs the "loftiest of likenesses" (Q 16:60; 30:27). In the larger context of divine otherness, this seems akin to the rider of Christian theology that, despite its being true to the extent of our capacity to comprehend, human language is ultimately inadequate when used of God. Though the Qur'an's denial of all humanization of God strongly discourages us from taking such anthropomorphic descriptions literally, they unmistakably imply divine-human analogy (Q 23:116; 38:75; 55:27).

Second, if God is not ethically oriented as we are—if he does not hate injustice, for example—what sense would we make of qur'anic ethics? As Izutsu says, each of the key concepts in the sphere of human ethics is "but a pale reflection—or a very imperfect imitation—of the divine nature itself."[29] Such a view of moral likeness brings God very near, and it bears repeating that the urgency of humankind's ethical choice is the fact to which everything else in the Qur'an points. The ethical polarity involved in that choice finds its source in God's moral character: it is because God is both merciful and just that paradise awaits the faithful and hell the unbelieving.

Third, since the prophet utters God's words, obeying him is obeying God, and he is to some extent entrusted with God's program on earth. We might even say that prophets and their followers in some sense *partner* with God in his work on earth—qur'anically speaking, the liberation of Mecca's Ka'ba from idolatrous worship, for example. While such biblical language as "God's coworkers" (1 Cor 3:9 HCSB) would be out of place there, the Qur'an does refer to believers as God's "helpers" (Q 61:14). This points to the intertwined concepts of humankind's being in covenant relationship with God—a relationship marked by *mutual* commitment—and being appointed to vicegerency or *representative* rule under God (Q 6:165).[30] All this indicates divine-human analogy.

---

[29]Toshihiko Izutsu, *Ethico-Religious Concepts in the Qur'ān* (Montreal: McGill University Press, 1966), 18. But as we will see, the Qur'an does make one major exception to this.
[30]For more on the vicegerency concept, see 86-87 below.

Sensing this, mystically or theosophically inclined Muslims have openly acknowledged divine-human analogy, but the Muslim mainstream views this as a dangerous threat to God's uniqueness. And qur'anically, the mainstream has a point. When al-Kirmani discusses special revelation's necessitating divine-human analogy, for example, he approaches it from the exact opposite direction of Christian theology, positing that Muhammad had to be *denaturalized* as a man in order to receive divine revelation.[31] Hence, so-called orthodox Muslims hold to the Qur'an's avoidance of any explicit affirmation of divine-human analogy, while Sufis gladly embrace the Qur'an's inability to avoid such analogy effectively. But while the Muslim scripture does not explicitly deny humankind's being made in the image of God, its omission of it should be understood in terms of the qur'anic refrain that God is like nothing in all of creation (e.g., Q 112:4). Divine-human analogy is inexplicably excluded. And that exclusion is confirmed by the Qur'an's restriction of its metaphorical palette to the nonintimate metaphors of the divine-human relationship with which we began. As we shall see, the implications of this are enormous for both theology and anthropology.

The Shape of Qur'anic Theism

From early on the great refuge of "orthodox" Islam here has been the unknowability of God, one aspect of his transcendence. Whenever anything has come too close to divine-human likeness, Muslim theologians have said that words are beyond human comprehension when used of God. Only God can comprehend God, after all. Cornelius Van Til expresses the contrasting biblical notion well when he speaks of covenant as "the idea of exhaustive personal relationship." Though mere humans cannot know all there is to know of God, we can know God perfectly *to the full extent of our capacity*.[32] In other words, while both scriptures are equally concerned with our ethical response to the revelation, the Bible views that response as being within the context of God's intimate revelation of himself as the God of covenant love (Ex 19:3-6; Deut 7:7-16; 10:12–11:32). By contrast, the Qur'an seeks to limit its context to God's intimate knowledge of humankind, making the intimacy involved in qur'anic covenant decidedly one-sided.

---

[31]In his famous *Sharh al-Bukhari*; cited in Izutsu, *God and Man in the Koran*, 167.

[32]Cornelius Van Til, "Covenant Theology," in *Twentieth Century Encyclopedia of Religious Knowledge*, ed. Leferts A. Loetscher (Grand Rapids: Baker, 1955).

Accordingly, Muslims typically assert that in the Qur'an God is not self-revealing in any real sense of the term, that he reveals only his *will*, not *himself*.[33] This is inherently contradictory, since one cannot possibly reveal one's will without also revealing something of oneself. But despite the contradiction, there is some truth to the assertion for, as already noted, the Qur'an evidences very little of the divine intimacy everywhere evident in the Bible. Rather, in the Qur'an God is much more remote, much further from view, reminding us that apophatic theology generates a sense of mystery and awe far more easily than cataphatic theology.

During the modern period many Westernized Muslims have adopted an individualistic version of Islam that grants them a personal relationship with God while often freeing them from the external demands of ritual and law. But as positive and reassuring as such an understanding of Islam is, it is far from what we find in the Qur'an, where God does not even reveal his word to his prophets—Muhammad included—except through intermediaries. Why then would such a God as that want a "love relationship" with ordinary, rank-and-file believers? According to the Qur'an, the divine master reveals to his servants just what they need to obey his will and nothing more.

However, two aspects of qur'anic theology evoke the shape of biblical theology in a way that obscures God's remoteness to Western readers of the Qur'an. The first is the Qur'an's emphasis on the intensity of God's involvement with humankind, which we have already seen: through his prophets, he urgently calls his wayward people back to himself. The second—the corollary of the first—is the very fact of the pronounced theocentricity of qur'anic thought. But however unexpected the combination is, it is nonetheless true that, though God is very much at the center of the Qur'an, he is in a very real sense necessarily "out of focus" compared to what we find in the Bible. The unique sense of divine otherness in the Qur'an inheres in the fact that the divine-human relationship is fundamentally impersonal, in the sense of nonintimate. By contrast, the Bible fully embraces the concept of God's self-revelation and, as we will see, defines his nobility and even his majesty in terms that are quite contrary to those of the Qur'an.

---

[33]See, for example, Ismail Ragi al-Faruqi, "A Comparison of Islamic and Christian Approaches to Hebrew Scripture," *Journal of Bible and Religion* 31, no. 4 (1963): 286-87.

Six

God's Justice *and* Mercy

The Qur'an agrees broadly with the Bible in saying that God is both just and merciful. His justice relates to a paradigm of reciprocity by which each of our actions—e.g. loving, forgetting—evoke a corresponding action from God. But the fact that our actions do not often evoke an immediate response from God points to his superimposition of another paradigm—one of reversal—on the paradigm of reciprocity. Flowing from God's mercy, reversal allows him to delay the fulfillment of his promises both to punish and to bless. This is in accord with the Bible. In contrast to the Bible, however, God's mercy is always conditional in the Qur'an, and his ethical attributes are not necessarily rooted in an essential holiness, a point that explains the absence of any concept of divine atonement like that of the Bible. This leaves God without an ethical core holding his moral attributes together and points to a possible duality in him by which he is now just and now merciful. The only real alternative is to take refuge in God's unknowability—as Muslims have done—and say that we humans cannot expect answers to our questions about God's ways. By contrast, biblically God's humility is what binds his mercy and justice together as one and allows for Christ's incarnation and crucifixion. The Qur'an's *jahili* notion of nobility, by which haughtiness and the refusal to submit are primary to God's character, allows for neither.

*E*verything in the Qur'an points to the urgency of humankind's moral choice, and the polarity of that choice is rooted in the character of God. Because God is the God of mercy and compassion, on the one hand, and the God of justice and wrath, on the other, paradise awaits the faithful and hell the unbelieving. Though the Qur'an may point to God as an ethical duality—a topic to which we will return—it also suggests the paradoxical oneness of justice and mercy similar to that found in the Bible. In both scriptures, the sinner is said to sin against herself (Q 2:54; 3:117; 7:160; 29:40; Deut 10:13; Prov 3:3-4). Proverbs 1:20–9:18 equates righteousness to wisdom and unrighteousness to folly. Similarly, the Qur'an refers to itself as both mercy and guidance, implying all the constraints of an external standard of righteousness in God (Q 31:3; cf. Q 7:154). This makes the apparently harsh, forbidding aspect of the divine character—with its prescriptions, prohibitions and in a sense even its punishments—an expression of divine mercy, since these things guide those who heed them to salvation. So while the qur'anic view of salvation may tend toward an ethical duality in God, much there points to divine unity as well.

The Opposing Paradigms of Justice and Mercy

The Qur'an is in broad agreement with the Bible on divine justice. It categorically assures us that God wrongs no one. He holds each of us accountable for our own sins and does not judge without warning (Q 6:164; 17:15-16; cf. Q 67:10-11). He invariably opposes the unbeliever's falsehood and injustice and upholds the cause of the righteous (Q 4:135; 22:40). God will faithfully reward and punish on the basis of his full knowledge of our deeds (Q 4:40-42; 18:48-49). He rules in wisdom according to his inscrutable decrees, which include directing the righteous and the rebellious to their chosen ends (Q 6:39; 7:30; 14:4; 17:16). He protects his servants and grants them success (Q 2:57; 3:104, 150). He also delivers the oppressed from their oppressors (Q 2:257; 93:6-8). And he will ultimately cause good to triumph over evil (Q 21:18; 24:55).

This points to a paradigm of reciprocity, from which the whole concept of covenant blessing and cursing flows. Being a God of justice, he returns only blessing for good and cursing for evil. He lavishes his care on those who obey him and punishes all who reject him and abuse his creation.[1] This paradigm is foundational to both qur'anic and biblical thinking.

---

[1]The Qur'an presents human action as evoking a corresponding divine action—for example, "helping" (Q 22:40; 47:7) or "forgetting" (Q 2:14; 9:67; 45:34)—reminiscent of biblical teaching (2 Chron 15:2; 24:20; Ps 18:25-27; Prov 3:33-35).

The world we live in does not consistently operate like this, however. In large measure, God overlooks the demands of his justice such that we may pursue rebellion if we choose. And as a result, a great war rages between good and evil in our world. Evildoers often know considerable success, and the righteous often suffer. This is the result of God's superimposition of another paradigm, one of reversal, on that of reciprocity. The paradigm of reversal points to God's mercy, revealed in both common and special grace in both the Bible and Qur'an. God still fundamentally orders his universe by justice, and much of the misery of our world points to that. However, he restrains the destruction inherent in sin such that it comes to the sinner only partially and incrementally in this life. God may not judge the sinner for years or even until the final judgment, when perfect justice again prevails. But in the paradigm of reversal, he has granted our race a reprieve, making salvation possible. On the other hand, it permits a great deal of suffering and injustice. Because God is just, he did not simply replace reciprocity with reversal. Instead, he has carefully limited each paradigm by the other, such that the two operate together in a tension, the resolution of which only he can effect.

This second paradigm points to God's love and mercy, evident in so many of his dealings with us. First, he extends his providential goodness to everyone—righteous and unrighteous—leaving our race utterly indebted to him (Q 14:32-34; 29:60-63; 36:33-40). And this reminds us of Jesus' words, "He makes his sun rise on the evil and on the good, and sends rain on the righteous and on the unrighteous" (Mt 5:45). As noted above, God grants humankind time to repent and sends prophets to guide our lost race, giving them reasonable moral requirements, warning and promise (Q 2:243, 251; 7:42; 76:3). He also grants believers his forgiveness, purification, well-being and ultimately the bliss of paradise (Q 3:146-48; 6:54; 24:21).

The modern period has seen divine mercy in the Qur'an both newly emphasized and deemphasized. In terms of the latter, mainly nonscholarly Christians contend that God is not genuinely merciful in the Qur'an, but this is groundless. In fact, the title "the Merciful" (*al-rahman*) sometimes "approaches . . . the status of a proper name."[2] On the other hand, the question of whether mercy and justice are equally weighted in God is well worth considering. According

---

[2]Richard Bell and W. Montgomery Watt, *Bell's Introduction to the Qur'an*, rev. W. Montgomery Watt (Edinburgh: Edinburgh University Press, 1970), 152.

to Fazlur Rahman, along with God's other divine attributes, mercy and justice "fully interpenetrate in the Qur'anic concept of God as an organic unity."[3] Others go even further, asserting that the message of the Qur'an is nothing but mercy from beginning to end.[4]

There is no denying that mercy is a key qur'anic attribute of God. However, the claims of these Muslim scholars belong to the modern trend to "Christianize" the Qur'an by washing out God's fearsome aspects and stressing his friendly ones.[5] Rahman proof-texts his position with "He has prescribed for himself mercy" and "My mercy embraces everything."[6] Read in context, however, Q 6:12 declares only that God has committed himself to a course of mercy for believers (Q 6:11-13). For like his heavens and earth, his mercy too is entirely at his disposal. Likewise, Q 7:156 specifies that God ordains his mercy for the God-fearing. Hence the Qur'an insists that God dispenses his mercy—like his punishment—only to those who deserve it. As Daud Rahbar has shown, the central qur'anic concept concerning God is that of his just judgment. "All themes," Rahbar concludes, "are subservient to this central theme."[7]

This means God's mercy is in no way unconditional, and his love for humankind is not indiscriminate. Rather, his mercy is always limited by the demands of his justice, for without repentance, faith and obedience there is no forgiveness.[8] God's love and mercy for the unbelieving are limited to his providential care, his readiness to forgive the repentant and his sending them prophets to enable them to repent—all this is reversal, God's giving sinners what they do not deserve, though such mercy also makes them more culpable. Beyond these things, God has no love or mercy for the unbelieving. As Rahbar says, "Unqualified Divine Love for humankind is an idea completely alien to

---

[3]Fazlur Rahman, *Major Themes of the Qur'an* (Minneapolis: Bibliotheca Islamica, 1980), 1.

[4]For example, Abul Kalam Azad, cited in David Marshall, *God, Muhammad and the Unbelievers: A Qur'anic Study* (London: RoutledgeCurzon, 1999), 80.

[5]J. M. S. Baljon, cited in ibid., 81-82.

[6]Rahman, *Major Themes of the Qur'an*, 6.

[7]Daud Rahbar, *God of Justice: A Study in the Ethical Doctrine of the Qur'ān* (Leiden: Brill, 1960), 223-25. According to Miroslav Volf, the Qur'an agrees with the biblical assertion that God is love. Volf supports his view with Q 85:14, which describes God as being "Full of Lovingkindness" (in Yusuf Ali's expanded paraphrase—but it is more accurately rendered "the Loving" or "the Most Loving"; cf. Q 11:90). Miroslav Volf, *Allah: A Christian Response* (New York: HarperCollins, 2011), 101. In context, however, God's love is reserved for deserving believers, not freely offered to every human being, as is the case biblically.

[8]Marshall, *God, Muhammad and the Unbelievers*, 82.

the Qur'an."[9] So also is any notion that God longs to see all included in his salvation or suffers anguish over the unbeliever's lostness.

By contrast, these are prominent features of biblical thought (Lk 13:34; Jn 3:16-17; 2 Pet 3:9; cf. Ezek 18:23, 32). Nowhere in the Qur'an does sin ever elicit from God the betrayed lover's lament voiced in both Old and New Testament.[10] "Such a piteous appeal for the love of a weak creature," says Rodinson, "would be inconceivable coming from the Master of worlds of the Koran."[11] In fact, the only clear qur'anic expressions of universal compassion come from prophets who discover that God does *not* condone their love for unbelievers.[12] This is especially so in Muhammad's case: each time he grieves over his idolatrous tribesmen, his concern elicits divine rebuke (Q 27:70-72; 58:22; cf. Q 4:88-89; 5:26; 7:93; 9:84; 11:36). Hence, while divine mercy is clearly qur'anic, it is undeniably far narrower than its biblical counterpart.

Both the Bible and Qur'an insist that saving grace belongs with faith in and submission to God. But the essential difference between the two scriptures with respect to the paradigm of reversal is that, biblically, God pours out his grace on sinners in advance of their submission to his lordship. Indeed, without such grace-in-advance-of-obedience, obedience is not possible, and the holy life God requires of us is but our grateful response to the saving grace that began its work in us when we had nothing to commend ourselves to him (Rom 5:6-8). Qur'anically, there is no thought of such saving grace in advance of obedience. That being so, we might think that the Qur'an's salvation relates more closely to the paradigm of reciprocity than reversal, since the believer's good deeds must outweigh his bad. But as we will see, it is not so straightforward.

Ethical Differences

Combined with its relatively slight assessment of sin and forgiveness,[13] the Qur'an's mention of God's misleading unbelievers (Q 7:186) has made some

---

[9]Rahbar, *God of Justice*, 172-73.

[10]Kenneth Cragg suggests Q 36:30 as an exception to this rule, translating the relevant clause "The pity of it in respect of my servants"; Kenneth Cragg, trans., *Readings in the Qur'an* (London: HarperCollins, 1988), 170. But his translation Christianizes the qur'anic text. Arberry's "Woe be to my servants!" makes more sense; A. J. Arberry, trans., *The Koran Interpreted: A Translation* (New York: Touchstone, 1996).

[11]Marshall, *God, Muhammad and the Unbelievers*, 86.

[12]What Abraham says in Q 14:36, for example, is corrected by the chronologically later Q 9:114.

[13]See chapters ten and eleven below.

question the depth of his commitment to truth and justice. The Qur'an refers to God as holy only twice (Q 59:23; 62:1), and the context does not specify whether it has ontological or ethical holiness in view. It similarly refers to God as truth ontologically—"Reality," as Yusuf Ali puts it (Q 22:6; 31:30)—and lacks any clear statement to the effect that God is truth ethically. On the other hand, it proclaims the truth of God, asserting that he is angered by the false values, beliefs and morals of unbelievers (Q 7:96-99; cf. Q 1:7). He is also fully committed to the overthrow of falsehood by truth, this being the cosmic battle in which Muhammad and his *umma* are engaged (Q 21:18). Further, the general fixity of qur'anic moral requirements points to God's ethical holiness.[14] And the Qur'an's primary emphasis on God's justice is in some ways like the concept of divine holiness that pervades the Bible.

That concept does take us beyond divine justice, however, for it roots the ethical character of all God's dealings with humankind in his essential separateness from evil. Combined with the biblical notion of divine-human analogy, the holiness of God becomes the ground of moral obligation: created in his likeness, humankind is designed to reflect the very character of God (Lev 11:44-45; 19:2; 20:26). And rooting our need to conform to God's will in essential likeness takes biblical ethics well beyond the motivation of mere reward and punishment.

Holiness and Atonement

God's self-revelation is the larger issue to which his holiness points. Biblically, sin offends God's holiness and thus demands his judgment. This concept of holiness gives rise to the notion of sacrificial atonement so central to the Jewish scriptures and fulfilled in the New Testament in Christ's death. The point is that "the one thing God could not do in the face of human rebellion was nothing."[15] As P. T. Forsyth writes, "The holiness of God . . . is meaningless without judgment. . . . He must either inflict punishment or assume it. . . . He chose the latter course, as honouring the law while saving the guilty. He took His own judgment."[16] According to the

---

[14]There is no thought that infanticide or adultery, for example, might be redefined as morally acceptable. Cf. 159-60 below.

[15]John Stott, *The Cross of Christ* (Downers Grove, IL: InterVarsity Press, 1986), 153.

[16]P. T. Forsyth, *The Cruciality of the Cross* (London: Independent Press, 1909), 98.

Bible, then, there can be no forgiveness of sin without what Dietrich Bonhoeffer calls "costly grace." The Jewish scriptures point to this grace in sacrificial offerings (Lev 17:11), while the New Testament fully reveals it in Christ's freely giving his life as a ransom for humankind. Biblically, then, God's holiness is the guarantor of all his ethical attributes, assuring us that his justice can never override his mercy and vice versa, not even in forgiving sin. Divine holiness, then, is what guarantees the ethical *wholeness*—in other words, the *unity*—of God.

By contrast, the Qur'an's concept of atonement limits it to human actions carried out by individual believers to secure their own salvation. While the Qur'an echoes the story of Abraham's sacrifice of his son (Q 37:99-111; 22:34-37), it makes sacrifice peripheral to salvation, suggesting not a biblical but rather a *jahili* view of it. But we traverse this entire region of qur'anic thought by mere inference, nothing having been stated clearly. The Qur'an does not challenge sacrificial atonement's centrality in the Bible. It simply lacks anything equivalent, setting forth its own minimalist view of it instead, as if its treatment of the theme—amounting to a radical reduction when compared to the biblical notion—should in no way dismay adherents of the biblical traditions. This may not have been particularly jarring for the Jews in Muhammad's audience, since Judaism's sacrificial offerings had long since been discontinued due to the destruction of the temple in Jerusalem. With regard to Christians, however, it suggests that Muhammad had limited direct dealings with them during his prophetic career.

Salvation and Divine Self-revelation

In terms of its broad concerns, the Qur'an's vision of salvation consists entirely of our race's return to the path of submission to divine revelation. Hence, in comparison to New Testament soteriology, with its major emphases on justification, sanctification and union with Christ, the Qur'an gives its hearers little indication of salvation's divine means. Its entire focus is instead on salvation's human means, on scripture's marking out the path of salvation the believer must walk in community with other believers committed to God's Cause in the world. Qur'anically, we need nothing more. Sin does require divine pardon, and, as we will see, our faith and good deeds may help us attain it. But the Qur'an does not elaborate on how God effects our salvation.

On God's side, qur'anic forgiveness requires only his merciful "overlooking" of our sins. Biblically speaking, due to God's holiness, such an act is possible only because of his mercy's satisfying the demands of his justice in Christ's atonement. With no concept of divine atonement,[17] the Qur'an leaves us just three ways to explain how God's mercy can override his justice to forgive believers. First, we can assign the duality to humankind, devaluing the sins of believers (but not of unbelievers) such that the believer's forgiveness does not actually contravene divine justice. Second, we may view God as an ethical duality, with now mercy and now justice prevailing. Third, we may conclude that when used of God, the words *mercy* and *justice* do not have their normal meanings—or more accurately, should be emptied of content to whatever degree they suggest duality in God. Muslims have historically chosen this third option, taking refuge from all such issues in the unknowability of God.[18] But regardless of which option we take, the net effect is the same: we inject a strong element of ambiguity and obscurity into the divine-human relationship.

This takes us back to the question raised earlier: Does God reveal only his will or himself also? As previously noted, the question does not really make sense, for how can he reveal his will without revealing himself? Biblically speaking, in the historical event of his incarnation and its Old Testament foreshadowings, God, as Covenant Maker and Covenant Keeper, relentlessly draws members of our wayward race into a relationship of intimate friendship, personal communion and oneness in company with the community of faith, or Christ's church. The Bible views that relationship as God's purpose in creation and hence humankind's final goal (Jer 31:33-34; Jn 17:3; Rev 21:1-4). The Bible further asserts that, as the "image of the invisible God," Jesus has disclosed God to the full extent of our understanding (Col 1:15).[19] All this is entirely out of place in the Qur'an, taking us back to the one-sided intimacy of knowledge with its inherent theological ambiguity as noted above.

---

[17]The Qur'an's only mention of atonement limits it to actions believers themselves take to make up for their sins. See 126-28 below.

[18]In fact, Muslim theologians generally disassociate God's forgiveness from his mercy, relating it to his omnipotence instead. That is, he forgives not because he is merciful, but simply because he can do whatever he wants; Christine Schirrmacher, *The Islamic View of Major Christian Teachings* (Bonn: Verlag für Kultur und Wissenschaft, 2008), 50. This, however, ignores the Qur'an's own clear connection of God's forgiveness with his mercy (e.g., Q 6:54; 24:21).

[19]See 92 below.

The Humility of God

But why does the Qur'an so consistently avoid metaphors for God that involve a two-sided intimacy? Why does it always subordinate his immanence to his transcendence, but not vice versa? Quite clearly—and this takes us to the root of the difference between biblical and qur'anic theologizing—it is its absence of divine humility. This is in sharp contrast to the biblical emphasis. While the Hebrew Bible does not explicitly attribute humility to God, it nevertheless makes it visible in countless expressions of divine condescension (e.g., Deut 7:7-11; Ps 138:6; Hos 11:1-4). It is also implicit in our race's being called to reflect God in holiness, something Micah 6:8 spells out for us in terms of not merely justice and mercy but humility as well. This becomes more visible still in the definitive act of divine humility, that of Christ's incarnation, life and passion (Ps 45:4; Is 42:2-3; 52:13–53:12; Jn 13:1-17; Phil 2:1-8; cf. Jn 1:18; 14:9). Jesus thus perfectly revealed God's character as well as his will. In his humble submission to sacrificial death, the full demands of God's justice were met by God's mercy. Biblically, then, neither his mercy nor his justice is subordinate to the other: in binding divine justice and mercy together, divine humility revealed God as not just numerically one but ethically one also.

We must grasp this concept of divine humility to understand the mutual incompatibility of the qur'anic and biblical views of Jesus, since the Bible presents him as both divine and God's humble servant. By contrast, the Qur'an's omission of divine humility explains its obvious reserve in dealing with divine-human analogy. In contrast to the biblical case, the human response of humility before God—the most basic of the Qur'an's ethical requirements and the definitive mark of genuine faith—mirrors nothing in God, for his role as master is altogether exclusive of servanthood. Like the Qur'an, the Bible presents God as immutably majestic in his nearness. Biblically, however, his divine authority and majesty are viewed as most fully revealed in Jesus' humility and voluntary submission, the means by which he triumphed over both evil and death. And since the three persons of the Trinity have from eternity past all served one another in love, Jesus' voluntary submission on the cross revealed God's greatness in this regard.

All the positive tenets of biblical theism imply divine condescension, a grand-scale stooping to our weakness on the part of God. That he would, for example, bother to create our race, take any notice of us and establish a personal—that is, a covenant—relationship with us: all this implies his gracious condescension. Further, the very concept of linguistic revelation requires humility on the part of God—that he, in Calvin's words, would "baby talk" with us, expressing his thoughts to us through the medium of language with all the historical limitations inherent in its cultural specificity.[20] Since the very act of communication always risks misunderstanding, to communicate invariably requires an element of humility, and that risk is not one from which God is exempt. The biblical category of divine humility enables us to see why he so freely assumes such a risk. But unlike the Bible, the Qur'an affords its hearers no category for such an admission, since the absoluteness of its master-servant distinction excludes the very possibility of God's being humble.

Monotheism in Jahili *Terms*

Three points require clarification here. First, the Qur'an's avoidance of any admission of humility in the character of God reflects the *jahiliyya's* essentially nonreligious appraisal of humility and self-surrender. The pre-Islamic Arabs considered these qualities "something disgraceful, a manifestation of weak and ignoble character," while they took "haughtiness" and a "refusal to submit" as marks of nobility. Hence Izutsu's statement that "with the advent of Islam, the balance was completely overturned" must be qualified.[21] For while it is true that the former weakness became the highest virtue in terms of the human response to God, the *jahili* appraisal of "haughtiness" and "refusal to submit" as marks of true nobility lived on in the qur'anic doctrine of God. The reason is that it was also intrinsic to the *jahili* concept of God, which answered to the *jahili* conception of nobility.[22]

Second, the omission of any notion of divine condescension is also to be understood in terms of the Qur'an's utter abhorrence of that humanization

---

[20]All such communication is inherently weak due to the fact that the speaker and listener never have the exact same backgrounds. This makes them give different shades of meaning to what they say and hear and makes normal language easy to misinterpret. The only exceptions here are, say, legalese or certain uses of scientific language, where both speaker and listener agree to restrict a particular use of language to prescribed contexts in which words possess one meaning and one only. Only thus do we artificially escape language's inherent weakness.

[21]Toshihiko Izutsu, *Ethico-Religious Concepts in the Qur'ān* (Montreal: McGill University Press, 1966), 22.

[22]As Block points out, some Muslim translators fail correctly to translate *al-mutakabbir* in Q 59:23, referring to God as "the Arrogant" or "the Proud"; Block, *The Qur'an in Muslim-Christian Dialogue*, 190. This represents an Arabization of God, akin to Bottéro's description of ancient Middle Eastern gods on 64 above.

and degradation of God so central to the theology of *jahiliyya*. In biblical terms, the divine condescension that culminates in Christ's crucifixion is divinely initiated throughout, even though unrighteous men seem to be the initiators (Is 53:3; Jn 10:17-18; Acts 2:23-26; 3:17-19; 13:27-30; Rev 13:8). Because the New Testament writers freely accept God's humility, the fusion of divine lordship and servanthood essential to a full acceptance of divine-human analogy becomes possible. Qur'anically speaking, such a fusion is unthinkable, as is the divine condescension needed for incarnation. Ironically, there is no room for God's humiliation, even when initiated by him.

Last, this leads to a basic but important point: the qur'anic author everywhere evidences a single-mindedness with regard to his corrective task. He limits his positive theologizing to that deemed vital to undoing *jahili* misconceptions of God, as well as what he perceives as their reflections in Christianity and Judaism. All other seventh-century concerns—e.g., Christian disputes over the precise nature of Christ—are clearly nonissues. In a religious context in which God was anything but unique, Muhammad called above all for faith in God's uniqueness. Hence, if the so-called Satanic verses signify a polytheistic compromise of that uniqueness, the resultant syncretism was only temporary. Regardless, the Qur'an's stress on God's numerical oneness is secondary to its emphasis on his uniqueness. By ascribing the *jahili* conception of nobility to God, however, the Muslim scripture renders him a kind of glorified "noble Arab," threatening his divine uniqueness. It also threatens his unity both ontologically and ethically, and its readers cannot help but feel this tension from beginning to end.

Seven

Adam *in* Stereoscopic Vision

Because we are related to God primarily as his servants, submission is to characterize our relationship to him. The Qur'an's multiple accounts of humankind's creation and divine appointment echo the biblical accounts in many respects. God creates Adam from clay, animates him by his breath and creates his wife from him. God also appoints Adam his vicegerent on earth and establishes his covenant with him. But despite the fact that the qur'anic worldview demands divine-human analogy, humankind is not said to be created in God's image, as the biblical narrative makes clear. In addition, it seems that humankind is not created on earth but in an extraterrestrial garden. Finally, Q 33:72-73 gives a far darker assessment of humankind's character and divine appointment than the Qur'an's other creation narratives, an assessment that connects Adam's appointment to vicegerency with hubris, the opposite of submission.

*T*he anthropological obverse of the qur'anic vision of God's peerless lordship lies in the concept of humankind's rightful submission (*islam*) to God. Qur'anically, we each stand before God first and foremost as his "servant" or "slave" (*'abd*). Hence every prophet before Muhammad is said to have pointed to the path of *islam*, since that is both the ideal for which we were created and our sole route of recovery from lostness. This self-surrender involves attitudes of reverent fear of God, humility, subservience and grateful dependence. As noted above, in contrast to the paganism of the *jahiliyya*, the Qur'an made this inner posture the religious ideal. And that amounted to an absolute ethical revaluation of humility and submission to God. One question we must answer is whether qur'anic *islam* produced a servile view of humankind.

We should note at the outset that the Qur'an has nothing comparable to the narratives that magisterially open the biblical canon and tell the creation story in a comprehensive fashion (Gen 1–2) such that they frame everything else that comes after them. Rather, we find multiple accounts as well as a few scattered mentions of humankind's creation, which altogether yield two very distinct narratives of primordial man. The first of these narratives is presented somewhat differently in each of its tellings, exemplifying that flexibility around a common core that is typical of oral-formulaic composition.[1] The Qur'an gives each new telling or oral performance variant a different emphasis depending on the specific situation it addresses,[2] but none of its tellings can be designated the primary one.

The popularity of the narratives of Adam's creation and his encounter with Satan (*al-shaytan*), or Iblis,[3] among Arabia's long-established Jewish and its widespread Christian communities ensures that Muhammad's audience would also have had some familiarity with them.[4] Ordered chronologically, these narratives are found in Q 15:26-48; 38:67-85; 17:61-65; 18:50-51; 7:10-27; 20:115-17; 2:29-39; 33:72-73. Because the last-recited passage, Q 33:72-73, views the primordial Adam from an entirely different perspective, I refer to it as the "minority position" on Adam.[5] But we begin with the Qur'an's "majority position," which we find in all the earlier narratives and narrative

---

[1] On the oral-formulaic composition of this narrative, see Andrew G. Bannister, *An Oral-Formulaic Study of the Qur'an* (Lanham, MD: Lexington Books, 2014), 57, 274.

[2] Ibid., 281.

[3] The Qur'an implicitly identifies Iblis with Satan in Q 20:115-24, and Muslims have accordingly identified them as one. It presents Iblis first in the role of heavenly prosecutor—like Satan in the book of Job—but as it retells the story, it makes Iblis more of a coded enemy to the human race in the person of *al-shaytan*; Whitney S. Bodman, *The Poetics of Iblis: Narrative Theology in the Qur'an* (Cambridge, MA: Harvard School of Divinity Press, 2007), 24.

[4] Bannister, *Oral-Formulaic Study of the Qur'an*, 6.

[5] I thus synthesize these qur'anic accounts into two stories. For a detailed study of the "majority position" accounts, see Angelika Neuwirth, "Negotiating Justice: A Pre-Canonical Reading of the Qur'anic Creation Accounts (Part I)," *Journal of Qur'anic Studies* 2, no. 1 (2000): 25-41; Angelika Neuwirth, "Negotiating Justice: A Pre-Canonical Reading of the Qur'anic Creation Accounts (Part II)," *Journal of Qur'anic Studies* 2, no. 2 (2000): 1-18; and Bodman, *Poetics of Iblis*.

fragments. Once we have seen both positions, we can decide whether the last passage signals a decisive shift in qur'anic thinking.

Adam's Divine Creation and Appointment—the Majority Position

While some versions of the majority account are highly condensed or differ between themselves on one or more points, they yield the following synthetic story line:

- Having created the *jinn* out of fire, God creates Adam out of clay, animates him with his breath and then creates his wife out of him (Q 7:11; 15:26-29; 4:1; 39:6; 49:13).

- When God tells the angels he intends to appoint man as his vicegerent on earth, they remonstrate; but when they ask why he would choose over them—who praise him continually—a race that will spread corruption and bloodshed, God says only that his knowledge surpasses theirs (Q 2:30-33; cf. Q 5:27-30; 38:26).

- Having taught Adam the natures (literally, the "names") of the lower orders of creation, he asks the angels whether they can name them all, and, when they admit they cannot, he has Adam display his knowledge (Q 2:31-33).

- God then commands them to bow before Adam, and all but Iblis submit; when God demands an explanation, Iblis indicates that he is scandalized that God would require him to revere a creature so inferior to himself— literally, made of slimy mud (Q 15:33).

- Expelling Iblis from the garden, God puts him under a curse until Judgment Day, but then he grants his appeal for respite until the resurrection; in response Iblis vows that, since God has led him astray, he will lead all of humankind astray, except God's devoted servants; God authorizes Iblis's program, assuring him that he will fill hell with him and his followers (Q 38:82-85; 17:16-17, 64).

- God then makes a covenant with Adam, allowing him and his wife to enjoy the bounty of the garden as long as they do not approach the forbidden tree; he also warns Adam not to let Satan drive them from the garden (Q 2:35; 7:19; 20:117-19).

Although it closely parallels rabbinic literature,[6] this creation account also parallels that of the Bible in a number of respects. Adam is made of clay, mud or dust[7] in the garden and is the last of God's creation. Adam is shaped by God's own hand, as it were, and animated by his breath.[8] God creates Adam's wife—named Eve (*Hawwa*) by tradition, but unnamed by the Qur'an[9]—out of Adam, to be the mother of the human race (Q 4:1; 7:189). No less than her husband, Eve is covenantally bound to God.

Adam's Vicegerency

Two great distinctions are lavished on Adam. First, God honors him above the angels and *jinn* by subjecting the earth to him as *khalifa*, or vicegerent, though the *khalifa*'s specific responsibilities are never spelled out (e.g., Q 2:30). While many Muslim commentators recognize that Adam is designated God's vicegerent, some assign to *khalifa* its alternate meaning of "successor" and, by extension, of "settler." But their rationales for these meanings are implausible.[10]

In addition, such treatment of *khalifa* ignores both its larger and its immediate qur'anic context. First, God's command that the angels bow down to Adam (Q 2:34)[11] follows on the heels of two clearly related actions: God's

---

[6]Abraham Geiger, *Judaism and Islam* (1898; repr., New York: Ktav, 1970), 75-77. The sole addition to the rabbinic story of the angelic remonstrance is that man will shed blood. John C. Reeves, "Some Explorations of the Intertwining of the Bible and Qur'ān," in *Bible and Qur'ān: Essays on Scriptural Intertextuality*, ed. John C. Reeves (Atlanta: Society of Biblical Literature, 2003), 52-54, 58-60. Given that this point is found only in Sura 2, which came in the militarized Medinan period, it clearly relates to the fact that Muslim and non-Muslim blood was then being shed in God's Cause.

[7]Qur'anic references to man's being created from a "blood-clot" or "base fluid" (e.g., Q 22:5; 77:20) clearly refer to human conception, not primordial creation.

[8]As Thomas O'Shaughnessy shows, we should read *ruh* in Q 15:29 and 32:9 as "breath"—i.e., the animating life force of God in creation—not as "spirit," which the Qur'an uses to refer only to Gabriel (*Jibril*), his agent of revelation; *The Development of the Meaning of Spirit in the Koran* (Rome: Pontificium Institutum Orientalium Studiorum, 1953), 26, 30.

[9]For the sake of convenience, however, I will refer to her as Eve. Consonant with all other Middle Eastern creation accounts save one—the Genesis account—the Qur'an gives us no special account of woman's creation, but this lack was readily supplied by the hadith.

[10]For example, some say humankind are "successors" since one generation succeeds another. Thus Mohsin Khan paraphrases it "generations after generations"; see "Verse (2:30)—English Translation," *Qur'anic Arabic Corpus*, accessed Nov. 21, 2013, http://corpus.quran.com/translation .jsp?chapter=2&verse=30. Similarly, Abdel Haleem renders it simply "settlers," since that is really all that is left here: the human race's settling the earth through successive generations; M. A. S. Abdel Haleem, trans., *The Qur'an: A New Translation* (Oxford: Oxford University Press, 2004). Others claim God first meant to give the angels the coveted role but replaced them with humankind, who thus became *their* successors.

[11]This idea of the angels' having to bow before man seems related to an idea found in Heb 1:6 or its

announcement of his choice of Adam as his *khalifa* and God's teaching him the names (Q 2:30-33). Hence God commands the angels to honor Adam not because of his special creation, but rather his singular appointment. And God teaches him the names to prove that only Adam is equipped to take on this role.[12] Second, the angels' reaction demonstrates that this appointment is no mere matter of location—and this is even more obvious in the case of Iblis, who refuses due to his offense over God's appointment of a creature he deems inferior to so highly coveted a post (Q 2:30; 15:33; 17:61-62). Last, the corollary of this, that the whole world is in fact made subject to humankind, is confirmed by many other passages (Q 14:32-33; 16:12-14; 45:12-13; cf. Q 38:26). Hence the Qur'an agrees with the Bible in making Adam heaven's vicegerent on earth: God chooses him not simply to settle the earth but rather to rule it under him.

Covenantal Anthropology

The other great distinction God bestows on Adam is that he calls him to live before him in a relationship of mutual commitment as expressed by the covenant. The beautiful garden God gives the first pair for their home is doubtless part of his covenantal obligation to them (Q 2:35). Characteristically Semitic, the qur'anic notion of covenant (*'ahd*, elsewhere *mithaq*) is basically like that of the Old Testament covenant (Hebrew *bərît*). In its primary theological usage, it is a formal expression of the sovereignly imposed religious bond between God and humankind, with the idea of mutual obligation at its heart.[13] This mutuality is evident in the later statement that God will fulfill his part of the Israelites' covenant if they fulfill theirs (Q 2:40).

While the contents of the Adamic covenant are never explicitly identified, Adam's disobedience is in direct violation of it (Q 20:115). Hence we should identify it with God's stipulation that he will punish disobedience with expulsion from the garden. Adam's being covenantally related to God meant he was responsible to conform to God's will within a context of

---

Septuagint source (Deut 32:43); its meaning in Hebrews is clearly christological, relating to Jesus' coming into the world as the firstborn of God's new creation.

[12] While God does grant Adam here a knowledge to which he alone is privy, the biblical account has God asking Adam to name the animals himself, pointing to his unique inherent ability—as *imago Dei*—to think God's thoughts after him (Gen 2:19-20).

[13] Toshihiko Izutsu, *Ethico-Religious Concepts in the Qur'ān* (Montreal: McGill University Press, 1966), 88.

divine-human reciprocity, although such reciprocity in no way signified ontological equality between Adam and God. On humankind's side, then, the covenant required *islam*—exclusive loyalty to God—within a clearly specified situation in which Adam and his wife were simply to abstain from the fruit of the one forbidden tree. On God's side, the covenant obligated him to provide for Adam and his wife's needs and to reciprocate loyalty for loyalty, rejection for rejection. This principle of divine requital is basic to the qur'anic notion of human responsibility.

This covenantal reading of the human situation is unmistakably clear throughout the Qur'an. In one passage, the race is taken from the loins of Adam's sons and covenantally bound to serve God (Q 7:172). We learn of various covenants mediated by the prophets also (e.g., Q 2:63-84). And even more, we see prophets reminding their hearers of their covenantal choice: blessing for those who submit, cursing for those who do not (e.g., Q 2:80-82; 3:76-77; 13:20-25). This seems close to the biblical assessment of the human situation (e.g., Deut 30:15-20; 2 Chron 26:5, 16; Heb 12:18-29). Adam's covenantal vicegerency, viewed as the highest of creaturely honors, then provides the interpretive framework for all developments in the divine-human relationship.

Thus we see humankind in both scriptures as God's servants, our great call to submission to God's will being rooted in both the nobility of our representing his rule on earth and our mutual commitment in covenant relationship. As servants of God, our human greatness is bound up in the greatness of the one we serve. On the one hand, Adam is infinitely inferior to God ontologically. But on the other, the greater the master, the greater the servant. To speak of God's greatness is inherently to speak of our dignity and nobility not as mere residents but as God's vicegerents on earth. Hence the qur'anic majority position on Adam joins together two complete opposites in the *jahili* assessment of things—nobility and servility—in its concept of *islam*.

These two concepts of vicegerency under God and divine-human covenant are the warp and woof of theistic anthropology, so to replace vicegerency with mere successorship or residence on earth is no small matter. Together with covenant, humankind's vicegerency counterbalances the Qur'an's predominant theocentricity with a corresponding yet subordinate anthropocentricity, reflecting the biblical situation.

Major Contrasts Between the Scriptures

There are, nonetheless, many significant differences between our scriptures' respective creation accounts. First, the Qur'an gives only the barest description of woman's origins, leaving the question of her status in relation to her husband unanswerable. Biblically, Adam's naming of the other creatures leads, as with theatric drumroll, to the recognition of the creation's singular lack: a partner "equal to" Adam (Gen 2:20).[14] That realization is followed by God's consummation of his previously incomplete creation with a special creative act, one meant to picture the intimacy and equality of the male-female partnership since Eve is taken out of Adam's "side" (Hebrew ṣēlaᶜ).[15] The Qur'an does say, however, that she was created to dwell with her husband in love (Q 7:189). But it does not tell us whether Eve is appointed with him to humankind's vicegerency under God, as the Genesis account makes plain (Gen 1:26-29). Furthermore, that the Qur'an leaves Eve nameless also suggests her inferiority,[16] even though the qur'anic author does make women equally responsible to submit to God.

Second, the Qur'an does not detail Adam's responsibilities as *khalifa*, as does the Bible's cultural mandate, or point to his creative abilities in his naming of the other creatures (Gen 1:28-29; 2:19-20). In the cultural mandate, Adam and Eve are commissioned to take care of God's creation, to keep the earth, extending God's wise rule from the garden to the ends of the earth and—as implicitly prophets and priests also—to fill the whole earth with God's glory.[17] That mandate involved bracing, invigorating and productive work. By contrast, no such component is so much as hinted at in the qur'anic accounts, which lack any positive description of what vicegerency entails and so leave us with a notion of ease without work.[18] Qur'anically, Adam's vicegeral appointment also takes on

---

[14]The Hebrew idea here is of "exact correspondence" and hence equal worth.

[15]The Hebrew word is "side," not "rib," as most English translations have it. Hence the phrase is better translated "a part of his side." This is why Adam breathlessly exclaims of Eve, "This at last is bone of my bones *and flesh of my flesh*": she truly completes him (Gen 2:23); Umberto Cassuto, *A Commentary on the Book of Genesis* (Jerusalem: Magnes Press, 1961), 134; Joseph Coleson, *Genesis 1–11: A Commentary in the Wesleyan Tradition* (Kansas City, MO: Beacon Hill, 2012), 108; Victor P. Hamilton, *The Book of Genesis, Chapters 1–17* (Grand Rapids: Eerdmans, 1990), 132.

[16]Eve's namelessness is unexceptional in the Qur'an. In the entire Qur'an, in fact, only one woman is named: Mary (*Maryam*), Jesus' mother.

[17]Harvie Conn, *Theological Perspectives on Church Growth* (Nutley, NJ: Presbyterian and Reformed, 1976), 1; Meredith G. Kline, *The Structure of Biblical Authority*, 2nd ed. (Grand Rapids: Eerdmans, 1978), 87.

[18]This notion is confirmed by the qur'anic view of paradise, with humankind's return to a supposedly ideal life of ease without work.

a negative, even fatalistic aspect, as being a precursor only to our race's catastrophic fall. Also, Adam's naming of the animals in Genesis 2:20 is not simply
about recalling what God has elected to teach him (cf. Q 2:31-33). It rather
displays humanity's God-given ability to discover the meaning the Creator has
invested in his creation. Hence the biblical Adam and Eve are not just "function-
aries in a heavenly bureaucracy of command and control but agents of creativity."[19]

Third, the qur'anic creation narrative omits two key biblical markers of
divine-human intimacy. The Genesis account says God himself planted Adam
and Eve's garden home. So in welcoming them to live there, he was inviting
them to live with him in his royal sanctuary, his home on earth, a point Ezekiel
picks up on when he calls Eden the "garden of God" (Ezek 28:13-16).[20] This
is not present in the qur'anic account. Neither does the Qur'an offer anything
comparable to the Bible's first image of divine-human friendship, where God
approached Adam and Eve to enjoy their company at the end of their workday
(Gen 3:8; cf. Gen 5:21-24). As we saw earlier, the biblical motif of divine-
human friendship is notably missing in the Qur'an.

Fourth, the Qur'an sets humankind's creation and appointment to vicegerency not in the world's creation but rather in Satan's fall, thus giving the story
a unique emphasis and moving the audience breathlessly from the fall of Iblis
to that of humankind. This makes it hard to see Adam and Eve apart from their
fall, since it is presented as the fruit of Satan's fall, in his determination to get
back at God by perverting our race (Q 7:16-17; 15:39-42; 38:82-83). Their fall
clearly repeats the pattern of Satan's fall: reasonable divine requirement, creaturely rebellion and retributive exile with respite. Since Adam's appointment
to vicegerency results in Satan's downfall, it clearly leads to his own downfall
as well. And that casts a negative pall over the Qur'an's entire story of humankind's genesis. Neither is this negativity offset by anything analogous to the
biblical stress on the creation's essential goodness and the first pair's having
no shame in the purity of their nakedness (Gen 1:9-31; 2:25).[21] Instead, the
creation is troubled by jealousy and rebellion, and Adam and Eve are clothed
from the start (Q 7:27; cf. Q 20:118).

---

[19]Andy Crouch, *Playing God: Redeeming the Gift of Power* (Downers Grove, IL: InterVarsity Press,
2013), 14.

[20]See Kline, *Structure of Biblical Authority*, 87.

[21]Elsewhere the Qur'an does indicate that the creation conformed perfectly to God's plan (e.g., Q 32:7),
but not in any of the narratives related to Adam's creation.

Fifth, this positioning of Adam and Eve's creation within the context of Satan's fall seems to make the location of their creation extraterrestrial. Hence, while the fact that their biblical counterparts' creation from dust indicates that they are made *on, of* and *for* the earth, none of that is clear in the Qur'an. As in the apocryphal Life of Adam and Eve and the Cave of Treasures, the qur'anic context of Iblis's fall is an extraterrestrial garden, with God's commanding him to "go down" to earth (Q 7:13).[22] Likewise, the garden from which Adam fell is the place where he was created (cf. Q 7:22, 24-25). This suggests that Adam's transgression is necessary for him to fulfill his destiny as vicegerent on earth,[23] which is in itself problematic.

The Absent Image

Last but not least, the qur'anic accounts contain no mention of the focal point of the biblical account: Adam and Eve's creation in God's likeness (Gen 1:26-27; cf. Gen 5:1; 9:6). On one hand, Adam's appointment as vicegerent in the context of covenant—with its basic principles of mutual obligation and reciprocity—makes any genuine avoidance of this concept impossible. Adam's mind is made to hold God's knowledge of the names, so we must assume that he is also perfectly fitted by God to fulfill his charge as creaturely representative of God's rule on the earth—though, as we will see, this is undermined by the darker picture of him found in Q 33:72-73. Indeed, as we saw in chapter five, everything about theism—qur'anic theism included—implies divine-human analogy. But however much the Qur'an implicitly affirms it, divine-human analogy nevertheless appears illegitimate in the larger context of the Qur'an's distinct sense of divine otherness.[24] This is borne out, for example, in Adam's being "taught" the names of the lower orders, as opposed to his simply being asked to name them, the latter implying divine-human likeness (Q 2:31; Gen 2:19-20). Hence the Qur'an does not grant human beings the same exalted status the Old Testament gives them: "a little lower than God" (Ps 8:5).[25]

---

[22]Bodman, *Poetics of Iblis*, 76-78, 81.

[23]Neuwirth, "Negotiating Justice (Part II)," 12.

[24]While the two scriptures give humankind unrivaled preeminence within the created order, biblically this points to our being made in God's image, while that is not the case qur'anically.

[25]Iain Provan, *Seriously Dangerous Religion: What the Old Testament Really Says and Why It Matters* (Waco, TX: Baylor University Press, 2014), 98-99.

From a biblical perspective, the real point here is christological, for two key ideas come together in Christ. Commenting on Paul's description of Jesus as "the image of the invisible God" (Col 1:15), N. T. Wright says, "Humanity was designed to be the perfect vehicle for God's self-expression within his world," and Jesus came as the perfect man, to do in human form what he had done perfectly from eternity past—namely, express the life and character of his Father. Wright connects these two points as follows: "It was thus appropriate for him to be the 'image of God' as man: from all eternity he had held the same relation to the Father that humanity, from its creation, had been intended to bear." Not only did God design Adam and Eve to reflect his image perfectly: he had always intended to come and live among our race *as one of us* and so to rule over us in love. Wright concludes that

> God made us for himself, as Augustine said with a different, though perhaps related meaning. The doctrine of incarnation which flows from this cannot, by definition, squeeze either the "divinity" or the "humanity" out of shape. Indeed, it is only in Jesus Christ that we understand what "divinity" and "humanity" really mean. . . . Paul's way of expressing the doctrine is to say, poetically, that the man Jesus fulfills the purposes which God had marked out *both* for himself *and* for humanity.[26]

This is why the biblical writers are so comfortable with the metaphor of God as Father and even refer to Adam as "the Son of God" (Lk 3:38), Adam's sonship having everything to do with inherent likeness and nothing to do with sexual reproduction. This is made abundantly clear by the fact that our likeness to God is boldly affirmed at the outset of a series of documents—the Pentateuch—that utterly deny our right to idolatry (e.g., Ex 20:1-6; Deut 6:4). As G. C. Berkouwer notes, it is precisely because Adam and Eve reflect God's image on earth—*exclusively*, that is—that the Decalogue declares any (idolatrous) alternative to that image illegitimate to us.[27]

By contrast, qur'anic man is perhaps best likened to the vizier whose unrivaled position in the land does not alter the fact that he is a mere slave, whereas biblically the metaphor of divine sonship always includes servanthood. Thus, though the divine image was twisted and distorted by Adam's fall, that image was restored to our race by Christ, who is uniquely God's Son. Hence, despite

---

[26]N. T. Wright, *The Epistles of Paul to the Colossians and to Philemon: An Introduction and Commentary* (Grand Rapids: Eerdmans, 1986), 70-71, italics original.

[27]G. C. Berkouwer, *Man: The Image of God*, trans. Dirk W. Jellema (Grand Rapids: Eerdmans, 1975), 77-84.

the radical Creator-creature distinction, in Christ we can be returned to our place as sons and daughters of God and simultaneously his servants.

Despite the fact that divine analogy is everywhere implicit in theism, the Qur'an never explicitly acknowledges it. Apparently, it avoids such analogy lest it compromise God's uniqueness and approach the line between truth and error. Here the biblical concept of truth is radically different: truth is itself the narrow line between opposing errors. Accordingly, this kind of risk taking was characteristic of biblical revelation from the very first.

Adam's Divine Appointment—the Minority Position

Before we conclude our discussion of the Qur'an's primordial myth, we must consider the Qur'an's figurative reframing of primordial man in Q 33:72-73. In this exclamatory narrative fragment, a fairly common occurrence in the Qur'an, Adam is referred to simply as "man." Here we are told that God asked the personified heavens, earth and mountains—symbols of created immensity, durability and strength—to accept "the trust" (*amana*). Sensing their inadequacy, they refused. Man then brazenly nominated himself to shoulder it. The passage reads as follows:

> We offered the trust to the heavens and earth and to the mountains also, but they refused to carry it and shrank back from it. And man accepted it. Signally sinful was he and foolish! So that God might punish hypocrites, both men and women, as well as polytheists, both men and women, and relent towards believers, both men and women. God is forgiving and compassionate!

The ambiguity of the key word *trust* has given rise to numerous interpretations, many of which belong to the time of not Muhammad, but rather the later commentators. For example, Baydawi takes it to mean obedience to the Muslim sharia, and some Shi'ite interpreters see it as referring to the Shi'ite imamate. Though the word *amana* could refer to the "covenant" (*'ahd*)—I believe Rahman is right to identify it with the vicegerency to which Adam was singularly appointed (Q 2:30-35).[28] In any case, the concepts of vicegerency and covenant are logically so close as to be inseparable. But however we read it, the word must refer to some uniquely human responsibility freely given by God and willingly accepted by primordial man. And most commentators' choices fit that description.

---

[28]Fazlur Rahman, *Islam*, 2nd ed. (Chicago: University of Chicago Press, 1979), 35.

The vital points in this brief pericope come in the pessimism of the divine commentary that follows the story. Here God states that man shouldered the trust because he was very sinful (*zaluman*) and foolhardy (*jahulan*, from the same root as *jahili*). This implies that God's plan required an act of rash folly and sin on Adam's part to "kick-start" it in the beginning. Since man's choice here leads to humanity's division into those who earn God's punishment and those who win his favor, this ill-thought-out decision resembles Adam's fall as presented by the majority accounts. But what is shocking is that here the disaster befalls humankind not from man's disobeying God's command, violating the covenant or compromising his vicegerency. Rather, it consists in his accepting of the vicegerency or covenant—or both.

Some commentators take the first divine comment to refer not to humankind's acceptance of the trust, but to our subsequent exercise of it. Perhaps we should see humankind's later abuse of the trust as organically contained in the presumption that led Adam to market himself so boldly for the exalted office of vicegerent. If so, this may justify God's decision to make Adam's self-exaltation over the other created orders the indirect cause of his self-abasement in the fall. But to take the divine comment as referring to Adam's yet-future disobedience, we must import two words into the text, effectively reading: "*But later* he was signally sinful and ignorant." Rahman's treatment of the passage also lessens the gravity of the divine commentary by making it an expression of divine pathos for Adam's unthinking blunder.[29]

However, that fails to do justice to the willfulness inherent in both *zaluman* and *jahulan*, both adjectives being derived from fertile and qur'anically crucial roots. The semantic field of the former has words like *evil*, *injustice* and *oppression* in it. And the latter adjective belongs to the *jahiliyya*, days characterized by "arrogance" (*istighna'*) and total lack of thoughtful moral self-restraint. That the Qur'an consistently opposes *istighna'* to *islam*—the duty of the entire creation—shows man's rash self-nomination here to be an implicit denial of his creaturehood.[30] And to concede that this act of brash self-assertion was a mistake, that

---

[29]Ibid.

[30]See Izutsu's study of the relationship between these key qur'anic words in Toshikiho Izutsu, *God and Man in the Koran: Semantics of the Koranic Weltanschauung* (Tokyo: Keio Institute of Cultural and Linguistic Studies, 1964), chap. 8.

Adam neither expected nor wanted its consequences, does not lessen its will-fulness any more than in his subsequent eating from the forbidden tree.

The point is that Adam plunged on with his stunningly presumptuous self-nomination, totally ignoring the moral prudence of God's own nominees for the charge, all of which were far better suited to it than he. What brought Adam down? Like that of his archrival Iblis, it was his act of headstrong overconfidence, his basic failure to know and accept his place. But if we are to view Adam's reckless acceptance of earth's vicegerency as an act of arrogant self-promotion, should we not also see it as an act of "catastrophic obedience"? That is, as his true fall? After all, it set in motion history's great examination of the race, beginning with the single covenant prohibition in the garden and ultimately issuing in the salvation of believers and the damnation of unbelievers. This also raises the question as to whether or not man's inherent rashness (*'ajul*) here implies that he was created flawed and blamably ignorant (cf. Q 21:37; 17:11).

Do any other passages substantiate this pessimistic outlook on our race? Yes, Q 12:53 and 70:19-21 seem to do just that. On the other hand, they could refer to our tendency to evil since Adam's fall, which would fit with other passages— Q 32:7 and 95:4, for example—that speak of man's being created flawless.[31] We must eventually deal with the tension thus produced by the majority and mi-nority positions. But for now it is enough to note the two poles basic to the qur'anic assessment of humankind. The very fact of the Qur'an puts humankind at the center of God's concern. The majority position is mixed in its assessment of Adam, reflecting a darker, more servile and diabolical view of humankind in some respects, but mainly restricting that view to the story's setting in Iblis's fall. By contrast, Q 33:72-73 moves the negativity from the story's periphery to its focus, such that Adam's acceptance of vicegerency becomes his grand liability, his colossal blunder, an act of folly not at all unlike that of his archrival Iblis.

The Complexity of Islam

To sum up, we can read the Qur'an's majority position on humankind in two ways. On one hand, we can see Adam's appointment as the prelude to all the prophetic history to follow. This is what the Muslim community has done,

---

[31]A third passage, Q 4:28, appears equally pessimistic, but it refers not to moral vacillation, rather his physical capacity, as Arberry's "weakling" brings out (cf. Q 8:66; 30:54; 31:14). A. J. Arberry, trans., *The Koran Interpreted: A Translation* (New York: Touchstone, 1996).

making Adam the first prophet, though the Qur'an never actually designates him one. On the other hand, we can begin with Satan's fall and see human history as its extended postlude. The latter view suggests the darker image of Adam, that of Q 33:72-73. This bifurcation of meaning yields two very different emphases and, really, two different Adams—the one noble in his self-surrender to God, the other servile in his diabolical self-exaltation. And this duality pervades qur'anic anthropology as a whole, its positive and negative strands being interwoven throughout. That being so, we cannot give a definitive answer to the question of what sort of servility under God the Qur'an demands of us. At least not without first considering how its portrayal of Adam and Eve's disobedience changed the picture.

Eight

Measuring Adam's Fall

In accord with Muslim scholarship's interpretation of Adam's fall, some Western scholars describe the qur'anic account as mythophobic, and a number of its features minimize its mythic aspects. Nevertheless, the qur'anic fall narratives present the fall as alienating the first pair from God, from each other—in the war of faith versus unbelief—and from their garden home. Furthermore, the Qur'an in no way suggests that these three effects are not universal and in many respects shows that they are. Even so, a number of cardinal differences distinguish the qur'anic from the biblical treatment of the fall, relating to both the scope of the fall and its remedy. Most importantly, the Qur'an has no concept that Adam's sin leads to the earth's being cursed, the human mind's being darkened or death's being sin's penalty, as is the case biblically. And without a matching redemption myth or truly messianic figure, the Qur'an's modified Adam myth is fundamentally unsatisfying, which partly explains the standard Muslim downgrading of it.

*H*aving seen the minority position on humankind's first act of arrogant folly, we turn now to the first pair's disobedience in eating the forbidden fruit. This obviously echoes the Bible's fall myth familiar to Muhammad's audience. Thus we must see what the Qur'an keeps, modifies and omits of the biblical myth. And the challenge is increased by the fact that the qur'anic, like the biblical, narrative often takes understatement to the level of a high art.

From what we have seen of the covenant concept, Paul Ricoeur's assessment of the biblical case is true here also: Adam and Eve's sin is "not the transgression of an abstract rule—of a value—but the violation of a personal bond."[1] This is why God forbids one particular kind of fruit, a kind he could equally have made permissible: it is breaking the bond that makes it evil. While each occurrence—in chronological order, Q 7:19-27; 20:117-23; 2:35-39—gives the narrative a slightly different application, its basic meaning remains the same throughout.[2] Despite God's abundant care and clear warning, Adam and Eve carelessly spurn God's word to them, choosing to follow Satan in defiance of God. Besides judgment, God extends mercy to the first pair in the form of guidance and forgiveness. So in broad outline, this is the same story we find in Genesis. One noticeable difference is that the biblical story presents Satan in the form of a serpent, but there are many more significant differences here between the two scriptures than that.

Qur'anic Mythophobia

The standard Muslim interpretation of the story amounts to a thoroughgoing de-emphasis of Adam and Eve's sin, such that it is strictly personal and quite minor. Some of the Muslim community's reasons for so emptying this myth of its mythological character are clearly theological. To begin, Muslims' belief in prophetic sinlessness leaves no room for a major sin on the part of Adam, whom they count a prophet.[3] Likewise, the story's mythological truth does not fit with Muslim belief in evil's being exterior to humans. For if sin is a simple matter of avoidance—at least for members of the Muslim *umma*—as one might avoid a foreign object, and of seeking forgiveness for past sins, then nothing can be so inherently wrong with us that we need a deep work of grace, and the Qur'an offers none. But if we must begin with the fall myth in order to determine how qur'anic the standard Muslim view of human nature is, we cannot fully decide the matter apart from assessing the qur'anic view of sin and salvation, as we will do in chapter ten.

---

[1]Paul Ricoeur, *The Symbolism of Evil*, trans. Emerson Buchanan (New York: Harper & Row, 1967), 52.
[2]On the applications of these narratives, see Angelika Neuwirth, "Negotiating Justice: A Pre-Canonical Reading of the Qur'anic Creation Accounts (Part I)," *Journal of Qur'anic Studies* 2, no. 1 (2000): 25-41.
[3]Interestingly, Pickthall, Yusuf Ali, Abdel Haleem and other Muslim translators obscure the narrative's pointed condemnation of Adam, while Arberry and Jones—lacking their theological precommitment—accurately convey the text's meaning. A. Yusuf Ali, trans., *The Holy Qur'an: Translation and Commentary*, 2nd ed. (n.p.: American Trust Publications, 1977); Mohammed Marmaduke Pickthall, trans., *The Meaning of the Glorious Qur'an: An Explanatory Translation* (New York: Penguin, 1991).

Our first task then is ask to what extent the Qur'an's treatment of the fall is indeed "mythophobic," as Neuwirth describes it. Consonant with the Muslim interpretation, her idea is that the qur'anic fall narratives shun myth to present Adam's fall as mere *exempla*.[4] Gustave E. von Grunebaum similarly views Adam's sin in the Qur'an as not the cause but just an example of human fallibility.[5] Hence we must hold up those narrative features that suggest a non-mythical interpretation against the rest of the narrative's data.

Five features of the qur'anic fall clearly minimize its effects on humanity:

- its larger, Satanic, context
- its irrelevance to Adam's vocation
- its irrelevance to earth's chaos and barrenness
- its less intimate break
- its irrelevance to knowledge or death

The Qur'an always sets Adam's fall within the larger story of Satan's fall, thus making humankind's fall a sort of replay of their false guide's fall. And this framing has the effect of diminishing the importance of Adam's fall, especially when the Qur'an gives Satan's fall more than double the attention.[6] By contrast, the biblical tempter appears out of nowhere in Genesis, with no backstory whatsoever. While this raises questions for us, it does keep Adam's story central.

Next, the garden's extraterrestrial location makes earth's destiny appear virtually unrelated to humankind's choice, making it a simple matter of personal destiny. For it is hard to see earth's destiny as hanging in the balance when the entire temptation scene is set elsewhere and the text makes no connection between their sin and their vicegerency.

Third, neither are we told of earth's being cursed on account of their sin (cf. Gen 3:17-19). Qur'anically, there is no sense in which the earth is not as it should be. Its chaos and barrenness apparently reveal God's intention relative to its human inhabitants. But Adam and Eve's sin does in fact bring a curse on the earth

---

[4]Angelika Neuwirth, "Negotiating Justice: A Pre-Canonical Reading of the Qur'anic Creation Accounts (Part II)," *Journal of Qur'anic Studies* 2, no. 2 (2000): 1-18, on 16.

[5]Gustave E. von Grunebaum, "Observations on the Muslim Concept of Evil," *Studia Islamica* 31 (1970): 117-34.

[6]The Qur'an gives the story of Satan or Iblis's fall a total of seven times. Its making that story the context of Adam's fall simultaneously minimizes Adam's fall and points to its mythological import, since Satan's fall is clearly of mythic proportions.

entrusted to them, for it enables the tempter to gain control over a great many of earth's future residents and effectively turn the earth into a "war zone." However, that earth is "offstage" during their temptation and that earth's barrenness is not specifically included in their punishment obscure the connection.[7]

Fourth, the qur'anic fall gives Adam and Eve's relationship to God a different character from that of the biblical account. While the Qur'an shows Adam conversing with God, this does not suggest the sort of friendship we see in Genesis 3:8. This means the Qur'an views the covenant bond they broke in a manner consistent with its minimization of humankind's intimate relationship with and knowledge of God. Having sinned, Adam and Eve now need God's mercy and corrective guidance (Q 2:37-38; 20:122; 7:23). But their lack of intimacy with God contributes to a minimization of the fall, especially when his warning relates to their loss of not relationship with God but only their beautiful home. Their disobedience does make them wrongdoers (Q 2:35; 7:19). But given the relatively slight dimensions of their relationship with God, the breaking of that covenant bond seems relatively minor.

Last, the Qur'an does not clearly connect Adam and Eve's fateful choice with any gain or loss in knowledge, nor with immortality or death. Its only mention of the possibility of increased knowledge, power and immortality comes from the lips of Satan, the story's one thoroughly untrustworthy character (Q 7:20; 20:120). As already noted, God warns only that Satan will drive them from the garden and they will be wretched (Q 20:117). When God does mention death, it is not specifically in relation to sin's punishment (Q 7:25). Consistent with this, eating the fruit does not result in any opening of their eyes (cf. Gen 3:7). And the Qur'an's failure to relate their disobedience to either knowledge or death also lessens the story's mythological import.

---

[7]The qur'anic presentation of an extraterrestrial garden seems contradictory on two counts. First, it conflicts with Q 2:30, which specifically relates Adam's vicegerency to his being sent to earth. On one hand, his vicegerency was a great honor, as we saw in chapter seven. But on the other, God warns Adam not to allow Satan to drive him and his wife from the garden (Q 20:117). If the garden were not on earth, then their punishment—being expelled to earth—becomes highly ambiguous, since being sent to earth is intrinsic to both the divine honor and the punishment. Thus the Qur'an lacks clarity on the relationship between the vicegerency and fall. Second, Q 21:104 promises that the creation will ultimately be restored: "As we began the first creation, We shall bring it back again—a promise binding on us. We shall do it." This seems to suggest that Adam's abuse of his trust resulted in earth's desolation, as is the case biblically, since God will restore earth to its original condition.

In Genesis, these features are central to the story, and two trees in the garden are named, the "tree of the knowledge of good and evil" and the "tree of life" (Gen 2:9). By contrast, the Qur'an entirely omits the latter and has Satan call the former the "tree of immortality" and promise that it confers unfailing supremacy (Q 20:120). In Genesis God also warns that eating the fruit of the former tree will lead to death (Gen 2:8-9, 17). By eating its fruit, Adam and Eve choose to experience not good but evil. This does open their eyes—as Satan had promised—but only to their shame and at the cost of their intimate knowledge of God in the darkening of their minds (Gen 3:7; cf. 2 Cor 4:4). Rather than abandon them to their darkness, God provides animal skins to cover their nakedness, clearly implying a sacrificial death on their behalf. He also expels them from Eden, lest they eat of the tree of life and make their other losses eternal (Gen 3:22).

The Primordial Sin's Seriousness

But while the Qur'an's reframing of Adam and Eve's fall definitely weakens its mythological character, it does not eradicate it. For by showing us that the offenders themselves take their sin with real seriousness, the Qur'an gives us good reason to do the same. They acknowledge that they have "wronged themselves," a qur'anic expression always associated with the moral folly of sin (Q 7:23; cf. Q 2:54, 231; 3:117; 65:1). And God in no way disputes their assessment (Q 7:24-25), for the various fall narratives then use five different words to refer to their sin and its effect on them: *khasirin, nasiya, 'asa, ghawa* and *zalim*. Each of these words presents it as willful—informed, free and avoidable but for their stubborn determination to rebel.

To begin, Adam acknowledges that without God's mercy they will be among "the lost" (*khasirin*, Q 7:23). The Qur'an consistently uses this word to signify those who set themselves in opposition to God and who he damns in the life to come (cf. Q 20:124-27; 5:30; 8:37; 10:95; 16:109; 42:45; 46:18). Further, Adam repents of his sin and is granted mercy on that basis (Q 2:37; 7:23; 20:122).

Q 20:115 tells us Adam "forgot" (*nasiya*) the covenant God made with him. This word is also used in the story's larger context, where we are told that, since the damned have forgotten—really, ignored—God, he will ultimately forget them (Q 20:126). Other passages say similar things. For example, Q 9:67-68 says, "They have forgotten God, and he has forgotten them. . . . God has cursed them, and a lasting chastisement awaits them." Q 25:18 tells us the idolaters forgot God in their corruption, and Q 45:31-35 says God will forget those who arrogantly forget his judgment to come. Just like the obstinate peoples who forgot what God had reminded them of, Adam and Eve willfully disregarded God's warning and embraced Satan's delusions (Q 6:42-45). Yet most Muslim commentators expect us to believe that the first pair's forgetting connotes a mere memory lapse. But why should we take only the primordial act of disregarding God lightly? Why would it have been any less deliberate than God's reciprocal act of forgetting, his casting the wayward into fiery oblivion? Thus Adam and Eve's forgetting God is an act of gross and deliberate carelessness, the product of willful indifference to his bounty and warning to them.

The Qur'an uses the three other words here to much the same effect. It uses 'asa (disobey) a total of thirty times, always to signify deliberate transgression (e.g., Q 2:61, 93; 49:7; 71:21). Taken in the story's larger context in Satan's fall, Q 20:121 uses 'asa to mean that Adam joined Satan in his evil rebellion against God. The verse also says Adam "erred" or "went astray" (ghawa). But the idea is not of a mere mistake or losing one's way, which connotes inadvertence or unintentionality. Q 20:123-24 parallels going astray with deliberately turning away, both actions leading to the wretchedness of damnation. And Satan uses aghwa (the fourth form of the same verb) twice in announcing his intention to pervert the race from God's plan and blaming God for leading him astray (Q 15:39; 38:82). Like Satan's rebellion, Adam and Eve's abandoning the true path is completely avoidable and deliberate. This is borne out by the fact that their offense made them "evildoers" (zalim) (Q 2:35). The Qur'an uses zalim 150 times, and it is derived from zulm, one of the most crucial terms in the whole qur'anic vocabulary related to evil.[8]

Hence the Qur'an indisputably ranks Adam and Eve's primordial sin as a deliberate deviation from God's revealed will, dire in its consequences. In that sense, it is very similar to what we find in the biblical account. Within its larger qur'anic context, the focus is not on God's responsibility as our creator but on humankind's responsibility as ungrateful wretches who flagrantly turn away from his goodness and warning (e.g., Q 7:189-90). If the Qur'an has human weakness in view in these narratives, it is only in connection with our tendency to moral vacillation (Q 20:115). So the Qur'an makes Adam's sin neither a mere

---

[8]For an introduction to the key qur'anic concept of zulm, see Toshihiko Izutsu, *Ethico-Religious Concepts in the Qur'ān* (Montreal: McGill University Press, 1966), 164-72; also Kenneth Cragg, "The Meaning of *Zulm* in the Qur'an," *The Muslim World* 49 (July 1959): 196-212.

accident nor the fruit of human finitude and weakness, like a child's unthinking heedlessness. To take it in either sense is to ignore the narrative's positive data in favor of mere inference, for the actual data constitutes it a free choice with profound consequences. Indeed, if the Muslim authorities are right to make it a minor fault, God's punishment of it in no way reflects that, as we will see.

God's Punishment of Their Sin

What then does the Qur'an present as the consequences of the first human sin? Though Q 2:37 tells us God relents and gives Adam "words"—meaning revelation—God's mercy does not mitigate all of the consequences of his rebellious servants' disobedience. Rather, he treats Adam and his wife as responsible adults, as it were, in his just administration of their sin's penalty, with multiple consequences. And a number of the consequences of their change of allegiance—from serving God to serving Satan—are immediate and permanent.

First, they suffer disgrace in the exposure of their nakedness (Q 7:22, 27; 20:121). Having been clothed by God at their creation, Adam and Eve are now physically disrobed by Satan in the fall.[9] The qur'anic narrative represents a standard Semitic reading of nakedness, associating public nakedness with evil. The Bible, by contrast, remarkably turns such Semitic thinking on its head, associating nakedness with primal innocence and sufficiency (Gen 2:25; 3:7-11), for in Genesis the prefallen Adam and Eve have no cause for shame, not even one of which they are blissfully ignorant or simply manage through the use of clothing. Rather, God has declared their creation—their nakedness included—very good. Their sense of shame and inadequacy is mediated only by their experience of evil (Gen 1:31; 2:25; 3:7). Hence, while both scriptures show Adam and Eve clothing themselves with leaves due to their newfound shame, in the Qur'an their shame is simply social, relating only to a loss of clothing—not to a fundamentally different self-perception.

Second, their sin affects them spiritually. As a result, they appeal to God for forgiveness, indicating their new awareness of moral defilement (Q 7:23, cf. Q 20:123-24). And as noted above, Adam and Eve now need God's corrective

---

[9]Q 7:27 says the first pair are ashamed when Satan strips them of their garments, and those commentators who take this figuratively fail to recognize that Q 7:26-27 uses the narrative to correct the practice of physical nakedness in pagan religion. Q 20:118 corroborates this, saying that the prefallen Adam and Eve experienced neither hunger nor nakedness.

guidance also (Q 2:37-38; 20:122; 7:23). For without revelation—knowledge of the true path—they are lost. Again, biblically this is highlighted by the fact that they hide not just their bodies but also themselves from God, their sense of shame in the presence of a holy God being foreign to the Qur'an (Gen 3:7-10).

Third, Adam and Eve's sin profoundly alters their interpersonal relations also. God informs them of a new social alienation, as husband and wife must now live in mutual hostility (Q 2:36; 7:24; 20:123). However, this hostility characterizes not just their marriage but human relations generally. So, losing their peace with God, they forfeit their communal peace as well. The verb in the divine command to "Get down (*ihbitu*), each an enemy to the other" is plural, not dual, indicating that the conflict includes Satan, who will continue his campaign of ambush and perversion on earth (Q 2:36; 7:16-17). Despite their repentance, then, Adam and Eve can expect neither marital nor societal solidarity. And they must set themselves in opposition to Satan in his war of evil against good. In other words, their sin turns the entire world into a war zone and bifurcates the race into believers versus unbelievers.

The last consequence of their fall is their expulsion from the garden, symbolic of all the ease of God's special favor toward them (Q 2:36; 20:117, 123). Though God bars them from the garden, he allows them to stay on earth for a time, only under far less prosperous circumstances (Q 2:36; 7:24; 20:117-19; cf. Q 2:35). This entails an element of shame also, as they are unceremoniously evicted from their glorious paradisal home to seek whatever makeshift shelter they can find. We should not, however, take this to mean that their tenure on earth will be altogether miserable. God promises them temporal livelihood there with enjoyment but bounded by human mortality, first mentioned here, and by the stern prospect of God's final judgment (Q 2:36; 7:24-25). Prosperity is promised to the righteous in this life also because none who follow God's guidance will be wretched (Q 20:123; cf. Q 2:38).[10] But it is prosperity amid the many hardships of both permanent exile and the war against evil. Their failure in their examination has thus made their probation a permanent state of affairs, but now without the garden's ideal conditions, in a world bracketed by the terrifying possibility of eternal damnation.

---

[10]Set over against the threat of hell, Q 2:38 promises an absence of grief and fear in the afterlife. The Qur'an promises this a dozen or more times, always related to the hereafter (e.g., Q 2:62; 7:35; 46:13). By contrast, the promises in Q 20:123-24 relate to both this life and the afterlife.

Humankind's Personal Alienation

Nothing could be more important from a comparative point of view than the scope of sin's effects. As we have seen, besides the public degradation involved in their nakedness, the Qur'an presents the fall as alienating the first pair in three different respects:

- spiritually, from God

- socially, between them and Satan

- spatially, from the garden

The question here is, Which of these aspects of God's punishment of Adam and Eve also relates qur'anically to their descendants after them? I believe they all do.

First, the Qur'an presents humankind as universally in need of God's forgiveness and guidance and nowhere suggests that believers are exempt (Q 1:6; 3:16; 29:69; 48:1-2; 57:23-24; 67:12). Without God's mercy expressed in these ways, all are lost. The Qur'an repeatedly says humankind is predisposed to rebellion, ingratitude and unbelief. It describes our race as self-seeking, vain, conceited, deceptive, impatient and arrogantly rash—"hasty" in qur'anic terms—and hence morally and spiritually irresponsible (Q 7:10; 17:100; 70:19-21; 89:15-30; 96:6-16; 100:6-8). This sinfulness is what produces the tragic monotony of history, qur'anically viewed, as one generation after another engages in idolatry and God sends prophet after prophet, each of whom is rejected, leading to the tragic outpouring of divine wrath. Even then, neighboring cities and subsequent generations seldom heed God's judgment as one dismal cycle follows another (e.g., Q 22:42-48; 28:58-59; 50:12-14; 53:50-54; 69:4-12; 91:11-14). Such repetition attests to the generic effect of humanity's alienation from God.

The only other possibility is that history's monotony evidences some limitation or flaw inherent in human nature from the first. In fact, all but some mystically inclined Sunnis espouse the idea that humankind is essentially good despite our chronic inclination to evil: that is, we are good, but flawed. Qur'anically, however, there are three basic problems with this. First, the concept back of it—that we are all predisposed at birth to *islam*—has virtually no qur'anic support and is based almost entirely on hadith.[11] Second, by

---

[11]On this, see D. B. MacDonald, s.v. "Fitra," in *EI*². In some ways, Islam's *fitra* concept seems to compensate for its lack of the biblical idea of *imago Dei*—e.g., despite our hostility to God, we are still related to him (Rom 1:18-23).

removing the source of humankind's deficiencies to the realm of design, we implicitly incriminate God, our designer. Last, this approach reduces the urgent question of Q 82:6-8 to divine mockery: "O man! What deceived you concerning your generous Lord, who created and shaped you and fashioned you in proper proportion and constituted you according to his intended design?" Rather, since God created humankind perfectly, lacking nothing, the blame for their waywardness was entirely theirs.[12]

Humankind's Social and Spatial Alienation

The Qur'an views the bitterness of Adam and Eve's social alienation as universal also (Q 7:43; 15:47). This relates directly to Satan's hostility toward them and manifests itself most basically in his tearing the race in two. Fundamental to all prophetic history is the qur'anic division of believers and unbelievers, with each opposing the other at every turn. Though Adam does not himself fulfill the angels' prediction that humankind will fill the earth with bloodshed (Q 2:30), his firstborn opens that floodgate by murdering his brother (Q 5:27-31). So Satan's heavenly rebellion breeds lawlessness and oppression on the earth. And this situation will clearly persist until the Last Day.

Finally, we cannot escape the fact that Adam and Eve's sin caused the entire race to forfeit the garden's bounty and liberality, and all the more obviously so since their former home is not even said to be on our planet. Hence they did not choose the forbidden fruit merely as private individuals. Rather, just as— between them—they constituted the entire race, so they chose on behalf of the entire race, which is why their exile (along with the fall's other enduring effects) defines the human situation throughout subsequent history. Only restored to the garden in the afterlife can we return to the rest and peace our first parents knew. We must thus acknowledge that it was as representatives of all humanity that Adam and Eve failed the test.

---

[12]Some Muslim theologians have argued that createdness necessarily implies imperfection. But while absolute perfection applies only to God, relative perfection must be applicable to created beings, otherwise God would not be a perfect creator. And the Qur'an does teach the perfection of God's entire creation and specifically of humanity's design (Q 32:7; 54:49; 65:3; 82:7). On the other hand, Sunni modernists often make the flaw inherent in human free will. But it does not logically follow that free will necessarily means inconstancy, for any will that *must* make at least some evil choices cannot be said to be free. Rather than so sidestepping the issue, we must return to the Qur'an, which teaches the universality of our spiritual alienation. As Q 95:4-5 says, God created man "in the fairest stature and [then in his fall] rendered him the lowest of the low."

Therefore, with respect to all three of its enduring effects, Adam and Eve's punishment is clearly generic to the human race. This is most obvious in terms of the third effect: humankind's physical exile to earth. But that exile is specifically to a battlefield since Satan, their nemesis, accompanies them. And the very fact of a war in which faith and unbelief are the polarizing factors suggests some racial predisposition to alienation from God. It only stands to reason then that the Qur'an makes all three effects—including those less visible and hence less demonstrably connected to their source—part of the one curse that came on the race in the fall.

Adam's Mythological Stature

Since we are equally exiled from the garden with Adam and Eve, it should be clear that our first parents represented us in their rebellion. Otherwise God has effectively punished us all for a sin completely unrelated to us. That Adam represented our race in his acceptance of the vicegerency and related covenant clearly supports this view.[13] We cannot then say that representative action per se is un-qur'anic: if Adam represented our race in accepting the covenant, he similarly represented us in its violation and abuse. If the former had the potential to bring God's blessing to our race, why would the latter not bring down his curse on us all?

There is nothing in the Qur'an militating against this unique case of representation. Indeed, representation is generic in the sense that each generation affects the next in, for example, how a mother-to-be treats her unborn baby and how well we steward the earth. An alcoholic mother, for example, delivers an alcoholic newborn, and irresponsible use of the land can turn the earth into a wasteland for generations to come. At the dawn of time and then only, two individuals constituted the entire human race and so represented us all, which by definition is what the primordial pair do. There is thus no reason why God would not singularly designate that point as the moment of destiny for the entire race. In that case Adam and Eve's fall represents the moment when the stream of persons to issue from them was polluted at its source.

Here some will object that the Qur'an's twin emphases on the individual specificity both of humankind's culpability and of God's judgment forbid such

---

[13] Recounting God's binding our race—extracted from the loins of Adam's sons—to himself, Q 7:172-73 refers only to a divine reiteration of the basic covenant previously established with Adam.

an understanding of Adam. But the oft-repeated statement, "No burdened soul bears the load of another," relates invariably to an individual's salvation or damnation on the Last Day (Q 6:164; 17:15; 35:18; 39:7; 53:38), in other words, to the postfall situation. So while we would not ascribe to Adam's sin Augustinian overtones, it is nonetheless of another order, being part of history's interpretive framework, not the picture within. Indeed, it is why we are all caught in the war of faith versus unbelief.

Like the Bible, then, the Qur'an clearly makes the fall an event of structural—as opposed to incidental—significance, notwithstanding Muslim assertions to the contrary.[14] In St. Paul's development of this, Adam's representation of the human race incurred on it both Adam's pollution—which Luther called the "bondage of the will"—and his guilt[15] and penalty. Admittedly, Paul's treatment of the first sin is far more explicit than the qur'anic author's (Rom 5:1–8:39; 1 Cor 15:21-22; cf. Jer 17:9; Mt 7:18; Mk 10:20-23; Rom 3:9-18). But while the qur'anic treatment of both guilt and pollution differs in various respects from its biblical counterpart, none of the differences nullify humankind's representation by Adam in the garden.

The Nature of Human Lostness

Biblically, guilt has two aspects: theological or objective (Lev 5:17; Deut 5:11; Josh 7:10-15) and psychological or subjective (Ps 51:3, 14; Jn 8:7; Heb 10:22), the former relating to how God sees us, the latter to how we see ourselves. By contrast, the Qur'an focuses entirely on our objective guilt, seen in God's judgment based on his infallible record of our deeds. It almost totally ignores the notion of our subjective guilt.

One reason the Qur'an can do this is that it bars us from any intimate knowledge of God. And sin is only as internally unbearable as the personal

---

[14]On the "orthodox" Sunni view, see von Grunebaum, "Observations on the Muslim Concept of Evil," 120-21.

[15]Most people who chafe against the doctrine of original sin perceive it as the arbitrary judgment of God's holding us responsible for other people's sin. They ask how he can hold us responsible for a choice in which we had no say. But Adam's representative headship is all about *shared* responsibility. For in a sense, we were there in our first parents—present in their genes—and their choice was every bit our choice too. We share responsibility for it just as, for example, we descendants of the British, Spanish and French in North America have a share in our ancestors' responsibility for their abuse of Native Americans. We had no say in what our ancestors did, but their sins are ours too, confirmed by the fact that we so often treat Native Americans similarly.

bond it violates is intimate. Related to this and to the Qur'an's keeping God somewhat "out of focus," as it does, it does not present him as intrinsically holy. And that makes our guilt somewhat arbitrary, connected to God's judgment more than his moral character, giving us no compelling reason to feel guilt. We find a third reason in the Qur'an's marked tendency toward exteriorizing human evil, which relates to the Qur'an's second picture of humankind.[16] That picture's emphatically sociological orientation also explains why sin's effect is far more one of shame than subjective guilt.

The qur'anic emphasis on humankind's universal need of revelation may suggest the darkening of the human mind. But the Qur'an emphasizes our need of revelation and forgiveness over any need of empowerment due to inner brokenness. By contrast, the Bible speaks clearly of all three: our minds are darkened, we are estranged from God, and our hearts are divided. Hence, we cannot please God or attain salvation in ourselves, our access to the necessary revelation notwithstanding (Gen 6:5, 11-12; Is 64:6; Jn 12:40; Rom 1:18-21; 3:9-20; 2 Cor 4:4).

The biblical situation differs categorically in that the human race is dealt with representatively in both Adam and Christ, the "last Adam" (1 Cor 15:45). This means Christ's accomplishments are structural also, his death and resurrection undoing what Satan accomplished in Adam's fall (e.g., Rom 5–8). But like the Qur'an, the Bible evidences the very same insistence on individual responsibility apart from these unique cases of representative action (Ezek 18:1-30; Mt 12:36-37; Rom 2:6; 14:11-12; 1 Cor 3:8; Gal 6:4-8).

Cardinal Differences

Thus, though the qur'anic fall and its universal effects are in many respects consonant with their biblical counterparts, seven cardinal features distinguish the qur'anic from the biblical narrative, the first five of which we noted above in relation to the Qur'an's minimization of myth:

1. The Qur'an always presents Adam's fall as the effect of Satan's fall.

2. It never specifically relates Adam's sin to his vocation as vicegerent.

3. It never relates earth's barrenness (or chaos) to sin's curse.

---

[16]On this qur'anic tendency, see 120-22 below.

4. It presents humankind's alienation from God in Adam's fall in much less radical terms.

5. It never makes either death or a loss of knowledge integral to sin's effects.

6. It shows God granting mercy to the first pair only after they repent.

7. It envisions no end to the war of good versus evil but the final judgment.

While some believe the Bible implies a relationship between Satan's fall and that of humankind, the fact is, if it says anything at all about the former, it does not specifically relate it to the latter. Its focus is consistently on the relationship between God and humankind, and no antecedent actions on the part of Satan are ever allowed to cloud that. The Bible's concern in the fall is rather Adam and Eve's greatness under God (e.g., as vicegerents), their attempted re-direction of their greatness, and the effects of that action on themselves, their progeny and the earth entrusted to them. Besides clearly connecting earth's barrenness to sin's curse, the Bible ultimately anticipates earth's eschatological recreation when the curse has finally been removed (Gen 3:17; cf. Rom 8:20-22). By contrast, the Qur'an omits this curse, although it does speak of earth's restoration, which may seem to imply a curse (Q 21:104).

Compared to the Bible, the Qur'an also scales down the divine-human relationship, since it views humans as categorically unable to know God intimately. Hence their alienation from God seems fairly minor relative to the biblical fall, and a number of its other effects are either omitted or almost so. And as we have seen, the Qur'an relates Adam and Eve's shame to their loss of clothing, not of innocence. It never makes either death or the darkening of the mind consequences of sin, despite the fact that these are key aspects of the biblical story. By contrast, in Genesis the first pair knows no shame until they sin, despite their nakedness. Genesis also makes death the fall's primary consequence (Gen 2:16-17; Rom 5:12-19; 6:23), underscoring the point by making the tree of life their alternative choice. This basic association of sin with death and righteousness with life is observable throughout the Bible (Gen 6:12-21; 7:17-23; 18:16-25; Prov 11:19; Ezek 18:4-31; 33:7-11; Jn 8:21-24; Rom 6:16-23; Rev 20:11-15). We see it especially in the great choice between covenant blessing and cursing Moses set out before the Israelites (Deut 30:15-20). Thus, while the Bible and Qur'an both view life as temporal, issuing in eternal states, the Bible gives death what we might call "metonymic" significance, as an image that represents the whole of sin's alienation. The Qur'an, by contrast, makes alienation central to the fall but omits death from it, presenting death as only the natural end of life's probationary choice.

This has profound christological significance. By making death peripheral to God's judgment on sin, the Qur'an makes death irrelevant to that judgment's removal. Seemingly, God's eradication of evil and his undoing the damage wreaked by it have nothing to do with either death or resurrection. By contrast, the Bible views Jesus' death and resurrection as salvation's triumphal one-of-a-kind bursting of sin's death-bonds on the race. The Bible inextricably links evil with death such that Christ's defeat of the latter establishes his victory over the former. Biblically, then, sacrifice provides for humankind's restoration to full communion with God by his covenant of grace in Christ. Hence, viewing Jesus' death as the fulfillment of the Mosaic covenant's sacrificial system, the New Testament refers to it in terms of the blood of God's new covenant (e.g., Mt 26:27-28; Mk 14:24; cf. Ex 24:8; Ps 50:5; Heb 8:1–10:18). But as already noted, the Qur'an gives sacrificial death none of the central significance it holds in the Bible.[17]

In addition, the Qur'an consistently portrays God as granting the first pair mercy only after they have repented (Q 2:37; 7:23; 20:122). By contrast, the biblical account shows God graciously clothing them without offering any indication of their repentance (Gen 3:10-13, 21). In other words, it is a case of God's granting his grace in advance of either repentance or obedience, whereas the Qur'an views divine mercy as granted only to those who deserve it.

The last major difference here is that, though the Qur'an points ahead to the age-long war in which humankind's sin has issued—between God's followers and Satan's—it foresees its conclusion only in the unbelievers' consignment to hell (Q 2:36, 39; 7:24, 27; 20:123). By contrast, Genesis 3:14-15 predicts the coming of the woman's descendant, a champion who does battle with the serpent: though the former suffers in the fight, he triumphs, crushing

---

[17]As noted above, the Qur'an prescribes sacrifice—traditionally understood to commemorate Abraham's sacrifice of his son (e.g., Q 22:36-37; cf. Q 37:102-7)—but never develops its broader significance. Mahmoud Ayoub's study of Shi'ite applications of such qur'anic materials in terms of the later death of Imam Husayn effectively corroborates this. Apart from citing Q 2:156, a reference to the believers' suffering in jihad, Ayoub presents no qur'anic basis for the Shi'ite view of redemptive suffering. See Ayoub, *Redemptive Suffering in Islam: A Study of the Devotional Aspects of 'Ashura in Twelver Shi'ism* (The Hague: Mouton, 1978), 15n1; on Twelver Shi'ite interpretations of Abraham's sacrifice, see 32-34; cf. 235-36, 246-47.

the serpent's head. The woman's "offspring" refers primarily to the virgin-born Jesus, who defeats Satan in his fatal encounter on the cross, and secondarily to all who are united with him.[18]

The Issue of Congruity

What motivated the qur'anic author to omit such things as earth's being cursed, the human mind's being darkened and humankind's being given a death sentence in his recounting of the fall? The answer is seemingly that they would have demanded a more radical work of salvation.

As Mircea Eliade has shown, a people's primordial myth is invariably fulfilled in the prospect of their full-circle return at the end of time, with the consummation constituting a recovery of creation's original design.[19] Accordingly, the garden of the Qur'an's final state promises believers the sort of pristine conditions Adam and Eve knew in the beginning. And any use of the Adam myth demands a divine corrective equal to its diversion. The problem is that, despite the way the qur'anic author chooses to exclude certain biblical elements in the Adam myth, the fall he presents still constitutes a radical diversion from God's original intent in creation. To present the Adam myth—even with the sort of modifications the Qur'an introduces—without offering an equivalent redemption myth is fundamentally unsatisfying. Furthermore, if Adam is our representative in the fall, we naturally look for his counterpart, our representative in redemption, a role the Bible assigns to the Messiah. But not only does the Qur'an include no redemption; as we will see, it includes no actual Messiah either.

Without a complementary redemption myth, its Adam myth stands like a bridge built from only one side of a chasm out to its midway point. Doubtless discomfort with this inherent incompleteness factored in the later Muslim downgrading of Adam's fall from a myth to a type. That is, Muslims view the story of Adam as a classic case of human free will gone awry. But they insist it conveys no fundamental truth about humanity, despite the fact that their demythologization of it requires them to ignore considerable qur'anic data in the process.

---

[18]Bruce Waltke, *Genesis: A Commentary* (Grand Rapids: Zondervan, 2001), 93-94. Satan's overthrow in Christ's death is to be seen as a present reality, culminating in the (yet future) final application of Christ's historic triumph (Rom 16:20; 1 Cor 15:24-25; Jude 6; Rev 20:1-3, 7-10). United with Jesus and empowered by his Spirit, Jesus' followers continue his fight.

[19]Mircea Eliade, *The Myth of the Eternal Return* (Princeton, NJ: Princeton University Press, 1954).

Nine

Divine Reprieve

God showed Adam and Eve mercy in two ways. His common grace deferred his judgment, allowing the continuation of humankind's probationary testing, now relocated to earth, where evil may temporarily triumph over good. Special grace, by contrast, comes to humankind as God reveals his Word to his prophets. The messages they receive guide humanity to the true path—with its moral precepts and beliefs, etc.—making the other component of special grace, divine forgiveness, possible. While the Qur'an and Bible similarly present humankind's situation as one where faith and submission to God do not always guarantee immediate visible success, the two scriptures differ dramatically in their understanding of special grace and how it comes to us.

As we have seen, Adam and Eve's choice to disregard God's warning to them and submit to Satan was neither private nor incidental. Rather, they represented the entire race such that their fall was humankind's fall. Hence, in granting Adam and Eve a reprieve, God showed mercy to humankind universally. We may view the ways he did so under two headings:

1. Common (or universal) grace
2. Special (or saving) grace

Grace signifies favor bestowed on those who in fact deserve the very opposite.[1] God grants special grace to believers to restore them to right relationship with himself and enable them to follow the true path. More basic
than that, however, his common grace permits the continuation of our race's
probationary testing. In other words, common grace gives Adam and Eve a
second chance to respond to God's special revelation and grants each of us
that same chance in them.

Common Grace

God gives Adam and his wife—and the human race in them—an extension
for an indefinite period of time on earth (Q 2:36; 7:24-25). This is what is
meant by God's choosing the fallen Adam in Q 20:122, for the alternative
would have been his rejecting him. Basic here is the notion of partially deferred judgment: though their high treason against God warrants their immediate destruction, he shows mercy by sending them to earth with the
possiblilty of escaping the final judgment. He alludes to that judgment in
the words "from there you shall be brought out"—that is, they will be
brought out of the earth in the resurrection (Q 7:25). But God does not
reverse his decision to make Adam his vicegerent. Adam's fall comes as no
surprise to God: he had known about Adam's weakness before the angels
told him. Yet he had deliberately chosen Adam as vicegerent, and mercy
now stays his hand.

This deferral of punishment has two implications for humankind. First,
the earth is our home for now. And second, good and evil frequently go
unrewarded in the course of the race's subsequent history. If this were not
so, the prophets would never have preached *impending* doom or held out the
hope that the believers' "wage awaits them with their Lord" (Q 2:274, 277;
cf. Q 2:112, 262). Hence the indiscriminateness of God's providential care
is integral to this notion of an extended time frame. Accordingly, God
promises Adam a livelihood (*mata*ᶜ) on the earth, implying some measure
of productivity and enjoyment. This concept of universal blessing is evident
throughout the Qur'an in that the bounty of God's creation, visible in his

---

[1]Since Muslims typically reduce Adam's sin to a mistake, they easily see his repentance as making
him deserving of divine mercy. Qur'anically understood, however, Adam sinned, and God is never
obligated to grant mercy to sinners.

omnipresent "signs"—his general revelation—is taken as a clarion call to humankind's debt of gratitude to him. Hence God's sovereign rule over his creation implies his overwhelming goodness in the general course of events (e.g., Q 10:60; 12:38; 14:34; 27:73).

This means that in this life God generally blesses evildoers along with the righteous. Indeed, this must be so if there is to be any genuine conflict between the communities of faith and unbelief. For the entire concept of "fighting for God's Cause" (*jihad fi sabil Allah*) requires a temporal measure of equality between believers and unbelievers here. The qur'anic concept of jihad allows that unbelievers can pose a physical threat to and even gain supremacy over believers by God's permission. Muhammad's need to emigrate to Medina and his army's defeat at Uhud clearly attest to this. The qur'anic concept of self-injustice (*zulm al-nafs*)—that all sin is against the self (Q 2:57, 117; 9:36, 70)—also suggests that this gracious deferral includes some restraint of sin's destructive powers over individuals and over society generally. Sin is generically the denial of God, the ground of all being, and so signifies a person's alienation from the whole of existence. For the sky to stay in position above our heads, then, implicitly calls for thoroughgoing divine restraint.

This deferral of sin's punishment does not rule out the possibility of either immediate retribution or reward. But for all their prominence in the qur'anic messages, outbursts of divine wrath are exceptional, representing only the occasional crises and climax points in unbelief's long history.[2] Likewise, the deferral of faith's eternal reward does not keep God from rewarding believers in this life. Indeed, the Qur'an emphatically holds out the hope that God may immediately demonstrate his favor toward believers and vindicate them in the face of their opponents. In a sense, believers' temporal blessedness is but a foretaste of their final reward, although their earthly lot often includes privation, mistreatment and sacrifice. This tension between the concepts of deferred and immediate reward and punishment accounts for much of the dynamic of the qur'anic concepts of submission (*islam*) and faith (*iman*).

---

[2]We can view such outbursts of judgment in this age of common grace after the model of Kline, as momentary intrusions of the eschatological Last Day into history; Meredith G. Kline, *The Structure of Biblical Authority*, 2nd ed. (Grand Rapids: Eerdmans, 1978), 154-58. But if we do, we must remember that they are rooted in nothing comparable to Jesus' death and resurrection.

Special Grace

The special or saving grace of God consists primarily of the guidance he offers humankind, conveyed by his prophets and their scriptures and efficacious to those who submit to it in faith. We need this special revelation—as well as creation's general revelation—since the fall has left us susceptible to Satan's counterrevelation, his whispering campaign urging us to rebel against God. The fall narratives explicitly mention God's guidance, presenting it as Adam's— and hence, humankind's—only means of salvation (Q 2:38-39; 20:123-27). By willfully defecting to Satan's cause, Adam and Eve denied God their rightful dependence on and submission (*islam*) to him. Hence humankind can only be saved by gratefully submitting again.

Integral to our submission is our genuine repentance—meaning our thoroughgoing reorientation from autonomous self-will to the will of God. We must abandon wrong, make amends and seek the special grace of God's forgiveness (Q 2:160, 199; 3:135; 4:110). We see both Adam's confession of sin and his plea for divine mercy in Q 7:23. And what God requires of him is required of us all. Hence God's guidance serves as the divinely appointed touchstone for humankind, the means by which we eternally seal our orientation either to or away from God.

God's guidance should doubtless be identified with the "words" Adam received (Q 2:37; 20:122) when his Lord relented toward him. The universal "signs" of God's goodness, greatness and majesty to our race are unmistakably clear despite their being nonverbal, since all of creation (e.g., sunshine and rain) attests to them. With regard to salvation's path, however, verbal revelation is required (Q 2:38; 20:123). Some Muslim commentators suggest that the words Adam received are those of the prayer that won him God's acceptance (Q 7:23). Some even put the Qur'an's opening sura, the *Fatiha*, in Adam's mouth.[3] While all this is possible, the Qur'an also allows for spontaneous prayer (*du'a*) in especially dire situations, and desperation certainly was not wanting here. In any case, Adam stood in need of far more than the appropriate prayer formula. In ascribing ten "Books" of revealed scripture to Adam, Muslim tradition evidences some awareness of the immensity of Adam

---

[3]Mahmoud Ayoub, *The Qur'an and Its Interpreters* (Albany: State University of New York Press, 1984), 1:84-85.

and his family's need. Looking broadly at the qur'anic concept of salvation, such revelations would have included at least three topics:

1. The continuing danger of Satan's perversion of truth

2. The renewed possibility of blessing for covenant obedience

3. What that obedience specifically entailed for humanity, facing all the challenges and possibilities of their new home

Hence, though our race had fallen, God extends mercy to them, especially to believers. God reserves for the afterlife the ultimate realization of his plan to bless believers (Q 2:38; cf. Q 7:25), when all their earthly trials will end in their readmission to the garden. However, he chooses, nurtures, shelters and blesses believers in this life. God's blessing is evident in the believer's removal from that sphere of Satan's authority also (Q 15:42; 16:99-100; 17:65). Satan's opposition to believers is limited and ideally accrues yet more divine blessing to their account through their perseverance in faith's testing. It follows then that unbelievers cannot ultimately triumph over believers. For while unbelievers' triumphs over believers are divinely authorized, they are in another sense quite clearly satanic in origin. Hence we must see the triumph of unbelief represented by the killing of a martyr (*shahid*)—whether a common believer or prophet—as an apparent triumph only and necessarily temporary, to be righted on the Last Day if not before (e.g., Q 2:154; 3:157-58, 169-71; 22:58-59).

The Biblical View Compared and Contrasted

There is general agreement between the qur'anic perspective and the biblical reading of the postfall situation. The paradigm of covenant reciprocity continues, but now with the paradigm of reversal superimposed on it. This produces the same tension between God's covenant faithfulness and his deferral of rewards—due to common grace's permitting evil—and hence a similar dynamic in which faith and submission to God operate in a hostile world.

Notwithstanding this basic agreement, there are also a number of major differences between the Qur'an and Bible, particularly in terms of the operation of special grace. Briefly, these relate to (1) the nature of saving grace, (2) how God gives that grace to our race and (3) the nature of the guidance by which believers are redeemed and rescued from their lostness. The point throughout is the same, biblically speaking: special grace—

indeed, grace of any kind—is impossible apart from Christ's incarnation and triumph over death.

We see some of these differences in the fall narratives, but they become fully apparent only in the larger qur'anic context. Hence we set the fall narratives aside for now, returning to them in the course of our larger discussion of the human situation and the nature of salvation. That discussion will require our reassessment of qur'anic anthropology, for the picture of humankind given by the fall narratives does not constitute the whole picture. The Qur'an also evidences a quite different view. Not only is this second picture equally qur'anic: it is the standard view of nearly all nonmystical Muslim interpreters and has profound implications for qur'anic soteriology.

Ten

Sin *and* Salvation in a World *of* Us Against Them

Along with its Adam myth, the Qur'an gives another picture of humankind, defined by the communal divide between believers and unbelievers, each presented in ideal terms. This points to a transposition of Hijazi tribalism into the Qur'an's religious register by which the tribe's moral value is ascribed to the new "supertribes" of faith and unbelief. Since God is on the side of the Muslim *umma*, loyalty to it in its great conflict with unbelievers is a major qur'anic emphasis. The Qur'an designates spiritual guidance as humankind's great lack and itself as the repository of that guidance. Salvation is viewed as synergistic, requiring the individual's faith and good deeds in combination with God's mercy. The Bible's very different assessment of the human problem produces an equally different solution. Another major difference between the two scriptures relates to the historical role they assign to Jesus. In keeping with its stress on divine transcendence, the Qur'an makes personal salvation attainable only on the Last Day, not issuing in a present-tense relationship with God through Christ, as in the Bible. Also unlike the Bible, the Qur'an never once speaks of God's revealing himself or the depths of his love for humankind. It also says nothing of humankind's need of a redeemer who bears the sins of the world. The two scriptures also differ greatly as to the means by which the faith community should fulfill its mandate and the character of that community's relationship to outsiders.

*E*choing the biblical Adam myth, the Qur'an evidences some key similarities to the Bible on the human predicament and its solution. Both scriptures present human beings as morally responsible for their choices and the human problem as primarily spiritual and moral. Both portray God as graciously extending his offer of salvation to humankind with a call for repentance, faith and obedience. In both, salvation involves the believer's following the divinely prescribed path to paradise within the context of the faith community's struggle against evil. In both, God judges on the basis of our moral choices. But despite this convergence, the two scriptures also diverge widely on the human problem and its solution. Nothing in the qur'anic view of salvation answers to a mythological fall, calling for redemption on a structural level: we see only individual sins for which each sinner must atone. While this affords believers a measure of hope, the Qur'an's negative theology makes friendship with God and any assurance of salvation in this life impossible.

The Qur'an's Second Picture of Humankind

To understand the Qur'an's view of salvation, we must return to its view of humankind, for besides its primordial myth, the Qur'an presents also a very different portrayal of humankind, distinguished by its essentially external assessment of sin. That is, unlike its Adamic picture, the Qur'an presents innumerable data suggesting that humankind—or at least believers—are not inwardly bent toward evil. And that means human nature remains unchanged since creation, that Adam's children are not naturally predisposed to rebel against God.[1]

Unlike its Adam myth, however, the Qur'an presents its second view of humankind not in story form but rather in its overall presentation of believers and the way of salvation. It does so partly by exteriorizing evil, making the fight between good and evil waged not mainly on the battlefield of the human soul but rather on a communally divided landscape.[2] Even the most cursory study of jihad and its cognates makes plain that the qur'anic concept is mainly to be taken in this sense, for jihad is nearly always associated with submission (*islam*)

---

[1]Hence most Muslims believe that at birth everyone is either morally neutral or else inclined to Islam; on this see 105n11 above.

[2]The Qur'an never gives any clear indication that the communal conflict begun in the garden (cf. Q 2:36-39; 7:16-17) issues from an even deeper divide within every human soul.

as the great communal watershed between faith and unbelief. That divide relates to such things as persecution, emigration, the military campaign to retake Mecca for God and the urgent need for communal solidarity in all of that (e.g., Q 8:74-75; 16:110).[3] The Meccan suras focus on the believer's perseverance amid adversity growing into open persecution. Then, once the *umma* emerges as a religio-political entity, the Medinan suras complement that theme with the *umma*'s military campaign to defeat its foes. Both themes make the Qur'an's second picture of humanity predominant.[4] But in the ongoing qur'anic diatribe against unbelievers—including Jews and Christians—and hypocrites, that picture holds glimpses of the other, darker view. Thus, because unbelievers are integral to the Qur'an's central contest between faith and unbelief, its darker, Adamic picture of humanity is never far from view, though it makes for a rather messy anthropology composed of competing perspectives.

Hence Muslims generally view the Islamic *umma* with real optimism, while often taking a far darker view of those resisting the *umma*'s God-given goals. That is to say, the Muslim community largely maintains the qur'anic spirit in its view of humanity's faith/unbelief divide. Thus the believers' *islam* demonstrates that humans are not basically askew in their spiritual orientation, though unbelievers' rebellion is harder to explain, and the Qur'an alternates between implying that they will convert as soon as they see the truth and making them denizens of hell by design.

Sin in a Socially Dichotomized World

When we say believers are not askew in their spiritual orientation, it is not that the Qur'an ever portrays them as sinless, for both rank-and-file believers and exalted prophets commit sins and need God's forgiveness (Q 3:31; 11:47; 28:14-17; 38:21-26; 71:28). But the Qur'an never depicts them as *sinful,* inherently wayward. Neither does it treat their sins with any of the passion with which it treats those of nonbelievers. Since nearly all the passages cited in chapter eight on the human bent toward evil address unbelievers' evil, Adam's fallenness belongs seemingly to unbelievers only.[5] So while the Bible makes sin pervasive in believers no less than unbelievers—the line between faith and

---

[3]On jihad, see 184-211 below.
[4]During Islam's first century the conquest made this picture primary.
[5]Q 12:53 is exceptional here, referring to the race generically, the prophet Joseph included.

unbelief running through every heart, and the war between faith and unbelief as much internal as external (Gal 5:17; Jas 4:1)—the Qur'an does the opposite. Its agenda is so sociologically as opposed to theologically driven that its concern is almost entirely the struggle's communal, as opposed to its individual, aspect.

Hence the Qur'an focuses primarily on sin's more deadly fruits—namely, those sins that define the *umma* negatively or threaten its existence.[6] The Qur'an vehemently condemns the unbeliever's refusal to submit to Muhammad and join his *umma* but says very little of pride's seemingly "nicer" side, such as the believer's pride of piety. It treats hypocrisy likewise: its focus is almost entirely communal, on the treachery of treasonous deception, while it says very little of that duplicity of heart afflicting even the best believers. This tends markedly toward a less insidious, more superficial view of evil than one might expect given the Qur'an's strong emphasis on the deceitfulness of sin and Satan (Q 3:14; 6:43; 15:39; 40:37). And that points again to the Qur'an's preoccupation with what we might call "watershed" sins—sins that define the line between the mutually antagonistic causes of faith and unbelief. For what makes a sin significant qur'anically is the degree to which it endangers the "Cause of God." And that deemphasizes any pollution of the believer's inner spring and makes sin appear exterior to her.

The effect of this is a thoroughgoing social dichotomy and, in the nature of the Qur'an's polemical thrust, the frequent idealization of both believers and unbelievers. Donner writes:

> The characters that populate the Qur'an's narrations are bleached out, because its focus on morality is so intense. The only judgment about a person that really matters, in the Qur'anic view, is whether he or she is good or evil, and most characters presented in the Qur'anic narratives fall squarely on one side or the other of that great divide. More often than not, it gives us "ideal types," with little suggestion that a single personality might be a mixture of good and evil impulses in constant tension. Moreover, it conveys no sense that the tension itself, being uniquely human, is of special interest. That is, there is little appreciation of the human moral struggle in its own right; there is only concern for its outcome. Hence one finds in the Qur'an no sympathy for the sinner as

---

[6]This is why Muslim ethics emphasize communal propriety far more than personal morality, let alone holiness.

someone succumbing . . . to all-too-human impulses in the face of overwhelming temptation, despite the valiant efforts to resist temptation. Rather,
the Qur'an portrays humanity in a strictly polarized way.[7]

Donner's point here is vital. I would qualify it only in that what bleaches the
qur'anic characters out is not the intensity of the moral lens through which
they are viewed. It is rather that the intensity is communally limited: the
failings of unbelievers—though never those of believers—are scrutinized
with extreme intensity. And among non-Muslims, the Qur'an only recognizes
goodness in those supportive of the Muslim cause or just about to convert.

This provides a major contrast between the Qur'an and Bible, which—especially in Jesus' teaching—focuses its moral intensity as much on believers
as unbelievers. As we will see, even those prophets the Qur'an shows as
sinning seem somehow untouched by their sin. The Qur'an essentially does
not take its prophets' sins seriously—merely giving them a sideways glance.[8]
Neither does the Muslim scripture take ordinary believers' sins with much
gravity,[9] at least not compared with those sins that define the line between
faith and unbelief. The believer's capacity to commit serious sin may be implicit in the qur'anic treatment of the so-called boundary (*hadd*) punishments
for theft and illicit sex, etc. (Q 5:33-39; 24:2-10). But the Qur'an does not
document the infraction of these proscriptions within the *umma*. The only
exception is the case of defectors, whose sin de-islamicizes them (Q 4:88-89;
5:33; 9:73-74; cf. Q 9:123). Neither does the Qur'an explain the need for these
punishments, whether it lies in the believer's rebellion or simple ignorance of
the divinely ordained bounds. In any case, the Qur'an's in-house guidance is
typically optimistic in tone, in sharp contrast to its vast offensive against unbelievers. The vital issue is always that of communal faith versus unbelief.[10]

---

[7]Fred M. Donner, *Narratives of Islamic Origins: The Beginnings of Islamic Historical Writing* (Princeton, NJ: Darwin Press, 1998), 75-76.

[8]This why the classical scholars were so easily able to expunge them from the record in their prom-ulgation of prophetic sinlessness. See 149-51 below.

[9]Bodman offers a fascinating study of the moral tension evident in the Qur'an's treatment of at least one of its primary characters. But ironically, the one character who displays this polarity and de-velopment is none other than Iblis and so not human at all; Whitney S. Bodman, *The Poetics of Iblis: Narrative Theology in the Qur'an* (Cambridge, MA: Harvard School of Divinity Press, 2007).

[10]Tor Andrae sees the Qur'an's outlook on humankind as largely pessimistic, while Dirk Bakker views it oppositely. This is because Andrae focuses on Muhammad's interaction with Mecca's poly-theists, while Bakker focuses on the Medinan suras' treatment of the *umma*'s early successes and hence the believer-oriented view of humanity. See Tor Andrae, *Der Ursprung des Islams und das*

The Tribal Rooting of Moral Value

This communal divide points to a rather significant omission in the qur'anic treatment of sin and moral value. The Qur'an never challenges the *jahili* concept of morality, according to which good and evil are seen as residing not in the individual per se but rather in the tribe—its either noble or ignoble heritage.[11] To be born into a noble tribe was thought to confer character and moral qualities on the individual. One's blood was what was believed to convey nobility or servility and link the Arab to his illustrious or ignominious ancestors. This bifurcated the world into one's tribe versus all its rivals. Since value inhered in the tribe, not the individual, tribal unity and survival were the greatest good and hence the tribe's primary focus.

The Qur'an tacitly endorses this tribal rooting of moral value in various ways. To begin, this is why everything in the Muslim scripture relates to the watershed between faith and unbelief and why absolute loyalty to its "super-tribe" of faith is paramount. Not only is the *umma* the locus of every believer's calling in the world, but it is the source of her nobility and hence her confidence before God. The Qur'an assures believers: "You are the best community ever raised up for humankind, commanding virtue and forbidding vice, and believing in God" (Q 3:110). Binding themselves to that community gives believers their best hope of salvation.

This is also what makes the Qur'an so stridently polemical in tone, its treatment of history—replete with prophetic panegyric and lampoon—resembling the tribal polemics of pre-Islamic poetry. The primary change the Qur'an introduces into Arab tribalism is that it redefines the beliefs and behaviors by which one proves one's nobility in terms of religious piety, making them the deciding factors in the great sociological contest it sets forth for our race.[12] Good and evil now reside in the "families" of faith and unbelief respectively. But otherwise, the old Arab conception of tribal nobility appears to have been transposed intact into the Qur'an's religious

---

Christentum (Stockholm-Uppsala: Kyrkohistorick Arsskrift, 1926), 88; Dirk Bakker, *Man in the Qur'an* (Amsterdam: Drukkerij Holland, 1965), 53-54. The same suras are equally pessimistic in speaking of unbelievers and Jews (e.g., Q 2:83-103; 3:176-84; 22:42-48). Whenever the qur'anic author addresses those opposed to God's Cause, he automatically reverts to his darker view of man.

[11]See 31 above.

[12]See Toshihiko Izutsu, *Ethico-Religious Concepts in the Qur'ān* (Montreal: McGill University Press, 1966), 58-61.

register—with nobility still being given ample room to express itself in valor in battle, for example. This communal rooting of moral value tends strongly to exclude the possibility of taking seriously either believers' sins or their continuing inclination toward evil, according to the qur'anic Adam myth.[13] This view is also consonant with the Arab concept of tribal solidarity, with its predilection for favoring insiders and resisting or attacking outsiders who refuse to submit (Q 5:54; 48:29).[14]

The Qur'an's rooting of morality in the supertribe may seem at odds with its urgency over the individual's responsibility on the Last Day. But the pre-Islamic poets also called members of the tribe to demonstrate its nobility personally as opposed to manifesting the despicable character of rival tribes.[15] Thus the Qur'an urges believers to emulate Abraham and the *umma*'s other noble "ancestors" and so conform to the supertribal ideal.[16] It also stresses total allegiance to the "Cause of God" and warns of alternatives in its denigration of unbelievers.[17] So while the true believer is in one sense essentially good, her true guarantee of goodness inheres in the *umma* and her absolute allegiance to it. Also, while the *umma*'s initial formation depended on conversion, that crisis experience tended to be

---

[13]Thus Muslim scholars demythologized its primordial fall, as we have seen. They made its two inescapably universal consequences—humankind's expulsion from the garden and the age-long communal contest between faith and unbelief—matters of mere locality and divine design, respectively, and diminished its other effects. They did this in order to downgrade Adam's sin to a mere mistake, the product of weakness or incapacity, and to minimize anthropological dissonance in the Qur'an by allowing its optimistic view of the supertribe of faith to override the Adam myth.

[14]By contrast, the biblical witness moves always in the opposite direction, with God judging his chosen people more severely than he judges outsiders, the idea being that with covenant favor comes increased responsibility. Since his people have more light, God holds them to a higher standard than outsiders (Lk 12:48; Jn 15:22; 1 Pet 4:17).

[15]The *jahili* Arab "felt himself charged with the sacred duty of transmitting [his tribal honor] unharmed, or even greatly increased, to his posterity"; Izutsu, *Ethico-Religious Concepts in the Qur'ān*, 62-63.

[16]Cf. 143 below.

[17]If there were any real conflict between individual responsibility and communal moral value— whether *jahili* or qur'anic—it would be at the points of conversion and backsliding. But Arab tribalism allowed for the possibility of a tribe's inclusion of alien individuals (or groups) who assumed a "client" (*mawla*) status and were thus granted member status in the tribe. Since changing one's tribal allegiance was possible, Muhammad's call for pagans to join the *umma* had the force of calling aliens to join the noble supertribe of *islam*. Hence the sins (e.g., idolatry) of a believer's preconversion days would all be erased by the fact of his conversion, since those sins belonged to the now-annulled state of his former alienness to the community. In terms of backsliding, the Qur'an repeatedly warns those wavering in loyalty of the grave danger of proving themselves to have been unbelievers all along (Q 2:8-20; 3:167-68; 29:10-11; 61:2-3). In that case both their conversion and its later undoing would be shown to have been apparent only.

forgotten in the life that followed, especially as one generation of Muslims succeeded another.[18]

Anthropology's Effect on Soteriology

This tribal rooting of morality goes a long way toward explaining why the Qur'an frames salvation so differently from the Bible, for any solution to the human problem is closely related to the way in which that problem is defined. Here the Qur'an gives us only faint traces of the Bible's strong emphasis on such interrelated concepts as human inability, sacrifice, salvation, redemption and atonement (e.g., Q 3:103; 40:41; 47:2).[19] It does present humankind as needing forgiveness (e.g., Q 2:177; 3:108; 7:43; 33:33; 62:2), but its primary need is for guidance, which leads them to repent, believe and do good deeds. Hence most Muslims view humankind's moral deficiency primarily in terms of the lack of knowledge, met simply and efficiently by the Qur'an, God's "criterion" for salvation (Q 25:1). The believer demonstrates her faith by observing the various communal markers—ritual prayer, almsgiving, fasting, etc.—living by the Qur'an's moral precepts and giving her unwavering support to "God's Cause."

The Qur'an also speaks of God's absolution of the believer's sins (Q 3:195; 8:29; 47:2; 48:5; 65:5; 66:8). But besides God's mercy and sovereign choice, his basis for forgiving sins and granting admission to paradise inheres in three things: repentance (Q 4:17-18; 39:17, 54), faith (Q 5:65; 10:103; cf. Q 2:136, 177, 285) and pious deeds (Q 2:277; 3:195; 5:94; 19:59-60; 24:47-56; 29:7; 33:35; 46:31). Q 11:114 says flatly, "Good deeds remove evil deeds" (cf. Q 13:22; 28:54). Ultimately, only the believer whose good deeds outweigh her bad merits God's pardon (Q 7:8-9; 21:47; 23:102-3; 101:6-9; cf. Q 3:30; 18:49; 54:52-53).

---

[18]Hence the Qur'an's stress on the irrelevance of tribal affiliation on the Last Day must be taken in the context of its conversion-aimed preaching (e.g., Q 80:33-37). It condemns not tribalism per se but only ethnic non-Muslim tribalism: the Qur'an's religious redefinition of tribalism is never in question—only tribalism as a barricade to conversion. Tribalism is a problem only when it hinders—never when it facilitates—submission to Muhammad's prophethood. Hence Izutsu overemphasizes the Qur'an's rejection of tribal for individual responsibility; *Ethico-Religious Concepts in the Qur'ān*, 59-62; cf. W. Montgomery Watt, *Muhammad at Mecca* (Oxford: Clarendon, 1953), 19, 25.

[19]The Qur'an does speak of the expiation (*kaffara*) of sin, but solely in terms of the believer's acts of charity and fasting, and so on. (Q 5:45, 89, 95); on this, see J. Chelhod, s.v. "Kaffāra," in *EI²*. The Qur'an does once speak of God's ransom (*fada*) of Abraham's son with a mighty sacrifice (Q 37:107). But elsewhere it uses *fada* and its cognates only to refer to human acts of righteousness. It also uses "deliver" (*naja* and *ajara*), but instead of hundreds, the Muslim scripture uses them only a few dozen times, few of which connect well with their biblical equivalents.

The Qur'an's focus on revelation also makes humankind appear morally neutral, neither willfully blind to the truth about themselves and God nor perverse with respect to seeking the good.[20] Believers commit sins through simple ignorance, forgetfulness or incapacity, their need of forgiveness at times appearing almost cosmetic,[21] for God appears to overlook and dispense with the believer's moral faults—especially her smaller sins—as one might "forgive" a child's inability to think or act like an adult.[22] She need only hear the prophetic word in order to respond with faith and submission. Self-transformation presents no insuperable challenge to believers, since "God will replace their evil deeds with good ones" (Q 25:70). Biblically, such an approach is perilously naive in its understanding of evil's power and human nature's compromised state.[23]

The Qur'an describes believers as those who avoid the major sins and indecencies (Q 42:37; cf. Q 53:32). Since the smaller sins do not in any sense threaten the Muslim *umma* or one's allegiance to it, they seem not to hinder believers from obtaining salvation either. "If you avoid the worst sins forbidden you," Q 4:31 says, "we will acquit you your minor sins and grant you a grand entrance" to paradise. Rahman concludes that God will pardon believers' lapses, "provided their overall performance is good and beneficial" (cf. Q 39:33-36).[24] The clear sense is that overlooking the believer's lesser sins is a minor matter, although the believer must still do her part—avoid the greater sins and do good deeds—in order for God to do his. And minus

---

[20]Al-Ghazali (d. 1111) took qur'anic statements stressing the utter impossibility of humankind's attaining salvation apart from the intervention of divine grace in terms of both revealed truth's objective light (e.g., in scripture) and subjective, inner sight, without which we cannot perceive the light. The qur'anic emphasis in such statements, however, is on either external guidance (e.g., Q 7:43) or divine sovereignty in salvation (Q 10:99; 24:35; 35:8; 42:8). But as we have just seen, on the human side the Qur'an stresses not our absolute need of spiritual sight to release us from our blindness but rather faith, good deeds and exertion for God's Cause.

[21]This seems not to fit with Q 3:17, which speaks of those who beg for God's pardon late at night, but since the Qur'an never once commands it, the practice may be that of Christian monks.

[22]This estimate of human moral capacity fits with what we saw of the Qur'an's categorical master-servant disjunction and its avoidance of divine-human analogy.

[23]Iain Provan, *Seriously Dangerous Religion: What the Old Testament Really Says and Why It Matters* (Waco, TX: Baylor University Press, 2014), 391. The Qur'an never emphasizes "the extent to which individuals are, in fact, compromised by evil or carry significant baggage from the past or face truly problematic structural evils in the present. . . . The scale of the problem of evil is not very large. Perhaps this is why Islam is unconvinced, too, about the need for radical divine action in the world (in redemption and atonement) . . . to deal with evil in general and with each individual's evil in particular" (161).

[24]Fazlur Rahman, *Major Themes of the Qur'an* (Minneapolis: Bibliotheca Islamica, 1980), 30.

the enormous biblical demands of loving God wholeheartedly and loving our neighbor as ourselves, this is well within the believer's power and requires no divine atonement.

The Qur'an says nothing of a covenant of redemptive grace due to humankind's inability to save themselves. And the Qur'an's minor concept of animal sacrifice does not relate to sin's expiation, except in that all good deeds are expiatory (Q 5:45, 89, 95). Unlike its biblical counterpart, qur'anic soteriology is centered not in sacrifice and priesthood[25] but exclusively in revelation and prophethood. "Belief in the redemptive sacrificial death of Christ, does not fit the Islamic view that humankind has always been fundamentally good, and that God loves and forgives those who obey His will."[26] Al-Faruqi says conversion to Islam takes the convert from a moral deficit to a zero balance and then "lays out before him the arduous road of the Shari'ah, or Divine Law, which he has yet to tread in order to lift himself out of the zero zone by his own efforts."[27] That is, believers by self-effort must accrue a sufficient positive balance to satisfy God. From conversion onward, the believer's good deeds must outweigh her bad in the Qur'an's synergistic approach to salvation (Q 7:8-9; 21:47; 23:102-3; 101:6-9).[28]

Biblically, by contrast, we either obey God's law perfectly, as Jesus did (Lev 20:26; Mt 5:48; Rom 3:10-20; Heb 4:15; 1 Pet 2:22), or we acknowledge our

---

[25]The Pentateuch's emphasis on priesthood and sacrifice finds its fulfillment in the New Testament's emphasis on Jesus as simultaneously our great high priest and our all-sufficient sacrifice (Heb 4:14-16; 9:11–10:14). On the biblical concept of sacrifice, see 295-97 below.

[26]Badru Kateregga and David W. Shenk, *Islam and Christianity: A Muslim and a Christian in Dialogue* (Grand Rapids: Eerdmans, 1981), 141.

[27]Isma'il Ragi A. al-Faruqi, *Christian Ethics: A Historical and Systematic Analysis of Its Dominant Ideas* (Montreal: McGill University Press, 1967), 226.

[28]Cf. Q 3:30; 18:49; 54:52-53. Biblically, by contrast, expiation is utterly impossible for believers to achieve. God's holiness demands absolute perfection every waking hour, something only Jesus ever achieved: it would never be enough for God to disregard our past sins provided we obey him from now on. Even if we could achieve absolute perfection for a whole day, it would meet God's requirements for just that day, leaving no surplus of merit with which to expiate our sins.

But while the Qur'an presents itself as God's saving "criterion," it does not comprehensively spell out what supplicants must do in order for God to do his part. Nor, indeed, could it. For even if it specified exactly how many of what kinds of deeds and of what quality were needed for which particular sins, such precision would still be only suggestive. Because who but God could apply his standards, accurately measuring both the sins' seriousness and the good deeds' quality? Hence those qur'anic passages that say what God requires can only be suggestive of whole masses of divine criteria (Q 5:89, 95; cf. Q 2:196). Traversing so vast an unmapped realm as this can lead only to uncertainty, especially given the divine obscurity so endemic to the Qur'an. Then again, such anxiety would only promote greater devotion to Muhammad's *umma* and cause.

inability to satisfy God and accept his gracious provision on our behalf. That is, being just, God accepts us either on the basis of our own perfect record—by the paradigm of reciprocity—or on the basis of Jesus' record on our behalf—by the paradigm of reversal. There is no other means by which God deals with us.[29] Thus the Bible presents Jesus as the author of a salvation that is wholly God's gift to us (Eph 2:8-9; Heb 2:10; 12:2). Jesus took our sin with its curse in order to share his blessing with all who are united to him. The basis of this salvation is his costly act of sacrificial love on our behalf (Jn 3:16; Acts 4:12; 1 Pet 3:18; 1 Jn 2:2). Believers must embrace that grace as if their lives depend on it, for they do—God's free gift of salvation comes with the moral imperative to live as Jesus lived (Acts 1:8; 1 Cor 6:19-20; Heb 8:10-12; 10:10; 1 Pet 2:21; 1 Jn 5:4). But it is pure gift nonetheless, and our good deeds add nothing to Jesus' perfect sacrifice.

Indeed, we are in no position to do so. With hearts contaminated by self-seeking, we naturally put ourselves, not God, at the center. Hence all of our own righteousness falls short (Is 64:6). So instead, God, our judge, declares us righteous—justifies us—and grants us eternal life *in Christ*. That is, not on the basis of our imperfect record of good deeds, but rather Jesus' perfect record, as God unites us with him (Jn 3:36; 4:14; 5:24; 6:27, 40, 47; Rom 3:23-25; 5:1; Gal 2:16). It is on the basis of Christ's life, death and resurrection on our behalf that God accepts us. "The determining factor of my existence," says Sinclair Ferguson, "is no longer my past. It is Christ's past."[30] Thus by his death, Jesus atoned for our sins (Mt 26:28; Lk 22:20).

The Bible's staunch refusal to compromise on the matter of God's absolute holiness excludes all notions of salvific partnership. Believers must abhor what is evil and cling to what is good (Rom 12:9), but faith and all its fruit in our lives come to us as pure gift, from Jesus' life in us (Jn 15:1-10; Eph 2:8-9).[31] God's freely accepting us, on the basis of not our good works but his on our behalf (Rom 3:21–4:17; Eph 4:1-8; Tit 3:4-6), leads not to moral indifference but rather to moral purity (Rom 6:1-14). For while "Faith alone justifies . . . a justified person with faith alone would be a monstrosity

---

[29]See 72-73 above.

[30]Sinclair B. Ferguson, "The Reformed View," in *Christian Spirituality: Five Views of Sanctification*, ed. Donald L. Alexander (Downers Grove, IL: InterVarsity Press, 1988), 57.

[31]All our good works, then, flow from his life in us: they do not add to it.

which never exists in the kingdom of grace. Faith works itself out through
love (Gal. 5:6). And faith without works is dead (Jas. 2:17-20)."[32] With
Christ's resurrection life in him, the believer produces the fruit of Christ's
faith, attitudes and behavior (Gal 5:6, 22-23). And without this fruit, there
is no salvation (Mt 6:14-15; 25:21-46). But because we please God simply
by allowing his life to flow through us (Jn 15:1-8), this is no do-it-yourself
project. As the Puritan divine Richard Sibbes wrote, since God knows that
we have nothing to offer in ourselves, "in the covenant of grace he requires
no more than he gives, and gives what he requires, and accepts what he
gives."[33] Giving us eternal life as pure gift, he simply asks for the fruit of that
life in us. So while—like the Qur'an—the Bible requires faith, repentance
and obedience, and bases the believer's final judgment on her deeds, it flatly
denies the sort of synergism the Qur'an everywhere endorses (Jn 10:9-15,
27-29; Rom 5:1-2, 6-11; Col 1:21-23).

Eschatology's Effect on Soteriology

Besides anthropology, eschatology shapes the qur'anic view of salvation. Biblically speaking, God takes on our humanity in Christ in order to do what we
cannot do for ourselves—namely, bear our sins and put our world to rights.
Though it clearly envisions an age-long battle between good and evil, the
Qur'an has no real affinity to this sort of cosmic drama. Since the human condition was not altered in the fall, no structural remedy is needed, and thus
Adam's sin calls merely for pardon and guidance. This leads to a far flatter view
of salvation, with no historical triumph of good over evil. Prophetic revelation
comes like a divine "intrusion" into human affairs. But though the Qur'an
presents itself as the ultimate revelation, Muhammad, its bearer, does not heal
an ancient breach opened up by Adam's sin, for that breach is not acknowledged to exist. So while "the role of the prophets is all-important [and] the
significance of Muhammad as their Seal exceeds description . . . yet they
remain 'accidental' figures, repeatable bearers of repeatable functions."[34]
Except perhaps in bringing the Qur'an (e.g., Q 3:81), Muhammad does not

---

[32]John Murray, *Redemption Accomplished and Applied* (Philadelphia: Presbyterian and Reformed,
    1950), 131.
[33]Richard Sibbes, *The Bruised Reed*, (1630), 38, Kindle edition.
[34]Gustave E. von Grunebaum, "Observations on the Muslim Concept of Evil," *Studia Islamica* 31 (1970):
    117-34, on 120-21. By "accidental" von Grunebaum means not unintentional but rather unstructural.

alter the human situation. With nothing to undo, God simply overthrows evil on the Last Day.[35]

Biblically, by contrast, Jesus came as the "last Adam" to undo the first Adam's forfeiture to Satan of the earth entrusted to him. By his life, death and resurrection, Jesus regained what Adam lost (1 Cor 15:45), making it possible for believers once again to enjoy the blessedness of communion with God. As John Scotus Eriugena put it so beautifully, Christ accomplished humankind's redemption *"profundissima vallis historiae,* deep down in the valley of history."[36] In word and deed, Jesus proclaimed the gospel or "good news" that he was restoring God's rule on earth. While his crucifixion seems to suggest that his mission failed, the biblical writers agree that paradoxically his resurrection demonstrated the exact opposite to be true. In its apparent strength, evil was completely overthrown by good in its apparent weakness (Rom 16:20; 1 Cor 15:24-25; Jude 5; Rev 20:1-3, 7-10). Having thus regained humanity's lost authority, Christ shared it with his people, the new humanity "in him" (Mt 13:31-33; 25:31-34; 28:18-20; Acts 2:16-21; 2 Cor 10:4-5; 2 Tim 4:1; Rev 11:17-18). Jesus' death thus made putting the creation to rights an already present—though partial—reality and so inaugurated the Last Day within history. When he returns as king, his victory will be fully realized (Rom 8:22-23; 2 Pet 3:13).[37]

Theology's Effect on Soteriology

Just as the Qur'an's anthropology and eschatology shape its view of salvation, so does its theology proper. Here soteriology's chief distinctive lies in God's

---

[35]Donner believes the Qur'an views Muhammad as inaugurating the final hour in some sense (Q 54:1; cf. Q 47:18); Fred M. Donner, *Muhammad and the Believers: At the Origins of Islam* (Cambridge, MA: Belknap Press, 2010), 81-82. But as noted above (57), the Qur'an often blurs the lines between the temporal and eschatological when referring to divine judgment. This blurring of the line may have enabled Muhammad's foot soldiers to live in the "eschatological now," clearly the place to be when riding a wave of conquest. Each new success would then tell them they were themselves involved in the in-breaking judgment scenario. And the later conquering Muslim armies may have seen themselves as eschatological inheritors of the lands of unbelievers by divine mandate (cf. Q 10:13-14; 14:13-14; 33:27); see 23n25 above.

[36]John Scotus Eriugena, quoted in Gustave E. von Grunebaum, "Islam: Experience of the Holy and Concept of Man," in *Studia Islamica XXXI-XXXII*, ed. Wilferd Madelung (Chicago: Variorum Reprints, 1976), XXXII:15.

[37]Mysteriously united with Christ in his life, death and resurrection, believers extend his victory to the ends of the earth as members of his church (Rom 12:3-8, 21; Gal 2:20; Eph 4:7-16; Col 2:15). So lived, their lives becomes a collaborative divine-human adventure in which God infuses what they do with his light, love and peace. All this and more is what it means to be "in Christ."

remoteness, including the Qur'an's ambiguity on the issue of his ethical holiness—how sin affects him and what is involved in his pardoning it.[38] Biblically, the believer is directly and personally related to God, who reveals himself to us as infinitely holy or intolerant of evil. Because he is holy, he does not simply decide to ignore our sins, as in the Qur'an. But, being as merciful as he is holy, he chooses to redeem humankind at great personal cost. In the Qur'an, by contrast, the very idea of God's being affected by human sin is unthinkable. He is often called merciful and grants blessing and forgiveness. But as noted above, being transcendent, the divine Master reveals to his servants nothing more than what they need to obey his will. The believer is called to his path, his *umma* and his Cause and, hopefully, admitted to his paradise, but God himself is distant throughout.

Directly related to this divine distance is the fact that the vast majority of qur'anic references to divine pardon use future tense or specifically project it to the Judgment Day (e.g., Q 8:74; 22:50; 24:26; 49:3).[39] If he so chooses, God can forgive sins prior to the Judgment Day (e.g., Q 2:52; 3:152, 155; 28:16). But barring a specific revelation informing believers of his pardon (e.g., Q 5:95, 101), they are not privy to the effect of their prayers and other good deeds until the end. Hence the Qur'an offers believers nothing like Jesus' gracious words: "I tell you the truth, those who listen to my message and believe in God who sent me *have* eternal life. They will never be condemned for their sins, but they have *already* passed from death into life" (Jn 5:24 NLT; cf. 1 Jn 3:14; 5:12). Biblically, God wants us to live our lives not endlessly seeking his acceptance but rather in joyful demonstration of his full present-tense acceptance of us.[40] Thus Jesus gave all who received him the right to become God's children, and his Spirit assures us of that fact (Jn 1:12; cf. Rom 8:15).[41] With its synergistic view of salvation, the Qur'an deems such confidence egregious

---

[38]These are not qur'anic questions due to the Qur'an's approach to divine transcendence. While, on one hand, we must avoid God's wrath over sin, on the other, he seems above being "affected" by human rebellion. In either case, as Master he does not include his servants in "his business."

[39]Abraham, for example, refers to his hope that God will forgive him at the Judgment (Q 26:82). Q 47:15 tells believers they will receive forgiveness from their Lord in paradise. The Qur'an repeatedly says they "will have forgiveness and a generous reward" on the Last Day (Q 5:9; 11:11; 33:35; 34:4; 35:7; 36:11; 67:12; cf. Q 8:29). And the Qur'an often contrasts the believer's forgiveness and reward with the unbeliever's punishment in the next life (e.g., Q 35:7).

[40]We find similar assurances in the Old Testament (Pss 32:1-2; 103:3, 11-12; Is 43:25; 44:22).

[41]As previously noted, unlike the qur'anic author, the biblical writers do not hesitate to use the language of divine fathering, never ascribing to it any of the processes involved in physical fathering.

(Q 5:18). Because of God's distance from his servants, the Qur'an reveals only two things about who will attain salvation. On the divine side, salvation awaits only those chosen by God (Q 2:269, 284; 3:129; 5:18, 40; 48:14). On the human side, the believer's piety, prayers and other good deeds will *hopefully* secure her salvation. The ambiguity here flows partly from the Qur'an's variable statements on the topic,[42] but partly also from the sheer impossibility of knowing this transcendent God's mind on such a matter.

Nowhere is salvation's futurity more grimly underscored than in Q 19:66-72, which envisions God making everyone who has ever lived[43] kneel around the gaping mouth of hell to await his verdict on their eternal destiny. The passage menacingly assures us that God knows best who deserves to roast in hell and spares only the God-fearing. Ultimately, then, salvation lies somewhere at the nexus of God's mercy, the *umma's* unequaled nobility and the believer's appropriation of it by piety and devotion to God's Cause. Nothing undergirds God's decision beyond the Qur'an's overwhelming sense of divine otherness. And with only that to fall back on, believers cannot possibly hope for assurance of salvation now. As stark as this soteriology is, there is an enviable "no fuss, no muss" aspect to it, since negative theology shields God from the sort of accusation and caricature positive theology allows skeptics to make.[44] Biblically speaking, negative theology clearly has its place. But without an equally robust positive theology, it collapses in on itself and makes God remote, as is the case qur'anically.

With regard to the biblical concept of a redeemer who bears the sins of the world (Is 53:3-10), the Qur'an seems sometimes expressly to reject

---

[42]Q 66:8, for example, makes the effects of the believer's striving for salvation probable but not certain. Other statements, however, go beyond the contingent: "Say, 'If you love God, then follow me. God will love you and will forgive you your sins'" (Q 3:31). Q 39:35 similarly says God will pardon believers' worst deeds and reward them for their best deeds (cf. Q 4:31). Some verses speak of God's being obliged to save his people (Q 3:93; 9:111; 10:103). But not even God's prophets obtain assurance of salvation in this life (e.g., Q 26:82).

[43]This would have to include Muhammad, Jesus and the rest of God's prophets.

[44]For example, the accusation that God's giving his Son to die for the world (Jn 3:16) represents a case of child abuse; Imam Mohamad Chirri, quoted in A. H. Mathias Zahniser, *The Mission and Death of Jesus in Islam and Christianity* (Maryknoll, NY: Orbis Books, 2008), 235. The imam's failure here is in viewing the Christian doctrine of redemption as Christians so often wrongly present it—that is, as a human-centered doctrine. Biblically, however, God's ultimate goal in sending his Son into the world is "that all may honor the Son just as they honor the Father" (Jn 5:23). In other words, God's concern is primarily positive, that we be the kind of people who center our lives in his Son. That allows God to spare us from the destruction inherent in dishonoring Jesus. And by giving his Son as he did, God revealed the very things about Jesus that make truly honoring him nonnegotiable.

that possibility, although the rejection may not be as clear as it seems (cf. Q 2:255; 10:3; 20:109).[45] Qur'anic denials of the possibility of one person's bearing the sins of another assert either the fact of individual responsibility (Q 6:164) or the impossibility of changing one's fate on the Last Day (Q 82:17-19). Disputing neither of those points (Ezek 18:4, 14-18; Lk 16:22-26; cf. 2 Cor 6:2; Heb 3:13-14; 9:27), the Bible clearly makes Jesus' redemptive death a unique case, in direct fulfillment of the Old Testament's sacrificial system. But as we will see in chapter sixteen, the Qur'an implicitly excludes Jesus' redemptive work.

Biblically, not only does God reveal himself to us, but in Christ's cross, he reveals the depths of his love (Jn 15:13; Rom 5:6-8; 1 Jn 4:9-10). And his faithfulness forms the entire basis of his covenant relationship with us (Deut 7:9; 32:4; Is 11:5; 49:7; 1 Cor 1:9; 1 Thess 5:24; 1 Jn 1:9). Hence the Bible invites believers to live out of the freedom and fullness of God's gracious present-tense acceptance of them in Jesus. By making salvation a partly human work to satisfy an aloof, hidden God, the Qur'an issues a strikingly different invitation. It effectively calls believers to strive perpetually to please God in the hopes of earning his pardon. While the Bible offers believers the confidence that comes from being "in Christ," the only security the Qur'an grants believers is that of being in the *umma*, the best religious community on earth (Q 3:110).

The Bible also presents Jesus as God's perfect self-revelation, assuring us that the God who spoke repeatedly through his prophets has now with finality spoken to us in Jesus (Heb 1:1-3). This is why Jesus is in himself the only way by which we come to God (Jn 1:1-18; 14:6; Col 1:15-20) and why no subsequent prophet can possibly replace Jesus. But in place of a God who willingly takes on our humanity to redeem us, the Qur'an substitutes itself as God's ultimate revelation. The believer who submits to it in the company of the *umma* walks on salvation's path. While that cannot guarantee her salvation, it gives her her only real hope of attaining it. Thus, in terms of the Qur'an's intention to reform the Christian faith, it ignores the centrality of Jesus and constitutes the believer's good deeds as the only expiation needed. It substitutes

---

[45]The qur'anic data on intercession (*shafaʿa*) suggests that representative action per se is not excluded from the qur'anic concept of salvation; Mahmoud Ayoub, "The Idea of Redemption in Christianity and Islam," in *Mormons and Muslims*, ed. Spencer J. Palmer (Provo, UT: Religious Studies Center, Brigham Young University, 1983), 111.

the Qur'an for Jesus as God's way of salvation and replaces Christ's body, the church, with Muhammad's *umma* as the locus of God's activity in the world. So qur'anic and biblical soteriology differ dramatically, even if the Qur'an never openly challenges the Bible on the subject.[46]

The Social Dichotomy Contrasted

Finally, we must contrast the biblical and qur'anic views of the social dichotomy between believers and unbelievers, insiders and outsiders, *us* and *them*. Since God's truth is to rule over every part of the believer's life, the divide is thoroughgoing in both scriptures. However, the Bible's approach to the dichotomy differs radically from that of the Qur'an in terms of

- the nature of the dichotomy;

- the means by which the faith community fulfills its mandate; and

- the character of that community's relationship to outsiders.

With respect to the nature of the division itself, while the Qur'an constitutes its *umma* as geopolitical in nature, the Bible emphatically does not make the church geopolitical. Jesus called his followers to engage fully with the world around them, just as he did, but as resident aliens, members of his kingdom, his counterculture on earth (Jn 17:14-19; cf. Rom 12:2; 1 Cor 5:9-13). He never sought political or military power, and neither did the early church. Neither can the sword spread the good news of Jesus' kingdom—not even by making the coercive influence of a Christian government and legal system unavoidable. Indeed, spread in that way, it ceases to be good.[47] As Paul assures believers, they fight against not their human opponents in faith's contest but rather against the spiritual powers behind them (Eph 6:12). Thus the New Testament's only call to arms is to spiritual, never physical, warfare.

The Qur'an, by contrast, presents its *umma* in geopolitical terms, as the singular state representing God's Cause on earth. In the Medinan suras, submission to Muhammad clearly required every able-bodied man to join his military campaign to defeat his Meccan foes. On Mecca's surrender, the

---

[46]The Qur'an's hesitancy to challenge the Bible's teaching on salvation in these regards makes it very unlikely that it then denies the centerpiece of biblical soteriology, Jesus' crucifixion, in Q 4:157-58. See chapter sixteen below.

[47]Christians have often strayed from their scriptures here—notably, for example, under Heraclius. But I focus here simply on the ideal to which each scripture calls believers, not its actualization.

umma's mandate expanded to include non-Muslim polities of every description. Neither did the *umma* need any provocation beyond a tribe or nation's refusal to submit to its divinely sanctioned rule in order to attack: that was sufficient affront. Just as Muhammad forcibly cleansed the Meccan Ka'ba of its idols, so he forced Arabia's pagan tribes to forsake their idolatry. After his death the *umma* fought the so-called wars of apostasy, purportedly to prevent Arabia's tribes from reverting to idolatry. As we will see in chapter thirteen, Q 2:256 makes an exception relative to fellow monotheists. But as it pertains not to subjugation but only conversion, the basic qur'anic model for the faith community's relationship to an unbelieving world is one of imposition, as opposed to the New Testament model of cultural infusion.

Second, while the Bible and Qur'an both call unbelievers to submit to God, the two scriptures are diametrically opposed in terms of the power by which believers exercise his rule over his world. Biblically, Jesus' followers fulfill their mandate to extend God's rule solely by living in love, which Jesus did perfectly (Rom 8:37; Eph. 5:2; 1 Jn 4:4–5:5; Rev 12:11). Just as Jesus' sacrificial love was indomitable, so his followers triumph over evil by that selfsame love. It alone enables them to seek peace in God's name (Rom 12:18-21; Jas 1:19-20; 1 Pet 2:21). The Qur'an similarly views the community of faith as commissioned to extend God's just rule on earth. But it rules not by the power of love, but rather by persuasion and subtle to overt coercion, including a readiness to challenge militarily any tribe or nation that resists.

Last, the Bible's approach to its social dichotomy differs radically from that of the Qur'an in terms of the character of the faith community's relation to outsiders. While both scriptures call believers to invite outsiders to share their peace, the peace the Qur'an envisions is geopolitical in nature and established largely by coercive means.[48] Biblically, by contrast, the human flourishing to which believers invite unbelievers is rooted in each individual's relationship with God and the unity Christ established in the new humanity, his church (Rom 5:1-2; Eph 2:14-22). We are called to live out of the peace he established even as we invite others to embrace it and look for the day when he returns to make it a universal, geopolitical reality. In accord with this,

---

[48]Only when conditions do not permit it to impose Muslim rule on resistant unbelievers should the *umma* forbear.

the New Testament fostered in the early church an openness to outsiders that is revolutionary even today.

To begin, the Christian community is exclusive not just for its own sake but very much also that it might be inclusive: it exists for outsiders too. New Testament believers are called to follow Jesus' example and offer themselves in costly service to others and to do so whether or not the objects of their love ever embrace their message (Mt 25:40; 1 Pet 2:21). We are to do good not just to the members of the "household of faith," but to everyone everywhere to whatever degree we can—and like Jesus, to do good for love's sake, no strings attached (Lk 6:35; Gal 6:10; 1 Tim 6:18; 1 Thess 5:15). And this includes seeking our society's renewal. Our exclusivity thus becomes "a springboard towards all humanity."[49] All that the New Testament then mandates of engagement with the world—including bold proclamation and humble invitation—is to be done for love's sake, leaving the results to God.

Pluralism in the Bible and the Qur'an

The New Testament also evidences its own distinctive approach to pluralism, linguistically, culturally and religiously. Jesus taught not in the hallowed language of Scripture—Hebrew—but rather in everyday Aramaic. And following his example, the apostles translated his message into vernacular Greek in the New Testament. Acts 2 shows the Holy Spirit embracing a broad multiplicity of languages at Pentecost, and Acts 10 presents the apostles as breaking free from Judaism's cultural absolutism.[50] Biblically, this means that "no one language or culture is privileged over any other"[51] and that God sees every culture as redeemable. The New Testament also provides the basis for freedom of belief within an atmosphere of healthy religious pluralism.

The gospel would not be good news if God had come to earth—in Jesus—as the one person in the room with the microphone or, worse, a military general issuing ultimatums. Rather, it shows us a God who assumed a position of vulnerability right from his birth in a lowly manger. Infuriated that an outsider would challenge their authority, the powerbrokers in his society mistook

[49]In order to embrace universal brotherhood, we must first love our own people; Jean Vanier, *Community and Growth* (London: Darton, Longman and Todd, 1989), 17.
[50]Lamin O. Sanneh, *Translating the Message: The Missionary Impact on Culture* (Maryknoll, NY: Orbis Books, 1990), 29, 47, 214-15.
[51]Tim Keller, *The Reason for God: Belief in an Age of Skepticism* (New York: Dutton, 2008), 254n19.

his humility for weakness and conspired to condemn him falsely and crucify him. In fact, they could not possibly have forced anything on him—he freely chose to endure it. What would induce an omnipotent God to endure such abuse at the hands of his subjects? Only love. Had he wanted mere submission, he could simply have silenced all dissenters. Had he been content with external conformity, he could easily have brought an army to enforce his will. But God desires our love, and you cannot mandate that. If it is not freely chosen, it is not love. God knew that safeguarding the freedom essential to love would cost him everything. But for love's sake, he willingly paid the price (Is 42:2-3; 53:1-12). Thus the life he asks of us is but "the joyful response of our whole being to his love"[52] (1 Jn 4:19), for God came to earth not to command our love, but to win it.

We find the very same thing in the apostles. It was not by accident that they went out as lambs among wolves, evangelizing from a position of weakness, as outsiders—even prisoners (Mt 10:16). For its first few centuries—until Constantine and his successors "domesticated" the gospel—the church displayed this same vulnerability-by-design. With no geopolitical ambitions, it never imposed its views on others. Hence the New Testament calls believers to destroy only their own idols, never those of others (Lk 16:13; 1 Cor 10:14; Col 3:5; cf. Mt 7:5). Instead it evidences a remarkable openness to the other. In Athens Paul freely recognized the polytheists' experience of God, limited though it was (Acts 17:23), and humbly acknowledged truth wherever he found it, quoting contemporary pagan writers and crediting his sources (Acts 17:27-28).[53] He evidently claimed no monopoly on either goodness or truth.

Though very different from that of the New Testament, the Qur'an's approach to religious pluralism[54] was in some respects exemplary in Muhammad's day. The main difference between our current concept of religion and that of the Qur'an[55] is that the latter is communal/tribal in orientation, whereas Western understandings are more theological/liturgical/canonical/

---

[52]Thomas R. Kelly, *Reality of the Spiritual World* (Wallingford, PA: Pendle Hill, 1942), 16.

[53]In addition, the New Testament writers frequently quoted (or referred to) the Old Testament writings, freely crediting them when they did so.

[54]For more on the topic of the qur'anic approach to religious pluralism, see Claire Wilde and Jane Dammen McAuliffe, s.v. "Religious Pluralism and the Qur'an," in *EQ*.

[55]I refer to the Medinan suras' use of religion (*din*), not the Meccan suras' use of it, where it usually refers to judgment; on this see 146n13 below.

juridical and more individualistic than communal. Q 5:48 acknowledges that
the Muslim *umma* is not the only God-ordained *umma*. "We could have made
you one *umma*," the verse says. But instead, "We have appointed to each of you
a right way and an open path." Hence the Jewish and Christian communities,
both born by divine revelation, continue to exist by divine permission, even
though their revelations have been abrogated by the Qur'an. Muslims are to
view this divinely ordained plurality as a case of God's testing them to see
whether they will obey his word to them through Muhammad and leave God
to decide which community is right on the Last Day.[56] In the meantime,
while all three communities are to compete in doing good deeds, Muslims are
to judge by what they have received from Muhammad and avoid friendship
with Jews and Christians in any way threatening the Muslim cause (Q 5:51).
I hasten to add that it is possible to obtain a more ecumenical reading of the
passage, but only by taking Q 5:48 in isolation from the rest of the sura, much
of which is agonistic in approach.[57]

As we will see, the qur'anic data supports Muslim tolerance of Jews, Christians and Sabians[58] (Q 2:62; 5:69; 22:17). But the Qur'an's stark idealization
of believers and unbelievers, combined with its characteristically polemical
approach, often fosters Muslim hostility toward non-Muslims. It is impossible,
for example, to see the Qur'an as urging believers always to honor Jews when
it so often attacks and vilifies them (Q 2:65; 5:60; 7:166) or to respect idolaters when it commands believers to kill them and even forbids praying for
them (Q 9:5, 113-14). Indeed, so dominant is the Medinan suras' geopolitical
focus that we can hardly imagine their calling believers to do good to outsiders
purely for love's sake. Neither does the Qur'an suggest any real openness to
other cultures. Indeed, so emphatic is the Qur'an about its own uniqueness
and inimitability that the Muslim consensus has always required Muslims of
every language to perform their required prayers in Arabic[59] and viewed

---

[56]But as stated above, the Muslim *umma* exclusively represents the "Cause of God" on earth.

[57]Ironically, Reza Shah-Kazemi uses parts of the verse to argue strongly against Muslims polemically
attacking non-Muslims, despite the fact that Sura 5 is itself so often polemical in tone; *The Spirit of
Tolerance in Islam* (New York: I.B. Tauris, 2012), 77-79. But while many Muslims throughout history
have favored Shah-Kazemi's more tolerant approach, they have done so precisely by ignoring the
Medinan suras' characteristic approach.

[58]The Sabians are most likely to be identified with the Manichaeans.

[59]"Islam may be considered a lenient, even lax, religion on many matters," yet for a non-Arab to
advocate approaching God in prayer in his mother tongue is an offense so great as to earn him the

translation of the Qur'an as undermining its authority. And we can conclude that the Medinan suras' approach to non-Muslims remains applicable today except where Muslims are in a minority. That approach was characterized by urgent call and polemical argument (Q 16:125) complemented by the military enforcement of both monotheism and Muslim rule.

The Qur'an is enigmatic regarding other sources of truth also. It does recognize the authority of the biblical scriptures, albeit ambiguously. But it never acknowledges its reliance on those scriptures or any other source and only rarely engages explicitly with a recognizable source outside itself.[60] All of this combines to make it appear at best ambivalent to the idea of truth outside itself, despite its claimed kinship to the Bible. This ambivalence is due largely to the Qur'an's unique approach to revelation, which we will consider in the next chapter.

---

designation of infidel; Sanneh, *Translating the Message*, 213.

[60]Q 5:44-45 presents a clear case of its referring to a passage from the Mosaic law (Ex 21:24).

Eleven

Prophets, Scriptures, Revelation

The Qur'an describes itself as a scripture revealed by God, putting Muhammad in the company of Moses, Jesus and other biblical prophets. Yet by presenting Muhammad as the "Seal of the Prophets," it also subordinates all his predecessors to him. It also claims to restore the pure religion of an Arabized Abraham before Jews and Christians corrupted it. In various respects, the qur'anic concepts of prophethood and revelation seem to be a biblical-pagan amalgam. The Qur'an's prophets, for example, are sinful, but seemingly only superficially so. And its concept of revelation seems to be inspired by a hybrid of biblical prophecy and Arab poetry. While it claims to confirm and clarify the biblical scriptures, it also seeks to correct their alleged misinterpretation by Jews and Christians. But its confirmation gives only token attention to the Bible, and its correction never deals with the biblical text directly, implying that it means not to supplement the earlier scriptures, but to replace them. Its approach to the earlier scriptures is thus radically different from that of the New Testament, which is vitally connected with both Old Testament concepts and text. And being uneasy with the very idea of divine self-revelation, the Qur'an allows no room at all for the divine incarnation at the very heart of biblical revelation.

Most basic to any understanding of the Qur'an is its claim to be a message revealed by God to Muhammad. Though Muhammad's name appears in it very infrequently, its messages repeatedly refer to their recipient as God's messenger (*rasul*[1]) and prophet (*nabi*). And once he had found his prophetic stride, his utterances were prophetic in both senses of the word: they claimed to be given by God and called for repentance in the face of imminent judgment.

The twin concepts of a messenger sent by God and of God's authoritative words preserved in scripture were simultaneously familiar and foreign to the Meccans: they were familiar as concepts, but concepts belonging to the Jewish and Christian traditions. Their missionaries had been vying for the loyalty of Arabia's tribes for well over a century, and both had made many converts. The contest required Christians and Jews to market not just the political but also the ideological advantages of conversion. Stories were normally traded along with goods,[2] as previously noted, and story is that part of a religious tradition that most easily crosses cultural lines. Hence we can reasonably assume that the Meccans had some awareness of the major biblical prophets, especially in a century in which religion was of paramount importance, dominating culture.

The Prophetic Tradition

Though prophethood was foreign to them, the Meccans did believe the *jinn* possessed and spoke through their poets, soothsayers and sorcerers. Hence they naturally put Muhammad into that category, and his messages insisted that he was not what they thought but rather a prophet in the biblical tradition.[3] The Qur'an names twenty-three biblical characters as Muhammad's predecessors, claiming that they all brought the same basic message: Adam (*Adam*),[4] Enoch

---

[1]Often mistranslated "apostle," the word *rasul* actually means "messenger."

[2]Since religion then dominated regional politics, it also dominated culture.

[3]Two points the Qur'an makes regarding its prophets peculiarly mark it as being addressed to pagans. It counters the objection that Muhammad cannot be a prophet since he "eats food and walks around the markets" with the insistence that all of God's prophets were human and lived normal lives (Q 13:38; 14:10-11; 16:43; 17:94-95; 21:7-8; 25:7-8, 20; 36:15). The Meccans also expected the God of the Bible to speak in Hebrew, Syriac or another language associated with it, prompting the qur'anic reply that God always addresses a people in their native tongue (Q 10:47; 12:2; 13:37; 14:4; 16:36, 103; 20:113; 26:195; 39:28; 41:3, 44; 42:7; 43:3; 46:12). Christians and Jews would not have needed these replies, which is why they appear only in the Meccan suras.

[4]The Qur'an does not specifically name Adam as a prophet, but he otherwise appears to be one.

(*Idris*),[5] Noah (*Nuh*), Job (*Ayyub*), Abraham (*Ibrahim*), Lot (*Lut*), Ishmael (*Isma'il*), Isaac (*Ishaq*), Jacob (*Ya'qub*), Joseph (*Yusuf*), Moses (*Musa*), Aaron (*Harun*), David (*Dawud*), Solomon (*Sulayman*), Elijah (*Ilyas*), Elisha (*al-Yasa'*), Ezra (*'Uzayr*), Ezekiel (*Dhu l-Kifl*), Jonah (*Yunus*), Zechariah (*Zakariyya*), John the Baptist (*Yahya*) and Jesus (*'Isa*). The Qur'an includes three extrabiblical Arab prophets also: Hud (*Hud*), Salih (*Salih*) and Shu'ayb (*Shu'ayb*).[6]

By placing Muhammad at the end of a long line of mostly biblical prophets and itself as the last in a series of God-given scriptures, the Qur'an claims for Muhammad and itself an honorable lineage and pedigree. It thus replaces the Meccans' idolatrous ancestors with biblical prophets, giving Muhammad and his *umma* a noble "ancestry." This was vital because Muhammad's denunciation of Meccan religion amounted to a wholesale rejection of a traditional society's tradition. Second, it gave Muhammad and his message all the weight of the former prophets and scriptures—a gravity not lightly dismissed—and conferred both legitimacy and authority on him and his scripture. Last, making Muhammad the final link in the chain of divine revelation points to his supremacy and makes his scripture replace its predecessors. Not only is it the final "volume" in the library of scriptures, but the Qur'an also refers to its heavenly archetype, thus seeking to gain purchase for itself and assert its ultimacy in an already scripture-rich world.

One common qur'anic refrain is that God makes no distinction between his prophets (Q 2:136, 285; 3:84; 4:150, 152). Calling Muhammad's hearers to accept *every* prophet it names, the Qur'an has in mind especially its three most controversial prophets. Jews would have rejected Muhammad, Ishmael and Jesus, and Christians the former two. Ishmael's prophethood would have jarred Jews and Christians because the Bible frames its presentation of him with the threat he posed to the fulfillment of God's covenant promise to Abraham through Isaac (Gen 21:12). But the Qur'an insists its list of prophets is nonnegotiable and implicitly calls Jews and Christians to forsake their narrowness for Muslim "inclusiveness." This insistence on no distinctions between its

---

[5]With little qur'anic data by which to identify *Idris*, some scholars contest the traditional view, identifying him as Esdras instead; James A. Bellamy, s.v. "Textual Criticism," in *EQ*.

[6]There is no reason to identify Shu'ayb as the biblical Jethro except that he was sent to the people of Midian (*Madyan*), but he was sent to *al-Ayka* also; Roberto Tottoli, *Biblical Prophets in the Qur'an and Muslim Literature* (Richmond, UK: Curzon Press, 2002), 45, 48-50; cf. Roberto Tottoli, s.v. "Shu'ayb," in *EQ*.

prophets does not mean the Qur'an does not rank them, however, though it never establishes what those ranks are (Q 2:253; 17:55).[7]

The Purity of Abraham

While Jews and Christians would have had no problem with Abraham's inclusion, the Qur'an departs from biblical teaching on him on a number of critical points. In particular, it

- nowhere mentions the Abrahamic covenant;
- views Abraham and Ishmael as the founders of the Ka'ba;
- makes Ishmael's line eclipse Isaac's line (in Muhammad);
- makes Abraham similarly eclipse Moses and Jesus; and
- has its Abrahamic prayer fulfilled in Muhammad.

Although the covenant (*mithaq*) concept so prominent in the Bible appears in the Qur'an, it is never specifically related to Abraham. This is not surprising when we remember that, biblically, the Abrahamic covenant is precisely what excludes Ishmael.[8] Furthermore, that covenant has a strong ethnic component to it, since it gives the Jewish people—Abraham's descendants through Isaac and Jacob—distinctive promises and responsibilities, for it is through them that God's salvation comes to the world. Viewing the Abrahamic covenant as fulfilled in Christ, the New Testament removes the Jewish-Gentile division in him, revoking Israel's seeming "monopoly" on salvation, as Isaiah and others had foretold (Eph 2:11-16; Is 11:10; 42:1-6; 49:1-6; Zech 2:11; Mal 1:11). By contrast, the Qur'an unites the human race by omitting the Abrahamic covenant altogether, implicitly denying that racial particularity was ever part of God's plan.[9]

---

[7]The Qur'an exalts Abraham, Moses and Jesus, for example. Many Muslim scholars make *rasul* an elite subcategory of *nabi*, but the reasons they give for doing so are unconvincing. In fact, the Qur'an uses the two words interchangeably, the only difference between them being that *rasul* is a native Arabic word used throughout the Qur'an, while the Hebrew loanword *nabi* is used only in Medina to appeal to its large Jewish population. Apart from Muhammad, *nabi* refers only to biblical characters, while *rasul* is used of extrabiblical ones too.

[8]Genesis excludes Ishmael not from God's blessing per se (cf. Gen 17:18-21; 21:12-17) but only from being God's conduit of salvation to humankind, since Jesus would come through Isaac.

[9]John Kaltner, *Ishmael Instructs Isaac: An Introduction to the Qur'an for Bible Readers* (Collegeville, MN: Liturgical Press, 1999), 104. For a helpful discussion of the biblical and qur'anic Abraham, see ibid., 106-26.

Biblically, the Abrahamic covenant also binds Isaac's descendants to a particular land, where God's house was to be built. The New Testament shows Christ as blessing and embracing the entire world and constituting the community of those indwelt by his Spirit (i.e., the church), his new earthly temple. By contrast, the Qur'an returns to Judaism's concept of sacred-versus-profane geography but removes earth's spiritual center from Jerusalem to Mecca.

All this is closely tied to the Qur'an's rehabilitation of the biblical Ishmael, which remains inconspicuous in the Meccan suras—while Muhammad still needs Jewish allies. The Qur'an Arabizes (and de-Judaizes) Abraham only after changing the direction of prayer from Jerusalem to Mecca (Q 2:144). Whereas Q 22:26-29 (Meccan) depicts him alone as purifying the Kaʿba for the worship of God, Q 2:125-29 (Medinan) portrays Abraham and Ishmael as its purifiers and founders. Q 37:100-111 (Meccan) relates the story of Abraham's sacrifice of his son, but without naming the son.[10] Q 3:67 (Medinan) states that Abraham was both upright (*hanif*) and truly submissive (*muslim*) to God but was neither a Jew nor a Christian. It also presents him as the model believer (*imam*) for *all* humanity, thus countering Jewish and Christian attempts to monopolize him. And by claiming that the Muslims truly walk in his pathway, it implies that they have a greater claim on him than Jews and Christians (Q 6:161). Q 3:96 goes still further, declaring that the first house of worship was founded in Mecca—named *Bakka* here. It thus associates with Abraham both the Kaʿba and Muslim forms of prayer and pilgrimage (Q 3:124-25; cf. Q 22:26), including prostration and circumambulation of the Kaʿba.

In close examination, however, the theological fault line leading to this break was already visible in Mecca. For example, in Q 14:35-42 Abraham prays for those of his family whom he has settled in Mecca,[11] implicitly putting Ishmael on a par with Isaac (v. 39). And as we have seen, much of the Qur'an's reformation of the biblical Ishmael happens by way of omission. For

---

[10]As long as Muhammad's need of refuge is dire, the Qur'an does not marginalize Isaac. By not naming the son Abraham sacrificed, it allows its Jewish hearers to assume that Isaac is intended. But it seems far likelier that Ishmael is actually intended, as Muslim commentators eventually agreed. Cf. Brandon M. Wheeler, *Prophets in the Qur'an* (New York: Continuum, 2003), 102-3.

[11]Though the passage refers to a city with a sacred house in a barren valley, which Mecca certainly was, it does not name the place—doubtless partly to minimize offense to Muhammad's potential Jewish allies. Biblically, Abraham never visited the Hijaz, and Ishmael and his mother settled not in Arabia but rather in the desert of Paran, in the Negev (Gen 21:8-20).

example, it gives no hint of his ignoble (i.e., slave) origins[12] and entirely omits both his having been divinely disenfranchised and his fractured relationship with Isaac (Gen 16:11-12; 21:8-20).

Framing Ishmael in this way is vital to the Qur'an's crucial shifting of the biblical focus from Jesus to Muhammad. The Bible emphatically designates Isaac the son through whom God would fulfill his foundational promise to bless the world (Gen 12:1-3; 21:9-21; 22:18; Heb 11:11-12, 17-19). The Qur'an, by contrast, depicts Abraham and Ishmael praying that God will raise up from among their descendants a messenger who will recite his revelations to them and purify them—that is, the Arabs—as a nation (Q 2:128-29). Qur'anically, God's answer to that prayer needs no introduction. Thus, when the Qur'an exclaims, "Who but a fool would forsake the religion of Abraham?"[13] (Abdel Haleem), its implicit idea is, Why build your life on the shifting sand of Moses or Jesus' teachings when the Qur'an puts you back on the bedrock of Abraham himself?

Hence the Qur'an gives only token attention to Moses' law and, as we will see, Jesus' teachings, bypassing both in order to restore the pristine religion of Abraham as the true path to salvation. That is not to say that the Qur'an portrays Jesus, for example, as having abandoned Abraham's religion. Rather, it broadly subsumes the teachings of Jesus and all the other prophets in what it calls the "religion of Abraham." That is, it effectively homogenizes their teachings into one basic message, the one Muhammad now proclaims (Q 2:135-36; 3:84; 4:163; 42:13). Muhammad's continuity with the true biblical tradition—of Abraham-Moses-Jesus—then makes him its rightful heir, as Jews and Christians should apparently recognize. The Qur'an takes itself and its prophet as normative of all the earlier scriptures and prophets, as we repeatedly discover.

So the Qur'an's universality makes it uninterested in genealogy relative to a chosen race, though it does make one lineal connection vital: Muhammad's descent from Ishmael, for that makes him the long-awaited messenger Abraham asked God to send. And as we have seen, that messenger brings God's salvation—the Qur'an—to the world.[14] Thus the Qur'an's

---

[12]While Genesis emphatically details his mother Hagar's being a slave (Gen 16:1-9; 21:9-13), the Qur'an entirely omits any mention of her; Kaltner, *Ishmael Instructs Isaac*, 131n10.

[13]The word translated "religion" here (*din*) actually refers to "God's right path for human beings on earth at all times"; Patrice C. Brodeur, s.v. "Religion," in *EQ*. As the *umma* took shape in the Medinan period (when Sura 2 was given), *din* also acquired communal dimensions.

[14]The Qur'an explicitly identifies Abraham as the Meccans' ancestor (Q 22:78) and, together with

Abraham-Ishmael-Muhammad axis decisively replaces the Bible's Abraham-Isaac-Jesus axis. But like so much of what it does, the Qur'an executes this critical change without ever explicitly owning it.

Muhammad's Unrivaled Supremacy

Thus, while the Qur'an makes Muhammad just one in a long line of prophets, it also clearly does three things to set him apart from all his predecessors. It establishes

- his preeminence;
- his finality; and
- his universality.

We see Muhammad's preeminence in Q 3:81, where God makes all the prophets before Muhammad—the messenger who will confirm their revelations—promise to believe in, witness to and support his prophethood. To underscore the point, God is said to make them prophets only on condition that they do so. The absolute nature of this—their agreement being prerequisite to their prophethood—makes Muhammad's preeminence over all of his predecessors unqualified.[15]

In keeping with this, Muhammad's prophethood is shown to be universal. Despite his having been sent to the Arabs with a message in plain Arabic, the Qur'an describes him as "a mercy to all created beings" and presents him as a bearer of good news and warning to all humankind (Q 21:107; 34:28). The Qur'an likewise calls itself "a reminder to all beings" and "a recitation for all humankind" (Q 12:104; 17:106; 38:87; 68:52; 81:27). So its having been given to the Arabs in Arabic in no way contradicts its universality.

Combined with these two points, the finality of Muhammad's prophethood renders his message supreme over the earlier scriptures, for, as the "Seal of the Prophets," his revelation is irreplaceable (Q 33:40). This is the sense in which we should understand Q 5:3, recited near the end of his life: "Today I have perfected your religion for you, completed My blessing upon you and chosen as your religion *islam* [total devotion to God]" (Abdel Haleem).[16] However

---

Ishmael, the founder of their sacred shrine. Furthermore, by making Muhammad the answer to Abraham and Ishmael's prayer in Q 2:128-29, it makes him their descendant.

[15] The only other condition of prophethood is to transmit God's revelations (Q 33:7-8).

[16] As noted above, "religion" (*din*) here is viewed in communal terms.

great Muhammad's predecessors—including Jesus—were, their greatness only increases that of Muhammad, since he stands on their shoulders, metaphorically speaking, as God's final prophet. Hence, while the Qur'an's approach to the earlier scriptures is somewhat unclear,[17] we cannot doubt its intention to supersede them with its own recasting of biblical truth.

Given its view of Muhammad's preeminence, universality and finality, the Qur'an thus presents him as unrivaled by anyone before him. Thus the clearest qualitative distinction it makes between its many prophets is that between the generality of Muhammad's forerunners—highly exalted though some are—and Muhammad, the bearer of God's last word to humankind.

The Prophets' Humanness

Despite their exalted nature, the Qur'an presents its prophets—Muhammad included—as being only human. In particular, they are shown to

- do miracles only by God's permission;

- sin and need God's forgiveness; and

- suffer for their faith, with some even dying for it.

Though the Qur'an says all God's prophets brought guidance and some worked miracles, it insists that all of their guidance and miracles were gifts from God. It asserts, for example, that Muhammad has no control over the words given to him (Q 10:15). The same is true of those prophets who worked miracles: they did so only by God's permission (Q 5:110; 40:78).

In keeping with that, when Muhammad's enemies ask him to produce a miracle to prove his authenticity, he cannot do so. The frequency of the Qur'an's response to this taunt tells us how seriously exercised by it Muhammad is. But he is told that he needs no sign since

- the whole of creation backs up his messages (Q 2:118);

- signs will never induce the wayward to submit, whatever they say (Q 2:145; 6:109); and

- God decides who will believe, and Muhammad is not responsible for the results (Q 13:27).

---

[17]See 260-69 below.

It further remonstrates that Muhammad is "only a warner and a guide," thus implicitly not a miracle worker like some other prophets (Q 11:12; 13:7). Hence, contrary to later Muslim teaching, the Qur'an makes it abundantly clear that Muhammad did no miracles. Its ultimate reply to those seeking a sign—and to Muhammad, who so longs to silence them—is that the Qur'an itself, being inimitable, is his sign (Q 2:23; 11:13-14; 17:88; 29:48-51).[18]

We find a similar situation with regard to prophetic peccability. Though God enables his prophets faithfully to convey his messages to their people, he does not keep them from all sin. As we saw above, the Qur'an does not deny the gravity of Adam's sin, despite the commentators' best efforts to the contrary. It presents a number of other prophets as guilty of sin too. Abraham asks God for forgiveness (Q 14:41), and Moses kills a man and asks God's forgiveness (Q 28:15-16; cf. Q 7:150-51). Q 38:24-26 portrays a repentant David recognizing that in his abundance he has stolen something precious from a "poor man." The passage does not say what he stole, but the hadith and early commentary saw it as referring to the sin of adultery (cf. 2 Sam 12:1-14). And the gravity of his sin is evident from God's warning that following his impulses like this will "lead him astray from God's path" to "extreme torment," a clear reference to hell (Q 38:25-26). There is, however, an evident lack of clarity on the prophets' sins,[19] making it quite easy for classical scholars to downgrade them, even as they did Adam's sin.[20]

---

[18]Qur'anic inimitability gradually developed into the idea of a miraculous and utterly perfect Qur'an. It became inappropriate for Muslim scholars to fault the Qur'an's style only around the middle of the ninth century, and the first seminal works on inimitability (*i'jaz*) were not composed until the late tenth century; Sophia Vasalou, "The Miraculous Eloquence of the Qur'an: General Trajectories and Individual Approaches," *Journal of Qur'anic Studies* 4, no. 2 (2002): 24. Theologians assigned the Qur'an's inimitability to such things as its perfect rhetoric, ethics and prophecy. See also Issa J. Boullatta, "The Rhetorical Interpretation of the Qur'an: *i'jaz* and Related Topics," in *Approaches to the History of the Interpretation of the Qur'ān*, ed. Andrew Rippin (Oxford: Clarendon, 1988), 138-57.

[19]As with David's sin, the Qur'an omits all detail of Solomon's sin, though it clearly implies his guilt, for God punishes him with wasting illness until he seeks forgiveness (Q 38:31-35). According to Razi, God reduces him to a walking skeleton; cited in Abdel Haleem, *The Qur'an: A New Translation* (Oxford: Oxford University Press, 2010), 292nb. The Qur'an similarly shows God judging Jonah for his sin by having him swallowed by a fish. If Solomon and Jonah did not actually sin, then God's punishment was out of all proportion to their deeds. But despite the seriousness of Jonah's sin—which makes him "blameworthy"—the Qur'an is again ambiguous about its nature, saying that he fled, but not why or from what (Q 21:87; 37:140-44).

[20]For example, Abraham came from a pagan family (Q 19:41-49), but most commentators maintain that he worshiped idols only as a child or else not at all—and the same went for Muhammad. They further said the "sins" (*khatiat*) to which Abraham refers were just "faults" (Q 26:82), but the very same word is used in Q 71:25 to explain why God drowned Noah's generation and sent them to

Beginning in the eighth century, the Shiʿa and the Muʿtazila made prophetic impeccability an integral part of their doctrinal systems.[21] That the rest of the Muslim community followed their lead points to three universal Muslim concerns—conscious or not—that they

1. defend Muhammad's honor against any aspersion;

2. safeguard the Qur'an's absolute authority; and

3. nullify Jesus' uniqueness.

Since the charges that Muhammad had sinned in taking Zayd's wife and compromised in the matter of the Satanic verses remained live issues among Muslims during the early period, there could be no better way to counter them than simply to dismiss *all* charges against *all* prophets.[22] Muhammad could more reasonably be made sinless along with all the other prophets than by himself. If he had been liable to sin, later Muslims reasoned, he could also have distorted God's revelations. And what better defense than a good offense—to assert that, being sinless, he could not possibly have distorted anything? In addition, Muslim theologians must have found the Qur'an's acknowledgment of Muhammad's sins especially bothersome due to the unfavorable contrast it produced between him and its sinless Christ. By "absolving" their prophets of sin en masse, they effectively denied Jesus' uniqueness.

But as we saw with other prophets, all the qur'anic data run contrary to the doctrine of Muhammad's sinlessness (ʿisma). Q 66:1 says that he prohibited what God had permitted in order to please his wives. More tellingly, God twice commands him to pray for forgiveness for his sins (Q 40:55; 47:19). A later sura explicitly says that God has forgiven both his past and future sins (Q 48:1-2). So while the Qur'an presents Muhammad as an

---

hell. Predating the development of the twin doctrines of prophetic sinlessness and Muhammad's perfection, however, the Qur'an commentary of Muqatil (d. 767) is exceptional here; Claude Gilliot, cited in Gordon Nickel, *Narratives of Tampering in the Earliest Commentaries on the Qur'an* (Leiden: Brill, 2011), 69-70.

[21]The Shiʿa, for example, developed the doctrine in tandem with their belief in their imams' sinlessness; W. Madelung, "*Isma*," in *EI²*; Paul E. Walker, "Impeccability," in *EQ*; A. J. Wensinck, *The Muslim Creed: Its Genesis and Historical Development* (London: Frank Cass, 1965), 94, 192-93, 217-18, 246-47; David S. Powers, *Muhammad Is Not the Father of Any of Your Men: The Making of the Last Prophet* (Philadelphia: University of Pennsylvania Press, 2009), 302n1.

[22]When Q 3:161 says God's prophets never act unfaithfully, it refers not to their every word and deed but rather only to the discharge of their prophetic task.

excellent example (Q 33:21), the idea that he was sinless developed after his death and contradicts clear qur'anic teaching.[23]

Finally, the Qur'an has a great deal to say about the prophets' weakness in the face of opposition. Unbelievers frequently mocked, persecuted and threatened them (Q 3:184; 6:10, 34; 13:32; 15:11; 21:41; 25:37; 34:45; 51:52-55). Some prophets were even killed for being faithful to God (Q 2:61, 87, 91; 3:21, 112, 181-83; 4:155; 5:70), making clear that prophets too are subject to the paradigm of reversal.[24] So the Qur'an in no way supports the later Muslim assertion that God would never allow his prophets to suffer dishonor or martyrdom: prophets do indeed suffer for their faith—perhaps even more than ordinary believers.

Biblical and Qur'anic Prophethood in Contrast

Hence, while the Qur'an's treatment of its prophets' sins resembles that of the Bible to some degree, it is radically different also, for the Old Testament is unflinchingly honest about its prophets' sins, presenting them "warts and all."[25] Its patriarchs and prophets represent a first-rate collection of antiheroes. Though they are undoubtedly exemplary in some respects, none are mythological heroes: they all sin, and some commit truly despicable crimes. The Bible even stunningly presents the Israelites as a nation of former slaves and, furthermore, insists that they perpetually rehearse their humble origins—which is the exact opposite of what one did in the ancient world. Hence, from beginning to end, the Old Testament gives us only ordinary people, none with impressive credentials.[26] It does this with deliberate purpose so that the story's hero is God alone.

The New Testament mirrors this situation closely, presenting all of its apostles as utterly fallible—self-centered, misguided and faithless—on their

---

[23]In each passage, the word for sin is *dhanb*, which consistently refers to sins that bring on God's stern judgment (e.g., Q 3:11; 6:6; 8:52, 54; 40:21). Q 55:39 even uses *dhanb* to speak of sins that damn the lost. Why should we give it a unique meaning only with respect to Muhammad?

[24]See 73 above.

[25]Adam squanders the whole of creation, Abraham lies to save his skin, Jacob cheats his brother by deceiving his father, Moses commits murder, David commits adultery and orders the murder of the unsuspecting husband, and Solomon embraces his wives' idolatry.

[26]In this the Old Testament differs radically from the literatures of all the surrounding cultures—ancient Egypt, Babylon, Greece, etc.—which present only heroes and god-kings towering over the world of mortals in their quest for glory, honor and revenge. Unlike the mythological landscape, the biblical landscape is entirely our own. Iain Provan, "The Scriptures Jesus Knew: History, Archaeology and the Reliability of the Old Testament" (lecture, L'Abri Canada, Bowen Island, Canada, n.d.), accessed January 12, 2013, www.labri.org/canada/lecture_109_493266219.mp3.

own, despite their many strengths. Even their transformation into men of
vision and valor at Pentecost does not change that: they are never heroes on
their own (e.g., Gal 2:11-16; cf. Rom 7). And as for the church as a whole, its
members are presented not as wise, noble or powerful, but rather weak and
despicable in the eyes of the world (1 Cor 1:26-31). Again, the story's only
true hero is God—God incarnate, that is, who himself identified with the
weak and lowly—fishermen, tax collectors and prostitutes.

Neither presenting humankind's fallenness unequivocally nor, as we shall
see, accepting Jesus' messiahship in the biblical sense of the term, the Qur'an
does not produce so sharp a contrast between human inability and divine
amplitude. While it gives us echoes of the biblical emphasis on prophetic
sin, they are invariably faint: the few vestiges of prophetic sinfulness that
remain leave the reader guessing as to what actually happened. And the
Qur'an never connects the prophets' failures with those of Muhammad's
followers. Rather it makes those sins the Israelites' property exclusively,
which is the exact opposite of what the New Testament writers do with them
(e.g., 1 Cor 10:6-11; Heb 3:11-13).[27] So while some traces of prophetic peccability survive the Qur'an's transposition of the biblical prophets into its
register, they are meager enough to allow the classical scholars easily to
purge them from the Qur'an.[28]

Prophetic Models

One striking difference between the qur'anic and biblical presentations of the
prophets relates to the fact that the biblical witness gives each prophet
distinct individuality and purpose within his or her divine appointment.

---

[27]The Qur'an mentions the Israelites' slavery in Egypt. But unlike the New Testament, it never identifies its faith community with the Israelites in the sense that the former represents the "New Israel"
and so shares in not just God's promises to Israel but also all its limitations and faults. In fact, the
Medinan suras so vilify the Jews for their spiritual intransigence that they make them the virtual
antithesis of believers. By contrast, the New Testament's use of Jewish example is always predicated
on the Christian's solidarity with the ancient Israelites: "what happened to them could happen to
you" (e.g., Rom 11:17-22). This emphasis on human weakness met decisively by the power of God's
grace is vital to the way the writers of both biblical testaments framed their salvation message, their
goal being to make salvation unattainable merely by human effort and to exalt God's name above
all. But despite its bluntness about the prophets' moral failures, the Bible balances the great need
of its prophets—which it clearly applies to all of humanity—with God's astonishing desire to engage
with them as friends in an intimate, dialogical and transformative relationship. See 290-95 below.
[28]They had merely to ignore a few hazy details and downgrade the meaning of a few words—*sins* to
mistakes, etc.

Conversely, the Qur'an structures its prophetology entirely around the model of Muhammad. It does so for three reasons. This enables it to

- reframe and "correct" biblical prophetology;

- make its prophet normative of all his predecessors; and

- decisively center everything in Muhammad as the consummate prophet.

To begin, "the Qur'an means not to retell the biblical stories, but ... to recollect them within the corrective framework of its own discourse."[29] This naturally reshapes its reminiscence of biblical prophets dramatically. Second, the Qur'an makes itself and its prophet normative of all their predecessors[30] and uses all its biblically inspired stories to enable Muhammad to meet his specific challenges. This leaves all the qur'anic prophets looking rather similar due to the fact that they all resemble Muhammad at whatever point in his story the Qur'an deems their stories relevant: their stories matter only insofar as they illustrate and validate his.[31] Hence all the earlier prophets—Jesus included— serve only as illustrations and "professional references," which from a biblical perspective amounts to a major flattening of them. Qur'anic prophetology is thus distinguished by its pronounced Muhammadocentrism,[32] replacing the New Testament's christocentrism.

Another notable difference is that, while the Bible and Qur'an evidence the same two basic prophetic models or templates, the order in the latter scripture is opposite from that of the Bible. That is, beginning with Moses and following him with Joshua, David and Solomon, the Old Testament presents a theocratic model of prophethood. This then gradually gives way to that of the outsider prophet, who effectively represents God's government "in exile."[33] Whether

[29]Sidney H. Griffith, *The Bible in Arabic: The Scriptures of the "People of the Book" in the Language of Islam* (Princeton, NJ: Princeton University Press, 2013), 70-71.

[30]Hence Griffith accurately characterizes the qur'anic prophet Joseph in Q 12:37-40 as "a double" for Muhammad; ibid., 76. The Qur'an repeatedly has the biblical prophets say to their people what Muhammad is saying to his.

[31]Q 4:163 says that God communicated with all his prophets as he does with Muhammad—presumably using the angel Gabriel (*Jibril*) as his intermediary (Q 2:97-98). Q 9:111 even says that, like the Qur'an, the Torah and the Injil promise that believers who die fighting for the Cause of God will win paradise.

[32]Josef Horovitz, Richard Bell, Rudi Paret and others have pointed out, for example, ways in which the qur'anic author's punishment-narratives "mirror developments in Muhammad's life"; cited in David Marshall, *God, Muhammad and the Unbelievers: A Qur'anic Study* (London: RoutledgeCurzon, 1999), 29.

[33]There are exceptions. The prophet Samuel, for example, may be viewed as transitional between the

this prophet plays social critic or national comforter or addresses other nations for God, he does so from outside the corridors of worldly power (e.g., Isaiah, Jeremiah, Jonah, John the Baptist).[34] In Jesus, however, the New Testament effectively fuses the two templates into one, since he obviously preaches as an outsider, but as God incarnate, he is himself the true center, representing heaven's rule on earth. Accordingly, he is an outsider on a surface level only.[35]

By contrast, the Qur'an reverses the order of these prophetic templates. The Meccan suras portray Muhammad and his predecessors as outsider prophets. Then, once Muhammad assumes the role of theocratic ruler, the Medinan suras generally align the biblical prophets they present—prophets who appeared in the Meccan suras—to the ruler-prophet template. But by presenting the two templates in the reverse order from that found in the Bible, the Qur'an effectively makes the paradigm of reciprocity normative, whereas the New Testament paradoxically unites it with the paradigm of reversal during the present age.[36] And the effect of the Qur'an's implicit normalization of reciprocity on Muslim spirituality has been profound.[37] While Jesus' reinstatement of the Old Testament ethic of love displaced its temporarily sanctioned sacred violence, the Qur'an resacralizes violence and without even the Old Testament's limits. This is what makes the Qur'an's sacred violence such a live issue for Muslims to the present day.[38]

---

two models. And Daniel, Ezra and Nehemiah also straddle the line in a sense.

[34]While an element of divine authority is inherent in any prophetic speech, there is nevertheless a marked difference between the ruler-prophet and the outsider-prophet.

[35]To the degree that the Old Testament's outsider prophets represented God truly, the same may be said of them. Likewise, to the degree that it submits to him and is led by his Spirit, Christ's church is like him here: though unimpressive by worldly standards, Jesus' followers reign with him, backed by all of heaven's authority (1 Cor 4:13; Eph 2:6-7). Jesus' perfect submission to God is what uniquely set him apart from the other representatives of God's rule.

[36]As noted above, reciprocity is the paradigm by which good merits blessing, while evil merits cursing. By contrast, the paradigm of reversal rewards good with cursing, evil with blessing. As Paul says, Jesus' followers constantly share in his death so we may also experience the power of his resurrection life (2 Cor 4:9-11; Phil 3:10).

[37]The Medinan template dominated Muslim thinking during the conquest until Sufism grew up to return the focus to Muhammad as outsider prophet. And even now the Medinan template remains dominant among Muslims for various reasons, the obvious one being that Muhammad's victory over the Meccans represents the climax to which his entire story led as well as one of the umma's defining moments in history. Accordingly, most Muslims view the umma's geopolitical success as normative and any failure on the part of Muslims to dominate geopolitically as a deviation from that norm.

[38]Since Medina's theocratic model so obviously replaced Mecca's persecuted prophet model, it would be asking a lot of Muslims to allow that God could reverse that climactic development and accept that his design for his umma today might in fact be their subordination to unbelievers.

Scripture in a World of Signs

To understand the qur'anic concept of scripture, we must begin with the noun *kitab*—usually translated "book"—which can refer to human writing as well as God's knowledge and decrees. Derived from the verb "to write" (*kataba*), the noun *kitab* refers in nearly all of its some 260 uses to an activity quintessentially divine.[39] The Qur'an speaks often of God's having given a *kitab* to Muhammad (Q 2:53; 3:48; 5:48), but also of a heavenly book and of books given to Muhammad's predecessors—the Torah (*al-tawrat*) to Moses, the Psalms (*al-zabur*)[40] to David, and *al-injil*[41] to Jesus (Q 4:163; 5:43; 17:55)— as well as "pages" to Abraham and Moses (Q 53:36-37; 87:18-19).[42] But the Qur'an gives little indication of the earlier scriptures' actual contents.

Hikma and *aya* (plural *ayat*) are key terms here also, often used in relation to *kitab* or to each other (Q 2:129, 151). Usually translated "wisdom," *hikma* is related to the verb *hakama*, meaning "to judge, rule or decide." So *hikma* is not the gnostic's esoteric wisdom but rather "the practical wisdom or the wise authority of the experienced ruler."[43] *Ayat*, usually translated "signs," refers to whatever reveals God's ways and will—namely, everything in nature, history, legislation, prophetic message or miracle (Q 24:1, 61; 30:46; 46:27). But since ingratitude blinds us to God's goodness and power evident in everything around us, he must give us verbal expressions (*ayat*) through his prophets, thus making his requirements clear to us.[44]

---

[39]Thus God's *kitab* refers to the finality, clarity and comprehensiveness of his knowledge and decrees; Daniel A. Madigan, s.v. "Book," in *EQ*, 242-45. Since God does not literally maintain physical, written inventories of his knowledge and decrees in heaven, we might conclude that the Qur'an's usage of *kitab* is only figurative. But in a largely oral culture, Muhammad's hearers observed no airtight divide between a physically written and a memorized text. So our modern "book" represents a mere subset of what *kitab* signified in seventh-century Arabic.

[40]This word can also be used as a generic designation of spiritual writings; Arie Schippers, s.v. "Psalms," in *EQ*.

[41]On the meaning of *al-injil*, see chapter seventeen below.

[42]Within this semantic field, Nicolai Sinai sees three distinct qur'anic usages of *kitab*: (1) a heavenly record book, which also functions as a revelatory source, generally with the definite article; (2) a revealed body of scripture such as the Qur'an, the latter being a work in progress during Muhammad's lifetime; and (3) a divine commandment or decree. Despite the close connection between the Qur'an's earthly manifestation in Muhammad's recitations (the second meaning) and its heavenly source (the first meaning), they remain ontologically distinct throughout the Qur'an; cited by Stefan Wild, "Qur'anic Self-Referentiality as a Strategy of Self-Authorization," in *Self-Referentiality in the Qur'an*, ed. Stefan Wild (Wiesbaden: Harrassowitz, 2006), 104-5.

[43]Madigan, "Book," 246.

[44]The Qur'an also uses *aya* to mean a qur'anic verse. See further Binyamin Abraham, s.v. "Signs," in *EQ*.

The Nature of Qur'anic Revelation

The prophet thus becomes God's mouthpiece, reciting God's words to his people. And scripture represents a body of divinely revealed messages or speech (*kalam*) in an authoritative text. The Qur'an speaks of God's "giving" (*ata*) his book, which his prophets all seemingly recite in serial form (Q 2:53). God also "reveals" (*wahy, awha*) his book to his prophets or "inspires" them (Q 4:163; 12:3; 20:114), though the idea is not that of biblical inspiration, by which the human author typically communicates to his audience in tandem with God.[45] Rather, the Qur'an speaks of God's "teaching" (*'alim*) the Torah and Injil to Jesus, the idea being that of an Arab teacher transferring his words to his student's memory for the student to reproduce them verbatim (Q 3:48; 5:110). And this is evidenced by the fact that the qur'anic recitations so often begin with the divine "Say:" or "Recall:" (e.g., Q 2:139; 19:51). It is also confirmed by the Qur'an's overwhelming lack of narrative framework, a point to which we will return. In the Qur'an, revelation allows no creativity—whether planning, research or editing—on the prophet's part. The revelations are *ipsissima verba Dei* precisely because they are in no sense human in origin.[46]

The most common qur'anic descriptor of the revelatory process is that of God's "sending down" (*nazzala, tanzil*, etc.) his messages (Q 2:174, 176, 213, 231).[47] This again suggests that the messages were in their final form when the

---

[45]While revelation may seem a more biblical than qur'anic idea, it is implicit in the central qur'anic concept of God's "signs" (*ayat*), whether verbal or visual. But since the Qur'an's spatial metaphor of scripture's descent (*tanzil*) proved more amenable to Muslim theology—both its avoidance of divine self-revelation and its exaltation of the Qur'an—that became its focus, and the qur'anic emphasis on verbal signs was thus downplayed.

[46]Some read Q 20:114 as giving Muhammad an active role in qur'anic composition; for example, G. F. Hourani, "The Qur'ān's Doctrine of Prophecy," in *Logos Islamikos: Studia Islamica*, ed. Roger M. Savory and Dionisius A. Agius (Toronto: Pontifical Institute of Mediaeval Studies, 1984), 179. Rather, the verse commands Muhammad to wait. Hence it actually calls only for increased passivity on the prophet's part in order for him to relay its messages faithfully.

[47]This relates to the "Preserved Tablet" (*al-lawh al-mahfuz*, Q 85:22) and the "Essence (or Source) of the Book" (*umm al-kitab*, literally "Mother of the Book," Q 3:7; 13:39; 43:4)—to most Muslims, the heavenly archetype of which the Qur'an is the earthly transcript.

For a fuller treatment of the Qur'an's semantic field on revelation, see Stefan Wild, "'We Have Sent Down to Thee the Book with the Truth': Spatial and Temporal Implications of the Qur'anic Concepts of *Nuzul, Tanzil* and *'Inzal*," in *The Qur'an as Text*, ed. Stefan Wild (Leiden: Brill, 1996), 139-53; and Toshikiho Izutsu, *God and Man in the Koran: Semantics of the Koranic Weltanschauung* (Tokyo: Keio Institute of Cultural and Linguistic Studies, 1964), chaps. 6-7. Together with the notion of its miraculous nature, the Qur'an's otherworldliness led to its being credited with not only perfection but eternity also.

Some scholars think the Qur'an's references to itself as a *kitab* show that Muhammad was driven to give his people their own written scripture—to make his community competitive with Jews and

angel Gabriel (*Jibril*) mediated them to the prophet. Hence the inspiration by which God gives the *kitab* to his prophets (Q 18:27) amounts to something like dictation, not his gifting the prophet to "coauthor" the text with him, as is the case biblically. Here the prophet only mentally registers and faithfully repeats God's words, making it closer to the pagan concept of inspiration—of the *jinn* giving words to the poet or soothsayer, often in a state of "possession"—than to the biblical concept.[48]

The qur'anic text comes in installments as God purportedly responds to the various situations Muhammad faces (Q 25:33). Rejecting the claim that it should be revealed all at once, the Qur'an "insists on being God's authoritative voice in the present" (Q 17:106).[49] Some qur'anic passages even seem to be provisional, since God reserves the right to amend the text.[50] And replying to objections raised about the qur'anic revelations themselves, the Qur'an is self-consciously and defensively scriptural to a degree unmatched by any other major scripture.

Though the Qur'an always refers positively to the biblical scriptures, it is otherwise ambiguous on its relationship to them. It uses three words to describe the relationship. It confirms (*tasdiq*) and clarifies (*tafsil*) them (Q 2:41; 3:3; 4:47; 10:37; 35:31). But it also presents itself as the protector (*muhaymin*) of the biblical scriptures (Q 5:48). For indeed, what religious reformer does not come claiming to defend the true faith against its falsifiers? Hence the Qur'an claims to guard the biblical text against its Jewish and Christian abusers, a topic to which we will return.[51] But since it so rarely interacts with the biblical text itself, we only vaguely know what is being confirmed and what defended.[52] That it gives such little explicit attention to the biblical text itself does, however, imply that it means to replace, not supplement it. Also, the

---

Christians, who each had their own books of scripture. What they apparently forget is that in Muhammad's largely oral culture, no memorized and recitable text needed to be written down to become a *kitab*; William A. Graham, *Beyond the Written Word: Oral Aspects of Scripture in the History of Religion* (Cambridge: Cambridge University Press, 1987), 79-80.

[48]Some hadith describe Muhammad's inspiration in terms associated with just such possession. And as with the Qur'an's descriptors of the process of revelation, so also words derived from the root *n-z-l* were used to describe the *jinn's* inspiration of the pre-Islamic poet. Izutsu, *God and Man in the Koran*, 169-71.

[49]Madigan, "Book," 250.

[50]See the discussion on abrogation on 160 below.

[51]See 264-69 below.

[52]See 260-64 below.

Qur'an implicitly completes the biblical scriptures, as the final sequel in the series, since it calls Muhammad the "Seal of the Prophets."

The Limits of a Serial Revelation

The Qur'an's serial nature results in the repetition of certain key stories, characterized by numerous slight variations, as occurs with folklorist oral transmission.[53] This has the effect of atomizing its major prophets, since we rarely get the larger picture of who they were and what they did but must piece that together ourselves as best we can. This is far different from substantially presenting their stories in context.[54] But it fits very well with the Qur'an's selective approach to Muhammad's predecessors and its granting them very subordinate roles.

This makes the Qur'an differ dramatically from the Bible in its basic approach to narrative. So central is narrative to the biblical text that we can describe the Bible as a grand narrative into which fit its multiplicity of smaller narratives and accessories.[55] The biblical writers nearly always make their context explicit, even if only in their book's opening verse (e.g., Amos, Jude). As with the smaller stories, all of the nonnarrative sections take their meaning from, illuminate and in some way further the grand narrative. When the Bible uses narrative illustratively, its references and allusions work precisely because both the original story and—at least partially—the metanarrative already exist within the biblical corpus (e.g., Ps 106:7-9; Lk 17:32). By sharp contrast, the Qur'an seems almost to have an aversion to narrative in the following ways:

- It reframes biblical narratives without reference to the Bible's grand narrative and gives no clear sense of a metanarrative of its own.[56]

- Instead, it recounts biblical narratives within a repetitive cycle of God's sending a prophet to a people, who reject him before God brings judgment down on them.

---

[53]Bannister, *Oral-Formulaic Study of the Qur'an*, 57, 274.

[54]Q 26:10-175 is exceptional in this regard.

[55]Though the Bible includes very significant nonnarrative sections—for example, most of the Psalms, Prophets and New Testament letters—all of them are built on and set within its larger story.

[56]The assumption that the Qur'an's often spare retelling of biblical narratives implies that Muhammad's audience needed few details since it was already so well versed in them runs contrary to what we know of the nascent Muslim community. It also fails to appreciate the dynamics of messianic-type leadership, by which a leader presents himself as the singular solution to the problems facing a people—and indeed, often facing *all* people—as the Qur'an presents Muhammad, in fact. See 40-41, 49 above.

- It implicitly connects Muhammad's mission with its extrabiblical narratives of Abraham and Ishmael in such a way that it represents God's penultimate intervention.

It affords no clear sense of history between creation and the Last Day, but only brief, scattered glimpses under the combined rubric of human rebellion and divine intervention. Thus the Qur'an is almost ahistorical, offering little awareness of how its prophets relate to one another beyond what would have been common knowledge to many hearers in a peninsula dominated by the Christian and Jewish stories. But the Qur'an itself gives no metanarrative beyond the primordial Adam, followed by an assumed sequence of Noah, Abraham, Ishmael, Moses and David and by the final sequence of John the Baptist, Jesus and Muhammad, the "Seal of the Prophets."

That the Qur'an claims to confirm the previous scriptures would seem to suggest that it builds on the Bible's metanarrative, including its grand narratives of Israel and the church. But in fact, it entirely omits those key biblical narratives. And to whatever extent it employs the Bible's various component stories, it invariably reframes and retools them—in substance or detail or both—but without ever acknowledging it.[57] Nevertheless, it presents them in such a way that it gives a fairly consistent understanding of both God and humankind, but one that is in many respects independent of the biblical text.

The Qur'an's Fixity and Plasticity

With this view of verbal revelation, the Qur'an teaches the permanence of God's words. Q 6:115 says none can change God's words, while Q 10:64 flatly states that they cannot be altered (cf. Q 6:34; 18:27; 50:29). So on one hand, God protects his word from any effort to distort it. But alongside this fixity and immutability, we find that God may exchange one verse (*aya*) for another (Q 16:101), although he clearly never alters his basic approach to unbelievers (Q 33:62; 35:43; 48:23). So God is seemingly not bound by what he says. Q 2:106 says, "For every verse (or sign) We abrogate or cause to be forgotten,

---

[57]This retooling conforms more often to midrashic materials than to the biblical text, as previously noted; Michael Lodahl, *Claiming Abraham: Reading the Bible and the Qur'an Side by Side* (Grand Rapids: Brazos, 2010), 18-20; and Joseph Witztum, "Joseph Among the Ishmaelites: Q 12 in the Light of Syriac Sources," in *New Perspectives on the Qur'an: The Qur'ān in Its Historical Context 2*, ed. Gabriel Said Reynolds (New York: Routledge, 2011), 425-48.

We bring something better or similar. Do you not know that God is sovereign over everything?" Judging by their contexts, these passages refer to God's replacing one revealed book with another. The Qur'an never openly states that God has replaced the Bible with the Qur'an, but it does repeatedly imply it.

It seems that Q 2:106 also meant to establish God's right to change what he had previously said. Classical scholars took this as an escape hatch, enabling them to reconcile contradictory qur'anic verses or to sideline verses contrary to their practice. The idea seems to be that God can replace one revelation with another since he is not limited by anything he has said. Q 16:101 speaks similarly of God's exchanging one verse (*aya*) for another, and Q 13:39 explains that God is free to blot out or confirm his words as he chooses since he possesses the master source of his revelations. How do we know which verses abrogate which? The Qur'an does not say, and thus Muslim scholars are divided on it, as on every other question related to abrogation.[58]

The Biblical Concept of Revelation

We find a direct affinity between qur'anic and biblical teaching on general revelation and humankind's inability to attend to it. However, the Qur'an views humankind's blindness to creation's revelation of God as being entirely corrected by verbal revelation through his prophets, whereas biblically that is not the case. The exact same blindness operates in terms of both general and special revelation, requiring a God-given miracle of sight: unless he opens our eyes to his truth, we simply do not "get it," no matter how clearly he words it (Is 32:3; 42:7; Lk 24:45; Rom 1:18-23; 1 Cor 4:4; Eph 1:17-23). This pertains to the two scriptures' different assessment of our spiritual capacity. While the Qur'an considers itself the sole remedy needed to combat humankind's blindness to God's truth, the Bible makes us reliant on God's saving action illuminating our hearts and minds so that we can see.

---

[58]An example of the sort of problem abrogation solves relates to gambling and the use of intoxicants. Q 2:219 strongly implies that believers should handle both with care. But Q 4:43 prohibits believers from coming to prayer drunk, suggesting that drinking alcohol was still permissible. Later, Q 5:93 describes both alcohol and gambling as evils believers must avoid. This particular progression may seem straightforward, but the problem is that no verse allegedly abrogating another ever identifies itself as such. And most Muslims take abrogation further, allowing that the *sunna*, or example of Muhammad and his Companions, can also abrogate qur'anic verses, which only magnifies the problem. For example, while the Qur'an prescribes one hundred lashes for the adulterer (Q 24:2-3), the sharia follows the *sunna*, requiring that adulterers be stoned to death. On this, see John Burton, s.v. "Abrogation," in *EQ*.

We see major differences between the biblical and qur'anic concepts of special revelation also. The Bible's concept of verbal revelation parallels its notion of divine incarnation, for the incarnation involved the perfect union of the divine and human in the person of Jesus, who is thus both fully God and fully man. Similarly, in the biblical understanding, revealed scripture is simultaneously the product of two authors, divine and human. Hence biblical revelation is about God's using all of the author's personality and experience in such a way that every word written expresses equally the divine and the human author. Only in rare cases, such as the Decalogue, is there any sense of God's being the sole actor in the process. Then in the incarnation, what was foreshadowed in earlier prophetic revelation reached its fulfillment in Jesus: he is the prophet who reveals God to us perfectly because he is God. To borrow Marshall McLuhan's phrasing from another context, Jesus is the medium who is himself the message, the very Word of God.

Finally, the New Testament concept of abrogation pertains to the old covenant's fulfillment in Christ and the new covenant's equal inclusion of every people—no more just Jewish believers (and proselytes). Thus the New Testament frees Christian believers from those aspects of Moses' law specifically designed to ensure Israel's cultural purity and exclusivism. It also releases us from the sacrificial system, which found its fulfillment in Jesus' death. But it does not release us from the Old Testament's moral principles, such as those enshrined in the Ten Commandments. And it releases us from the burden of Moses' law only to take that law's principles to an even higher level in Jesus' royal law of love. Thus "the Christ event has introduced an interpretive lens that leads to some texts being set aside and others given new meaning," but in such a way that the new scriptures sit side by side with the old and "the canon of Scripture is a mutually interpreting or dialogical collection of texts."[59] The idea that one verse may abrogate another within a single covenant, however, would suggest a political expediency and relativism altogether foreign to God's being immutable in holiness, faithfulness and love.

---

[59]Steve Moyise, "Intertextuality and Historical Approaches to the Use of Scripture in the New Testament," in *Reading the Bible Intertextually*, ed. Richard B. Hays, Stefan Alkier and Leroy A. Huizenga (Waco, TX: Baylor University Press, 2009), 23-24.

Twelve

Qur'anic Spirituality's Devotional *and* Social Dimensions

The Qur'an calls believers to express their submission to God both devotionally and socially and repeats most of the Decalogue in some form. Two core devotional requirements are reciting the creed and prayers. Unlike New Testament creedal statements, the Muslim creed is supremely simple, in not just its words but ostensibly its concepts also, and centers Muslim life in obedience to God and Muhammad. The Muslim prayer rite combines devotional simplicity and rigor in a way that powerfully pictures the believer's relationship to both God and the Muslim community. But involving no true communication, the Muslim prayer rite is radically different from the biblical concept of prayer as talking with God. Like these components of Islamic devotion, so also Islamic social laws hold great appeal to many today—though not typically Westerners. For example, by limiting polygyny, the Qur'an mitigates some of the effects of Arab patriarchy, but never challenges its essential gender inequality. The Qur'an takes a similar approach to marital breakdown, commanding husbands to apply corporal punishment "as needed," and when that proves ineffective, allowing for easy divorce. This amounts to an implicit denial of New Testament teaching on marriage and divorce. All these differences flow from the Qur'an's marginalization of the two laws Jesus so decisively put at the center.

*T*o survey qur'anic spirituality, we must first define *spirituality*, an often nebulous word nowadays. Under this rubric I include qur'anically guided morals
and practices, as well as the religious experience that flows from them. And
since that experience cannot be properly appreciated without some awareness
of the institutions or "trappings" that have grown up around Islamic practice, I
also include brief descriptions of the mosque, the faith community's spiritual
"home," and the sharia, the moral pathway classical Muslim scholarship set out
for society.[1] I thus deliberately depart in these two chapters from my strict
focus on the qur'anic text to include present-day Muslim experience. But since
current Muslim religious understanding and practice involves a wide range of
diversity, my treatment of them can be only suggestive. Still, I believe it is vital
to my threefold goal of unpacking something of

- the richness and the continuing appeal of Islamic spirituality;

- the challenge of being Muslim in a century so dominated by Western ideas;
  and

- the similarities and differences between biblical and qur'anic faith and
  practice.

My overarching goal in these chapters is to offer readers a sympathetic understanding of Muslim spirituality today. But I see no value in abstracting that
spirituality from the real crisis facing Muslims in this century as opposed to
the seventh century.

Qur'anic Faith and Practice in Three Dimensions

To discern the overall shape of qur'anic spirituality, we must reckon with its
three dimensions: devotional, social and political. Individuals and groups
often focus on one of them, depending on which vision of Islam they find
most compelling. For example, Sufis typically focus on the devotional, while
Islamists focus on the political dimension. But while these dimensions are
different, they are not really separate one from another. Rather, qur'anic
spirituality is of a piece, each dimension interpenetrating the others, which
is why Muslims across the spectrum are generally able to share a common
life despite their different emphases.

---

[1]On the sharia, see 172-73 below.

For example, everything about the believer's devotional life has profound social and political implications. Profession of the creed (*shahada*) determines who is inside and who outside the "House of Islam." Together with Islam's other core devotional practices—ritual prayer (*salat*), almsgiving (*zakat*), the fast (*sawm*) of Ramadan and pilgrimage to Mecca (*hajj*)—it also firmly establishes the believer on the Muhammadan foundation of this "House."[2] Commitment to every qur'anic social ideal is a matter of personal submission to God's Cause in the world. Since the "House" is geopolitical in nature, one's being inside or outside it is as political and social as it is devotional. To say the creed or perform any of Islam's other core devotional practices is in a sense to commit or re-commit to the Qur'an's religio-political vision for the world. Hence we see an integration in qur'anic spirituality that embraces the whole of life. And that unity and wholeness has great appeal to Muslims the world over.

Muslim Devotion Begins with Two "Words"

While the Qur'an never combines the creed's two "words" in their precise creedal form—"There is no God but God, and Muhammad is God's messenger"—all Muslim spirituality begins with this brief profession of faith. The Qur'an clearly attests that there is no God but God, even as it witnesses to his having sent down his revelation to his prophet or messenger, Muhammad (Q 3:18; 4:166; 6:19). The Qur'an also unequivocally urges obedience to both God and Muhammad, which is the creed's practical import.[3]

There is something simultaneously easy and hard, simple and severe, about the creed, which every new convert—whatever her language—must say in Arabic. There is certainly no theological intricacy here, nor subtlety like we find in the Christian Trinity or incarnation. There is no real mystery either—at least not in the Christian sense of something scandalously counterintuitive, like a God who suffers and dies for love's sake. This makes the Muslim creed highly appealing to millions, for here is theology anybody can grasp, not that qur'anic

---

[2]It is impossible to know precisely when these five mandatory practices, often referred to as the "Pillars of Islam," took on their familiar shape. For more on Muslim devotional life, see John Renard, *Seven Doors to Islam: Spirituality and the Religious Life of Muslims* (Berkeley: University of California Press, 1996), 35-72 especially.
[3]The Qur'an asserts the need to obey (God and) Muhammad fully eighteen times, making this one of its top ethical priorities: Q 3:32, 132; 4:13, 59, 69; 5:92; 8:1, 20, 46; 9:71; 24:47-56; 33:33; 49:14; 58:13; 64:12.

theology does not have serious incongruities, for, as we have seen, it does. But the Muslim creed wastes no time on them: it is as clean as it is succinct. And if we find in Q 2:177 a secondary qur'anic creed—as most Muslims do—it has only five cardinal beliefs: in God, the Last Day, angels, scripture and prophets. It is simply intended to give Muslims a basic framework for belief.

For submission is ultimately the key point, with or without understanding. Like belief in God, Muhammad's prophethood is something believers must simply accept. The same can be said of Islam's prayer rite and its other three core devotional practices. We need not understand why God demands *salat*. Obedience alone is required, meaning that once one learns what to do and say, there is real simplicity to it so long as one makes the effort to do it. On the other hand, some argue that no other world religion demands so much of believers: ritual prayer five times daily, performed according to precise rules, to say nothing of a month-long fast every year.[4]

This sort of simplicity-severity marks the whole of qur'anic devotional life as most Muslims practice it today. What is true of Muslim devotion's general orientation (in the creed and almsgiving) and its daily rhythms (in ritual prayer) is also true of its dramatic moments (Ramadan and the pilgrimage). Due to Ramadan's complete fasting during daylight hours[5] and its relative feasting during the night, it is simultaneously the year's most challenging, hallowed and celebratory month. Likewise, as demanding as pilgrimage to so extreme a location as Mecca is, most pilgrims testify to the *hajj*'s being the high point in their life.

The Muslim Prayer Rite

Space permits examination of just one more of Islam's five core devotional requirements, that of prayer, the daily practice that is the heart and soul of Muslim spirituality. Indeed, together with faith and almsgiving, prayer may almost be said to define true *islam* (e.g., Q 27:3; 31:4; 98:5). While the Qur'an omits any concept of a sabbath day, Q 62:9-10 does fix the weekly congregational prayer at midday on Friday, Medina's market day. Though every

---

[4]The Qur'an refers to just three daily prayer times: at dawn, midday and night (Q 2:238; 24:58). It seems the early *umma* added two more prayer times after Muhammad.

[5]Ramadan's fast is total abstinence from food, drink, smoking and sex from sunrise till sunset, posing a major challenge, particularly in extremely hot, dry climates.

Muslim's experience of prayer differs somewhat from that of the next, certain aspects of it are common to all:

- its essential spiritual focus

- its challenge and simplicity

- its visualization of communal solidarity

- its pervasiveness in Muslim life and society

- its marginalization of women

- its richness and dominance in the mosque

- its sense of space and serenity

Some grasp of these aspects is vital to any appreciation of *salat*'s power in Muslim life.

First, prayer requires a certain focus, expressing itself in the worshiper's purity, direction and posture. The practice of leaving shoes and sandals outside the mosque clearly attests to the desire to "hallow and be hallowed" in approaching God.[6] Beyond the removal of footwear, there is each participant's ritual ablution with water (Q 4:43; 5:6). Q 2:149-50 mentions another prominent aspect of *salat*'s requisite attentiveness, the participant's physical orientation in prayer: only *salat* facing the Meccan Ka'ba counts.[7] The prayer posture is another important part of the worshiper's focus in prayer: her prescribed prostration says that she approaches God in the manner of a slave to her master, the formality of prayer's various positions representing the imperative distance between her and the deity. Prostrating, purified yet facedown, in the direction of Mecca multiple times a day embodies a refocusing and reorientation of the worshiper in humble submission to God and all that the qur'anic vision requires.

A second distinctive is the combined challenge and simplicity of the physical and mental, the oral and visual, in *salat*. This makes proficiency in all the technical aspects of the physically demanding rite—what to do and say—

[6]Kenneth Cragg, *Faiths in Their Pronouns: Websites of Identity* (Portland: Sussex Academic, 2002), 94.
[7]When praying outside the mosque, the believer's intention to pray facing Mecca matters more than her precise geographic accuracy. What I refer to as attentiveness in prayer Muslim scholars dealt with under the category of "intention," which pertains to all five pillars and, indeed, all of Muslim devotional life; on this see Renard, *Seven Doors to Islam*, 37-40.

critical. But having once memorized its postures and Arabic words,[8] the believer can perform his prayer without being distracted by them, meaning that each times he performs it, it becomes a matter of confident familiarity and reassurance. While the rite involves no true communication, Islam's minimization of the believer's knowledge of God shifts the emphasis to prayer's ritual enactment of the divine-human relationship.

Another striking aspect of the prayer rite is that it is both personal and corporate, as each member of the group shares it identically.[9] That makes the community's religious solidarity highly visible, as participants stand "in neat lines and bow in precise unison as token of their personal and corporate submission to the will of God."[10] Socially, this has a leveling effect too. For regardless of how generally pious a participant is or is not, his reverent, proficient performance of the rite at least momentarily "covers a multitude of sins" and in that sense makes him fully equal to all the other participants in the community's eyes. Because before their heavenly Master all obedient Muslims are equally his submissive slaves, that is what establishes their oneness. Hence, regardless of what divisions may wrack the community and what guilt may dog the individual participant, his performance of prayer gives him a momentary sense of being spiritually united with other Muslims all over the world and right back to Muhammad.

Fourth, "one witnesses among those Muslims that fulfill the obligation a striking sense of individual responsibility even if the time and place are less than ideal."[11] Thus prayer punctuates the entire day, interrupting virtually any activity under way. It can also be offered almost anywhere the believer is, and it requires the presence of neither a group nor a leader—and in any case, leading normally involves little more than establishing the pace.

Another distinctive of *salat* is that, although women are required to observe the same five prayer times as men, seventh-century Arab attitudes to women continue to restrict them in prayer down to the present. Women are nearly universally relegated to the back of the mosque (or else to the home), where their devotions will not breach the demands of modesty and distract male

---

[8]The prayer must be said in qur'anic Arabic, regardless of what language(s) the worshiper speaks.
[9]Cragg, *Faiths in Their Pronouns*, 95.
[10]Wilfred Cantwell Smith, *The Faith of Other Men* (Toronto: CBC Publications, 1962), 27.
[11]Daniel A. Madigan, "A Christian Perspective on Muslim Prayer," in *Prayer: Christian and Muslim Perspectives*, ed. David Marshall (Washington, DC: Georgetown University Press, 2013), 67.

worshipers. They are also almost universally excluded from leadership in prayer, minimal as it is. All this "offers a dramatic demonstration of a de facto exclusion from public life."[12] And that such exclusion shapes the Muslim community's religious life strongly encourages women's marginalization, if not their exclusion, from the rest of public life.

Sixth, in order to grasp something of the power *salat* typically exercises in Muslim societies, we must recognize that prayer's primary venue has always been the mosque, where it is accompanied by the call to communal prayer. Both of these features add significantly to *salat*'s appeal. Continually punctuating the day, the call to prayer asserts the legitimacy of communal prayer by making it a dominant part of public life, an activity about which one need never feel embarrassed or defensive. The call's restriction to the sonorous Arabic of the Qur'an proclaims the relevance of Muhammad's revelation to the present. The central location of the mosque and the prominence of its minaret visually reinforce both points. Performing his prayers in such a setting, or even just living his life against such a backdrop, can only increase the pious Muslim's sense of satisfaction with his devotions. With now some fourteen centuries of architectural development, mosques can be absolutely stunning in their reflection of the combined beauty, richness and simplicity of Islam.[13] And the mood created by good mosque architecture reflects the sort of solemnity, dignity and oneness "conducive to the non-competitive, coordinated effort of one people surrendering in unison to the one God in whom they believe."[14]

One last distinctive of *salat* bears mentioning here: despite its marked elements of negativity, the prayer rite conveys a clear sense of space, security and serenity. By its negativity, I refer to the fact that fully half of the creed—

---

[12]Ibid., 69.

[13]The qur'anic text is central throughout, whether visually in the graceful calligraphy adorning the mosque's walls and ceilings, aurally in the chanted artistry of its full-voiced recitation, or personally in the participant's prayer. In each respect, scripture provides believers with a sensuous feast, even if they do not understand its Arabic medium. And since the Qur'an is believed to be the only means by which the divine touches earth, all such expressions can become supercharged in Muslim experience. Oneness is communicated by the open, unbroken nature of the space designated for the practice of elbow-to-elbow ritual prayer and sitting. Though mosques are in many respects minimalist in their basic design and furnishings, they typically spread rich carpets beneath the believer's feet and mosaics, stained glass, beautifully carved wood and other forms of artistry before his eyes. From dawn to dusk, day after day, year in and year out in all the rhythms of the Muslim calendar, the mosque is typically home to the beauty, simplicity and richness of Islam in a manner both tangible and compelling. For a brief description of mosque architecture, see Renard, *Seven Doors to Islam*, 44-52.

[14]Renard, *Seven Doors to Islam*, 47.

"There is *no* god *but* God"—and a number of other lines repeated during prayer are negations or have strong negativity attached to them.[15] Despite that negativity, the prayer rite communicates peace by virtue of its steady physical rhythms and the power with which it penetrates public and private space. Everything from the familiar sound of the muezzin's call to the group's moving in unison through its measured motions in the stillness of the mosque gives *salat* an almost mesmerizing appearance of stability and peace. Reinforcing this multiple times each day doubtless helps Muslim believers prepare to meet a largely unknowable God amid the terrors of the Last Day and to do so with a remarkable sense of calm and serenity. So we might say that whatever *salat* lacks in intimacy with God it makes up for in calm predictability and—especially in large assemblies—in aesthetic power.

Creeds and Prayer in the Bible

If there is anything in the New Testament equivalent to the Muslim creed—that is, a simple litmus test of faith or unbelief—it would be the single statement that "Jesus is Lord," with all it means of Jesus' historical triumph over evil and the dark powers of this world by his death and resurrection to glory (Rom 10:9; 1 Cor 12:3). Other biblical affirmations echo that simple belief. First Corinthians 15:3-4 says that Christ died for our sins, he was buried and then raised on the third day, all according to the Old Testament scriptures. And Philippians 2:6-11 gives Jesus' whole story in brief, climaxing in statements telling why Jesus came to earth and died: to make the whole of creation one again, when every knee bows at his name and every tongue confesses that "Jesus Christ is Lord to the glory of God the Father."[16] It all comes down to Jesus' absolute triumph in history and how it will ultimately restore everything to the glory for which God created it. Clearly these essentials of faith leave no room for another prophet to disregard both Jesus' teachings and his triumph over evil in order to declare himself God's ultimate prophet instead.[17]

---

[15]For example, multiple times during prayer Muslims refer to avoidance of God's wrath and the path that leads astray (Q 1:7). Though not mandatory, most Muslims also recite Sura 112—with its double rejection of God's having begotten a son—every time they pray (!). And in keeping with that, *salat*'s multiple repetition of *Allahu akbar* often includes the notion of the triumph of the Muslim *umma* over all other religions and hence implicitly the defeat of all other religions.

[16]Other creedal statements likewise focus on the full humanity of the triumphant Christ (Jn 1:14; 1 Tim 3:16; 1 Jn 4:2), a highly controversial point when they were written.

[17]See chapters fifteen and sixteen below.

With regard to prayer, one has only to turn to the Psalms, the Bible's prayer book, to see how different the Bible's understanding of prayer is from that of the Qur'an. The psalmists are not opposed to ritual formulations, but unlike *salat*, their prayers are always centered in real communication with God. The psalmists also meant their prayers to be sung. Indeed, they designed them to partake of the full range of instrumental and choral music and, at least some of them, of sacred dance, all of which would have been unacceptable to the qur'anic author. Like the real communications they are, the psalms are "rough-hewn from earthy experience" and run the full range of the emotional spectrum—from the depths of despair to the heights of joy. Though the psalmists often rejoice with God and celebrate his goodness, they also cry out to him for help and comfort in their need and lament or even chide him over the injustice they see.[18]

But as Eugene Peterson observes, the psalms' very messiness helps correct our thinking about God. We think he would want to hear from us only when we are on our very best behavior, but the psalms tell us he is most concerned with our being honest with him. He knows our inmost thoughts, after all. So prayer is not "what good people do when they are doing their best," but rather "the means by which we get everything in our lives out in the open before God."[19]

Prayer's intimacy and ordinary everydayness make sense only because, biblically, God seeks real friendship with the believer, a relationship in which she comes to know him and opens her heart to him in prayer. Jesus' pattern prayer evidences the same sort of intimacy when it teaches believers to come to God as children to their heavenly Father, to center their lives in him and his concerns for the world and, so centered, to bring their needs to him, believing that he will hear them (Mt 6:9-13; 21:22). Jesus also strongly warns his followers against public prayer aimed at impressing others with its piety and emphasizes the need to persist in prayer (Mt 6:5-6; Lk 11:5-13; 18:1-7). Most of these points fade into insignificance in the Qur'an, if they appear there at all. Like the Qur'an, the Bible encourages believers to devote regular times to prayer, both privately and corporately. However, prayer has been

[18]Sebastian Moore, quoted in Kathleen Norris, *The Cloister Walk* (New York: Riverhead, 1997), 91.
[19]Eugene Peterson, *The Message: The Bible in Contemporary Language* (Colorado Springs: NavPress, 2002), 910-11.

called the Christian's "vital breath,"[20] since God also desires communion with his people moment by moment (1 Thess 5:17).

Morality, Society and Culture in Islam and Christianity

In addition to rightly relating individuals to their divine Master, the Qur'an seeks to establish a just and well-ordered society under God's rule. Among other things, this includes (1) addressing socioeconomic inequities by prohibiting usury (Q 2:275-80; 4:161) and (2) improving the lot of women by mandating an ex-husband's obligations to divorced wives and reforms to Arab inheritance laws (e.g., Q 2:228, 4:11, 65:4). While the Qur'an corrects many of the ethical failings of Muhammad's society,[21] it does not challenge Arab tribalism so much as enlarge it, as we have seen. And though the Qur'an would decry Judaism's ethnic tribalism, yet the Qur'an is no less culture bound than the Mosaic law.[22] Both give primarily contextualized ethics.[23] The Qur'an is reminiscent of Moses' law in another respect also: both view every area of life as falling under its jurisdiction—everything from the personal, devotional, dietary, domestic and social to political, economic and criminal.

This is what impelled Muslim scholars after Muhammad to produce their life-encompassing sharia, founded largely on the Qur'an's correction and moderation of seventh-century Arab tribal culture and on Muhammad's inspired example, or *sunna*. That is, the sharia is built on the conviction that the single moment in time—roughly two decades—during which Muhammad uttered his recitations and established their meaning in the life of the Muslim *umma* would forever after be normative for all of humankind. Then, for some three centuries after Muhammad, Sunni jurists gradually filled in many of the

---

[20]From James Montgomery's nineteenth-century hymn "Prayer Is the Soul's Sincere Desire."

[21]Among other things, the Qur'an thunders against female infanticide, the oppression of orphans and widows, and the evils of usury (e.g., Q 4:2, 10, 19; 16:59; 81:8-9). It calls for the avoidance of pork, carrion and all forms of alcohol. It also specifies that a thief's hand should be amputated and an adulterer flogged (Q 2:173; 5:3, 38; 6:145; 24:2-5). As noted above, the sharia makes adultery a capital offense, thus preferring the hadith over the Qur'an.

[22]Muhammad's call to supertribalism under God's rule represented monotheism in an entirely new configuration. For if Judaism exemplifies monotheism in its ethnic tribal aspect and Christianity in its universal multicultural aspect, Islam—specifically, the sharia—represents it in its universal supertribal and culture-specific aspect.

[23]Thus the qur'anic author either assumes that moral stipulations relevant to seventh-century Arab culture will apply equally everywhere and always—or else simply responds to current conditions in the knowledge that he can change his stipulations whenever the situation changes. But since Muhammad's death marked the end of revelation, that proviso came with an expiry date.

numerous remaining gaps in the law by means of consensus and analogical reasoning—before locking the door to any new legal rulings in the tenth century.[24] But the vast majority of Muslims do not view its culture specificity as in any way limiting Islam's universal applicability due to the fact that the Qur'an presents all of its teachings with a finality that logically implies it. While the doctrine of abrogation allowed for change within the qur'anic text, nearly all Muslims view the Qur'an's nonabrogated strictures as timeless. This "timelessness" still commits the religious establishment in both Sunni and Shi'ite camps to resisting all but minor religious changes. But such sharia rulings as those on female dress, concubinage and prepubescent marriage are problematic to many Muslims today.

The Christian response to biblical ethics has historically been radically different. The Old Testament establishes some of its norms—the Decalogue, for example—with a clear sense of their permanence, making them keys to understanding all the rest. However, a great many Old Testament legal stipulations are bound to their particular culture, time and place. The New Testament, by contrast, puts moral principles at the heart of its ethics. It does give some of its principles culture-specific applications, but most Christians agree that not all biblical norms are timeless. Although there is considerable agreement within the global Christian community as to how we should approach these issues, we by no means have unanimity on which biblical norms are timeless and precisely how contextualization is to be done. In some cases, we need to discern a norm's developmental trajectory, which gives us clear signs of God's gradual education of his people throughout biblical history.[25]

---

[24]While Shi'ite jurists did not follow them there, Shi'ite legal practice is also largely bound in the distant past.

[25]Christians find help here because their faith is rooted in a three-thousand-year-old tradition, enabling us to discern the contours of God's dealings with his people diachronically. Only on the basis of that trajectory can we venture further than Scripture's explicit teaching. For otherwise, we cannot distinguish between following God as he continues to guide his people into truth and allowing the incessant pull of idolatrous human culture to weaken and erode his moral standards. For example, while the Bible prescribes corporal punishment for children, we have reason to see this as a temporal application of a timeless value and, while the Bible never directly forbids slavery, it does establish a clear trajectory toward its total abolition; William J. Webb, *Corporal Punishment in the Bible: A Redemptive-Movement Hermeneutic for Troubling Texts* (Downers Grove, IL: IVP Academic, 2011); William J. Webb, *Slaves, Women and Homosexuals: Exploring the Hermeneutics of Cultural Analysis* (Downers Grove, IL: IVP Academic, 2001); cf. Harvie M. Conn, *Eternal Word and Changing Worlds: Theology, Anthropology and Mission in Trialogue* (Grand Rapids: Zondervan, 1984). This approach is radically different from that of Muslims in interpreting the Qur'an, for with only

Limited Polygyny Within a Patriarchal Society

Especially in the social sphere, the qur'anic author enjoins right and forbids wrong (Q 7:157; 9:71). Not only is this necessary if the Muslim *umma* is to please God: it is essential to the community's well-being. The social dimension of qur'anic spirituality is an extensive topic, so we will limit our discussion of it to just two features: the Qur'an's regulation of both marriage and marital breakdown, key aspects of its concern for social cohesion. While polygyny, a man's concurrent marriage to multiple wives, was previously unrestricted, the Qur'an limits Muslim practice of it to a maximum of four wives. Not surprisingly, given the Westernization of many Muslims today, the issue of polygyny is highly controversial among them, but that was never the case before the modern period.

Beginning with Syed Abul A'la Mawdudi (d. 1979), modern Muslims influenced by Western ideas have sought ways to make the Qur'an prohibit polygyny. Q 4:3 does say that if men are afraid they cannot deal with up to four wives fairly, they should limit themselves to one wife and any concubines and female slaves they have. The monogamist interpretation combines this rider with the statement in Q 4:129 that no man can deal fairly with multiple wives. In other words, since equitable polygyny is an oxymoron, it is forbidden to all. But Q 4:3 does not forbid polygyny. It makes any restriction here only self-imposed, depending on each husband's self-assessment. Furthermore, Q 4:129 simply urges that, since absolute equality in a polygynous marriage is impossible, husbands should at least avoid *utterly* neglecting their less favorite wife or wives.

In any case, any preference for monogamy found in Q 4:3 includes the possibility of a man's having an unlimited number of concubines, who were in many respects like slaves, purchased or taken as war booty. That is, the cultural context of this verse is a two-tiered system in which a man acquires sexual rights to women with either full or limited responsibility, in marriage or concubinage respectively. So even if Q 4:3 were to be taken as prohibiting polygyny, it fully legitimizes the practice of a Muslim's concurrently having multiple sexual partners provided he acquires them legally and acts responsibly toward them. But like its cultural context, the Qur'an permits this privilege to men only, never to women. Muhammad's practice of both concubinage and polygyny became normative among his followers

---

twenty some years of salvation history to go on—not to mention their use of abrogation to dismiss bothersome texts—they would be very limited in establishing ethical trajectories to be followed.

as soon as their military success allowed.[26] As elsewhere, Muhammad was his *umma's* primary model, his polygyny being exceptional only in that he was not required to observe the four-wife limit established for everyone else.[27]

Thus the qur'anic author institutes what he considers the most practicable approach to marriage a society can take. He has two concerns in mind. On the one hand, he knows that few seventh-century Arab men will be satisfied with just one sexual partner if they can afford more. Hence he leaves the door open to both polygyny and concubinage to stave off adultery. On the other hand, he views stable marriages as vital to a stable social structure and so seeks to enhance their stability by limiting polygyny to four wives and urging husbands to take proper care of unfavorite wives or otherwise to forego polygyny in favor of monogamy. Within the context of a male-dominant society, the qur'anic concern that husbands treat multiple wives fairly was exemplary. The Qur'an thereby limits polygyny's complications without vetoing the institution itself. But though it thus trimmed the plant's foliage somewhat, it left the root of its seventh-century Arab gender inequality untouched.

Marital Breakdown in a Patriarchal Society

Male dominance becomes equally clear in the Qur'an's approach to marital breakdown. Counseling women to guard their chastity, Q 4:34-35 instructs husbands who fear that their wives are "unruly" or "misbehaving" on how they should discipline them. Verse 34 outlines a three-stage approach to making such a wife submit. This involves the husband's progressively

- admonishing her verbally;
- withdrawing from her sexually; and
- beating her physically.

Hence, if the first two measures fail to control her, the Qur'an commands corporal punishment. Finally, if a husband's beatings are ineffective at alleviating

---

[26]The *umma's* military successes provided its men with booty, including both female slaves and the wealth with which to afford multiple wives. Likewise, Muhammad himself remained monogamous only until his first wife, Khadija, died, embracing polygyny and concubinage soon afterward. That polygyny has not been normative among Muslims throughout history relates to not ethical but rather economic factors. For some time now most Muslim societies have discouraged concubinage, and some have made both it and polygyny illegal, but both are permitted by the sharia.

[27]Most Muslims take Q 33:50 to exempt Muhammad from the four-wife limit.

his fears, arbitration is his last resort, after which he is free to divorce his wife if he chooses. That husbands alone decide whether their wives are "unruly" is made clear by the words "if *you* fear [*takhafuna*] their misconduct." This makes the husband's interpretation of his wife's behavior and even his fears concerning it the sole grounds for his following the corrective process. Furthermore, husbands are not told how severe their beatings should be.[28] Either way, in some cases the husband's God-given rule over his wife necessitates the husband's corporal punishment of her. Such coercion guarantees patriarchy within the family and hence within society at large.

Three points are worth noting with regard to qur'anic divorce. First, the Qur'an sets no limits as to its grounds. In fact, it never addresses the topic, effectively making divorce easy. For example, it evidences no concern to establish what sort of situations effectively break the marriage covenant and so warrant divorce or, indeed, ever to limit divorce to cases where it has already been broken.[29] Second, in divorce the husband has an automatic right to full custody of his children (Q 2:226-32, 236-37, 240-41; 33:49; 65:1), according to the sharia, at age eight for boys and at puberty for girls.[30] This would inhibit any wife with children from initiating divorce lest she lose them. But it does not limit divorce in marriages without children, and it clearly weights things in favor of the husband. Third, while the Qur'an seems to assign a passive role to the wife in a marriage gone bad, it may allow her to initiate a divorce, provided a male judge sanctions it.

A Biblical Approach to Marriage and Divorce

From a New Testament perspective, concubinage is totally ruled out. There is no room for any institution between marriage and singleness. For all but converts already in plural marriages, the New Testament prohibits polygyny of all

---

[28]One husband may take a lenient approach to his wife's behavior, while another beats her harshly for refusing to wear the veil. Classical interpretations of Q 4:34-35 are consonant with hadith, documenting both Muhammad's behavior—striking his favorite wife ʿAisha on the chest hard enough to cause her pain—and the early Muslim husband's use of physical punishment to subdue his wife as directed. Yusuf Ali and other modern translators insert the word *lightly* after "beat them," although they have no textual basis for doing so.

[29]By annulling Zayd's adoption, the Qur'an condones not only Muhammad's desire to marry another man's wife (legally), but also easy, no-fault divorce (Q 33:36-37; see 18 above). In both respects, the teaching of the Qur'an runs directly counter to that of Jesus.

[30]The sharia qualifies this in that the divorced mother loses custody of even her young children (e.g., boys under the age of eight) if she remarries.

kinds. This is clear from Jesus' teaching on marriage in Matthew 19:4-6. He argues that since God created one woman and one man—not a multiplicity of either—his original design was to make the two one in marriage. The monogamous model is the only guarantor of male-female equality. While God overlooked polygyny and concubinage to some extent in the Old Testament, Jesus calls us back to God's original intention for his creation. And the situation with regard to divorce is similar. God permitted divorce under Moses, but Jesus calls husbands and wives to respect their divinely constituted oneness: "what God has joined together, let no one separate." The only exceptions are when the marriage covenant has already effectively been broken, as in a case of adultery (Mt 19:6-9). Biblically speaking, allowing love for one's spouse to grow cold is not a valid reason.[31]

Furthermore, the New Testament takes a radically different approach to marriage when it commands mutual submission, the husband submitting to his wife no less than her to him (Eph 5:21). Everything else Paul says about marriage in Ephesians 5:21-33 must be understood within that context. While Paul calls the wife to submit to her husband as the church submits to Christ, he also calls the husband to lead precisely by laying down his life for his wife as Christ did for his bride, the church. In other words, Jesus' sacrifice is the model for the husband's leadership, so such leadership is never about domination (Eph 5:22-33). The husband leads by giving up his rights for his wife, while she submits to his leadership by choice.[32] If the other fails to obey Scripture in this regard, this does not exempt the other from fulfilling his or her obedience in the hope that God will yet bring husband and wife to a place of unity in him. Elsewhere Paul establishes a husband's love for his wife as normative (Col 3:18-20). So the picture that emerges is of true intimacy and gender equality within marriage. Nowhere does the Bible condone, let alone command, a husband's corporal punishment of his wife.

---

[31]Though we might assume that a tribal society like Muhammad's offered enough inbuilt familial resistance to make divorce difficult, Zayd's divorce of his wife at Muhammad's request in order to allow Muhammad to marry her gives us pause to question that. In any case, Muhammad's example suggests that marriage was never considered permanent per se. It also implies that since the qur'anic approach is so different from the biblical approach and yet never has to contest the latter, the milieu of the Qur'an is not a biblically oriented community at all.

[32]With so costly a model of marriage—costly to both partners—it should not surprise us that the Bible gives us no simple three-step approach to marital breakdown. (In a sense, a dysfunctional marriage is no less costly than the model marriage—it is just a question of how we choose to pay.)

The Appeal of the Sharia Today

For obvious reasons, Westerners are repelled by much of qur'anic spirituality's social dimension today, though they would not have been so repelled by it in the seventh century, when gender equality existed no more in Europe than Arabia. However, the situation is very different in much of the developing world, where the Muslim sharia has great appeal for many reasons. To begin, it offers a comprehensive social law and the only alternative to Western Christian permissiveness in the eyes of many who find such permissiveness as unattractive as it is fashionable in the West.

One certainly need not look far to see the vacuous lives of many Westerners and their imitators riding the wave of international fame and fortune. Likewise, the effects of Western moral decadence—gross materialism, pornographic advertising, open disdain for marriage, escalating divorce rates, an increasing acceptance of our drug culture, and so on—are impossible to miss. None of this can enhance a nation's social solidarity or stability for long. Against such a backdrop, the Islamic option has great attraction to many, representing moral strength and certainty as opposed to the West's evident moral decline. One need not reinvent the wheel. Challenging though it may be, a family or tribe's acceptance of Islam instantly settles a million and one social and legal questions. And the sharia is quite compatible with actual customary law in many developing nations—in which case, converting simply requires minor adjustments.

Toward a Right Relationship with God

To round out our treatment of qur'anic spirituality's devotional and social dimensions, we must briefly consider how the Qur'an's teaching relates to the Bible's ethical core—the Decalogue and the two great commandments Jesus put at the heart of his ethics.[33] Despite clear similarities between the Qur'an and the Bible, especially the Decalogue, the prominent place given to love in the Bible produces a significant ethical divide between the two scriptures.

Like the Bible, the Qur'an emphasizes the need to have no god but God (Q 4:116; 112:1-4; cf. Ex 20:3; Deut 6:4). Neither does it permit idolatry (Q 6:74; 14:35; cf. Ex 20:4-6). This requirement to let nothing encroach on God's unity, his unrivaled supremacy and glory is foundational to the ethics of both scriptures.

---

[33]See Scot McKnight, *The Jesus Creed: Loving God, Loving Others* (Brewster, MA: Paraclete, 2004).

The Qur'an repeatedly mentions that God possesses the most beautiful names, and it objects to the misuse of his name, though its understanding of what that involves differs from that of the Bible (Q 6:108; 7:180; 20:8). Though nothing in the Qur'an is exactly equivalent to the Decalogue, the Qur'an does include precepts akin to nine of its ten commandments. Only one is entirely omitted, the sabbath law. Biblically speaking, this is no minor omission, since the sabbath command envisioned a community accepting God's limit to production and consumption and thus centering itself on "an enactment of peaceableness that bespeaks the settled rule of [God]."[34] Nor is the biblical requirement simply Godward: it granted one's employees, slaves and animals rights too.

With regard to the imperative Jesus made foundational to his ethics—the command to love God supremely—the gap between the Bible and Qur'an widens (Mt 22:36-40; Ex 20:1-11; Deut 6:5; 10:12). The qur'anic version of the *Shema* entirely omits the command to love God, something that is in no wise coincidental, for not once in all of the Qur'an are believers commanded to love God. While the Qur'an mentions seeking "God's face," it gives us no sense that it involves real intimacy (Q 6:52; 18:28).[35] It twice calls God *al-Wadud*, the "Loving One" (Q 11:90; 85:14; cf. Q 20:39), and frequently names those whom he loves and does not love.[36] But compared to the biblical emphasis on God's love for humankind[37] and our need to love him in return, qur'anic references to God's love for us or ours for him do not point to a deeply

---

[34]Walter Brueggemann, *Theology of the Old Testament: Testimony, Dispute, Advocacy* (Minneapolis: Fortress, 1997), 185.

[35]Mention of "hearts that soften to the remembrance of God" in Q 39:23 refers simply to the willingness to yield to God's revealed word (i.e., in the Qur'an).

[36]God loves those who repent, the patient, good-doers, the God-fearing, the just, etc. (Q 2:222; 3:146; 5:93; 9:4, 7; 49:9), and, conversely, he does not love the guilty ingrate, the proud or boastful, the prodigal, transgressors, workers of corruption, unbelievers, etc. (Q 2:276; 4:36; 6:141; 7:31, 55; 28:77; 30:45). This is similar to certain biblical passages (e.g., 2 Cor 9:7; Prov 6:16). But the Bible differs dramatically from the Qur'an in emphasis. Lacking an equal or greater emphasis on undeserved love, the Qur'an teaches that God's love operates freely only within the paradigm of reciprocity, in that he loves only the deserving. His love operates only very guardedly within the paradigm of reversal: he gives rain and sunshine, life and breath, to the evil along with the good, and he sends prophets to call unbelievers back to the path of submission. But the Qur'an never says God unconditionally loves the unrighteous or unrepentant. Indeed, it rather says that God grants them time so that they may increase their guilt and doom (Q 3:178). And it does so without ever balancing that with the biblical depiction of God demonstrating deep compassion for sinners still estranged from him (Lk 15:11-24; Rom 5:7-10).

[37]The biblical corollary of God's love is his jealousy for our love: because he loves so deeply and intimately, the Bible portrays him as jealous when his love is not returned. The total absence of jealousy in qur'anic theology confirms the very different nature of God's love in the Qur'an.

personal and mutually intimate relationship between God and humankind. The Qur'an's occasional references to God's "love" for humanity and humanity's love for him are really just to mutual loyalty (Q 2:156; 3:31; 5:54): God is loyal to those who are loyal to him.[38] So it should not surprise us that we find no equivalent to the command to love God with all one's heart, soul, strength and mind (Deut 6:5; Mk 12:30), so fundamental to Jesus' understanding of Moses' law.

Like the Bible, the Qur'an frequently refers to the need to fear God (e.g., Q 2:2; 3:102; 4:131; 70:27; 98:8; cf. Pss 19:9; 111:10; Prov 9:10; 1 Pet 2:17). But when fear is commended apart from its biblical corollary of intimate personal love, it becomes servile and cringing, concerned not to cherish the relationship so much as to survive it as best one can. Thus, compared to the biblical focus, the qur'anic focus points toward human servility.[39]

This raises questions about the open letter placed in the *New York Times* by 138 Muslim scholars in 2007, titled "A Common Word Between Us and You," for that document states that the principles of love of the one God and love of neighbor are "the very foundational principles" of Islam and are found "over and over again in the sacred texts of Islam."[40] It also claims that the two commandments of love are "what is most essential to [Muslim] faith and practice." The letter's Muslim signatories are certainly to be commended for the grace and courage evident in their initiative to seek interfaith harmony. But frankly, the letter's attempt to make love central to qur'anic spirituality makes sense only in light of the hadith's Islamization of biblical teachings and a sustained effort to read the Qur'an through the lens of those hadith.[41]

---

[38]This is very much in keeping with what Bottéro says of the ancient Middle Eastern polytheist's "love" for the gods. See 64 above. Further, aside from the nature of God's love in the Qur'an, it speaks only of his loving those who love him (cf. n36 above), which clearly reverses the biblical emphasis on our loving God in return for his undeserved love (1 Jn 4:19).

[39]This, again, strikes one as being closer to polytheism than to biblical monotheism. Bottéro writes that the gods "always remained enveloped in majesty, distant and fearsome," which was why the polytheists' fear of the gods "always outweighed everything else"; Jean Bottéro, *Religion in Ancient Mesopotamia* (Chicago: University of Chicago Press, 2001), 40.

[40]While this designation includes the hadith, the statement is simply not true of the Qur'an.

[41]Ghazi bin Muhammad, "The ACW Letter—A Common Word Between Us and You," October 13, 2007, www.acommonword.com/the-acw-document. According to Seyyed Hossein Nasr, Prince Ghazi's interpretation of the Qur'an encapsulates its "inner meaning"; Seyyed Hossein Nasr, foreword to Ghazi bin Muhammad, *Love in the Holy Qur'an* (Chicago: Kazi Publications, 2010), xxv. And that meaning is found only by Christianizing qur'anic references to love. For centuries Sufis have been doing this, reading the Qur'an very selectively through the lens of profoundly Christianizing hadith.

As previously noted, it is always tempting for Westerners to give qur'anic references to love the biblical meaning of deep personal affection—even before leading Muslim scholars band together ostensibly to legitimize such an approach. But the Qur'an's original audience would not have taken them in that sense. And the same holds true for most Muslims today. Few if any of the Muslim countries represented by the ACW letter's signatories grant their people full freedom of religious belief, for example. As chapter thirteen will show, this attests to qur'anic spirituality's inherent coerciveness, as opposed to the letter's hadith-inspired approach. The Common Word initiative clearly aims to oppose radical Islamist interpretations, and some signatories doubtless hope it will have a trickle-down effect in their societies. The question is how that can work if the letter's redefinition of qur'anic spirituality cannot be reconciled with the coerciveness of the Muhammad of history. Admittedly, the hadith give love for God and neighbor a far greater emphasis than the Qur'an. But then, the Qur'an cannot be said to emphasize them at all.

Toward a Rightly Ordered Society

Relative to the Decalogue's commandments governing human interactions (Ex 20:12-17), the Qur'an teaches the importance of honoring parents and condemns murder, adultery, theft, lying and coveting (Q 2:283; 4:32; 5:32, 38-39; 15:88; 17:23-24, 32; 20:131; 25:68; 45:7). These six commandments obviously relate to the biblical call to love one's neighbor as oneself, which Jesus highlighted as the second greatest commandment in all of the Law (Lev 19:18; Mt 22:36-38). But the Qur'an never actually commands love of neighbor. The closest it comes to doing so is to give what we may take as applications of the golden rule (Q 2:267; 24:22; 83:1-4; cf. Q 4:8-9). Neither does it ever command love of one's enemies. Indeed, why would God require such love in his subjects when the Qur'an never once credits him with loving his enemies? The Qur'an does mention love between

---

As noted above, many Westernized Muslims have followed suit during the modern period, but with an individualistic version of Islam that grants them a personal relationship with God, devoid of the strictures of ritual and law. But while the hadith tell us how some Muslims in Islam's early centuries viewed their scripture, they do not tell us what the text meant to Muhammad's first followers (cf. 48 above). As previously noted, whatever meanings we see in the Qur'an must be grounded in its original and primary meaning—what its first audience understood when they heard or read it.

human beings a few times, but it never makes love the basis for all our inter-actions, as Jesus does.[42]

This points to another fundamental difference between the Qur'an and Bible: humility is a large part of loving one's enemies, and its absence is a major reason why our world is beset by so much conflict, from interpersonal to inter-national. All of the New Testament writers are intent on subverting the status quo on lordship, rights and subservience. For biblically, "God's way of looking at the world is upside down from ours." But not so in the Qur'an. Everything "stays right side up (which is, from a Christian perspective, wrong side down). The Muslim path is obedience and submission to God's will, but it is not God emptying himself and taking on the form of a servant. In Islam, God never leaves his heavenly throne."[43] Biblically speaking, merely recommending for-giveness as the Qur'an does (Q 24:22; 42:40; 64:14) fails to grasp either the extremity of our situation apart from God's grace or the indivisibility of love for God and love for neighbor (Mt 18:23-34). Further, the Qur'an calls be-lievers to be humble only toward each other, not categorically toward unbe-lievers too (Q 5:54). This clearly points to the qur'anic author's rejection of the biblical teaching that God not only universally commands love and for-giveness of us but also perfectly demonstrated it in Jesus' death on the cross (Lk 23:34).

Muslims often complain that the New Testament's demand that we love and forgive our enemies raises the bar impossibly high. And they are right, unless God intends to push us to trust him for resources beyond our own— for his grace to enable us to do what we cannot possibly do on our own. Paul views such an ethic's impossibility not as a minus but a plus, for our inability to love our enemies becomes God's opportunity to love them through us, which is all part of the process of our being united with him in love (2 Cor 12:9).

---

[42]Accordingly, the ACW letter cites only one qur'anic reference here, which equates piety with generosity to one's kin and to the marginalized, among other things (Q 2:177).

[43]David Capes, Rodney Reeves and E. Randolph Richards, *Rediscovering Jesus: An Introduction to Biblical, Religious and Cultural Perspectives on Christ* (Downers Grove, IL: IVP Academic, 2015), 186.

Thirteen

Qur'anic Spirituality's Political Dimension

We can truly understand the Qur'an's political dimension only within its seventh-century Arab context, in which virtually all religion was geopolitical. Military jihad, religious tolerance and the law of apostasy are three practices vital to this dimension of spirituality. Despite efforts on the part of moderate Muslims today to collapse this entire dimension into a modern notion of pluralism, historically, Muhammad's struggle (*jihad*) against unbelief in the world became militarized within two years of his coming to power in Medina. Hence the tolerance promulgated by the Qur'an extended only limited religious rights to subjugated monotheists protected by treaty within a context that ensured their communities' steady decline. In addition, the law of apostasy made Islamization a one-way street, since conversion from the Muslim faith was punishable by death. Though eminently practical, all three spiritual practices fit within a success-oriented, externalized ethic. And they diverge widely from the nonviolence, religious pluralism and freedom inherent in the New Testament, at the core of which is a kind of humility and love absent from the Qur'an.

*M*ost non-Muslims find Muslim spirituality's political dimension difficult to view sympathetically. Our best help here is doubtless to view it in terms of Islam's seventh-century origins, for the qur'anic author approached religion as virtually anyone in seventh-century Arabia did—as *necessarily* geopolitical.[1] That his paradigm does not fit the twenty-first century should not surprise us. But in their tension and interplay, the qur'anic concepts of jihad and religious tolerance went a long way toward making Islam what it is today. An equally integral feature of political Islam is the law of apostasy, the standard Muslim approach to which most Westerners today find deeply troubling.

At the very outset, we must note that for most of Islam's history it has been spread by peaceful means,[2] during which time most Muslims have seen no need to engage in religious violence. The balance of history thus supports the insistence of many Muslims on Islam's being a peaceable religion.[3] However, three equally solid historical facts counterbalance their claim. Written right into Islam's founding document—a scripture nearly all Muslims believe pre-existed creation—is a strong element of violence in God's name, as we will momentarily see. Second, this led the Muslim community to disempower, drive out or destroy anyone resisting its rule for much of Islam's formative period, from the early 620s—under Muhammad himself—to 750 CE. Indeed, that conquest was what put Islam on the world map, enabling it virtually to obliterate Mazdaism, for example. Last, the hadith, *sira* and sharia, which have played such a vital role in shaping all Muslim cultures, clearly reflect this militaristic mindset.[4] Thus, in an age given to stereotypes driven by sound bites and tabloid headlines, we must give all the scope we can to Muslim pacifism. But on the other hand, we cannot let this keep us from addressing the issue of qur'anic militarism, despite the risk of being perceived as Islamophobic or as distorting Islam.

---

[1]Monasticism was the primary exception to this rule. While the Qur'an evidences esteem for Christian monks (Q 5:82), it in no way advocates monasticism as a way of life (Q 9:34; 57:27), but rather embraces the marriage of religion and state.

[2]However, we cannot equate "peaceful" with "noncoercive" (see 190n19, 196-200 below).

[3]Moderate Muslims thus object to extremists' "hijacking" of their faith. See Khaled M. Abou El-Fadl, *The Great Theft: Wrestling Islam from the Extremists* (New York: HarperOne, 2007).

[4]Moderate Muslims counter this orientation by viewing the Qur'an and the rest of the hadith through the lens of hadith that effectively "redeem" the entire Islamic tradition for them by focusing on peaceful jihad while marginalizing military jihad. Abou El-Fadl, for example, makes the sweeping claim that Muhammad "repeatedly taught that the greatest form of jihad is to struggle against one's own base desires." Yet Abou El-Fadl uncharacteristically offers no support for his assertion; *The Great Theft*, 221. Perhaps generalization serves him better here because the hadith moderates usually use to make this point is so historically weak (see 185 below).

The Jihad Against Jihad

Horrified by modern-day jihadist brutality, moderate Muslims often assert that jihad has nothing whatever to do with violence and instead make jihad basic to the peace they see as the "true meaning" of Islam. They thus draw a principled distinction between the religious and political spheres.[5] But that distinction is nowhere to be found in the Medinan suras—before which the absence of an Islamic polity made the distinction impossible. And that fact strongly supports the classical (and Islamist) position on the indivisibility of religion and politics.

Those trying to demilitarize "Islam" marshal the following evidence to support their case:

- the greater-jihad versus lesser-jihad hadith
- Qur'anic verses on tolerance and self-defense
- the essential meanings of *jihad* and *islam*

It is not hard to see why moderate Muslims love the hadith categorizing the struggle to pray, fast, etc., as the "greater jihad" and militarism the "lesser jihad." But none of the classical traditionists included this hadith in their collections, let alone assessed its authenticity. This strongly marks it as a fabrication that did not exist in the ninth century. By contrast, numerous authentic hadith promote military jihad.[6] Only one very doubtful hadith contests that perspective.[7]

In terms of qur'anic texts, Q 2:256, a verse to which we will return, is the one quoted most often: "There is no compulsion in religion." Q 109:6—"To you your religion and to me mine"—sounds similarly broadminded. But coming in

---

[5]With costly wars under way and volatile electorates to manage, Western politicians have rushed to pronounce the moderate Muslim view correct. And many of us have cheered them on. Aside from the fear factor, who wants to think a world religion as impressive in so many ways as Islam could have sacralized violence at its core? But this points to the problem of letting our needs filter the qur'anic data on jihad. We must reckon with the classical evidence also. To deny the Muslim conquest or its religious cause "for the sake of peace" is like denying one's medical history to enhance one's health. (Denying formative events in one's history is no more life giving for cultures than for individuals.) On the other hand, to say that the Qur'an makes war in God's name integral to its communal vision does not mean everything the jihadists preach is qur'anic.

[6]One says that "standing for an hour in the ranks of battle is better than standing in prayer for sixty years." Another asserts that anyone who dies neither fighting for God's Cause nor ever having expressed a wish to do so dies a hypocrite—i.e., is not a true Muslim.

[7]Not only does this hadith not appear in any of Islam's major hadith compendiums, but it originates not from Muhammad or his Companions, rather from the generation after them. So shaky a tradition cannot provide solid grounds for discounting the rest of the hadith on military jihad.

the Meccan suras when the Muslims were being pressured to return to their native polytheism, it simply asked pagans to leave the Muslims be. Moderates also cite Q 2:217 in condemnation of military aggression, but it labels only fighting during the sacred month—something forbidden even by pagans—a great offense. Q 2:190-95 mentions fighting in self-defense, but also urges believers to fight against the Meccans until the Ka'ba is given to the worship of God alone—which is what the early *umma* actually did, and that was hardly self-defense. Those downplaying qur'anic militancy typically offer these few milder passages in an attempt to shut down meaningful exploration of the Qur'an on jihad. But these verses by no means encompass qur'anic treatment of the topic.[8]

Since it comes from the verb *jahada*, "to struggle or strive," moderates claim that the *essential* meaning of *jihad* (read: *true* meaning) has no military associations. Then, by combining their demilitarized *jihad* with *islam*, the *true* meaning of which they claim is "peace" (*salam*), they argue that jihad is simply the Muslim's struggle for peace. While it is true that *islam* and *salam* are etymologically related, the former does not mean "peace" at all but rather "submission."[9] Furthermore, words with more than one meaning do not have an "essential" meaning in the sense that one meaning is legitimate while other meanings are less so. That the Qur'an uses *jihad* with more than one meaning simply requires us to determine which meaning its original audience would have understood in each case. Surveying the current controversy, Michael Bonner observes that "Islam, through jihad, equals violence and war; or else, through jihad, it equals peace."[10] Since this situation has generated much

---

[8]Gordon Nickel, "Islam: A Religion of Peace?" *National Post* (June 13, 2006), www.canada.com /nationalpost/news/issuesideas/story.html?id=c53fc4cd-528a-42a9-b092-2b7b0ccce158. For example, "Whoever kills a person . . . it is as if he had killed all of mankind" is used but extracted from the extremely violent verse following it (Q 5:32-33).

[9]On this see Martin Accad, "Islam Means Peace? A Brief Etymological Reflection," The Institute of Middle East Studies, February 4, 2016, https://imeslebanon.wordpress.com/2016/02/04/islam -means-peace-a-brief-etymological-reflection/#more-3409. If the mere fact of an etymological connection made words synonyms, then *bless* and *blood*, as well as *rhyme* and *rhythm*, would be synonyms, since these pairs are also related.

[10]Michael Bonner, *Jihad in Islamic History: Doctrines and Practice* (Princeton, NJ: Princeton University Press, 2006), 2. Apologists at both ends of the spectrum, both Muslim and non-Muslim, invariably reify "Islam" as if it exists as some unchanging essence in the world down through the ages. In fact, Islam is simply the faith of the world's many Muslims and the civilization to which their faith gave birth; Wilfred Cantwell Smith, *The Meaning and End of Religion* (New York: Macmillan, 1963). Naturally, a reified approach is most useful for apologetic purposes.

confusion, we must ask—whether convenient or not—whether the Qur'an promotes an ethic of sacralized violence or peace. Muhammad's concept of jihad was clearly unrelated to present-day attitudes some fifteen centuries later. So we can solve the riddle only by reading the Qur'an in its historical context.

Qur'anic Uses of Jihad

In terms of the meaning of *jihad*, those denying the Qur'an's militancy are right to say the word derives from *jahada*, "to struggle or strive." However, as just noted, no word has an "essence" in the sense that just one of its meanings is its *true* meaning. A word like *jahada*, rather, has a range of meaning that depends on the contexts in which it occurs. All use of *jahada* in the Meccan suras is admittedly nonmilitaristic and can refer to prayer, almsgiving, etc. Q 29:6, for example, says those who struggle to please God do so to their own gain. However, the Qur'an's clear us-against-them divide runs through the Meccan suras too, since that struggle dominated Muhammad's entire prophetic career. So we should not be surprised to see that the Qur'an uses *jihad* and its cognates to refer to all struggle against those who openly reject Muhammad's claim to prophetic authority. Thus Q 25:52 (Meccan) urges Muhammad not to give in to his unbelieving opponents but to struggle hard against them. Although the Qur'an never sanctioned warfare—guerilla or otherwise—in Mecca,[11] it was only natural that this struggle—and with it, the word *jihad*— would take on geopolitical dimensions when the band of Muslim believers was transformed into the Medinan polity. As soon as the struggle between good and evil issued in war between Muslim Medina and pagan Mecca, qur'anic usage of the word *jihad*, too, was militarized.[12] The Muslims' initial objective was the conquest of Mecca. But no sooner had Mecca surrendered than their goal became expanding the *umma*'s dominion in all directions.

Thus the Medinan suras urge believers to pour everything at their disposal—their wealth and their lives—into the *umma*'s do-or-die war effort for God's Cause (Q 8:72; 9:20, 41, 44, 81; 49:44). Q 9:19-21 promises those who

---

[11]That even Muhammad was never authorized to attack non-Muslims before he had a state argues against any nongovernmental licensing of violence. But that argument has the hollow ring of impractical theory to puritanical Muslim groups who need only claim statehood in order to legitimize their violence.

[12]This war is justified on two bases: that the Meccans' having "exiled" the Muslims is more heinous than the war and that the Ka'ba, God's house, must be cleansed of idols (Q 2:190-95).

believe and participate in Muhammad's military campaigns forgiveness and a tremendous reward—not to mention victory over their enemies. It also warns against putting anything (e.g., one's business) ahead of the military struggle (*jihad*) for God's Cause. And since nonparticipation earned God's punishment, it was not an option for believers (Q 9:24; cf. 4:95; 8:65, 75; 9:24). Thus *jahada's* Meccan usage in the sense of "to struggle" complements, rather than discounts, its frequent military use in Medina.[13]

Jihad Is Far Bigger Than Jihad

However, the question of peace versus sacralized violence goes far beyond qur'anic usage of *jihad* and *jahada* and must be viewed within the Qur'an's larger military emphasis. The Medinan suras command believers to "kill" (*uqtul*) five times and to "fight" (*qatil*) twelve times (Q 2:190, 191, 193, 244; 4:76, 84, 89, 91; 8:39; 9:5, 12, 14, 29, 36, 123; 49:9). Those to be killed are variously unbelievers, polytheists and "Satan's friends." And those are just the imperatives. The Qur'an uses other forms of the same Arabic root (*q-t-l*) often also. For example, Q 2:216 tells believers that God has ordained warfare (*qital*) for them, despite their distaste for it, and Q 61:4 assures believers that "God loves those who fight for his cause" (*yuqatilu*).[14] When Q 5:33 speaks of "those who wage war against God and his messenger," it refers to physical enemies engaged in a real war against the *umma* over their refusal to submit to Muhammad's rule. It goes on to say the unrepentant among the believers' enemies should be slaughtered (*yuqattalu*), exiled, crucified or suffer alternate hand and foot amputations. In Q 33:60-61 God assures Muhammad that he will soon overpower Medina's accursed hypocrites, arrest them wherever he finds them and utterly massacre them (*quttilu taqtilan*). And Muslim historians tell us he did just that to the Jewish Qurayza tribe. Some Medinan passages even famously promise those who die while killing (*yaqtaluna*) God's enemies immediate admission to paradise (Q 9:111; 61:10-12).

Classical Muslim scholars singled out Q 9:5 and 9:29 for special attention, calling them the "sword verse" and the "tribute verse" respectively. Verse 5

---

[13]We can, therefore, hardly fault the Muslim community's later jurisprudents for using *jihad* to refer to that "full, complex doctrine and set of practices relating to the conduct of war." Yohanan Friedmann, *Tolerance and Coercion in Islam: Interfaith Relations in the Muslim Tradition* (New York: Cambridge University Press, 2003), 22.

[14]Nickel, "Islam: A Religion of Peace?"

commands Muhammad's men: "Kill (*uqtulu*) the polytheists wherever you find them, capture them, besiege them and ambush them." Verse 29 authorizes believers to fight against (*qatil*) the Jews and Christians—"until they pay tribute (*jizya*) willingly and have been humbled." So while polytheists who refused to convert were to be shown no mercy, monotheists were only to be subjugated.

A few verses later, Q 9:33 states the overall purpose of the war: God "has sent his messenger with guidance and the religion of truth, to make it prevail over all religions," including those of the Jews and Christians, who have just been accused of polytheism (Q 9:30-32).[15] Demonstrating that such supremacism is no passing sentiment on the part of the qur'anic author, this statement is repeated verbatim from two earlier passages (Q 48:28; 61:9). And since the Qur'an presents Muhammad as universally relevant, his message addressed to humankind, it makes sense that the politico-military course on which he set his community to "retake" Mecca, the Hijaz and Yemen for the true faith during his lifetime would ultimately include the rest of the world. Its mission is to ensure that the Muslim *umma* achieves its goal of universal dominion.[16]

Since qur'anic teaching must be understood in relation to key events in Muhammad's prophetic career, no credible scholar of early Islamic history can deny the Qur'an's sacralization of violence. In fact, by their principle of abrogation, Muslims have understood its later revelations to supersede earlier ones. Hence Gordon Nickel observes the following progression in the Medinan suras:

- permission to fight
- instructions on defensive warfare
- conditional permission to engage in offensive warfare
- open warfare without restriction

Authorization of the final approach—which carried the Muslims through the conquest—came only when Muhammad's position was secure enough to warrant it.[17] The classical commentators agreed that the Qur'an's later militant passages, especially the sword verse (Q 9:5), abrogated its peaceful Meccan

---

[15]On religion, see 146n13 above.
[16]Most classical Muslim scholars divided the world into two realms, that of "Islam" and of "War," meaning that any lands not yet under Muslim rule should ultimately be subjugated.
[17]Nickel, "Islam: A Religion of Peace?" Cf. Reuven Firestone, *Jihad: The Origin of Holy War in Islam* (New York: Oxford University Press, 1999), 67-91.

passages. And an indisputably clear witness to how the early *umma* understood the Qur'an comes in the form of early Islamic history, which was characterized by offensive warfare for well over a century after Muhammad's death.
Early Muslim accounts corroborate non-Muslim testimony in saying that the
Muslim conquest was not defensive only. Expunging the Qur'an of its sacred
violence by means of word games and the denial of early Islamic history is
disingenuous.[18] Violent struggle for the "Cause of God"—the expansion of
the Muslim state—is a major emphasis in the Medinan suras, vital to Muhammad's conquest of Mecca as well as his followers' turning his provincial faith
into a world religion.[19]

Hence Mawdudi and the Muslim Brotherhood (*al-Ikhwan al-Muslimun*) read
the Qur'an "with the grain"—according to its inner logic[20]—when they assert
that, since the *umma*'s goal remains universal Muslim sovereignty, believers must
"snatch power from wrongdoers" (i.e., unbelievers) whenever possible.[21] For
moderates to call the Islamists' application of the qur'anic principle of abrogation—by which peaceful commands were replaced by militaristic ones—
"a very whimsical way of dealing with Qur'anic teachings" is unreasonable because that is precisely what happened with the *umma* under Muhammad in
Medina. Abou El-Fadl is right to assert that the Qur'an calls Muslims to exercise

---

[18]Having grown frustrated with the Muslim world's political fragmentation, some Islamists have
freely invoked jihad, while others have proclaimed their leader caliph, thus "legitimizing" his call
to jihad. Though such Islamists deviate from classical Muslim understandings—which allowed
only the caliph of the worldwide *umma* to invoke jihad—they deviate less than those moderate
Muslims who claim that warfare is an un-Islamic response to a genuine threat. Ironically, for them
to mention only those few qur'anic verses that support a sanitized, Westernized version of Islam
"does violence" to the sacred text itself in the name of peace.

[19]That is not to say that Islamic religion per se spread largely by means of forced conversions in Byzantine
lands. Rather, the Muslims' military subjugation of fellow monotheists allowed for the more sustained
psychological coercion-attraction by which most subjects gradually converted to Islam, from Syria to
Andalusia. Further, while the Qur'an provided the Arabs with their vital religious rationale, historical,
economic, cultural and other factors combined in the success of their conquest. See Robert G. Hoyland, *In God's Path: The Arab Conquests and the Creation of an Islamic Empire* (New York: Oxford University
Press, 2015); Hugh Kennedy, *The Prophet and the Age of the Caliphates: The Islamic Near East from the Sixth
to the Eleventh Century*, 9th ed. (London: Longman, 2004), 59; M. A. Shaban, *Islamic History AD 600–
750 (A.H. 132): A New Interpretation* (Cambridge: Cambridge University Press, 1971), 24-25.

[20]David Marshall, *God, Muhammad and the Unbelievers: A Qur'anic Study* (London: RoutledgeCurzon,
1999), 193-94; cf. 154 above.

[21]Abul Aʿla Mawdudi, quoted in Christian W. Troll, *Dialogue and Difference: Clarity in Christian-Muslim
Relations*, trans. David Marshall (Maryknoll, NY: Orbis Books, 2009), 113. Sayyid Qutb urged his
followers similarly; John Calvert, *Sayyid Qutb and the Origins of Radical Islamism* (New York: Columbia University Press, 2010), 204-27.

temperance in their warfare, with peace—not annihilation—as the final goal (e.g., Q 2:190; 5:2; 6:108; 8:61; 41:34-36).[22] Restraint in war is never a given: dastardly war crimes have been committed by soldiers drunk on religion no less than on power, greed, racism or political ideology. Since they aimed to subjugate their foes, the more easily the Muslims achieved their goal, the easier the ensuing relationship would be for all concerned. But it is no less true that the Qur'an urges Muslims *not* to sue for peace as long as they still have the upper hand: they are to do so only when it is politically prudent (Q 47:35).

One reason the Qur'an justifies such aggression is that it is vital to evil's restraint in the world (Q 22:40). It never deems such warfare in the Cause of God unspiritual, but rather always the very opposite. Otherwise Muhammad would never himself have engaged in it.[23] Its spirituality is further confirmed by the qur'anic promise that martyrs for the cause immediately attain the bliss of paradise. If their violence were in any sense less spiritual, as the dubious hadith suggests, martyrs would never have been singled out for such honor. While the Qur'an demonstrates that some of Muhammad's followers were reluctant to participate in jihad, it roundly condemns such feeble, halfhearted faith. Indeed, its urgent attempts to secure the full commitment of such believers represent a major Medinan emphasis. Thus the reluctance of some Muslims in the nascent *umma* to engage in warfare in no way lessens the Qur'an's commitment to sacred violence.[24]

---

[22]Abou El-Fadl, *The Great Theft*, 233-41. Abou El-Fadl effectively turns qur'anic warnings against *unrestrained* aggression (e.g., Q 2:190) into a rejection of all but defensive warfare; see 235-36. His belief in the defensive nature of the Muslim conquest is the result of his making his particular understanding of qur'anic ethics the lens through which to view the entire historical record—not vice versa, with the historical record (i.e., the context) as the lens through which to view the Qur'an, including its ethics. That is not to say that the Qur'an can be held responsible for everything the conquering Muslims did, but the idea that the conquest was purely defensive is simply untenable, historically speaking. See 22-24, 36 above.

[23]Shabbir Akhtar rightly says that Islam in no way debased its own ideals after the *hijra*; *The Final Imperative: An Islamic Theology of Liberation* (London: Bellew Publishing, 1991), 31-32. We should not criticize Muhammad for his post-*hijra* politicization of religion, as if he were faithful to God in Mecca but then sold out to gain worldly power in Medina. He simply accepted religion's politicization as then practiced by Christians and Jews. The Meccan suras' apolitical nature is merely a matter of political prudence, their silence on politics pointing to their latent politics. The Meccans were possibly more averse to his preaching's political implications than its religious ones, concluding early on that Muhammad hoped to execute a bloodless coup in the name of religion.

[24]Firestone, *Jihad*, 77-84. None of the qur'anic references Firestone marshals as evidence for members of the *umma* who resisted the Qur'an's militarism say anything good about them. And the relevant hadith literature supports the idea that the "nonmilitaristic Muslim"—i.e., one with no valid reason to abstain—was essentially an oxymoron during the conquest.

Surprisingly, Q 33:62 says that all Muhammad's predecessors carried out massacres like the one to which the preceding verse refers. It assures him he "will find no change in God's practices" (Abdel Haleem). Lest we think Jesus is an exception to this, Q 9:111 envisions a militaristic Injil, stating that the promise of paradise given to martyrs (i.e., those slain in battle for God's cause) is found not only in the Qur'an but in the Torah and Injil also. While the Hebrew Bible has its strong militant streak, no one can accuse the New Testament of that, all of its calls to combat being metaphorical. This raises the question of how the qur'anic author could have understood Jesus so (cf. 2 Cor 10:3-5; 2 Tim 4:7-8).[25]

Where Jesus and Muhammad Part Ways

The New Testament actually agrees with Shabbir Akhtar's assessment that "power is no more inherently corrupting than sexuality or knowledge, or the appetite for food."[26] The Bible endorses the legitimate use of all these gifts from God, good in themselves. But as with sex, knowledge and food, so also with power: we humans have a strong tendency to render it just another form of idolatry. And idols invariably "ask for more and more, while giving less and less, until eventually they demand everything and give nothing."[27] For the New Testament writers, it was not that Jesus was "allergic to worldly power," as Akhtar contends.[28] The choice in Jesus' third wilderness temptation was not between embracing or rejecting worldly rule—for, biblically, there is no question that Jesus will yet rule the nations. Rather, his choice was between two radically different paths to power. He could either submit to his Father's will—costly though it was—and redeem the gift of power, or reject his Father's will in order to tap into Satan's illegitimate power. Political power is not inherently evil or corrupting, but any alternative to God's path to power is idolatry (Mt 4:8-10). Unlike Adam, who bowed down to Satan's hand, Jesus chose the path of submission to his Father. And the New

---

[25]Though Jesus appears to sanction the use of swords in Luke 22:36, the context makes a literal interpretation untenable, since two swords would not have helped his disciples resist his enemies (Lk 22:37-38). Being determined to offer his life in sacrifice, he sternly rebuked Peter's violence and healed his victim's ear (Lk 22:49-51; cf. Mt 26:39-46, 51-54). Jesus may have wanted swords on hand simply so he could be accused as a lawbreaker (Lk 22:37). As well, the sword he refers to in Matthew 10:34 is figurative, referring to the social divisions his teachings bring.

[26]Akhtar, Final Imperative, 31-32.

[27]Jeffrey Satinover, quoted in Andy Crouch, Playing God: Redeeming the Gift of Power (Downers Grove, IL: InterVarsity Press, 2013), 56.

[28]Akhtar, Final Imperative, 27.

Testament affirms that Jesus chose well. Forfeiting his spiritual oneness with his heavenly father for a shortcut to worldly power would have been failure (Mk 8:36). It was success, not failure, for him to give his life for the world.[29]

However, none of Jesus' disciples understood that until after his resurrection. Earlier, on realizing that Jesus was not the violent nationalist hero he had longed for, even John the Baptist had wondered whether he had been wrong to identify him as the Messiah (Mt 3:7-12; 11:1-19).[30] But it was precisely because Jesus went like a lamb to his death for sinners (Is 53:7; Acts 8:32) that he will one day rule lion-like over the nations, eradicating all evil and renewing the earth (Ps 2:6-9; Is 9:6-7; Mt 16:27; 2 Thess 1:5-10; 2 Pet 3:9-13; Rev 11:15; 19:11-21). He is the only man qualified to rule because he is the only one in all of history who never once employed his power selfishly but perfectly demonstrated God's love instead. Only thus could he win the right to exercise God's power over the earth (Is 2:1-4; 40:10-11; 42:1-4; Zech 9:9-10; Rev 5:1-10).

So while Muhammad sought to return to an Old Testament–style theocracy—with a military mandate like that of Deuteronomy 20:10-15—Jesus reframed the Old Testament prophecies such that meekness alone qualified him to exercise his power. Jesus and Muhammad both knew how hostile unbelievers can be in opposing good, but only Jesus emphasized the equal proneness of even the best of believers to self-deception and hypocrisy.[31] Beside the fact that he sought his people's freely given love, Jesus knew three things that kept him from forcing his people or the Romans over them to submit to him:

- Violence cannot ultimately defeat violence any more than evil can undo evil.

- His enemy was not Rome but rather the dark powers behind it and evil itself.

- Winning love's battle called for his "dying rather than killing."[32]

---

[29]In cleansing the temple, Jesus used precisely the force needed to dismantle misplaced "shops" and restore the space to its sacred use (Mt 21:12-13; Jn 2:14-16). Biblically, since God's people had misappropriated his house for their own selfish ends, he sent his Son to represent his interests, pronounce judgment, temporarily secure his property and await his people's response, which came soon after in their definitive rejection of Jesus. Hence, a key aspect of Jesus' mission was to seek his people's love, and, when they refused, he loved them to the end.

[30]This makes it easy to see why Muhammad did not appreciate Jesus' approach to power. Further, Muhammad would have assumed that the gospel should be viewed through the lens of the Byzantines, who had long since adapted it to meet their own need for divinely sanctioned power.

[31]The Qur'an does emphasize hypocrisy, but only that of its "hypocrites" (*munafiqun*), who comprise the worst of unbelievers (see 122 above). It thus effectively counteracts Jesus' emphasis.

[32]Tremper Longman III, "The God of War," *Christianity Today*, May 1, 2003, www.christianitytoday .com/ct/2003/may/30.62.html.

Jesus reveals the same God whose mercy and justice, goodness and severity, made him take the field as the mighty Warrior-King against evil throughout the Old Testament, but now on an entirely different level. Jesus' enemy was far bigger than Rome, but he knew of a power that nothing can resist. That is why he went to the cross.

Generals and dictators can all restrain evil to some degree. But they can also use their weapons to commit evil acts, obliterate cultural treasures and, worse, sever bodies limb from limb. Because those issuing the orders and wielding the weapons are themselves imperfect, any effect they have for good will be imperfect. By contrast, love is perfect, and even the simplest believer led by God's Spirit can wield it effectively, whether by life or by death. Violence has an amazing ability to perpetuate itself. It can proliferate, and it can penetrate good things. But the one thing it cannot do is defeat violence. Only one power in the world can do that, namely love.

That is why Jesus' Father called him to counter human falsehood, injustice and violence with only love, expressing itself in humility, mercy and justice. As gracious as Jesus was toward the fallen, he was never limp-wristed in the face of evil. To establish God's just rule on earth, he fought passionately but without engaging in violence (Is 42:1-4). He refused equally to coerce others to submit to him and to stop loving in the face of cruel and sustained opposition. And therein lay his victory. Though that victory still awaits its full realization, it was nevertheless decisive, allowing him to unleash the power of his invincible love to his followers. So their being limited to the same weapons he used—love, truth lived and proclaimed, and believing prayer—does not actually handicap them in fight: there simply are no better weapons to be had (2 Cor 10:3-5). This is what makes the news of God's kingdom rule perfectly expressed in Jesus so very good despite all its challenges: the meek shall indeed inherit the earth (Ps 37:11; Mt 5:5).

Ultimately, the New Testament and the Qur'an are at loggerheads over the nature of the human problem and its solution. The Qur'an, confidently asserting that it is the perfect scripture, claims to be all we need. According to its guidance, Muslims can overcome collective evil by military, political and legal means, knowing that—however imperfect—the results are far better than the alternatives. The New Testament, however, insists that human depravity runs far too deep to make that project feasible and that there can be no true theocracy without God himself present.[33] For that reason, until Christ returns, his followers should simply throw their energy into supporting and reforming existing human governments with a view to society's renewal.

Discounting Jesus' choice (Mt 5:5), the Qur'an quotes not Psalm 37:11, "The meek . . ." but rather Psalm 37:29, "The righteous will inherit the earth" (Q 21:105). For meekness simply is not the virtue in the Qur'an that it is in the Bible. Many things follow from this. The Qur'an implicitly views might as the only way right can win in the world and makes fear and social stigma primary spiritual motivators. It also makes respect for unbelievers occasional, since its essential coercion represents their objectification—and violent coercion the ultimate objectification—despite its supposedly being in their best interest.[34] On some level, the Qur'an's constituting the *umma* a state makes coercion intrinsic to religion, and a single language and culture essential to all.

In sharp contrast to Muhammad, Jesus willingly surrendered his rights and rejected the struggle for physical domination. He modeled radical humility for us so that we might give up on all our "god playing" (Phil 2:5-11). And he thus redeemed the gift of power, revealing our often well-intentioned abuse of it for what it is.[35] While the New Testament writers present a God who cares deeply about peace, they would utterly reject any human effort to unite the world by violent means in God's name. In fact, they would view it as parody of what God has so decisively done in Jesus.

Religious Tolerance in the Qur'an

In view of the early Muslim understanding of jihad, the question arises: What place did the early *umma* give to the idea of religious tolerance? As noted

---

[33]In a theocracy, it is not enough for God to give his law, as he did at Sinai. He must also oversee its interpretation and implementation. Otherwise, it is all too easily rendered a tool of oppression in the hands of sinful rulers and judges, as Israel's subsequent history attests.

Concerning biblical teaching on state-sponsored violence, the Hebrew scriptures authorize only defensive warfare, with one major exception—that being the three-century window from Joshua to Solomon. That particular case of warfare was exceptional in every sense. By contrast, the New Testament endorses the rule of law but does not identify God's kingdom with any human state. Christians may resort to physical force only when all other defensive options have failed and must contain its use as much as possible. This understanding flows from an awareness of the anomalous place legitimate violence has in God's economy. And the very same holds true for engaging in violence out of personal self-defense; John G. Stackhouse, Jr., *Making the Best of It: Following Christ in the Real World* (New York: Oxford University Press, 2008), 247.

[34]In the West the Spanish Inquisition took the same approach and with similarly tragic results.

[35]Crouch, *Playing God*, 73-75.

above, while Q 109:6—"To you your religion and to me mine"—seems very tolerant, it was really just an appeal to Mecca's pagans to let him and his followers be. Ironically, once Muhammad was in a position of power, he did not show the same tolerance of pagans that he had asked them to show him. And even the key verse on tolerance, Q 2:256, implicitly distinguishes between monotheists and polytheists, many thousands of whom were forcibly converted by Muhammad's armies in Mecca and beyond.

Regarding the precept that "there is no compulsion in religion," most Muslim scholars take one of two different approaches. Some view it as having been abrogated by various later qur'anic calls to war, noted above, while others believe it expresses the Qur'an's abiding concern that no Christian or Jew who willingly submits to Muslim rule be forced to convert to Islam. The actions of Muslim armies to cleanse the Arabian Peninsula of its Christians and Jews may be used to argue for the first view, while the second view is in line with most of the larger history of the conquest outside Arabia. Fortunately, this second interpretation is held by the majority of scholars,[36] although it is hard to know what that will count for in the interpretive free-for-all into which modernity has now plunged the Muslim world. Ironically, the Muslim "occasions of the revelation" (*asbab al-nuzul*) assign the verse's revelation to the expulsion of Medina's Jewish tribe of Banu Nadir. Whether or not that was its real context, we must read it in its seventh-century historical context. It clearly cannot be taken to establish full freedom of religion for all monotheists in twenty-first century, pluralistic terms.

On the Muslim concept of tolerance, there was significant toleration of fellow monotheists in that they were allowed to keep their religion and practice it openly to some extent, although toleration did not come without its price.[37]

---

[36]A third approach is that of Muslim modernists. North African Qur'an commentator Ibn Ashur (d. 1973), for example, turns the debate on its head, arguing that Q 2:256 completely abrogates any notion of jihad aimed at conversion. Not only is this in contravention of the entire exegetical tradition, which views Sura 2 as preceding Suras 4 and 9 chronologically, but it also flies in the face of the history of the Muslim state under Muhammad and his successors. See Friedmann, *Tolerance and Coercion in Islam*, 103.

[37]Their public practice of religion was limited to churches and synagogues. Some versions of the "Covenant of ʿUmar" even prohibited subjugated Christian and Jewish parents from teaching their own children about the Qur'an; Andrew Rippin, "Western Scholarship and the Qur'an," in *The Cambridge Companion to the Qur'an*, ed. Jane Dammen McAulifffe (New York: Cambridge University Press, 2006), 237. Indeed, even today there is no chance that a book such as this could legally be published in countries where the sharia remains in effect.
Practically speaking, allowing their fellow monotheists to coexist with them enabled the Muslims to learn from their much more advanced civilizations. And this made a great deal of cultural

Under the *dhimma*, or treaty of subjugation, Jews and Christians were required to accept religious, social, legal, cultural and economic subordination in return for protection from the state and the right to own property, worship and exercise considerable intracommunal autonomy. For example, Jews and Christians were permitted to drink alcohol, forbidden to Muslims, and allowed to maintain parallel courts in which many of their laws were applied within their ghettoized communities.[38] By seventh-century standards, this was fairly generous. Negatively, however, the *dhimma*'s humbling visibly chastised non-Muslims for refusing to convert, while positively encouraging conversion. Non-Muslims were simultaneously forbidden either to hinder their members from converting to Islam or to encourage Muslims to convert to their faith. So their position was one of public humiliation and subordination, the breach of which could threaten their property and even their lives. In practice, these restrictions were not always enforced, leading to extended periods of relative equality and peace between Muslims and subjugated Christians and Jews. But "inferiority and insecurity were the essence of the arrangement"[39] and were never far from the life of the *dhimmi*, or subjugated monotheist.[40]

That situation characterized the Muslim world until colonialism led to the demise of the *dhimma* in the nineteenth century. Since decolonization, Muslim governments continued formally to endorse the principle of equal citizenship by law, although long-established cultural patterns did not disappear. For decades, formal reinstatement of the *dhimma* was inconceivable. But the success of Islamist groups has made possible the crossing of that

---

borrowing on the part of Muslims possible. As the Muslims' approach to non-Muslims evolved, they gave Mazdeans and even Hindus who surrendered to their armies a treaty (*dhimma*) making certain demands and granting them certain rights and exemptions. Qur'anically, such protection was extended to fellow monotheists alone. While many Muslims held to that position during the early period, ultimately pragmatism won the day, and a much broader application of the *dhimma* prevailed—at least, until radical Islamism was born.

[38] Some sharia laws overrode Christian or Jewish laws, however—for example, the law of blasphemy, by which any ridiculer or blasphemer of Muhammad (or God) must face the death penalty. While there is no basis for the law of blasphemy in the Qur'an, there is historical precedent in Muhammad's assassinations of poets Kab ibn al-Ashraf and Asma bint Marwan and his killing of his most vocal Meccan opponents when the city surrendered. For more on this, see Friedmann, *Tolerance and Coercion in Islam*, 149-52.

[39] Mark Movsesian, "Religious Freedom for Mideast Christians, Yesterday and Today" (lecture, Lanier Theological Library, September 26, 2014), www.laniertheologicallibrary.org/videos.

[40] For more on this topic, see Yohanan Friedmann, *Tolerance and Coercion in Islam*, especially chap. 3. Friedmann limits his focus to Sunni practice during the classical period.

key psychological barrier to institute formally the public humiliation and oppression of non-Muslims again.[41]

However, the Muslims' tolerance was at least initially restricted to Christian and Jewish communities who had made treaties submitting to Muslim rule. It did not necessarily apply to Christian or Jewish women and children regarded as property—those taken in war, concubines or female or child slaves separated from their families. Sunni scholars differed somewhat on these various points, but they agreed that Q 2:256 did not apply to all monotheists—only to those under treaty protection. And as already noted, most jurists agreed that religious tolerance did not apply to nonmonotheists. That notion is supported by the history of Muhammad's armies sweeping across Arabia and giving its pagan inhabitants the choice of either conversion or death. Neither does the sharia deem religious tolerance relevant to apostates, as we shall see.

Further, acceptance of the other monotheistic communities never meant full equality with Muslims under the law. Jews and Christians were allowed to retain their faith, but their practice of it was carefully restricted to ensure its ultimate demise. For example, in the decades after Muhammad there was some Muslim practice of expropriating churches and synagogues at will. And with that came the prohibition of building new or enlarging existing ones. Furthermore, all public practice of Christianity or Judaism was restricted to those buildings. Jewish and Christian tribes and towns that had surrendered to the Muslim armies were also required to pay the *jizya* in exchange for their safety and protection of the rights they were accorded. This was a part of their being visibly humbled (Q 9:29), as was the sharia's requirement that they wear distinctive clothing in public. Further, the sharia forbade non-Muslims from testifying in court against Muslims. The idea, then, was to allow them to live under Muslim rule, but on two bases. Those were that they accept their place as second-class citizens—barred from enjoying the full rights of citizenship until they converted to Islam—and that their religion was doomed to decline, as it inevitably has.

The Law of Apostasy

As noted above, despite the prevalent Muslim interpretation of Q 2:256, Islamic jurisprudents produced a great deal of material discussing who should

---

[41]Movsesian, "Religious Freedom for Mideast Christians."

actually be forced to accept Islam. One group consistently targeted for coercion is apostates (*murtaddun*), those who have renounced their Muslim faith in favor of another. The jurists considered the apostate's infidelity worse than that of an infidel who has never been a Muslim. Legally, in fact, the apostate's position is like that of a deceased person, with no rights at all. In fact, conversion from Islam to another religion is not technically deemed possible from a legal standpoint, since the apostate's conversion leaves her "religionless."[42] While Muslims should not kill an unbeliever who is not a combatant, killing an apostate who refuses to repent is mandatory and is the responsibility of her family, thus maximizing psychological coercion aimed at restoring the apostate to the Muslim fold. Hence the sharia effectively makes profession of the Muslim faith irreversible, ensuring that many profess faith in Islam for no other reason than that they are not free to do otherwise.

What is the basis for the sharia's ruling on apostates? The sole qur'anic basis for it is the Qur'an's warning that God will send valiant soldiers against apostates and punish them harshly in the world to come (Q 2:217; 3:86, 90; 9:74; 47:25). But using a wartime threat to justify peacetime executions is suspect. The main basis for the sharia's ruling on apostasy comes from the *sunna*, or example of Muhammad, because some traditions describe as apostates three of those he executed when Mecca surrendered.[43] The hadith also make "a sustained effort to demonstrate that the qur'anic view according to which apostasy is punishable only in the hereafter began to change while the Prophet was still alive." This suggests that the tribal rebellion after Muhammad's death prompted the change of attitude and highlights the degree of coercion used during the early period and the level of instability it produced.[44]

In any case, a majority of jurists from every school of legal interpretation agree that apostates from Islam deserve the death penalty. Most schools require that the apostate be given a chance to repent, but there is considerable disagreement over how that should be done and whether the same standard

---

[42]Friedmann, *Tolerance and Coercion in Islam*, 123-24.

[43]Some hadith tell of people whom Muhammad spared when they repented of their apostasy; ibid., 125. But none tell of his sparing any apostates who refused to repent.

[44]Only those Christians and Jews who submitted to Muslim rule without contest were permitted to keep their religion. The rest of the subjugated population in the rapidly expanding empire—including the wives and children of Christians and Jews killed for resisting Muslim rule—were coerced into becoming Muslims; ibid., 126.

200 THE QUR'AN IN CONTEXT

applies to all Muslims. For example, most say that, unlike men, women apostates are not to be killed but only imprisoned and forced to convert.[45] Regardless, there is no doubt that in classical Muslim thinking, while non-Muslims are permitted to convert *to* Islam, Muslims are not free to convert *from* Islam. For centuries this posed no apparent problem for Muslims, but under the impact of Western values, many Muslims today find the law of apostasy troubling, with some granting Q 2:256 the ability to override the sharia's approach to apostasy.[46]

Based on the hadith and the *sira*, Muslim jurisprudents began to treat blasphemy under the rubric of apostasy. By the ninth century a consensus had developed that anyone blaspheming Muhammad deserves to die. And so it found its way into the sharia. While the Qur'an does not specifically say that blasphemy or slander of Muhammad must be punished, it does give us a clear sense that words uttered against the Prophet were taken as acts of treason.[47] In many Muslim countries today the sharia is either not applied or only partially implemented in favor of a postcolonial system based on European law. Despite that fact, more than twenty Muslim countries currently make apostasy a crime, usually a capital offense.[48] Others without apostasy laws—Pakistan, for example—have such broadly defined blasphemy laws that they work in virtually the same way. Even in secular Turkey, contrary to Turkish law, Muslim families applying the death penalty to apostate family members are never prosecuted.

The Biblical Approach to Tolerance and Apostasy

Having already spoken of tolerance in the New Testament,[49] a summary statement will suffice here. Though Christians intoxicated by worldly power have often ignored biblical teaching on it, three truths about the New Testament church make religious intolerance unacceptable:

- The church is not a geopolitical entity with the right to enforce religious conformity.

---

[45]Ibid.

[46]For example, Abdullah Saeed and Hassan Saeed, *Freedom of Religion, Apostasy and Islam* (Burlington, VT: Ashgate, 2004).

[47]See 197n38 above.

[48]The Library of Congress, "Laws Criminalizing Apostasy," accessed October 21, 2014, www.loc.gov/law /help/apostasy/index.php.

[49]See 136-38 above.

- Its Lord has demonstrated how personally committed God is to religious freedom.

- All coercion in religion is ruled out by the New Testament's law of love.

Commanded to love and respect everyone and do to their enemies as they would want done to them, Christians are given no room whatsoever to coerce anyone in matters of faith or spirituality.

While the Mosaic law makes an Israelite's participation in idolatry, blasphemy or witchcraft an offense punishable by death (Ex 22:18; Lev 20:27; 24:14-16; Deut 13), such laws were in force only when Israel exercised political sovereignty. The New Testament views these sins no less seriously than the Old Testament, as infringements on God's exclusive right to our love and trust (Rom 1:23; Gal 5:19-21; Rev 21:8). But it nowhere makes them capital offenses. Instead, after multiple warnings, the believer who flagrantly sins or denies the faith is simply to be excluded from the community of faith. That amounts to its releasing her to God's judgment in the hope that she will repent and be restored to faith and fellowship again (1 Cor 5:5, 7, 9, 11, 13; 2 Thess 3:14-15; 1 Tim 1:20; Tit 3:10), for the punishment of unbelievers belongs to God alone (Rom 12:17-21; 2 Thess 1:5-10). This follows the example of such prophets as Moses, David and Paul—not to mention Jesus—who left their defense to God (Num 12:1-15; 2 Sam 15–18; Lk 22:47–23:43; 1 Cor 3:4-14; Col 1:23-2:3).[50] Further, while the New Testament does warn believers sternly about the dangers of rejecting God's grace, it has no concept of an irreversible profession of faith, a religious version of the Eagles' Hotel California, where guests are perfectly free to check out so long as they never leave. And it grants the believer no role in judging unbelievers beyond that of prophet, whose unheeded words and deeds may seal their eternal fate.

The Dynamics of Communal Spirituality

The Qur'an and Bible agree that faith cannot mean mere mental acceptance: true faith invariably expresses itself in corresponding action. Accordingly, the Qur'an repeatedly couples good and bad belief with corresponding behavior (e.g., Q 2:82; 18:30, 88; 22:50, 56; 29:7, 9, 58). In the Gospels Jesus likewise

---

[50]That is, the biblical prophets typically left the defense of their own honor to God. Again on this point, the qur'anic text is clearly aligned more with Hijazi culture than with biblical thought.

emphasizes oneness of thought and deed, and James insists that faith without corresponding actions is dead (Jas 2:18-26). Both the Qur'an and Bible champion a holistic spirituality, by which one's faith and moral values speak to every sphere of human life, permitting no secular-sacred dichotomy.

The Qur'an rejects many pagan values, calling believers to conform to the values and norms modeled by Muhammad. In place of *jahili* egocentrism with its resultant hedonism and injustice, the Qur'an mandates absolute loyalty to the prophet's *umma*, mercy and justice for the poor, and a disciplined approach to mainly traditional lifeways. As previously noted, there are many similarities between qur'anic and biblical values and spirituality. However, the Qur'an's supertribalism combines with its geopolitical vision to externalize faith and yield an ethic of external communal success. As we have seen, the Qur'an focuses on "watershed sins" and gives relatively little attention to the duplicitous nature of the human heart—the believer's heart too. Given that outer conformity is all that law can regulate in a community's members, this qur'anic emphasis and deemphasis externalizes faith in the sense that the more observable a behavior is, the more it matters. By the same token, the more observable a proscribed behavior is, the more intolerable. What matters supremely is the community's *visible* success.

The Qur'an does warn that God will punish our secret thoughts, not just our visible deeds (Q 2:284; 6:120, 151; 7:33). However, al-Ghazali says that private sins are more tolerable than public sins, that adultery or any other sin committed in secret is less evil than the same sin indulged in with public knowledge. Though the Qur'an never explicitly endorses it, Ghazali's position is broadly consistent with qur'anic teaching. And most Muslims would agree that the moral tone of the community is far more important than either the individual's deceit or the motives behind it. Though the Qur'an never disparages personal piety before God, it almost seems as if the individual exists solely for the sake of community. This is the result of its stress on morality's communal dimensions, its acceptance of Arab tribal culture's distinct orientation toward shame, as opposed to guilt, and its avoidance of personal relationship with God.

By contrast, though Jesus' culture was similarly shame based, he takes various Mosaic prohibitions and goes the opposite direction with them, stressing the importance of what happens in the heart and mind before anything gets acted out or seen (e.g., murder and adultery in Mt 5:21-30). So while both scriptures are equally intense in handling moral issues, they differ dramatically in how they focus that intensity. The Qur'an stresses communal solidarity around Muhammad's leadership and propriety as defined by tribal Arabs, while Jesus stresses the sins of the heart within the context of right relation to him and each other.[51]

On jihad, apostasy, blasphemy and even tolerance under the *dhimma*, the sharia reflects the severity by which Muhammad's *umma* defended its power and cardinal values. Though the Qur'an says little specifically about either apostasy or blasphemy, its emphasis on obedience to God's messenger probably made that unnecessary. During his Meccan period, Muhammad reasoned patiently with unbelievers and endured their ridicule without retaliating (Q 33:14). But the Medinan suras reflect a radically different approach toward unbelievers and view hypocrisy—often equivalent to apostasy—as one of the most heinous of sins.[52] In Arabia's shame- and honor-based culture, a leader's public ridicule was to be endured only if he was powerless to stop it. And the hadith confirm the Medinan picture of Muhammad as a leader who— once he had the power he lacked in Mecca—became intolerant of ridicule, ordering the assassination of those who attacked him only verbally.

---

[51]Today's secular model, by contrast, largely disparages communal morality. That model often implicitly endorses Jesus' criticism of hypocrisy, but free from any fixed moral standards. This means an individual's right to define morality as she chooses is enhanced if she does so openly—regardless of her motivation—for no other reason than that she publically owns her choices. The New Testament firmly refuses the notion that individuals are free to choose their own moral standards, in rejection of the law of love Jesus modeled for us.

[52]For example, Muhammad is urged to fight against oath breakers (Q 8:12-13; 9:72; 59:2-7).

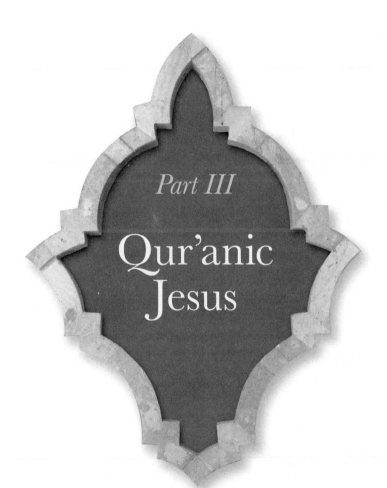

Part III

Qur'anic
Jesus

Fourteen

Jesus' Origins *and* Person

Theologically speaking, Jesus' identity was at the heart of Late Antique Arabia's great Jewish-Christian contest. Not surprisingly then, he is one of the Qur'an's most controversial prophets and is central to its reformed version of monotheism. To counter the Jewish polemic and insist on Jesus' inclusion, the Qur'an devotes much of its attention here to establishing Jesus' nobility, his mother's purity and his virgin birth. It also calls him the Messiah and gives him other titles, although such honorifics add little substance to his person. The Qur'an has the devout John the Baptist endorse Jesus and presents Jesus as sinless to establish the sterling credentials on which his unqualified backing of Muhammad rests. But honored as Jesus is, he is essentially no different from any other prophet before him. Since he is human and God's "servant," he cannot be divine, for qur'anically, it is unthinkable that God would cross the Creator-creature divide or ever humble himself. Hence the Qur'an impugns orthodox Christian belief on Jesus' deity, and it does so through a mixture of serious attack and lampoon. It also carefully limits Jesus' stature to ensure that he does not eclipse Muhammad.

*T*he topic of Jesus was a hot one in Muhammad's Arabia because religion was then all-important, the contest being between Christianity, Judaism and paganism. Also, Mecca was a pagan town close to a trade route with large Jewish and Christian populations at both ends. Christians and pagans knew Jesus, who the Qur'an calls *'Isa*, as the "Son of God," but with very different mean-ings.[1] Christians also called him the "Word of God," and everyone knew of Jesus' disputed title "Messiah," though pagans may not have grasped its bib-lical meanings.[2] Everyone also knew of the Christians' annual celebrations of Jesus' life—Christmas and Easter—celebrations local Jews likely considered anti-Semitic. In fact, next to Muhammad himself, Jesus was the most contro-versial figure in the Qur'an. It did not speak into a vacuum when it spoke of him. Everything it said about him either confirmed or challenged prevailing views. And its reformation of both Judaism and Christianity related crucially to beliefs about Jesus' person, among other things.

Despite widespread disagreement on Jesus, Muhammad's entire audience would have agreed on a number of points about him, two of which were that he was born under morally suspect circumstances and had earned a reputation for performing healings and other incredible feats, whether by miracle or magic. (Jesus' death by crucifixion is another point of agreement, one to which we will return in chapter sixteen.) Hence we should not be surprised to find those two points at the heart of qur'anic teaching on him. In fact, both are integral to its two major affirmations about him: his prophetic greatness, on the one hand, and his prediction of Muhammad, on the other. In fact, Jesus' virgin birth, moral purity, miracles and honorifics are what establish the sterling credentials on which his endorsement of Muhammad rests.

Jesus' Background

The Qur'an devotes more than two-thirds of its total number of verses on Jesus to his origins,[3] beginning with narratives of the childhood of Mary (*Maryam*) and the birth of John the Baptist (*Yahya*) to Zechariah (*Zakariyya*; Q 3:33-41; 19:2-11; 21:89-90).[4] The primary significance of the former is that Mary's

---

[1]Used some twenty-five times and of uncertain origins, *'Isa* is Jesus' proper name in the Qur'an; Arthur Jeffery, *The Foreign Vocabulary of the Qur'an* (Baroda, India: Oriental Institute, 1938), 219. On the Qur'an's use of *'Isa*, see 259 below.

[2]The Qur'an's echoing of various Jesus narratives, whether biblical or apocryphal, does not neces-sarily tell us how familiar the Hijazi Arabs were with them. See 40-41 above.

[3]Of its ninety-three verses about Jesus, the Qur'an devotes fewer than thirty to his ministry, teaching and death; Kenneth Cragg, *Jesus and the Muslim* (London: George Allen & Unwin, 1985), 25.

[4]*Maryam* represents the Syriac (and Ethiopic) version of her name. The names John (*Yahya*) and Zechariah (*Zakariyya*) may be of Mandaean origins; Geoffrey Parrinder, *Jesus in the Qur'an* (Oxford: Oneworld, 1995), 55.

mother dedicates her to God before birth and commends her and her offspring to his protection from Satan at birth (Q 3:36). Implicitly, then, Mary and Jesus were protected from evil, he from before birth. Mary is raised in the temple by Zechariah, a righteous prophet (Q 3:37-39, 44; 6:85; 19:11). Mary's faith encourages that of the aged Zechariah, who prays for a son despite its impossibility.[5] Hence the Qur'an pictures Mary, born into a pious family, as a model of faith and purity from birth and raised by a devout prophet within a sacred precinct.[6] As in the Bible, when Zechariah asks for a sign, he is struck mute. He likewise breaks with tradition in naming his son John, characterized as chaste and devout (Q 3:38-41; cf. Q 19:2-11; 21:89-90). The Qur'an defines John's role as confirming "a word from" God, referring to Jesus (Q 3:39; cf. Q 3:45). So John's story points to his spirituality and his endorsement of Jesus.

The Annunciation and Birth

While it has no female prophets, the Qur'an honors Mary by making her the only woman it names. Mary's pregnancy out of wedlock leaves her open to accusations of immorality and her son to accusations of illegitimacy. Striving to counter Jewish slander, the Qur'an aims to establish the purity of Jesus' conception.[7] Hence the Qur'an prefaces the annunciation with the assurance that God has purified Mary and, as in the biblical account, has chosen her "above all women" (Q 3:42). Frightened at the appearance of what seems to be a man, Mary casts herself on God's protection. When the angel informs her of his mission to give her a faultless boy, she replies, "How can I have a son when no man has touched me?" And the angel answers, "It is easy for me" (Q 3:42-51; 19:16-21).

After going into seclusion, Mary delivers her son under a palm tree. Exhausted and afraid to face her family, she wishes for death and is counseled by her newborn to drink from an as-yet-unseen rivulet at her feet and shake the palm tree overhead for fresh dates. This echoes elements found in the

---

[5]These stories faintly echo stories from "The Protoevangelium of James," in R. McL. Wilson, *Gospels and Related Writings*, vol. 1 of *New Testament Apocrypha*, ed. Wilhelm Schneemelcher, 2nd ed. (Louisville: Westminster John Knox, 1991), 426-30.

[6]For more on Mary and her role in the Qur'an, see Barbara Freyer Stowasser, *Women in the Qur'an, Traditions, and Interpretation* (New York: Oxford University Press, 1994), 67-82; and Jane I. Smith and Yvonne Y. Haddad, "The Virgin Mary in Islamic Tradition and Commentary," *The Muslim World* 79 (July/October 1989): 161-87.

[7]Q 66:12 calls Mary "the daughter of Amram ['Imran] who guarded her chastity." Implicitly, the Qur'an is insisting that she is not the kind of woman who would ever have had unlawful sex.

Gospel of Pseudo-Matthew, an apocryphal birth narrative.[8] The Qur'an takes the idea of a talking baby further when it has Jesus command his mother to keep silent on her return home and leave all the explaining to him (Q 19:22-26). Mary thus counters the accusations of her kinfolk simply by pointing to her baby, who eloquently replies, "I am the servant of God. He has given me the scripture and made me a prophet. And he has made me blessed wherever I am and charged me to pray and give alms as long as I live." He then describes his own exemplary character and pronounces a triple blessing on himself (Q 19:27-33).

Parallels with John the Baptist

Though in one sense the stories of Jesus' origins and birth are meant to honor him, Sura 19 also employs three parallels to limit Jesus' honor by putting him on a par with John:

- Zechariah and Mary ask how the promised conception can be possible, and the angel replies to both: "It is easy for me . . ." (Q 19:8-9, 20-21).

- The character of John and Jesus is described in strikingly similar terms: obedient, not overbearing or rebellious (Q 19:14, 32).[9]

- A virtually identical blessing is pronounced over each, blessing the birth, death and resurrection of each man (Q 19:15, 33).

These parallels imply the prophetic sameness of the two men. Jesus' birth becomes like John's since both are impossible and yet easy for God. Jesus' character is essentially the same as John's. Likewise, Jesus is put on the level of John with respect to his comprehensive blessedness.[10]

We saw above that two points are made emphatic with regard to John: his spirituality and his role as endorser of Jesus' prophethood. The parallels just seen tie in with this, since Jesus' primary role is precisely that of John: just as the Qur'an establishes John's moral stature in order to make him a trustworthy

---

[8]Drawing on earlier materials, Pseudo-Matthew tells how Joseph worried about their lack of water on the flight to Egypt, while Mary sat under a palm tree, wishing for its fruit. The infant on Mary's lap then commands the tree to share its fruit and water with Mary, and it immediately complies; a spring appears at Mary's feet. Both Q 19:26 and the Gospel of Pseudo-Matthew mention Mary's joy on eating and drinking; the Qur'an's echoing of this nonessential detail demonstrates the direct connection between the two accounts. Wilson, *Gospels and Related Writings*, 463.

[9]Sura 3 offers a similar parallel, describing each man as "one of the righteous" (vv. 39, 46).

[10]Q 4:157-58 aside, Q 19:33 gives no indication that Jesus' death or resurrection is extraordinary.

endorser of Jesus' prophethood, it says even more of Jesus' moral caliber. Being sinless, Jesus is still more trustworthy in his dual task of confirming the essential sameness of his revelation with earlier revelations and endorsing Muhammad's prophethood—and thus the Qur'an. Jesus' authority in each depends on his prophetic nobility and greatness.

Similarities and Differences

We find three key points of similarity between Jesus' birth narrative in the Qur'an and the Bible:

1. Jesus' miraculous conception is preceded by that of John the Baptist.

2. An angel tells the exemplary Mary that she will conceive Jesus without a father.

3. She gives birth to him while still a virgin.

However, the qur'anic image of an eloquent and authoritarian newborn baby is radically different from anything we find in the Gospels and makes Jesus look very odd—freakish, even.

There are many other differences between the biblical and qur'anic accounts of Jesus' background and birth. True to its overall approach, the Qur'an says nothing of the historical context of Jesus' birth. Q 66:12 tells us only that Mary is the daughter of Amram ('*Imran*). Since the Bible makes Amram the father of Aaron, Miriam—also *Maryam* in Arabic—and Moses, it seems the qur'anic author confuses the two women (Num 26:59).[11] The Qur'an has Jesus born in the desert and says nothing of Joseph or the census that took him and Mary to Bethlehem, Herod's hostility to Jesus, or the flight to Egypt (Mt 2:13-23). Neither does it include the Magnificat, the angelic chorus, Simeon and Anna's blessings or the visit of the magi, since they present Jesus as Messiah or savior of the world (Mt 2:1-12; Lk 2:8-38).

With regard to Jesus' birth, the Qur'an focuses on Jesus' conception as a display of God's miraculous power.[12] Biblically, however, it goes beyond just

---

[11]Later commentators field numerous explanations. For example, Baydawi surmises that the fathers of the two Maryams were both named Amram. But the qur'anic author also calls Mary the sister of Aaron (Q 19:28), doubling the coincidence and stretching plausibility still further. Muslim believers, however, view Mary's being called "Aaron's sister" as a teknonym (*kunya*) meaning Aaron's descendant; Parrinder, *Jesus in the Qur'an*, 64, 78.

[12]Qur'anically understood, however, Jesus' virgin birth in no way suggests his divinity.

the miracle. Jesus is conceived without a human father because Jesus is the "descendant of the woman," promised so long before to Eve (Gen 3:15). Mary is honored "above all women" because her faith and humble submission to God lay hold of his promise of true greatness, in contrast to Eve's rebellious embrace of the serpent's proffered delusion of grandeur. It is thus that she bears the Christ child, "God with us" (Is 7:14).[13]

A Prophet, but Only Human

Although the Qur'an gives Jesus a variety of titles, none of them exceed the category of prophethood. Hence the Qur'an most frequently calls him either God's messenger (*rasul*) or prophet (*nabi*). Like a number of other prophets, Jesus is sent to the children of Israel, suggesting that the scope of his mission was only national (Q 3:49). While *nabi* and *rasul* are synonymous, the Qur'an unquestionably ranks Jesus as being among its greatest prophets.

But exalted as he is, Jesus is not essentially different from any other prophet before him. And as we have seen, this has the effect of homogenizing all their messages. So against the Jewish rejection of Jesus, the Qur'an insists that God alone determines who is and is not his prophet—for to deny a prophet is to usurp the place of God. But likewise, against Christianity's deification of him, it insists that Jesus is "just a messenger of God" (Q 4:171; 5:75).

One of Jesus' commonest titles in the Qur'an, used twenty-three times, is "son of Mary" (*ibn Maryam*).[14] In the Qur'an this title alludes to three things:

- Jesus' noble origins (including his mother's purity)

- his miraculous birth

- his nondivinity, for having a mother means he cannot possibly be God

Since the Qur'an views "human" and "divine" as mutually exclusive categories, the "son of Mary" is emphatically not the "Son of God."[15] But that is not to suggest that "son of Mary" is in any way negative. While Arabs typically go by

---

[13]Just as Eve's unbelief under ideal circumstances introduced sin to our race, it is through a young woman's faith under highly onerous conditions that the Savior comes to us. Poor girl though she is, she is called to bear a child conceived out of wedlock in a society utterly intolerant of such rule breaking. It is specifically that child who crushes the serpent's head (Gen 3:15; Lk 1:32).

[14]By contrast, the New Testament refers to Jesus as the "son of Mary" just once (Mk 6:3).

[15]Neither does the Qur'an ever use Jesus' preferred self-designation in the Gospels, "Son of Man," with its truly messianic (i.e., redemptive) meaning.

their patronymic, a matronymic signifies no inferiority if one's mother holds a particularly noble status, as Mary certainly does in the Qur'an.

Another title meant to deny Jesus' divinity is that of God's "servant" (*'abd*). Q 43:59 says Jesus is "only a servant on whom we have bestowed favor." Jesus' servanthood is not meant to detract from his prophetic greatness, for no prophet is greater than he is submissive to God. Thus Q 4:172 says, "The Messiah will not disdain to be a servant of God." But as we have seen, God must never be confused with his servant. For the Creator emphatically submits to no one, submission belonging exclusively to the category of creature. By contrast, the Bible presents Jesus' lordship and his servitude as inherently one: it was precisely his willingness to humble himself as God's servant—even dying a criminal's death—that made him the exalted Lord of all (Phil 2:5-11).

Jesus the Messiah

In fact, the Qur'an piles mores honorific titles on Jesus than on any other prophet apart from Muhammad. It calls him the Messiah or Christ (*al-masih*, from the Hebrew *mašîaḥ*) some eleven times (Q 3:45; 4:157, 171-72; 5:72, 75; 9:30-31). But lest this be thought to ascribe divinity to Jesus, the Qur'an insists that "The Messiah . . . is nothing but a messenger" and "They have disbelieved who say, 'God is the Messiah, son of Mary'" (Q 5:17, 72, 75). Hence, again, the Qur'an seeks to strike the balance between what it sees as Jewish deficiency on the one hand and Christian excess on the other: though Jesus is indisputably one of God's great prophets, even the Messiah, he is emphatically not divine. The qur'anic position is nonnegotiable on both counts. But what is actually meant by the term *Messiah* is unclear. Fairuzabadi's Arabic dictionary says there are over fifty explanations of *al-masih*.[16] Even those commentators who relate it to the Hebrew verb "to anoint"—its biblical derivation—explain it not in terms of God's anointing Jesus as redeemer but rather Jesus' anointing the sick with oil. That the early commentators should be so divided over the word's meaning leaves us wondering what Muhammad's ordinary hearers could be expected to make of it. Baidawi's suggestion, that it is simply Jesus' surname, is likely the most helpful in that it shows qur'anic usage of the term to be essentially content-free.

---

[16]For example, Razi connects it with a verb meaning "to travel," saying it refers to Jesus' itinerancy, while others connect it with the verb "to touch," since he often healed by touch; cited by Parrinder, *Jesus in the Qur'an*, 31-32.

Jews in Muhammad's audience would doubtless have taken *al-masih* to mean Israel's long-awaited redeemer and assumed Muhammad was siding with Christians, though he never connected the term with redemption. On the other hand, Christians may initially have thought the Qur'an's use of *Messiah* signified an acceptance of Jesus as Savior. But listening on, they would surely have known it did not. For it presents humankind as needing no atonement they cannot make for themselves and Jesus as not *himself* God's revelation but just one of its many stewards. Nor does any qur'anic prophet accomplish for our race that great reversal signified by the new covenant in Jesus' blood. Given that the Qur'an never once describes what the Messiah is or does, we can only conclude that the term functions as an empty honorific.[17]

Other Honorifics

The Qur'an's use of two other biblically related words seems almost playful. Twice Sura 3 calls Jesus "a word" (*kalima*) from God (Q 3:39, 45). But if this reminds Christians of the *Logos* of John's Gospel, there is no doubt that it conveys far less than what John had in mind. For to John, the Word simultaneously "was *with* God" and "*was* God." He was, in fact, the Creator, without whom no created thing was made and whose life is "the light of all people" (Jn 1:1, 3-4). But the passage in Sura 3 ends by stating that "in God's eyes Jesus is in the same position as Adam," who was created from dust and animated by God's word (Q 3:59). Q 4:171 likewise calls Jesus "his word which he conveyed to Mary." That is, as Adam came to life by God's word, God similarly spoke Jesus into being in Mary's womb. Only in that sense is Jesus a word from God.

    Q 4:171 likewise calls Jesus a "breath" (*ruh*) from God, although the word is often mistranslated a "spirit" from God, that being *ruh*'s other meaning.[18] This use of breath (*ruh*) also ties in with Jesus' miraculous conception, for

---

[17]The text evidences no awareness of the term's Jewish or Christian meanings; John Kaltner, *Ishmael Instructs Isaac: An Introduction to the Qur'an for Bible Readers* (Collegeville, MN: Liturgical Press, 1999), 243. But with both communities well represented in Arabia, the qur'anic author cannot be unfamiliar with such usage. That he opts for his own undefined use of it (and does so only after Muhammad's relations with Medina's Jews are in sharp decline and he has increased contact with Christian tribes) seems to relate to the effect it has on Jewish and Christian hearers.

[18]On *ruh* see 86n8 above. We confuse the matter when we connect this with either "the spirit of holiness" or "his spirit," who he sent to Mary in the form of a man (Q 2:87, 253; 19:17). Some Christians have even tried to turn this into the Holy Spirit. In both cases, *ruh* refers to the angel Gabriel (*Jibril*), God's agent of revelation.

twice the Qur'an says God "breathed some [of his] breath" into Mary (Q 21:91; 66:12). Just as a spoken word is one with the breath vocalizing it, so when God spoke Jesus into existence in Mary's womb, Jesus was simultaneously that word from God and the breath conveying it. Jesus was thus animated by God's breath, as was Adam.

Among the Qur'an's other designations for Jesus, it calls him "blessed" (*mubarak*), "one of those brought near" to God (*min al-muqarrabin*), "one of the righteous" (*min al-salihin*) and "eminent (*wajih*) in this world and the next," all of which relate to his moral purity and prophetic nobility (Q 3:45-46; 19:31). The Qur'an calls him a "sign" (*aya*) to all beings, a distinction he shares with his mother and which likely relates to his virgin birth (Q 19:21; 21:91; 23:50). He is also a "witness" (*shahid*) to his people during his lifetime and against the un-believing among them on the Last Day, a role every prophet has (Q 4:159; 5:117). Last, he is called an "example (*mathal*) to the Children of Israel" and a "mercy" (*rahma*), both titles coming with insufficient context to give them clear meanings (Q 19:21; 43:57-59). All these titles are doubtless meant to honor Jesus. But considering that *Messiah* has no discernible meaning, while the re-maining titles relate either to his virgin birth, his moral character or his prophethood, they add only luster and shine to the qur'anic estimate of Jesus. But as we will see, the Qur'an also exercises a measure of limitation with respect to Jesus unparalleled in its treatment of any other prophet.

Leveling Features

The Qur'an essentially sets for itself two corrective tasks with regard to Jesus' person. It seeks to counter Jewish denials of his prophethood by vehemently defending Mary's purity and Jesus' legitimacy against Jewish slurs. But it also seeks to counter Christian belief in Jesus' divinity and redemption. This means it must walk a knife edge, carefully "containing" Jesus even as it honors him. Its clearest means of containing Jesus are flatly rejecting his deity and limiting him to prophethood. In terms of the latter, it says Jesus is "only" a messenger, "only" his word conveyed to Mary, "only" his breath and "only" a servant of God (Q 4:171; 5:75; 43:59).

The Qur'an also uses subtler means to render Jesus of like stature to others. For example, it makes him share his honors with others in six cases, some of which we have already seen:

- Jesus shares with Adam the distinction of his creation by God's creative fiat, without normal human conception (Q 3:59; cf. Q 3:45-47).

- By implication, Jesus is variously likened to John the Baptist (Q 19:8-33), suggesting that his real greatness, like that of John, lies in his endorsing his greater successor.

- Jesus shares the spotlight with Mary, since both are called a sign to all created beings, that constituting his only universal role apart from endorsing Muhammad (Q 21:91).

- Jesus is like Muhammad in that they are both called a "mercy" from God for the world (Q 19:21; 21:107; 28:46).

- Q 4:172 suggests that he is no more exalted than the angels when it says he does not refuse to serve God any more than the angels who are close to God.

- Q 5:17 even reduces Jesus to the level of all humankind when it insists that, if God chose to do so, no one could keep him from destroying the Messiah along with everyone else on earth.

Jesus' Divinity in Rhetoric and Ridicule

Those who struggle to understand the qur'anic polemic against Jesus' deity do so because it alternates between straight rebuttal and biting caricature, often in the same breath.[19] For example, after saying that "Christians say, 'The Messiah is the son of God,'" Q 9:30 calls on God to attack them for so perverting the truth. The passage then faults Christians for taking Jesus, along with their monks, as lords.[20] The qur'anic assertion that "Those who say 'God is the Messiah, son of Mary' are unbelievers" (Q 5:17) renders belief in Christ's deity unbelief. And it underwrites that equation with the verse's spectacular final claim, just mentioned, that God could snuff out Jesus' very life if he ever had a mind to do so (cf. Q 5:72). As previously noted, Jesus' expendability derives from the fact that he is a mere creature and thus totally at God's disposal.

---

[19]That is how the most biting satire works, mixing serious and ridiculous accusations together.

[20]Q 9:30-31 parallels this accusation with a more bizarre one against the Jews for calling Ezra the son of God and taking their rabbis as lords, which again represents prophetic parody.

Despite the urgency of its point, the Qur'an deliberately caricatures Christian belief in Jesus' deity as polytheistic. The point is that the Qur'an is not remotely concerned with presenting Christian belief on its own terms. Rather, it seeks to make it look as bad as possible. Later in Sura 5, God grills Jesus as to whether or not he told his followers to take him and his mother as gods "beside God" (Q 5:116), as if Christians believe in three gods, Jesus and Mary among them.[21]

So we can say either that, technically, the Qur'an rejects not the Trinity at all but rather its tritheistic distortion or that any Christian in Muhammad's audience would have known not to take such attacks literally. For the Muslim scripture repeatedly accuses Christians of believing in three gods in terms of the pagans' carnally conceived "daughters of God." Q 4:171, for example, says, "Do not say 'Three!'" Being only one, God is far above having a son.[22] It thus casts Christian belief in terms of the polytheistic notion of God's having offspring. The early Meccan Q 112:3-4 refers to the Meccans' daughters of God when it insists that God "neither begets nor is begotten, and no one is comparable to him." (cf. Q 53:19-21). Only in the Medinan suras is this denial explicitly applied to Christian belief (Q 4:171; 9:30; 19:34-35).

Taking such invective literally, Parrinder suggests the Qur'an may have been attacking Collyridianism, a syncretistic Marian heresy said to have existed in northwestern Arabia some three centuries before Muhammad.[23] Based on his woodenly literalistic reading of it, Parrinder thus turns Muhammad into a hero of Christian orthodoxy. The Qur'an, he claims, rejects not the Trinity per se but only its heretical distortions. He views Q 5:116 as "a simple rebuttal of a practice . . . repugnant to any monotheist."[24] But as we will see, the Qur'an leaves no room for Jesus to be more than created. Neither does it "misunderstand" the Trinity, as some suppose. Rather, it simply uses parody to drive home what it deems the folly of Christian orthodoxy.

---

[21]The only real alternative to this is that the qur'anic author misunderstood the Christian Trinity in polytheistic terms. But as we will see, that is highly unlikely.

[22]While the text uses the word *walad* for "son," we can be sure the Christian Trinity is meant here (on *walad* see 218 below). However, translators who substitute the word *Trinity* for the text's *Three* misleadingly flatten qur'anic diatribe in an attempt to reduce its dissonance; see 46n27 above.

[23]Averil Cameron, however, questions whether such a sect ever existed; "The Cult of the Virgin in Late Antiquity: Religious Development and Myth-Making," *Studies in Church History* 39 (2004): 6-7.

[24]Parrinder, *Jesus in the Qur'an*, 134-35.

A Hypothetical Acceptance of Jesus' Sonship?

Some Western scholars cite Q 43:81 in support of the Qur'an's openness to orthodox Christian doctrine, positing at least the theoretical possibility of God's having a Son. The source of the ambiguity is the text's initial "*in*," which may be taken in two very different senses:

1. "*If* the All-merciful has a son, then I am the first to serve him." (Arberry)

2. "The Merciful does *not* have a son; I am the first among [His] servants." (Jones)[25]

While the majority of English translators opt to take it as a conditional, with Arberry, this is problematic since *in* is a simple conditional, as opposed to *law*, which introduces an impossible or unrealizable condition (cf. Q 39:4). Three things, however, argue strongly for taking this *in* as a negative, along with Jones (cf. Muhammad 'Ali), for that is equally possible.

First, the larger context—verses 15-20, 58-60 and especially verse 82, which concludes with God's being "far above their false descriptions"—show that the passage is directed against polytheism. Second, the noun for "son" is *walad*. Related to the verb *walada* (bear, give birth, beget), it clearly connotes the process of physical conception-gestation-birth. With only two exceptions, the Qur'an consistently uses *walad*, not the more respectful *ibn*, to refer to divine sonship.[26] Arab Christians would have considered God's having produced a *walad* a serious distortion. Hence its connotation is intentionally derogatory, after the manner of poetic lampoon, there being a direct correspondence between a term's formality and the object it designates.[27] This tells us the qur'anic author does not have in mind a trinitarian view of Jesus, but rather means to equate that belief with the pagan notion of God's having sex to produce a "godling" (cf. Q 6:100-101; 72:3).[28] Third, together with its equivalents,[29] the phrase "the first among his servants" (*awwal al-'abidin*) is always renunciative. It invariably represents a

---

[25]Cf. Muhammad Ali, trans., *Holy Qur'ān: Arabic Text, Translation and Commentary*, 4th ed. (Lahore: Aḥmadiyya Anjuman Ishāʿat Islām, 1951).

[26]The sole exceptions are those cases where *ibn* is either employed in the standard *nasab*, "son of ___" construction or paired with its feminine form, *ibna* (Q 5:18; 9:30; 6:100; 37:149, 153).

[27]The English words *child* or *son* would, for example, be more respectful of the offspring of royalty or high office than the colloquial *kid*.

[28]Thus the Qur'an repeatedly counters the degrading claim that God has produced a *walad* by sexual means with the exclamation *subhanahu*, "glory to him!" (Q 2:116; 4:171; 10:68; 19:35).

[29]Its equivalents are "the first of those that surrender" and "the first of the believers."

formal rejection of polytheism, addressing the issue of alternative loyalties with an emphatic declaration of unequivocal devotion to God (e.g., Q 6:163; 7:143; 26:51). So Jones is right: the *in* negates what follows it.

This means that, though conceived miraculously and distinguished as a prophet, Jesus is only human. Q 4:171 allows that he is special but warns against taking his honor to excess. Since the Qur'an views the Christian's central article of faith as the most damnable act of unbelief possible, this can only mean that Jesus faithfully conveyed the message given to him but his followers concealed the truth about him to make him equal to God, for qur'anically, belief in Jesus' deity is polytheism (*shirk*), putting a created being on the level of the Creator.[30]

Jesus, the Perfect Muslim

We thus observe two opposite movements in the Qur'an with reference to Jesus. It honors him as God's prophet. It adds a number of honorary titles to that designation, though most of them carry little substance. It also attributes to Jesus sinlessness, which is not to be discounted. In fact, since the Qur'an presents him as perfect in his submission (*islam*) to God, it gives Christians and Muslims one key point on which they can wholeheartedly agree: Jesus is the perfect *muslim*, in the sense of "servant" of God. But while the Qur'an frequently honors Jesus, it usually does so with a marked element of qualification, limitation or equalization. Its implicit point throughout is that, exalted though he is, Jesus is nowhere near as great as Christians imagine. In fact, only two of Jesus' distinctions are unique: his virgin birth and his sinlessness. They alone set him entirely apart. But with so many precautions, parallels, empty honorifics and denials in its presentation of Jesus, the Qur'an is eminently successful in exalting Jesus in just such a way as to guarantee his inferiority to Muhammad.

Hence the Qur'an consistently rejects Christian belief in Jesus' divine Sonship, even though the latter excludes any concept of physical paternity, and the terms *Father* and *Son* are strictly analogical here. As the Nicene Creed puts it, the Son of God is "*eternally* begotten" of the Father, has always existed in a relationship of Son to Father. Thus the incarnation of the Son of God in Mary's

---

[30]Hence, when the Muslim preacher's fiery rhetoric leads him "to hurl epithets like 'infidels' and 'idolaters' in the direction of Christians," his language is informed by passages like Q 5:72-76, warning that all who hold to the Trinity will go to hell; Kaltner, *Ishmael Instructs Isaac*, 271.

womb was simply God's way of revealing himself to us as he has always been, Father and Son. But the Qur'an leaves no room for this. Divine incarnation is ruled out by the Qur'an's inviolable master-servant distinction no less than its Creator-creature distinction.

Other qur'anic references underscore the impossibility of the Christian doctrine. Q 5:75 notes that Jesus and Mary both ate food. Everything about the category of creature is contingent, including the needs of creaturely corporeality of food or sleep—or indeed, of anything at all. They all categorically deny one the status of deity (Q 2:255; 6:14; cf. Q 21:7-8). Not only that—eating involves hunger, mastication, digestion and voiding waste, all of which are far beneath God's exalted dignity. Q 5:116 has Jesus telling God, "You know what is in my mind, though I do not know what is in yours." He seems annoyed that God would think he could have promoted so outrageous a belief as Christians hold. Since God knows everything, for Jesus to confess his ignorance puts him decidedly on the servant side of the master-servant divide. Finally, when Jesus repeats the command he gave his followers to "Serve God, my Lord and your Lord," he implies that his relation to God is not fundamentally different from anyone else's (Q 5:72, 117).[31] Although Jesus is perfect in his submission to God, he is simply human, like Muhammad.

The Bible and Qur'an Compared on Jesus' Person

While no New Testament writer affords us an array of handy prooftexts on the topic, each in his own way presents Jesus as fully human and yet also fully divine. The Evangelists tell us that, in Jesus' birth, God became human in order to save his people from their sins (Mt 1:20-22; 2:11; Lk 1:30-35; 2:4-12, 35-38). They present us with a Messiah who both deserves and accepts worship (Mt 14:22-33; Mk 5:6; Lk 24:36-52; Jn 9:38). The great conflict they depict between Jesus and the nation's leaders is in large measure over his claims, implicit and explicit, by which he exercised the prerogatives of God (Mt 9:1-8; Mk 14:60-62; Jn 8:56-58; 10:30-33). The authorities saw it as blasphemy and ruled that he deserved to die. Had he not been all he claimed to be, they would have been right to condemn him. But Jesus' apostles saw his resurrection as validating all of his claims. It led them to write his story as God's good news for the world (e.g., Mt 28; Lk 24),

---

[31]John 20:17 uses similar phrasing to say that Jesus has opened the way for humankind to share his intimacy with his Father, while the Qur'an uses it oppositely, to say that Jesus is only human.

since the Messiah is both David's descendent and also David's Lord (Mt 22:41-46).[32] In Revelation, John portrays Jesus as the omnipotent Lamb of God, who died to overcome evil in our world and who will return to fulfill the rest of messianic prophecy as earth's Lord and King (Rev 1:7; 5:1-14; 19:11-16). Paul says similar things (Phil 2:5-8; Col 1:16; 2:9; cf. Heb 1:6-8). And since the Bible presents the Holy Spirit as divine also (Mk 3:29; Jn 15:26; 1 Cor 6:19), it ascribes to God a triune nature that in no way compromises his unity.[33]

Though this understanding of Jesus is clearly central to the message of the New Testament, the qur'anic author views it as a violation of God's oneness and grants Jesus the title of Messiah, but minus its biblical meanings. He acknowledges Jesus' prophethood but views his humanity as inherently denying his divinity. Implicitly rejecting the Bible's more nuanced view of God, the Qur'an uses poetic lampoon flatly to equate it with polytheism. This sets the Qur'an in direct opposition to much biblical teaching.

Conclusion

The Qur'an is silent on the biblical topic of God's self-revelation in Christ. However, its consistent aversion to divine self-revelation tells us it would have patently opposed it. But again, it rejects biblical Christology through a combination of serious and satirical arguments. To discern in the Qur'an's polemical arguments concerning Jesus the beliefs of such marginal Christian sects as the Nazoreans, Collyridians or Patripassians entirely misses the point: rather, the Qur'an attacks only mainstream Christian belief. However, it often does so through parody, by which it reduces Christianity to an imported version of the domestic paganism the Hijaz already had in excess, but this version masquerading as monotheism (!). This explains the Qur'an's apparent inclusion of Mary in the Trinity (Q 5:116). Some Christians in Arabia venerated Mary as the "Mother of God," which resembled the pagan concept of the family of the gods sufficiently—albeit superficially—so that the qur'anic author could not resist recasting the Trinity in such terms.[34] Tragically, though,

---

[32]For example, as noted above, John begins his Gospel by presenting Jesus as the creator of all things, one with God, his Father. He makes similar points throughout his Gospel and concludes it with one of Jesus' disciples recognizing him as God (Jn 1:1-3; 20:28).

[33]God's oneness is emphatically taught in Mk 12:29-33; Jn 17:3; 1 Cor 8:4-6; Eph 4:4-6; Jas 2:19.

[34]Similarly, many Muslims today claim that the Trinity represents the Christian belief in there being simultaneously one God and three gods, a notion as unbiblical as it is illogical.

the one thing the qur'anic author never once does is seriously engage with the biblical idea—an idea he seems unwilling even to consider—that God came to earth in the person of his Son for the set purpose of taking his rightful place as king over his creation.

Hence, when we compare Jesus' origins and person in the Qur'an and Bible, we see some important similarities but radical differences also. The Qur'an clearly means to honor Jesus as a prophet and messenger. Accordingly, it emphasizes his virgin birth, moral character and miracles. However, it means to reform not just paganism but clearly Judaism and Christianity also. Its purpose in presenting Jesus as it does is therefore radically different from that of the New Testament. The Qur'an's purpose is ultimately to establish Jesus' unqualified endorsement of Muhammad's prophethood. And that explains its exclusion of anything from the biblical presentation of Jesus that would in any way undermine Muhammad's supremacy. Anything threatening that must be either avoided, altered or emptied of meaning.

Fifteen

Jesus' Words *and* Works

The qur'anic presentation of Jesus' words and works contains not one narrative clearly resembling a Gospel account. Instead, Jesus' life as portrayed here begins with the miracle of his infancy speech, echoing an apocryphal birth gospel. By having the newborn Jesus assume a heroic role, that incident makes him look oddly self-important and, in fact, freakish. The Qur'an tells of another childhood miracle and speech that repeat that effect. It mentions his healing the sick, raising the dead and providing a meal from heaven but none of his nature miracles. And it insists that Jesus performs miracles only by God's power. The Qur'an states that Jesus confirmed the scriptures before him and foretold Muhammad's coming. It also refers to Jesus' relaxation of the Jewish law and his cursing the Jews who reject him. It speaks of his wisdom but gives such limited coverage of Jesus' teachings that they are shorn of all the beauty they have in the Gospels. It essentially ignores his distinctive teachings in the Gospels or else subverts them but without acknowledging it. It consistently describes Jesus' interactions with his disciples in such a way as to make him appear needy, dependent on them and in fact less spiritual than they. It otherwise only presents him in ahistorical situations in which he stands on the level of all the other prophets. In one case, God requires him to swear to support Muhammad's prophethood as the prerequisite to his own commissioning as prophet. In another, God makes him defend himself against the charge that he is responsible for his followers' "polytheistic" worship of him and his mother. The cumulative effect of all this is to discredit Christian beliefs, make Jesus subordinate to Muhammad and, in fact, to marginalize Jesus.

*T*he most striking difference between the Qur'an and Bible relates to the amount and kind of attention they give to Jesus' ministry and death. While these topics occupy most of the four Gospels, the Qur'an refers to Jesus' deeds in barely fifteen verses. About the same number cover his words and even fewer his death. Furthermore, the references in all three categories are scattered and lack substantive detail. In fact, the Qur'an gives no extended account of Jesus apart from his birth. Nor does it give any extended narrative of Jesus' adult ministry comparable to those of Noah, Abraham and Moses (e.g., Q 7:103-57; 10:75-90; 11:25-49; 37:83-112; 71:1-28). Even Joseph receives nearly a hundred consecutive verses of qur'anic narrative (Q 12:3-101). Only if Jesus is a B-list prophet does such treatment of him make sense. And lacking any longer narratives of his ministry, the Qur'an cannot possibly give us a sense of who Jesus really is.

Focusing on Jesus' ministry, this chapter has a threefold goal:

1. To examine the qur'anic presentation of Jesus' words and works[1]

2. To compare the Qur'an's presentation of his words and works to that of the Gospels

3. To ask why the Qur'an and Bible portray Jesus so very differently

Only by considering all three topics can we gain a true picture of Jesus' ministry in the Qur'an.

On the question of the qur'anic author's choices, it should be clear that— whether in oral or written form—various apocryphal texts and pieces of Judeo-Christian lore were available to him. Biblical materials would have been equally available in some form.[2] Jesus' wisdom sayings in the Gospels and the stories of his miracles, for example, were specifically designed for an oral society's easy remembering and retelling. Thus the question of whether or not the qur'anic author had access to a written Arabic translation of the New Testament is moot.[3] And his exclusion of biblical materials bears no less authorial import than his inclusions.

---

[1]Unlike in Christian theology, the Qur'an does not view Jesus' death as any "work" of his.
[2]For more see chapter seventeen below.
[3]He clearly had access to the "interpreted Bible" and such tales as that of the Seven Sleepers and the Alexander legend (cf. 38, 41 above). There is no reason to think he would not have had the same access to the New Testament. Furthermore, written texts are often deemed superfluous in oral societies.

Words Distinctive to Jesus

While separating Jesus' words and works is artificial—since they are so often inseparable—doing so will make the topic more manageable. So we will begin by considering the Qur'an's ten direct quotations of Jesus in the order in which they were first recited. Only the first two quotations, being Meccan, present him as truly heroic, a child prodigy in the extreme. Though just newborn, Jesus miraculously takes the lead. He comforts his exhausted and terrified mother by telling her where to find sustenance and silencing her accusers when she appears with a baby conceived out of wedlock (Q 19:24-26). Jesus eloquently defends his mother's honor and his own legitimacy by giving a litany of his prophetic credentials and pronouncing a comprehensive blessing on himself (Q 19:30-33). Though the speech makes him appear both unattractively adult and self-important, Jesus is nonetheless clearly the hero on the day of his birth.

The remaining quotations, all Medinan, present Jesus as increasingly weak. Though the text does not specify its context, the first quotation is likely from Jesus' childhood, since he says he will bring clay birds to life, a miracle that tradition says he worked as a child (Q 3:49-51). As in the quotation from Sura 19, Jesus again presents a litany of his future miracles and teachings. But instead of a blessing, it ends with a request that his hearers fear God and obey him in order to walk in the straight path. Evidencing the same odd self-importance we saw in Sura 19, this quotation makes Jesus look slightly weaker, since his telling people to obey him implies that some may not find him compelling—which is all the more understandable since he is so young.

Q 3:52-53 confirms that, with Jesus perceiving his people's unbelief and appealing for "helpers" and his disciples volunteering.[4] Three features combine to make Jesus look weak here:

- The context is one of Jesus' extreme vulnerability.

- Jesus' question makes him appear dependent on others.

- His disciples' response is one of unmistakable rebuke.

To begin, surrounded by "wolves," Jesus feels vulnerable enough to seek help (Q 3:54-55). Since a question's rhetorical force depends largely on things the

---

[4]Thus Jesus' disciples are usually called his "helpers" (*ansar*), notably the same term as is used for those who helped Muhammad by granting him asylum in Yathrib. Otherwise, the Qur'an uses *hawariyun*, an Ethiopic loanword meaning "disciples."

text does not supply—tone of voice, body language, etc.—it is difficult to know how to read it. But there are definitely stronger ways to recruit others than by asking a question. The Gospels, by contrast, show Jesus commanding men to follow and their simply doing so, even men who seem to have shown no previous interest. There Jesus always acts, while everyone around him re-acts.[5] He is also the one with the incisive questions and answers, whereas the Qur'an always leaves the adult Jesus looking decidedly needy, with the ball in the other person's court and him struggling to keep up.

The clearest feature here minimizing Jesus' importance is the disciples' re-sponse. Not only are they the decisive ones and he dependent on them: they respond to his question of who will be *his* helpers in God's Cause, stating that they are *God's* helpers. Thus they implicitly reprimand him, advising him to be more God-centered in what is a reversal of roles.[6] They then command Jesus to bear witness that they are submitters (*muslimun*) before spontane-ously declaring their faith to God and asking him to record them among the witnesses. The disciples' response then implies that, compared to Jesus, they are more decisive, more committed to God and more spiritually perceptive. All this inevitably reduces Jesus' greatness. This is confirmed by the only other incident from Jesus' adult ministry the Qur'an narrates, that of the miracle of the banquet (Q 5:111-15). As we will see, that story similarly presents him as being led by his "followers."

We next come to Q 61:6, which has Jesus proclaiming, "Children of Israel, I am God's messenger to you," and then referring to what are doubtless his most vital tasks, qur'anically: confirming the Torah before him (cf. Q 3:50; 5:46) and bringing good news of a messenger to come. Far from straight-forward, this third quotation must be examined in detail. But regardless of how we deal with it, the prophet Jesus predicts is none other than Muhammad. So while his opening line makes him seem self-important, Jesus goes on to announce that he brings good news of Muhammad, who in the context of the Qur'an towers over him in importance.

To appreciate the qur'anic role assigned to Jesus, one needs to understand that to "confirm" the earlier scriptures is to accept their divine origins. But

---

[5]Even in his moments of extreme weakness—in Gethsemane and on the cross—he is the only one who chooses to do what he does, while everyone around him is driven to behave as they do.
[6]Kaltner, *Ishmael Instructs Isaac*, 252-53.

qur'anically, it is always combined with replacing those scriptures—in Jesus' case, with the Injil.[7] And by the same token, his endorsement of Muhammad— recounted now centuries later by the Qur'an—effectively replaces Jesus' God-given revelation with the Qur'an, which purportedly carries the same message as the Injil. Hence the importance of what Jesus does here lies in his decommissioning of his own message in favor of the Qur'an. That point was clearly vital to Muhammad given the number of Christian tribes in the Hijaz and beyond. Then, a few verses later, Q 61:14 repeats verbatim Jesus' question from Q 3:52, calling for help and underscoring his need.

Sura 5, the last sura chronologically, contains three Jesus quotations, two appearing in the story of "The Banquet," after which the sura is named. The passage begins with God's granting Jesus' disciples faith and their replying that they do believe (Q 5:111). When they ask Jesus to provide a miracle meal for them, he fears their request is irreverent (Q 5:112). However, when Jesus hears their reasons, he backtracks on his initial reply.[8] Jesus' prayer for God to supply the meal forms the sura's second Jesus quotation (Q 5:114). The story then ends abruptly without ever recounting the actual miracle, suggesting that the qur'anic author's concern here was not so much with Jesus or his disciples as with the Jews, against whom the Jesus narrative becomes the foil to condemn them. For besides promising the miracle, God also warns that anyone who afterward disbelieves in Jesus will be punished unspeakably—the warning clearly directed against Medina's Jews who persist in rejecting him (Q 5:115).

Relative to Jesus, however, it is important to see that from the outset the narrative gives the disciples the lead role, since the miracle was their idea. Considering that the disciples' reasons for requesting the miracle are not very impressive (Q 5:113), Jesus' easy capitulation makes him look even less sure of himself. And God's readiness to grant the miracle Jesus had cautioned against requesting shows Jesus to have initially been mistaken, making him look both weak and unspiritual, undiscerning of God's will. Hence we find the very same sort of role reversal and depreciation of Jesus as compared with his disciples that we saw in Q 3:52-53.

---

[7] Jesus' confirmation of the previous prophets and scriptures (cf. Q 3:50; 5:46) is only what every prophet before him—Adam excepted—did. On the Injil's identity, see 260n6, 264-67 below.

[8] This is quite contrary to the picture we get from the Gospels. Not only did Jesus usually do miracles there without specifically praying, he also refused to grant requests for miracles of provision (Jn 6:25-40), which he took as a sign of unbelief, not of faith, as is the case in Sura 5.

The Qur'an's last quotation of Jesus, chronologically speaking, comes in a narrative fragment immediately following the story of the miraculous banquet. Q 5:116-18 is Jesus' longest speech in the Qur'an and represents his self-defense, presumably at the final judgment. The scene opens with God's questioning him on whether he told people to take him and his mother as gods "beside God." We could paraphrase his reply as follows:

> Glory be to you! I would never have said what I had no right to say. And if I had said it, you would already know it! For you know all my hidden thoughts, though I do not know yours. . . . I said nothing to them except what you commanded me to say: "Worship God, my Lord and your Lord." I was responsible to witness against their folly as long as I was with them. But when you caused me to die,[9] that responsibility returned to you. . . . Since they are your servants, you have every right to punish them. But being exalted in power and wisdom, you can also forgive them if you choose.

The issue here is the Christian worship of Jesus and exaltation of Mary, presumably to the status of "Mother of God." Besides denying that he ever encouraged such heinous things, Jesus almost reproaches God for putting so outrageous a question to him. He then concludes by washing his hands of any of his followers who so exalt him and his mother and turning them over to God to judge them as he sees fit.

In terms of how Jesus' words in Q 5:116-18 portray him, Jesus is given a defensive posture by the very fact that God has him in the dock, arraigning him on such an accusation. This makes Jesus look small enough that even the strength of his self-vindication takes him from a negative only to a neutral rating. Jesus highlights his relative insignificance when he ends his self-defense with three points that show his mortal limitations:

- unlike God's knowledge, Jesus' knowledge is limited.

- unlike God's timelessness, Jesus' responsibility is limited to his earthly term.

- unlike God's sovereignty, Jesus' power to influence his followers has ended, since he is neither their master nor judge.

In all three respects, Jesus' reply makes him look miniscule before his infinite and exalted Judge, making it needless for the Qur'an to say how seriously his followers have twisted his message.

---

[9]For a discussion of this controversial verb, see 246-49 below.

Other References to Jesus' Words

Besides these direct quotations, the Qur'an refers to Jesus' speech or teaching in an expository manner three times in the Medinan suras. An angel predicts that Jesus will speak both as an adult and from the cradle, as we earlier saw (Q 3:46; cf. Q 5:110). Q 5:46 says Jesus confirmed the Torah and received the gospel God gave him. Last, Q 5:78 says Jesus (along with David) cursed the children of Israel. In typical qur'anic style, each of these references omits the specific context of the event in question. None really adds to the picture we have of Jesus, except perhaps Q 5:78, which—lacking relevant context—seemingly makes him anti-Semitic.[10]

Two Medinan suras also include Jesus in words spoken by the prophets generically. Q 3:81 is pivotal to our understanding of Jesus in the Qur'an. In it God requires all the prophets solemnly to pledge that they will believe in Muhammad and support him. This makes Jesus' very prophethood contingent on his endorsement of Muhammad. Furthermore, it makes Muhammad superior to Jesus. The only other binding commitment God takes from the prophets— found in Q 33:7-8—includes both Jesus and Muhammad. Here all the prophets are required to make themselves accountable to God for their stewardship of the truth he reveals to them.

With regard to the Injil Jesus received from God, it was law oriented and proclaimed the same flat monotheism as the qur'anic revelations. Beyond that, the Qur'an gives only the slightest hints as to the contents of Jesus' teaching. Q 3:49-50 suggests that he was a lawgiver, presumably in the same sense that Muhammad was. It tells us he told his people—the Jews—what they should eat and store in their houses and that he made lawful some things formerly forbidden. This may very faintly echo Jesus' teaching in Matthew 6:19-21 and 15:11, but either way, it puts Jesus' focus on mundane laws. It also presents Jesus as abrogating laws revealed presumably to Moses, just as Muhammad's revelations abrogate those of his predecessors. We can also assume that the Injil taught the ritual prayers (*salat*) and almsgiving (*zakat*) God required of Jesus (Q 19:31). The only other qur'anic description of Jesus' teachings comes in the single word *wisdom* (Q 43:63; cf. Q 5:110), but since the Qur'an gives us no examples to inspire us with its character, this adds nothing new.

---

[10]If Q 5:78 is to be connected with Jesus' cursing of the fig tree, it seemingly mistakes the tree symbolic of the nation for the Jews themselves (Mk 11:12-26), whereas Jesus showed only compassion and forgiveness to his Jewish persecutors (Lk 23:34).

Jesus' Ahmadu *Prediction*

We return now to the most vital Jesus quotation in all of the Qur'an, Q 61:6, which reads: "Children of Israel, I am God's messenger to you, confirming the Torah revealed before me and giving you good news of a messenger to come after me whose name will be more praiseworthy [*ahmadu*]." The first question is whether *ahmadu* here is a word or a proper name. Virtually all Muslims today are firmly convinced it is the latter, claiming that Ahmad was Muhammad's alternate name. There are good reasons, however, to doubt this claim:

- Though Ahmad is from the same root (*h-m-d*) as Muhammad, the names are very distinct.

- While Muslims named their boys Muhammad from the first, it seems they began naming their boys Ahmad in the 740s, more than a century after Muhammad's death.[11]

- Commentators only took Ahmad to be Muhammad's name after the year 815.

- A variant reading of Q 61:6 substitutes for *ahmadu* clearer descriptions of Muhammad.

The variant reading is particularly telling, for if Muhammad had actually gone by the name Ahmad, such clarification would have been needless.[12] Thus it seems clear that Muslims took *ahmadu* as an adjective during Islam's first century, in which case Jesus only predicted the coming of one "worthy of more praise."[13] Essentially, when they realized they could take *ahmadu* nominally instead of adjectivally by crediting Muhammad with a second name, the verse packed a much stronger polemical punch.[14] But this does not change the fact that Jesus here foretells Muhammad's coming, in which case Muhammad is said to be worthy of more praise than Jesus, for no other referent is given, and that is in accord with what we saw in Q 3:81.

---

[11]Geoffrey Parrinder, *Jesus in the Qur'an* (Oxford: Oneworld, 1995), 98-99.

[12]Ibid., 96-97.

[13]W. Montgomery Watt, "His Name Is Ahmed," *The Muslim World* 43 (1953): 110-13.

[14]Further, Ibn Ishaq and his editor Ibn Hisham connected the Syriac word for "Comforter" in John's Gospel (*muhahhemana*) with Muhammad. That they completely omitted the name "Ahmad" from their discussion of Jesus' prediction suggests that they did not take *ahmadu* to be their prophet's name; Ibn Ishaq, *The Life of Muhammad*, trans. Alfred Guillaume (Oxford: Oxford University Press, 1995), 103-4.

Whichever way we take *ahmadu*, the fact remains that Q 61:6 does not correspond to anything in the Gospels. This would have made it difficult for the Muslim community after Muhammad, when it ruled ever-larger numbers of Christians. In John 14:26, Jesus does promise to send his followers the "Helper" or "Advocate" (Greek *paraklētos*), but he clearly states that he is the Holy Spirit and never suggests that another prophet would replace him—as if his revelation of God were somehow incomplete. The ingenuity of the early Muslim commentators comes through again here, though, in their assertion that the Greek word in John 14 was not originally *paraklētos*, but rather *periklytos*, meaning "praised" or Muhammad.[15] But there are real problems with this:

- Not one of the thousands of extant manuscripts of John's Gospel gives *periklytos*.[16]

- The Greek word *periklytos* was no longer in use in the first century when John wrote his Gospel, making the word substitution theory completely untenable.

Furthermore, John 14 presents Jesus specifically preparing his disciples for his imminent departure, news of which struck terror in them (Jn 14:1, 18, 25). Predicting the coming of a prophet six centuries later would not have helped them face the challenges ahead, as would the coming of the Holy Spirit just weeks later (cf. Acts 1:8). We cannot simply extract a single word and claim it was changed, totally ignoring its context.[17] For the verse to speak meaningfully of Muhammad's coming would require that Christians had changed not just the text's key word but rather the entire passage. And in that case, any Muslim use of it would be of dubious value.

To sum up, the Qur'an's fifteen verses dealing with Jesus' words give us little sense of what he taught and use his words primarily

- to draw attention to him and his prophethood, often in ways that make him seem oddly stilted and self-serving, biblically speaking; this evidently fits

---

[15]We find evidence for the *paraklētos* claim as early as Leo III (c. 719); N. A. Newman, ed. *The Early Christian-Muslim Dialogue: A Collection of Documents from the First Three Centuries (632–900 A.D.): Translations with Commentary* (Hatfield, PA: Interdisciplinary Biblical Research Institute, 1993), 71-72.

[16]That would have to mean that the Christians had expunged the alleged "original" version from the record not only thoroughly but very early also, and that simply did not happen.

[17]For example, Jesus said *he* would send the Advocate, who he claimed already lived *with* the disciples and would soon be *in* them (Jn 14:16-17).

with the qur'anic idea of honoring Jesus, which is not at all meant to make him winsome;

- to disavow strongly his ever having encouraged his followers to worship him; and

- to support the Qur'an's own homogenized view of prophetic revelation and Muhammad's commanding place in it—especially predicting his coming.

Beyond that, the Qur'an mentions Jesus' adjustment of Mosaic laws but with little sense of what that meant. It mentions Jesus' wisdom but without giving us so much as a glimpse of it. And in terms of its direct quotations of Jesus, the Qur'an evidences a clear progression from a bizarrely heroic infant Jesus to a man who looks progressively weaker.

Works: Jesus' Miracles

While the Qur'an repeatedly mentions the miracles Jesus performed, it recounts only one miracle story in any detail. Since that miracle, his defense of his mother's honor as a newborn, presents Jesus at his very best, we might call it his signature miracle (Q 19:24-26, 30-33; 5:110). As noted above, that account echoes a story from the apocryphal Infancy Gospel of James. Jesus was also a child when he made birds out of clay and then breathed life into them, a story with obvious parallels to God's creation of humankind (Q 3:49; 5:110). This echoes stories from the apocryphal Infancy Gospel of Thomas.[18] In addition, the Qur'an summarily states that Jesus healed the blind and lepers and raised the dead (Q 3:49; 5:110).

Furthermore, as noted above, the Qur'an alludes to a miracle feeding of the crowds. That is, it gives the lead-up to the miracle but not the miracle itself (Q 5:112-15). The figurative use of a banquet "table," which Jesus asks God to send down, also makes it difficult to say whether or not this miracle resembles the Gospels' feeding of the crowds. If the qur'anic story alludes to one of the miracle feedings from the Bible, then by portraying the disciples as the story's initiators, it clearly reverses the Evangelists' accounts of the event, where the disciples are anything but initiators (Mt 14:13-21; 15:32-39; Mk 6:31-44; 8:1-9; Lk 9:10-17; Jn 6:5-15). Some scholars think Jesus' concluding words in the qur'anic

---

[18]Peter E. Kirby, "Infancy Gospel of Thomas," verse 2, *Early Christian Writings* (website), accessed September 12, 2013, www.earlychristianwritings.com/text/infancythomas-a-roberts.html; R. McL. Wilson, *Gospels and Related Writings*, vol. 1 of *New Testament Apocrypha*, ed. Wilhelm Schneemelcher, 2nd ed. (Louisville: Westminster John Knox, 2003), 444.

account—that this meal should be "a festival for the first of us and the last of us"—refer to the enduring celebration of the Eucharist (Q 5:114). But this could just as easily refer to a single meal that excludes no one present. Others think the miracle conflates a miracle feeding with the Eucharist, while still others relate it to the Bread of Life discourse in John 6:22-71 or the story of Peter's vision in Acts 10:9-16,[19] all of which tells us that the story is so fragmentary and so unlike anything in the Gospels that we cannot possibly identify it with certainty.

Three general points stand out with regard to the qur'anic treatment of Jesus' miracles:

1. The Qur'an credits Jesus with doing many miracles and Muhammad with none apart from the "miracle" of the Qur'an (Q 11:16; cf. Q 2:23-24).

2. Jesus performed every single one of his miracles solely "by God's permission."

3. The qur'anic author's preference for nonbiblical sources is apparent.

Although Muslim traditions credit Muhammad with many miracles, the Qur'an does not, for it could hardly claim miracles for him that he could not perform. On the other hand, it was widely held that Jesus was a miracle worker (and by Jews, a sorcerer). By so crediting Jesus, the Muslim scripture does honor him. But since it offers no narrative account clearly from the Gospels and only one full miracle account from a nonbiblical source (his infancy speech), it definitely honors Jesus only on its own terms, terms that specified that he must be carefully limited to a supporting role. To that end, the Qur'an repeats the phrase "by God's permission" almost every time it mentions Jesus' miracles—four times in Q 5:110 alone.[20] By so doing, it stresses that Jesus is merely human, with no miraculous powers of his own.

The Bible and Qur'an on Jesus' Words

As noted above, the qur'anic author consciously and strategically chose not only to include what materials he did on Jesus, but also to exclude others equally available. The New Testament devotes a great deal of space to Jesus' teachings. His many parables, for example, expound on the meaning of the

---

[19]Michel Cuypers, *The Banquet: A Reading of the Fifth Sura of the Qur'an* (Miami: Convivium Press, 2009), 416-19.
[20]The only exceptions are Jesus' infancy speech, performed by the power given him by Gabriel or the "holy spirit" (Q 5:110), and the miracle feeding, where Jesus simply prays for a miracle.

kingdom he came to inaugurate. But the Qur'an does not so much as mention Jesus' preaching on the kingdom of God—and neither any of his parables nor his "I am" statements in John's Gospel (e.g., Jn 8:12; 10:7-8; 11:25; 14:6).

The Gospels show Jesus' ethical teachings simultaneously internalizing, externalizing, intensifying and simplifying Moses' law, and by so doing he fulfills the law in the sense that he meets all of his requirements and reveals its true meaning (Mt 5:17-20). Jesus internalizes it by relating its prohibitions and positive commands to our hearts and minds, not merely external actions. He insists that matters of the heart determine our relationship to God, and he makes external purity and ritual observance secondary to our thought life (Mt 15:1-20). Jesus' ethics also address the ubiquitous peril of spiritual pride, which can render all our best religious efforts mere ego faith, the use of religion to serve and glorify the worshiper more than the supposed object of worship (e.g., Mt 23:1-36). In fact, no morality—religious or otherwise—not centered in humility can save us from an overweening sense of superiority. That is why Jesus so faithfully modeled humility, showed us how lost we are apart from his grace and even recommended secrecy in our devotional practice lest we forfeit God's approval for the fleeting enjoyment of human praise (Mt 6:1-18; cf. Gal 1:10). Jesus also says sins like murder and adultery must be addressed at the level of heart and mind, where they are conceived before issuing in our observable actions (Mt 5:21-30). Jesus had no interest in that superficial morality that comes from controlling sin on the level of deeds only because it misses the larger point of God's law—that we be remade in his moral likeness, from the inside out (Mt 5:48; cf. Lev 11:44-45).[21]

By contrast, not only does the Qur'an not mention Jesus' emphases on the centrality of the heart, the primacy of love, humility as the essence of spirituality and becoming like God in our moral character, it offers nothing remotely comparable. Rather, apart from emphasizing loyalty to "God's Cause," it typically emphasizes observable actions and views hypocrites as unbelievers who infiltrate the *umma* from outside in order to weaken or attack it from within.[22]

---

[21]Besides faulting Christian practice of it, Akhtar calls Matthew's version of Jesus' teaching on adultery (Mt 5:27-30) "extremely unrealistic"; Shabbir Akhtar, *A Faith for All Seasons: Islam and Western Modernity* (London: Bellew Publishing, 1990), 236n30. Akhtar is certainly right to say that Christians do not perfectly attain this level of moral purity. But the Jesus of the New Testament would reply that, while it is true that we cannot attain God's standard for sexual purity on our own, that does not justify his lowering the standard. For God gave the standard in the full knowledge that we could only attain it by his power, which he is more than ready to supply.

[22]While Q 2:264 does not use the word *hypocrite*, it does warn of the danger of giving alms in such

Being impostors, the sooner they are exposed and ejected or killed the better (Q 4:88-90, 145; 9:64-68). In fact, the Gospels' entire emphasis on the heart is strikingly out of place in terms of what we have seen of qur'anic spirituality's focus on external conformity to supertribal norms.

Jesus also externalizes Moses' law by applying its ethical values practically in ways that demand a supernatural level of love and personal growth. For example, he tells us to love not just our neighbors as ourselves but also our enemies. He makes this love utterly practical, saying that it can involve turning the other cheek, walking a second mile, loaning without expectation of return and blessing those who curse us (Mt 5:38-48; Lk 6:31-36). Jesus also refuses to allow "spirituality" to trump justice and mercy (Mk 7:8-13) and insists that we forgive others as freely as God has forgiven us (Mt 6:14-15; 18:21-35). He washes his disciples' feet to model the kind of humility by which his upside-down kingdom operates (Jn 13:1-17). He holds firm to a position of monogamy and condemns an easy attitude to divorce (Mt 19:3-9). He also relates to women in ways that challenge societal norms, ways on which we do not see the Qur'an building. Like the Hebrew prophets before him, Jesus emphasizes acts of mercy and justice over ritual observance (Mt 23:23) and refuses any substitute—however good—for the justice, mercy and humility to which the entire law points (Mic 6:8). Radically intensifying the law's demands for body, mind and heart, Jesus condemns any attempt to weaken his standards.[23]

But besides intensifying God's requirements, Jesus offers a grace that welcomes any sinner who humbly cries to him for mercy while excluding proud, self-righteous "saints" (Lk 18:11-13). This is why his signature story tells of the prodigal whose father warmly embraces him despite his son's total rejection of him (Lk 15:11-32). Jesus intends the story to shock precisely because God's love is scandalous: it is the morally compromised but humble, not the self-righteous, who God welcomes at his table (Mt 11:19; Lk 7:34). The Qur'an, by contrast, offers not the slightest whiff of the scandal of God's love as we find it in the gospel.

But in the course of Jesus' radical refocusing of the law, he simplifies it too. In his teaching, the law no longer stands as six-hundred-plus competing regulations, but now as just two requirements that encompass all the rest, and those two being inseparable. By loving God supremely and loving our neighbor as ourselves, we

---

a way as to draw attention to oneself. But again, it links such behavior to unbelievers.

[23]On the New Testament view of divorce, see 176-77 above.

fulfill God's entire law (Mt 22:36-40). Since our neighbor is the image of God, loving her is integral to loving God. And we love our neighbor truly only when we also love the God in whose likeness she is made. Jesus thus removes the partition between heaven and earth, simultaneously revealing God's heart for us in his law and our desperate need of his enabling to obey it. Our pleasing God is thus about his loving us first and our loving him only in response (1 Jn 4:19).

Finally, as previously noted, Jesus' teaching leaves absolutely no room for the marriage of "church and state" as envisioned by either the seventh-century Byzantines or the nascent Muslim empire under Muhammad. Rather, Jesus says his kingdom is not that kind of kingdom, established by neither the sword nor the power politics of this world (Jn 18:36). Jesus sternly warns that "all who take the sword will perish by the sword" (Mt 26:52).[24] Neither does he endorse any worldly government or system that defines "truth" for its subjects and then coerces them into accepting its definition (Jn 18:36-38).[25] In fact, such substitutes for God's kingdom are diametrically opposed to the good news Jesus preached (1 Jn 2:15-17). Jesus knows well the ease with which ambitious leaders can use religion to turn sincere people—whole communities—into battalions of foot soldiers. And nothing is more vital to that enterprise than the sort of divine namedropping by which they stamp their empire building—including violence in which God has no part—with his imprimatur. Jesus will have none of it. "If my kingdom were from this world," he says, "my followers would be fighting to keep me from being handed over to the Jews. But as it is, my kingdom is not from here" (Jn 18:36).

One would naturally expect that any book claiming to honor Jesus would focus on and interact with his ethical teachings. And all the more so, given the Qur'an's marked orientation to praxis. But its author chose not do so. Here the Qur'an's silence on Jesus is truly deafening. It clearly has no interest in Jesus' teachings, whether from the Bible or other sources. Besides ignoring Jesus' ethics, a number of qur'anic teachings run directly counter to his teachings in the Gospels.[26] The primacy he gives to loving one's neighbor without distinction—as the outworking of God's universal love—is utterly lacking in the

---

[24]On the biblical view of violence, see 192-95 above.

[25]N. T. Wright, "Called to Be Human: Agenda for Tomorrow's Church" (lecture, Christian Life Assembly, Langley, BC, November 16, 2010).

[26]The Qur'an is in direct conflict with Jesus' teaching on marriage, divorce and the nonsexual nature of heaven's eternal bliss.

Qur'an. Neither does the Qur'an ever present God as loving unrepentant un-believers, as previously noted. And that being so, it is unthinkable that it calls believers to a higher standard of love than God himself demonstrates.[27]

The Bible and Qur'an on Jesus' Works

If it is true that separating a person's words and works is artificial, it is espe-cially so of Jesus. As the Gospels present him, no one ever practiced what he preached as did Jesus. As noted earlier, in Jesus the medium was the message as in no one else who has ever lived. His words and works flowed as one from the wellspring of who he was. That is why he is called the Word of God: he is *in himself* God's message.

The Gospel writers' intermingling of Jesus' miracles with his private con-versations and public teaching is not random. Rather, it is aimed at demon-strating the liberating power of God's reign as it touches the whole of human life. That kingdom is at the heart of Jesus' preaching. In effect his miracles reveal who he is and momentarily undo the curse in some respect.[28] Jesus' interactions with people invariably demonstrate his compassion. His teaching the crowds or engaging in scholarly repartee with the nation's religious leaders reveals not merely his intelligence but also his wisdom: Jesus understands life like no one else does. Hence the Gospels present Jesus as the master of every situation, utterly unlike the qur'anic portrayal of him as an adult.

Finally, there is the fact that the four Evangelists tell a story like no other, giving us four separate portraits of Jesus. This is vital, given that they wrote under the conviction that Jesus changed the course of human history forever. Part of the Gospels' appeal is also "the complexity of their central character—the mix

---

[27]The Common Word initiative asserts that Muslims are required to love their enemies just as Chris-tians are, but it presents no qur'anic support for this claim. See Ghazi bin Muhammad, "The ACW Letter—A Common Word Between Us and You," October 13, 2007, www.acommonword.com/ the-acw-document. Miroslav Volf similarly backs his claim up with a hadith and one qur'anic verse describing piety in terms of giving material aid to family, travelers and the marginalized, including setting slaves free (Q 2:177). But as similar to Jas 1:27 as the verse is, it nevertheless falls far short of commanding universal love to neighbors, including one's enemies, which is simply nowhere in view in the Qur'an; Miroslav Volf, *Allah: A Christian Response* (New York: HarperCollins, 2011), 108.

[28]For example, by turning the water into wine, he shares his kingdom's endless joy with the poor (Jn 2:1-11). By his miracles of healing, he releases people from the degenerative processes of mortality (e.g., Mk 2:1-12; 10:46-52). By touching lepers, he reveals God's heart for outcasts (Mk 1:40-45). By healing a Canaanite girl, he anticipates God's opening of faith's door to the Gentiles (Mt 15:21-28; Lk 7:1-10). By feeding the poor, he extends God's bounty to all (Jn 6:1-14). By stilling the storm, he shows his mastery over creation (Mk 4:35-41).

of gentleness and zeal, strident moralism and extraordinary compassion, the down-to-earth and the supernatural," the simple and the unfathomably deep.[29] Extracted from that context and presented in the typically truncated, non-chronological and unframed style of the Qur'an, Jesus stands there as a stock character with no real personality. Add to this the Qur'an's clear aversion to most of the content of the New Testament, and we are left with a thoroughly ahistorical Jesus, a lonely prophet who makes a few brief appearances, some within human history and some outside it. The Qur'an obviously sets out to honor Jesus in some respects, but it carefully restricts that honor to just what is needed for its portrayal to achieve its primary purpose, that is, for Jesus simultaneously to endorse Muhammad's prophethood and to decommission himself as prophet.

The two most stunning aspects of the Qur'an's treatment of Jesus' words and works are its dearth of narrative on Jesus himself and its disconnection from the Bible. In terms of the latter, the qur'anic treatment of Jesus' words and works evidence a deliberate choice to echo almost nothing from the Gospels. In fact, the only narratives common to both the Qur'an and New Testament are those of Zechariah's encounter with the angel before John the Baptist's birth and the annunciation (Q 19:2-23). Tellingly, Jesus is invisible in both narratives. Otherwise, the Qur'an echoes an apocryphal story, details ahistorical events and makes general summary statements, pointing in the general direction of Gospel events.

By now the reason for the strong qur'anic aversion to the New Testament should be clear. The Qur'an barely echoes it because not only the writings of Paul but also the Gospels themselves run directly counter to qur'anic teaching on so many points.[30] That is, since so little in the New Testament aligns with the qur'anic author's message, he simply has no use for it.

---

[29]Ross Douthat, "Return of the Jesus Wars," *New York Times Sunday Review*, August 3, 2013, www.nytimes.com/2013/08/04/opinion/sunday/douthat-return-of-the-jesus-wars.html?smid=tw-share&_r=0.

[30]Though some theologians have argued that Paul and the Gospel writers held very different theologies, they actually held the same basic theology, though they approached it differently. See N. T. Wright, *What Saint Paul Really Said: Was Paul of Tarsus the Real Founder of Christianity?* (Grand Rapids: Eerdmans, 1997).

Sixteen

Jesus' Death *and* Beyond

Most Muslims believe the Qur'an teaches that, instead of allowing Jesus to die, God supernaturally made someone else look like Jesus and die on the cross in his place, while translating Jesus to heaven. They base this on Q 4:157-58, a passage whose meaning is very obscure. For many reasons, however, the passage does not support the surrogacy theory at all, but rather Jesus' historical death and resurrection, although with no redemptive significance. However, in keeping with the surrogacy theory, most Muslims use a variety of methods to manage the remaining qur'anic references to Jesus' death, for example, giving a standard qur'anic word a unique meaning only in relation to Jesus. They also graft Jesus' second coming into the Qur'an to allow for the "yet future" actualization of Jesus' death and resurrection spoken of in Q 19:33. But carefully scrutinized, the Qur'an does not actually teach Jesus' second coming at all. Hence, by adhering strictly to the qur'anic text, Jesus simply died a martyr's death, one accompanied by divine vindication in his resurrection and ascension. Still, what is most important here is not that the Qur'an likely presumes the historicity of Jesus' crucifixion and resurrection, but that it so greatly marginalizes those events so central to the New Testament.

Of all our topics, none is more controversial than the end of Jesus' earthly mission in the Qur'an. Christians unfamiliar with Islam are invariably surprised to learn that Muslims almost universally deny that Jesus died on the cross. But one verse, Q 19:33, speaks clearly of Jesus' death and resurrection.

It quotes him as saying, "Peace be upon me, the day I was born, and the day I die, and the day I am raised up alive!" (Arberry). As Sayyid Qutb (d. 1966) says, this "leaves no room for explaining-away [ta'wīl] or for dispute."[1] To reconcile this verse with their denial, most Muslims assert that before the Judgment Day, Jesus will return to earth, die and be resurrected. With respect to the crucifixion, they believe God delivered Jesus from his foes and translated him to heaven; that his betrayer, Judas, died in his place; and that Christians mistook Judas for Jesus because God made Judas look like Jesus. Muslims base this belief on a particular interpretation of Q 4:157-58, verse 157 being the Qur'an's so-called crucifixion verse. But, as we will see, polemically expedient or not, that interpretation is beset with exegetical difficulties.

This topic is not only controversial but also challenging for various reasons:

- By referring to Jesus' death only a few times, the Qur'an makes it very peripheral.

- Q 4:157-58 is very obscure and easily misunderstood.

- Many interpreters use a semantic ploy to deny the normal meaning of related passages.

Furthermore, since Muslims tie their understanding of Q 4:157-58 to their belief in Jesus' second coming, we must consider qur'anic teaching on Jesus' place in the eschaton also.

Death or Deliverance?

Before examining Q 4:157-58, we must consider Muhammad's original audience, composed of pagans, Jews and Christians, virtually all of whom accepted the historicity of Jesus' death. The Christians clearly did.[2] Jews, too, have always acknowledged it, though without granting it messianic significance. Pagans never denied the fact of Jesus' crucifixion either. Tacitus and Lucian of Samosata wrote of Jesus' execution within a century of it. They did not invest it with religious meaning, but they did accept its historicity, as Arabia's pagans would have done. Hence Muhammad's audience universally believed that Jesus died on a

---

[1]Sayyid Qutb, quoted in Joseph L. Cumming, "Did Jesus Die on the Cross? Reflections in Muslim Commentaries," in *Muslim and Christian Reflections on Peace: Divine and Human Dimensions*, ed. Mustafa Köylü, John Dudley Woodberry and Osman Zümrüt (Lanham, MD: University Press of America, 2005), 47.
[2]Since the Qur'an neither promotes nor attacks dualism, it is unlikely that Mecca or Medina had any docetics or other gnostics.

cross. Thus, for the Qur'an to assert that his death was an illusion would have meant challenging a universal Arab belief. So we must ask, If the Qur'an actually meant to do that, why would it do so in only one brief enigmatic passage? That would suggest the denial was unimportant, whereas among succeeding generations of Muslims it has been anything but. Furthermore, Q 4:157-58 is directed at Jews, not Christians at all, making the Qur'an's denial of so central a Christian belief there even less credible.

Q 4:157-58, the cornerstone of the standard Muslim interpretive edifice, says:

> And because they said, "We killed *al-Masiḥ*, Jesus, the son of Mary, the messenger of God."—They did not kill him nor crucify him, but it was made to seem so to them. Those who disagree about him [or it] are clearly full of doubt about it. They have no knowledge of it and only follow conjecture. Certainly, they did not kill him. No, God raised him to Himself. God is Mighty and Wise. (Jones)

The idea that the Jews crucified not Jesus but rather a double supernaturally made to look like him is found in the oldest extant Muslim commentaries.[3] It is apparently attested earlier by John of Damascus[4] and possibly even by an Arabic Christian document from the 690s.[5] While Wahb ibn Munabbih (d. 732) interprets Q 4:157-58 in terms of a surrogate's death, he explains Q 3:55 in terms of Jesus' death for a duration of just three hours.[6]

But Q 4:157-58 is not the only qur'anic passage referring to Jesus' death. In fact, depending on how you interpret them, a total of four passages— Q 3:54-55; 4:157-58; 5:116-17; 19:33—refer to either Jesus' death or his translation to heaven.[7] Two others, Q 2:87 and 5:75, imply that Jesus died. These passages admit a number of interpretations, two of which—those of the

---

[3]Early commentaries attribute it to such authorities as Mujahid ibn Jabr Maliki (d. 722) and Qatada ibn Diʿama (d. 736); Geoffrey Parrinder, *Jesus in the Qur'an* (Oxford: Oneworld, 1995), 109; and Todd Lawson, *The Crucifixion in the Qur'an: A Study in the History of Muslim Thought* (Oxford: Oneworld, 2009), 44-55.

[4]Lawson suggests that John may be offering his own reading of the verse, but he gives us no reason to doubt that Muslims held this interpretation in John's day; Lawson, *Crucifixion in the Qur'an*, 7-8.

[5]Mark N. Swanson, "'Folly to the Hunafa': The Crucifixion in Early Muslim-Christian Controversy," in *The Encounter of Eastern Christianity with Early Islam*, ed. E. Grypeou, M. Swanson and D. Thomas (Leiden: Brill, 2006), 239.

[6]The surrogate was presumably crucified during that interval; A. H. Mathias Zahniser, *The Mission and Death of Jesus in Islam and Christianity* (Maryknoll, NY: Orbis Books, 2008), 34; Lawson, *Crucifixion in the Qur'an*, 50-52.

[7]In order to simplify the issues, I do not group Q 4:159 with the preceding verses, 157-58. I will return to it in my examination of the qur'anic data on Jesus' assumed eschatological role.

Ahmadi and Isma'ili Muslims—are highly implausible.[8] Thus the Qur'an refers here to either

- Jesus' historical death, resurrection and ascension by the power of God; or

- his translation to heaven, followed by his end-time return to earth and subsequent death and resurrection.

The grammar of Q 4:157-58 allows three distinct answers to the question of what it negates. Most people think the negation must be limited to the verb's object—that is, they did not kill *him* (i.e., *Jesus* never died). But that is not the case. It is equally possible that the negation limits the subject "they" or the verbs "kill" and "crucify."[9] If it negates the subject, then it does not deny Jesus' historical death at all.

The Illusory Death's Contextual Problem

The passage's context is hortatory teaching on the topic of unbelief (*kufr*), which Izutsu defines as faithlessness rooted in ingratitude.[10] And that gives us another reason to doubt the popular interpretation of it. Qur'anically, unbelief is not honest doubt but rather a willful refusal to let go of merely human ideas and embrace revealed truth instead. The passage begins with verse 153, when the Jews allegedly challenge Muhammad to have a book of scripture sent down to him from heaven. In response, the passage has God taking unbelieving Jews as a negative example. It lists ten of their sins, including violating his

---

[8]Ahmadis believe Jesus did not fully die on the cross but swooned, was revived and died of old age in India, a notion first taught by Mirza Ghulam Ahmad (d. 1908). But the historical evidence for Jesus' crucifixion rules out such a position since all of Jesus' crucifiers knew he had died. On the swoon theory's impossibility, see Martin Hengel, *Crucifixion in the Ancient World and the Folly of the Message of the Cross*, trans. John Bowden (Minneapolis: Fortress, 1977). By contrast, and in accord with their Neoplatonism, Isma'ilis, such as Abu Hatim al-Razi (d. 933/34), believe that while Jesus' body died, the "real" spiritual Jesus never died but went straight to God; Lawson, *Crucifixion in the Qur'an*, 81-83. But the basis of this dualistic approach is Isma'ili invocation of the text's "hidden meaning" (*batin*).
[9]Negation can be similarly ambiguous in English. If we say, "You never killed Emma," we usually limit the scope of our negation by emphasizing the subject, object or verb through vocal inflection, body language or both. In writing—barring the use of a cleft construction or an adjacent clarification—we do the same by means of an orthographic marker such as italics. Thus, "*You* never killed Emma" implies that someone else did. "You never *killed* Emma" allows that you may have hurt her, but she never died. "You never killed *Emma*" suggests that you may have, for example, killed Chloe, but not Emma. Without such markers of suprasegmental stress as italics and vocal inflection, we leave others guessing at the meaning, which is precisely the case here.
[10]Toshihiko Izutsu, *Ethico-Religious Concepts in the Qur'ān* (Montreal: McGill University Press, 1966), 105-7.

covenant, disbelieving his signs, murdering his prophets, slandering Mary and boasting that they had killed the Messiah (vv. 155-62). The passage ends with a warning of punishment for those who persist in these sins and a promise of great reward for those who submit to God instead (vv. 161-62). So the denial in Q 4:157-58 comes in an aside meant to silence the Jewish boast.[11] The passage's focus is thus not Christian doctrine, nor yet its imprecision, but rather Jewish unbelief, pure and simple.[12] And it is directed generally to Medina's Muslims and Jews during a time when relations between them were worsening. Hence its concern is not at all the historicity of Jesus' death.

The Illusory Death's Textual Problems

Sandwiched between the denials, we find the phrase *wa-lakin shubbiha lahum*, which can be translated, "But it was made to look like it to them." Most Muslims, however, take it to mean, "But he [the surrogate] was made to look like him [Jesus] to them [the Jews and Christians]," and make it the text's controlling phrase. There are, however, three problems with this:

1. It requires a divine deception of colossal proportions.

2. Its context points to the Jews' spiritual, not physical, blindness to what happened.

3. The grammar does not allow the phrase to refer to a surrogate.

The surrogacy theory makes historical Christianity "based on a divine deception which was not disclosed until the Qur'an was revealed centuries later."[13] Such a scam is both unprecedented in the Qur'an and unworthy of God. It also contradicts God's description of Jesus' disciples as divinely

---

[11]Nearly all the early commentators agree that the passage faults the Jews specifically for boasting that they had killed the Messiah; Zahniser, *Mission and Death of Jesus*, 18-23. We need not take this boast literally, for Jews hold the very idea of the Messiah in such esteem that that they would never boast of killing him and would never call Jesus Messiah either. Rather, this is prophetic parody, deliberately presenting the Jews in the worst possible light.

[12]Both Zamakhshari and Ibn Kathir explain Q 4:157 in terms of Christian heresiography to demonstrate the confusion of Christians. But the only confusion referred to is that of Muhammad's Jewish opponents; Gabriel S. Reynolds, "The Muslim Jesus: Dead or Alive?" *Bulletin of SOAS* 72, no. 2 (2009): 143-44. Precision on Christian theology is no more a qur'anic concern than is conformity to biblical detail in its recounting of narratives about past prophets. The sura does contest with Christians in vv. 170-75 on other theological issues, but not in verses 153-62.

[13]Mahmoud Ayoub, "Towards an Islamic Christology, II: The Death of Jesus, Reality or Delusion?" *The Muslim World* 70 (1980): 97.

inspired and his promise to make them victorious till the resurrection (Q 3:55, 5:111; 61:14). As al-Razi (d. 1210) says, if God misled Jesus' disciples, how can we know he has not misled the *umma*?

The statement immediately after *shubbiha lahum* reads, "Those [i.e., the Jews] who disagree are clearly full of doubt: with no certain knowledge about it, they follow mere conjecture." Their knowledge is based on mere "conjecture" (*zann*) and, according to Izutsu, the Qur'an consistently uses *zann* to refer to the unbeliever's futile efforts to understand the world apart from God. Hence it connotes thoroughgoing spiritual blindness.[14] The same faulty thinking that made the Jews reject Jesus also kept them from seeing God's wisdom and power or sovereignty displayed in his death.[15] Far from positing some act of divine deception, the text simply says that, being spiritually blind, the Jews completely mistook what happened there.

Finally, since Arabic has no neuter, the verb *shubbiha* means either "he was made to look like him" or "it was made to look like it." The substitution theory makes it the former, referring to the surrogate made to look like Jesus. As al-Zamakhshari (d. ca. 1143) shows, however, this does not work grammatically. For the subject would require a previously mentioned antecedent and, since only Jesus is mentioned, we cannot introduce a surrogate here.[16] Hence, Joseph L. Cumming says the verb *shubbiha* can only be an impersonal passive,[17] making the clause mean "it was made to look like it." In fact, the basis of the surrogacy theory lies solely in the highly conflicting hadith. So Q 4:158 must mean that God had the resurrected Jesus ascend to heaven.[18]

---

[14]Toshikiho Izutsu, *God and Man in the Koran: Semantics of the Koranic Weltanschauung* (Tokyo: Keio Institute of Cultural and Linguistic Studies, 1964), 59-62.

[15]The Jewish misunderstanding is contrasted with the certainty of revealed truth: the word translated "certainly" (*yaqinan*) opposes conjecture.

[16]Substitution stories say not that Jesus was made to look like someone else, but rather that some-one was made to look like him, an interpretive option the text does not give us; Ayoub, "Toward an Islamic Christology, II," 101.

[17]Cumming, "Did Jesus Die on the Cross?," 28.

[18]Some leading Muslim commentators take the qur'anic data as permitting belief in Jesus' actual crucifixion. The founder of the Yemeni Zaydi Shi'ite legal school, al-Qasim ibn Ibrahim al-Rassi (d. 860), affirms the historicity of Jesus' death, even referring to it as "a ransom to God." The great Sunni theologian al-Ghazali (d. 1111) also affirms the historicity of Jesus' crucifixion, as do the tenth-century Brothers of Purity (*Ikhwan al-Safa*); Lawson, *Crucifixion in the Qur'an*, 76-77, 86. Though neither al-Tabari (d. 923), nor al-Razi (d. 1210), nor al-Qurtubi (d. 1272), nor al-Baydawi (d. 1291) favor the historical interpretation of Q 4:157, all four plainly list Jesus' literal death (*wafat mawt haqiqiyya*) and resurrection among the possible interpretations of Q 3:55 and give supporting hadith; all cited in Cumming, "Did Jesus Die on the Cross?," 6-30. And lest anyone doubt which

The Meaning of Q 4:157-58

What Q 4:157-58 denies is not the fact of Jesus' death but rather the Jews' alleged boast that they essentially overpowered God in Jesus' crucifixion.[19] As Reynolds says, the two themes here are Jewish infidelity and divine sovereignty. On the former, and specifically on the Jews' killing of God's prophets, the Qur'an has much to say.[20] As we saw in chapter eleven, it is unequivocal here, making the point fully seven times—including in Q 4:155, a mere two verses before our text.[21] This means the common Muslim claim that God would never allow his prophet Jesus to be killed or dishonored by unbelievers belongs to later Muslim theologizing, not at all to the Qur'an. In fact, Q 2:87 names Moses and Jesus as prophets the Jews had mistreated or killed.[22]

On the theme of divine sovereignty, Q 8:17 tells the Muslims it was not they who killed their enemies in battle but God. Indeed, even a symbolic gesture Muhammad made before the battle—throwing sand at his enemies— is said merely to have manifested God's throwing sand at them. Q 4:155 likewise counters the Jewish assertion that they are impervious to the divine plan with the claim that God has sealed them in their unbelief (cf. Q 61:5). As previously noted, the Qur'an teaches that nothing we do happens without God's willing it. Reynolds concludes that the Jews in Q 4:157 are doubly at fault: "they both schemed against the Messenger of God [Jesus] and arrogated to themselves God's power over life and death."[23] Hence the verse does not contest the fact of Jesus' crucifixion. It insists only that God was in control, not

---

interpretation al-Baydawi means here, he adds, "And this is the view of the Christians." Though Rashid Rida (d. 1935) writes extensively on his objections to Christian belief in Jesus' atonement, he says, "The actual fact of the crucifixion is not itself a matter which the Book of God [the Qur'an] seeks to affirm or deny"; Cumming, "Did Jesus Die on the Cross?," 25, 30. Sayyid Qutb is open to the possibility that Q 4:157-58 means Jesus died a martyr's death and that, like all martyrs in God's Cause, he is now alive with him in heaven (cf. Q 2:154; 3:169); Sayyid Qutb, cited in ibid., 30, 34. Finally, Mahmoud Ayoub argues that Jesus did die physically on the cross; Ayoub, "Towards an Islamic Christology, II." But unfortunately, the judgment of all these scholars has gone largely unheeded amid the polemical maelstrom in which the Muslim masses are caught.

[19]To claim that Q 4:157 simply joins the Gospels in affirming that the Romans, not the Jews, crucified Jesus disregards the verse's context: Why ever would the qur'anic author interrupt so impassioned an exhortation with so mundane a clarification?

[20]Reynolds, "Muslim Jesus," 255.

[21]The others are Q 2:91; 3:21, 112, 181, 183; 5:70.

[22]Its concluding words, "some you called impostors and others you killed," suggest that Moses was included in the first group and Jesus the second; Kenneth E. Nolan, cited in Zahniser, *Mission and Death of Jesus*, 26.

[23]Reynolds, "Muslim Jesus," 255.

the Jews. This repeats the essential qur'anic motif of God as eternal subject as opposed to object: he acts on his enemies—never the reverse. The honor of God is at stake here far more than that of his prophet Jesus. But even so, Jesus' resurrection and ascension restore his honor (cf. Q 3:55).

Hence it was the sovereign God who ordained Jesus' death by crucifixion. The Jews merely fulfilled God's plan for him. They never for a moment held the power to terminate Jesus' life. God alone exercises such power and, being God's obedient servant, Jesus willingly accepted his will for him in it. This is also corroborated by Q 3:54, which as we will see similarly says it was the plan of God, not the Jews, that played out in Jesus' death. Thus the grammar and context of Q 4:157-58 both point to Jesus' crucifixion in terms of a faithful martyr's death.

Negative Measures to Support the Illusory Death

Thus far we have examined one passage referring to Jesus' death or—as most Muslims believe—his escape to heaven. "The classical commentators generally began with the questionable premise that Q 4:157-9 contains an unambiguous denial of Jesus' death by crucifixion," Neal Robinson points out. They then made all the other qur'anic references to Jesus' death fit their interpretation of that one passage.[24] In fact, to make three of the four passages—Q 3:54-55; 5:75, 116-17—fit with it, they had to work hard—and harder still to harmonize Q 19:33 with it.

Most Muslim scholars solve the problem in Q 3:54-55 and 5:116-17 by denying their key word *tawaffa* its standard lexical meaning, "cause you to die." The first passage reads as follows:

> They plotted[25] and God plotted too, and God is the best of plotters. And [recall] when God said, "Jesus, I will cause you to die [*mutawaffika*] and raise you to myself and purify you from those who do not believe and put those who follow you over those who do not believe until the Resurrection Day. Then to me you will return and I will judge between you regarding your differences."

The Qur'an uses *tawaffa* twenty-six times in all. God—or an angelic intermediary—is always the subject and, in all but two cases, it means "cause to die."[26]

---

[24]Neal Robinson, s.v. "Jesus," in *EQ*.
[25]The pronoun refers back to the Jews mentioned in verse 49 and referred to in verse 52.
[26]A. H. Mathias Zahniser, "The Forms of *Tawaffa* in the Qur'ān: A Contribution to Christian-Muslim Dialogue," *The Muslim World* 79, no. 1 (1989): 19-20. Interestingly, three occurrences of *tawaffa* refer to the possibility of Muhammad's untimely death (Q 10:46; 13:40; 40:77). The sole exceptions to this usage are in Q 6:60 and 39:42, where *tawaffa* is used to mean "receive a soul in sleep."

Hence God tells Jesus he will take his soul in death, raise him to himself and purify him from the Jews who reject him.[27] Since the subject of Q 3:35-57 is Jesus' historical origins and ministry, we are unjustified to project Jesus' death to the eschaton. The passage says that the Jews plotted against Jesus, but God outflanked them, an idea integral to Q 4:157-58 too. Besides raising Jesus, as he does in Q 4:158 also, God purifies him from the shame the Jews brought on him—but only after letting him die.[28]

Similarly, Q 5:116-17 has Jesus declaring that, while he was responsible for the message he proclaimed on earth, he cannot be held responsible for his followers' message since his death:

> And when God said, "Jesus, son of Mary, did you say to people, 'Take me and my
> mother as gods beside God'?" He replied, "Glory to you! It is not for me to say what
> I had no right to say. . . . I was a witness over them as long as I was among them.
> When you caused me to die [*tawaffaytani*], you were the watcher over them and
> you are a witness to everything."

Concerned about the worship of Jesus by Christians, Muhammad's contemporaries, this passage seemingly describes a scene from the Judgment Day. That God asks Jesus whether or not he was responsible for such worship means he is asking him about his historical ministry on earth. Accordingly, Jesus denies that, during his lifetime, he encouraged any such thing. But he also reminds God that he, Jesus, cannot be held responsible for whatever his followers did after his death.

The two passages are really quite straightforward. But due to their precommitments relative to Q 4:157-58, most Muslim commentators find them problematic and expend considerable energy seeking solutions. Some fall back on the verb's second meaning, producing a hadith that has Jesus falling asleep briefly between his arrest and translation to heaven. Another commentator cites a hadith that has Jesus die—though not by crucifixion—and then rise and ascend to God three

---

But even in those cases, the sleep is related to death; Q 1:16.

[27]Tarif Khalidi asserts that Q 3:55 refers to Jesus' being purified from "the perverted beliefs of his followers," evidencing a failure to connect the verse with both its context and Q 4:157-58. As Q 3:52 makes plain, the unbelievers to which Q 3:55 refers are also Jewish; Tarif Khalidi, *The Muslim Jesus: Sayings and Stories in Islamic Literature* (Cambridge, MA: Harvard University Press, 2001), 12.

[28]Since this passage precedes Q 4:157-58 chronologically, Muhammad's hearers had no way of knowing then what the later sura would say. They would thus have understood Q 3:54-55 in terms of their culture's universal belief in Jesus' death.

days later. Unimpressed by these solutions, some early commentators give the verb a meaning unique to these two occurrences, though they cannot agree on what that might be.[29] Another explanation is that it was Jesus' *work* that God received as having been completed, but this imports an object into the text that is not there. One commentator who grants that here as elsewhere *tawaffa* means "cause to die" reverses the word order, so that Jesus ascended to heaven before returning to earth and dying.[30] But the vast majority of commentators refuse to understand *tawaffa* according to its normal usage.[31]

The other passage in this category, Q 5:75, only alludes to Jesus' death. It says, "The Messiah, son of Mary, was only a messenger, before whom other messengers had passed away. His mother was a virtuous woman. They both ate food." The issue here is the Christian deification of Jesus and allegedly of Mary. Q 5:72-73 says, "Those who say God is the Messiah, son of Mary, certainly blaspheme [lit. have disbelieved]. . . . Indeed, anyone who associates others with God will certainly be barred by God from the Garden. The Fire will be his home. . . . Those who say 'God is the third of three' have actually abandoned faith," and the passage continues on with the theme of false worship to the end of verse 77. Verse 75 mentions the passing away of other prophets before Jesus because, being merely human, all prophets die. The words the Messiah "was only a messenger, before whom other messengers had passed away" then imply that he died just like others. Hence the passage marshals two proofs of Jesus' humanity. For qur'anically, mortality and corporeality—his eating food—are altogether exclusive of divinity.

Some Muslim exegetes avoid this conclusion simply by ignoring the verse's implication. Others deny the verb *khalat* its usual qur'anic meaning when used of individuals—"had passed away"—making it mean "are no longer present" instead. For example, Hasan Qaribullah renders it "had gone," while Tarif

---

[29]Some of the meanings advocated are "take in full" (i.e., take both soul and body to heaven), "seize from the earth" (i.e., physically), "complete my life" (i.e., not cut it short by an untimely death) or "make me like someone received in death."

[30]Parrinder, *Jesus in the Qur'an*, 106; Zahniser, "Forms of *Tawaffa* in the Qur'an," 14-24.

[31]Suleiman E. Mourad, "Does the Qur'an Deny or Assert Jesus' Crucifixion and Death?," in *New Perspectives on the Qur'ān: The Qur'ān in Its Historical Context 2*, ed. Gabriel Said Reynolds (New York: Routledge, 2011), 351. Tarif Khalidi and Laleh Bakhtiar's translations of these two verses give *tawaffa* its standard meaning. Mahmoud Ayoub allows that *mutawaffika* (in Q 3:55) could mean "causing you to die" also; "Toward an Islamic Christology, II," 106-7; Tarif Khalidi, trans., *The Qur'an* (New York: Penguin Books, 2008); Laleh Bakhtiar, trans., *The Sublime Quran* (Chicago: Kazi Publications, 2007).

Khalidi translates it "had come and gone," thus removing Jesus' implied historical death and allowing for his future death.[32] But unlike his mortality, the mere fact that Jesus was on earth for a limited time does not disprove his deity, qur'anically. The implicit argument carried weight with the Christians to which it was directed only because they knew Jesus had in fact died.

Positive Measures to Support the Illusory Death

As we have seen, there is no dodging Jesus' death and resurrection in Q 19:33. What is more, both Q 3:55 and 4:158 clearly affirm God's raising Jesus to himself. But the standard Muslim reading of Q 4:157-58 denies the New Testament teaching that Jesus died. And that interpretive choice forces them to relocate Jesus' death to the future, helping to foster the movement in the early Muslim period to Islamicize in their hadith literature various Christian traditions on Jesus' second coming. For as we will see, the Qur'an nowhere teaches that Jesus will come again.

Muslims use at least eight qur'anic references to establish Jesus' role in the eschaton. However, one of them, Q 5:110, actually speaks of Jesus during his lifetime, not in the future. And four others, though of some eschatological import, do not mention Jesus at all.[33] They only provide a means, however tenuous, of tethering the legendary Jesus of the hadith to the far more ordinary Jesus of the Qur'an. The sixth eschatological reference, Q 43:57-61, speaks only of the need to *believe* in Jesus to survive the Last Day. The other two, Q 3:45-46 and 4:159—both Medinan—actually do refer to Jesus' future, and we will consider them briefly in turn. A passage already examined above, Q 5:116-17, also refers to Jesus on the Last Day. As we will see, however, all these references ascribe to him a very normal prophetic role, nothing like the dramatic end-times role the hadith give him.[34] Our interpretation of these qur'anic texts,

---

[32]Hasan Qaribullah, "Surah Al-Maida," accessed on March 7, 2014, http://theonlyquran.com/quran /Al-Maida/English_Prof_Shaykh_Hasan_Qaribullah/?ayat=1&pagesize=0. Interestingly, both Qaribullah and Khalidi render the same verb as "have passed away" when it alludes to Muhammad's dying like the other messengers before him (Q 3:144).

[33]They are Q 17:1, the supposed qur'anic basis for Muhammad's legendary Night Journey; Q 18:21 and 21:96 on Gog and Magog; and Q 9:33 on Islam's triumph over other religions.

[34]The hadith literature tells us Jesus will, among other things, return in power to kill the antichrist, slaughter pigs, destroy crosses, churches and synagogues, and kill any Christians and Jews refusing to convert to Islam. He will then enjoy a long reign over the earth before himself dying, being buried in Medina and rising at Muhammad's side on the Last Day.

however, must stand or fall on their own apart from the highly contradictory exegetical hadith.[35]

Most Muslims believe Q 43:61 teaches that Jesus' second coming will usher in the Hour, or end time. However, the text refers to Jesus' future only if we accept a noncanonical reading of it. To understand the verse properly, we need to see it in context (Q 43:57-61):

> [57]When the Son of Mary is presented as an example, your people laugh out loud [58]and say: "Who is better, our gods or him?" They cite him to you simply for argument. Indeed, they are a contentious people! [59]He is merely a servant on whom We bestowed our favor, and We made him a model for the Children of Israel. [60]Had We wanted, We could have appointed angels as vicegerents among you on earth. [61]It [or He] is indeed knowledge for the Hour. Do not be in doubt about it, but follow me. This is the straight path.

There are two reasons why this does not carry the eschatological payload most Muslim commentators think it does. First, they usually take the initial pronoun in Q 43:61 to be "he," referring back to Jesus (vv. 57-59). They do this because they read the sentence's key word as "sign" instead of "knowledge." These words are distinct, but a noncanonical version of the text gives "sign" (*'alamun*) instead of "knowledge" (*'ilmun*). However, a second variant gives the word as "reminder" (*dikhrun*), and Tabari comments that this variant supports the authenticity of the canonical version.[36] Hence the canonical reading is more likely the authentic one. Second, while commentators in the classical period knew the Last Day to be many years distant from Muhammad, his original audience did not. The Qur'an never once presents the Hour as distant. Indeed, inherent in the very idea of the Hour is the fact that nothing would presage its arrival: the whole point is that it is frightfully imminent and will strike without warning.[37] Hence Q 43:61 was never meant to tell believers how to recognize the Hour's inception.

Instead it simply tells Mecca's polytheists they must accept Jesus' prophethood to be ready for the Last Day. Robinson takes the initial pronoun to be "it" and

---

[35]For example, some say Jesus' point of return will be outside Damascus, others in Jerusalem. Some say he will reign for forty years, others one thousand years. The classical scholars' designation of some hadith as authentic versus inauthentic did little to eliminate such contradictions.

[36]Tabari's point seems to be that "reminder" works as an interpretive gloss for "knowledge" only, not for "sign"; cited in Neal Robinson, *Christ in Islam and Christianity: Representation of Jesus in the Qur'an and the Classical Muslim Commentaries* (London: Macmillan, 1991), 91.

[37]This urgency is particularly evident in the Qur'an's Meccan suras—for example, Sura 43.

sees it as referring back to the fact of Jesus' servanthood mentioned in verse 59.[38] In other words, it refers to the issue under discussion, of Jesus' being a servant chosen by God. When the Meccans balk at the idea of accepting Jesus—a foreign god to them (v. 58)—the Qur'an insists that accepting his prophethood is essential. Only those who accept it will be ready for the Hour. Not only does this interpretation fix the verse squarely in its preceding context, it also fits its concluding call to the simplicity of faith and obedience. Again, the divine response to Meccan resistance to Jesus is clearly, "Human though he is, Jesus is no optional add-on. You either accept him as prophet or perish."

Q 3:45-46 and 5:116-17 deserve mention also. The former comes in the Qur'an's treatment of the annunciation, when the angel tells Mary she will give birth to Jesus, "highly honored in this world and the next, one of those brought near." That is, he will be among God's most highly ranked prophets and so will be brought close to him in paradise. Besides showing Jesus as submissive to God, Q 5:116-17 makes him answerable to him, as a defendant before a judge. So these passages cancel each other out, the one elevating, the other humbling him.

Still we have seen nothing to suggest that Jesus will return to earth again. Only Q 4:159 remains to be considered in this regard, a verse most Muslims believe refers to Christ's return. This verse, however, is just as ambiguous as the two immediately preceding it. What makes it so challenging is its use of no less than five personal pronouns: "And [there is] not [one] of the People of the Book *who* will not believe in *him* before *his* death and on the Resurrection Day *he* will be a witness against *them*." Having seen that Q 4:157-58 implicitly accepts Jesus' historical death, we must now determine whether Q 4:159 supports that interpretation or not. To do so, we must answer these five questions:

1. Is God here making a statement of fact or a threat?

2. *Who* will all believe?

3. They will all believe in *whom*?

4. They will believe before *who* dies?

5. *Who* will witness against them on the Resurrection Day, and to what end?

---

[38]Robinson, *Christ in Islam and Christianity*, 92-93. Commentators taking the pronoun to be "it" say it refers to the Qur'an or knowledge of the Qur'an needed to survive the Last Day. But while authentic hadith support this interpretation, "the Qur'an" in no way fits the verse's context.

First, to read it as a simple statement sends us in the wrong direction entirely. Zamakhshari argues that it is a threat, referring to the punishment of the grave (*'adhab al-qabr*). The idea is that in the moment of their death these people will realize to their horror that the prophet they rejected was indeed sent by God, and it is now too late to accept him. This interpretation fits the point of the larger passage: a painful punishment awaits the Jews who boasted about crucifying the Messiah, etc. (Q 4:153-61). Only those who repent now will be spared then.

Second, those who will all believe are the "People of the Book." But while that term can include Christians along with Jews, it does not include Christians here because the entire passage is directed against the Jews. Since Christians inherently believe Jesus was sent from God, to insert Christians here requires another insertion, the idea that Christians will see that their worship of Jesus has disqualified them from true faith and admission to paradise. That insertion takes us even further afield of the context and makes no sense apart from its obvious polemical appeal.

Skipping ahead to our fifth question, we answer the third as well. The notion in this threat is of a Last Day witness who seals his people's doom by testifying to God of their unbelief. This then is none other than Jesus (Q 4:157), a point on which the early commentators are agreed. But this does not give Jesus a unique role in the eschaton. Prophets typically testify against those who refused to listen (Q 4:41; 16:84, 89; 28:75; 50:21).[39] This means the one in whom they will believe is Jesus, and most early commentators agree here also. Suggestions that the object of their faith is either God or Muhammad miss the point. The passage does not mention Muhammad, so the *he* cannot refer back to him. Jews already believe in God, so it makes no sense to say they will believe in him. No, the Jews will believe in Jesus as God's prophet, but too late.

Finally, does the *his* in "his death" refer back to the preceding *him*—so Jesus' death—or distributively to the earlier, implied *one*—meaning each individual Jew's death? The hadith unhelpfully support both answers. But while a textual variant substitutes "their death" for "his death," a majority of early commentators take the *his* to mean Jesus' death.[40] This appealed to them, since a mass conversion of Jews before Jesus' death would have to mean his death was yet future,

---

[39]Ibid., 87.

[40]Arthur Jeffery, *Materials for the History of the Text of the Qur'ān* (Leiden: Brill, 1937), 127.

supporting the surrogacy reading of Q 4:157-58. But while the verse may not actually prove that Jesus had already died, seeing it as a threat decides the issue in favor of its referring to the death of each individual Jew. That is, it refers to the dying souls' being made to see the truth about Jesus. Thus the verse says nothing about Jesus' death. Neither does it give him a unique eschatological role. He is just like other prophets who will testify against their obdurate people.

To sum up, the Qur'an makes just three points about Jesus on the Last Day:

1. He will adamantly deny ever having encouraged his followers to worship him or his mother.

2. To their eternal loss, he will testify against the Jews who rejected him.

3. He will be highly honored by God and brought near to him.

The Qur'an says nothing truly exceptional of Jesus' role or place on the Last Day, nothing it might not also say of Abraham or Moses. It does not allude to Jesus' second coming[41] or ascribe to him any key eschatological role, whether those he holds in the Bible or in the hadith.

Though Minimalist, the Qur'anic View of Jesus' Death Is Historical

To sum up, we have solid evidence for accepting the historical-death interpretation of Q 4:157-58 and rejecting the idea that a denial of Jesus' death can be based on the passage:

- The Qur'an would not deny a universally held belief in one single obscure verse.

- The passage calls Jews to repent—it does not inform Christians of their misbelief.

- The grammar of Q 4:157 does not support the surrogacy interpretation.

- It is far more qur'anic to view Q 4:157 as negating the subject than the object.

- The honor at stake in the passage is that of God more than his prophet.

---

[41]Two of the Qur'an's central emphases combined to make any need for such eschatological drama unthinkable during Muhammad's lifetime: the imminence of the Last Day and the finality of Muhammad's prophethood. It is ironic that the hadith reversed the Qur'an here by establishing Jesus as a significant figure in the eschaton.

- The Jews were confused by their spiritual blindness, not an act of divine deception.

- The idea of divine duplicity is quite unprecedented in the Qur'an and dishonors God.

- The rest of the qur'anic data on Jesus' death supports the historical-death interpretation.

- Q 4:159 in no way challenges the historical-death interpretation.

The passage does not deny the crucifixion's historicity nor decide on Christian doctrinal issues. The size and shrillness of the debate over Jesus' crucifixion that has raged between Muslims and Christians through the centuries make it difficult to see that. Everyone in Muhammad's audience knew Jesus had died centuries before. The Qur'an's very first mention of Jesus, in Sura 19, spoke of his death and resurrection without qualification. No later passage—least of all, Q 4:157-59—qualified those events as yet future. Thus, when the Qur'an referred to Jesus' death and resurrection, it referred to the historical events. But the fact that it has so very little to say about them has enabled the Muslim community to force those round pegs into square holes.

The Qur'an and Bible Compared

The key point here is that the Qur'an gives Jesus' death, resurrection and ascension none of their biblical importance. While God was the one who took Jesus' life and gave it back to him in resurrection, those events relate simply to Jesus and his opponents, not to any redemptive plan of God. The Qur'an views Jesus' death as it does the death of other martyrs in God's Cause—that is, while accepting its historicity, it makes it only peripheral to God's purposes for humankind.

By contrast, the New Testament puts Jesus' historical death and resurrection at the heart of God's plan for his world. None of Jesus' followers or his enemies saw the significance of his death at the time. He alone knew it represented God's subversive redefinition of his redemptive work (Is 53:5-12; Mt 20:28; 2 Cor 5:19; 1 Pet 3:18). For by it, God executed judgment on evil and injustice, as Jesus, the sinless one, took the entire history of human evil and oppression onto himself and then triumphed over them by the power of his perfect love (Acts 2:24; Col 2:15; Heb 2:14). God, who is love, had always known what Jesus' total submission in a world ruled by egotism would cost him. But because of his love, God—Father and Son acting together—accepted that cost before Jesus ever came into the world. Still, as A. H. Mathias Zahniser says,

> Jesus did not want to die. Jesus even prayed that God would make this seemingly inevitable event unnecessary. Nevertheless, Jesus ended his Gethsemane struggle accepting what God willed for him (Mk. 14:32-42). Neither did God want Jesus to die.... God wanted Jesus to be fully human, to live out the love that is central to life under God's reign. Because that project made Jesus a threat to the entrenched interests of Roman and Jewish leadership, it entailed his death.[42]

Because Jesus loved to his very last breath, he was, as Herbert McCabe puts it, "the first member of the human race in whom humanity came to fulfillment, the first human being for whom to live was simply to love."[43] But evil men would have none of it. They condemned Jesus falsely and then heaped on him the abuse their own sins so richly deserved. So in his wisdom, God mysteriously took their evil and "turned it into" good by accomplishing in his Son's death the reversal inherent in grace (Rom 6:9; 2 Cor 5:21; Gal 3:13). In his death, good paradoxically triumphed over evil, as he, the sinless one, took the sinner's curse so that he might offer her his own eternal blessing.

Hence, biblically speaking, Jesus' death and resurrection are the central facts of human history. Without them, there is neither forgiveness nor hope for the future (Jn 14:6; 1 Cor 15:17; Eph 1:7; 1 Pet 1:3-4). Jesus' resurrection represents the beginning of God's recreation of his world, including his offer to us of his indestructible life and irresistible authority (1 Cor 15:20; Eph 1:15-23; Col 1:15; Heb 7:16). And Jesus' second coming is that moment when everything his life, death, resurrection and ascension accomplished—the inauguration of God's reign on earth—becomes fully visible and all is made new (Mt 16:27; Acts 1:11; 2 Thess 2:1-3, 8; Heb 9:8; Rev 1:17; 19:11-16; 21:5). That is why the New Testament refers to it hundreds of times.

Since the Qur'an differs so radically from the Bible in its take on the human problem and its solution, it should not surprise us that the Qur'an moves the very events the Bible makes central—Jesus' death and resurrection—to the

---

[42]A. H. Mathias Zahniser, "The Death of Jesus in Islam and Christianity," last modified April 1, 2010, www.catalystresources.org/the-death-of-jesus-in-islam-and-christianity.

[43]Herbert McCabe, *God Matters* (Springfield, IL: Templegate, 1991), 93.

margin and completely omits his second coming. This created a problem for the nascent Muslim community, however. For what worked for Muhammad and his followers in the Hijaz did not work so well after the conquest of the Fertile Crescent, where Christianity remained a major ideological, though no longer political, force. The Muslims needed solid answers to the theological objections of the Christians surrounding them. They also needed to know how to think of Christians and their scripture. As we will see in chapter seventeen, the Qur'an did not give them clear answers. And when polemical concerns drive a community magically to transmute its scripture's obscurity into perfect clarity, unusual interpretations arise. Lacking the clarity they so needed, Muslims looked for a knockout punch. But as we have seen, Q 4:157-59 does not deliver the punch most Muslims believe it does.

Seventeen

Jesus' Community *and* Scripture

The Qur'an often refers to Christians as "People of the Book," a term that includes Jews also. Its usual specific designation for Christians is "Nazarenes" (*nasara*), not the standard Arabic term in use then. Likewise, it calls Jesus *'Isa* and the Christian scripture *al-injil*, all unusual names. Such choices facilitated their Islamicization and may have made their inclusion in qur'anic theology slightly less repellent to potential Jewish supporters. The Qur'an leads readers to expect the Injil to resemble it closely, prompting most Muslims nowadays to resolve discrepancies between the New Testament and the Qur'an by alleging that Christians have falsified their scriptures. But a number of leading Muslim scholars have acknowledged that this theory is unfounded. The Qur'an gives no real indication of its author's familiarity with the contents of the Injil, which evidently refers to the New Testament. In fact, nothing suggests that the Qur'an has any real interest in either the Injil or Torah beyond using them as an endorsement of Muhammad. Followed chronologically, the Qur'an's approach to Christians moves in stages from sympathy to censure, ending with a condemnation of their "polytheism" and a mandate to subdue them militarily. Hence, as Muhammad's political power grew, so did his intolerance of those who rejected his prophethood. On the whole, the Qur'an proclaims its compatibility with the Bible but provides little support for that claim. Most of the pagans in Muhammad's audience would have been aware of Jewish and Christian beliefs in broad outline but would have had little knowledge of the Bible's detailed contents. This made it possible for the Qur'an to claim continuity with a Bible many of its teachings actually subverted.

*B*uilding on what we established in chapter four concerning the identity of the Qur'an's Christians and its approach to the biblical scriptures, we now consider five questions vital to anyone seeking to respond to the Qur'an with both grace and truth:

1. Why does the Qur'an present Christians as it does?

2. What is the Injil it claims to confirm?

3. Do Muslims have any basis for their charge of biblical falsification?

4. How does the Qur'an view Christians?

5. How should we understand the Qur'an's claims concerning the Bible?

How the Qur'an Refers to Christians and Why

The Qur'an uses various descriptions—e.g., "those who received the Book before you"—and names to refer generally to Jews and Christians. It calls them either the "People of the Book" (*ahl al-kitab*) or the "Children of Israel" (*banu isra'il*) some ninety-five times and the "People of Remembrance" (*ahl al-dhikr*) once (Q 21:7). But since these designations may refer to either Jews or Christians or both, we cannot say how many times they are specifically directed at Christians. This is part of the Qur'an's tendency to treat Jews and Christians as a single entity. On the other hand, the Qur'an emphasizes their division into two separate communities and implies that it should not be so (e.g., Q 6:156; 10:93; 23:52-53; 27:78; 43:63; 45:16-19). It refers explicitly to Christians fewer than twenty times, usually by the name *al-nasara*.[1] The Qur'an also accuses both Christians and Jews of polytheism (Q 9:30) and considers their rejection of Muhammad no less damnable than that of pagans, making the great choice before all his hearers crystal clear.

Scholars have suggested various meanings for *al-nasara*, but al-Tabari is likely right to say that it simply refers to Jesus' origins in Nazareth.[2] Assuming

---

[1] The Meccan suras refer to them as Romans, or Byzantines (*al-rum*, Q 30:2). The Medinan suras call them *al-nasara* some fifteen times and the "People of the Injil" (*ahl al-injil*) once (Q 5:47); they are also described as "those who followed [Jesus]" (*alladhina ittaba'uka*) once (Q 3:55).

[2] *Al-nasara* is derived from the Syriac *nasrare* (Nazarenes), a name for Christians used in eastern Syria primarily by non-Christians; Griffith, s.v. "Christians and Christianity," in *EQ*. Al-Tabari also connects the term to the word "helpers" (*ansar*), since Christians were those who volunteered to "help" (*nasara*) the Messiah as his disciples did (Q 61:14); Jane Dammen McAuliffe, *Qur'anic Christians:*

that *al-nasara* refers to standard Christians, the question is not how widely the term had penetrated Arabic. The point is that it would have been less offensive to Muhammad's Jewish hearers than the usual "Christians" (*al-masihiyyun*) since that term designated the latter by their belief in Jesus as Israel's Messiah.

The larger context for the Qur'an's name choice is key here—that is, its choice of unusual names for both Christianity's founder (*ʿIsa*) and scripture (*al-injil*). The increasing dangers of Muhammad's Meccan years required that he keep all his options open. He had always known that he and his followers might well need to seek refuge elsewhere. With Mecca's Kaʿba integral to his religious vision, he doubtless hoped a Hijazi town like Yathrib might welcome him. For the qur'anic author to appeal to its mixed Jewish and pagan population while simultaneously challenging both polytheism and Judaism required a bold and sensitive strategy. His inclusion of Jesus was naturally very problematic to Jews, making it vital that he adjust things slightly. And the names by which one designates an antagonistic community and its founder are vital. This was doubtless one reason he used the names *al-nasara* for Christians, *ʿIsa* for Jesus—not the standard *Yasuʿ*—and *Yahya*, not *Yohanna*, for John the Baptist. In fact, the less standard these names were the better. Not that any Jewish hearers would have been unsure of whom Muhammad meant by *ʿIsa*, the son of Mary.[3] But they would have found a de-Christianized name for Jesus slightly more tolerable—at least, that was the hope. Likewise, the use of *Yahya* was not meant to render the Baptist unrecognizable, only a bit less sequestered and polarizing. In minimizing the offense to potential Jewish supporters, this renaming of Jesus and his community also granted the Qur'an freedom to present them more fully on its own terms, that is, to Islamicize them.

Two things alert us to this tendency to appeal to Jews. First, the Qur'an delays declaring Jesus the Messiah until Muhammad sees that his overtures to Medina's Jews are a lost cause and changes his strategy toward them, as signaled by the changing of the *qibla* to Mecca. Second, until then the Qur'an had typically referred to both Jews and Christians by nonsectarian terms—it only once referred to Christians by name and then only by the nontheological term "Romans" (*al-rum*).[4] In Medina he distinguishes Christians mainly by

An Analysis of Classical and Modern Exegesis (Cambridge: Cambridge University Press, 1991), 95.

[3]There was no point for the Qur'an to rename Mary (*Maryam*) since her virginal purity—contra the Jewish charge of Jesus' illegitimacy—was such a key point in its anti-Jewish polemic.

[4]Despite all the negative associations of Byzantines to Jews in the seventh century, this would have been slightly less theologically charged for them than "Christians," as previously suggested.

his use of the equally nontheological "Nazarenes." Hence it seems reasonable that his desire both to avoid offending Jews and to achieve maximum control over his presentation of Christianity led him to rename its founder and his supporting prophet already during the Meccan period.[5]

The Injil of Muslim Polemics

Before examining the qur'anic view of Christians further, we must consider the identity of the Christian scripture mentioned by the Qur'an. Namely, to what exactly does al-injil refer? The problem here derives from a number of irreconcilable facts. The Qur'an

- uses al-injil to refer to the Christian scripture;
- leads us to expect al-injil to resemble the Qur'an closely;
- declares that Muslims believe in that scripture, implying that it agrees with the Qur'an; and
- is radically different from the New Testament in both form and theology.

Regarding the second point, the Qur'an seems to conceive of the Christian scripture as a book sent down to Jesus by God in the same manner that Muhammad claims to receive the Qur'an (Q 3:3, 65; 4:163; 5:46-47, 66-68; 57:27; cf. Q 3:48; 5:110). But this follows naturally from the fact that the Qur'an takes itself and its prophet as normative of all the earlier scriptures and prophets.

With respect to the name injil itself, its most likely philological ancestor is the Ethiopic wangel, itself derived from the Greek word euangelion ("gospel" in Middle English; "good news" in today's idiom). But a name's etymology does not determine its meaning and, unlike "gospel," injil only appears in the singular. Hence we should not assume that Injil in the Qur'an means "gospel" in any standard Christian usage.[6]

---

[5]By contrast, the qur'anic author did not rename the Jews (al-yahud), the Torah (al-tawrat) or any of its major Jewish prophets, since none of their names were objectionable to Christians.

[6]In Christian usage, Gospel or gospel may refer to (1) Christ's teachings generically, (2) the message of salvation through him or (3) a record of Jesus' life, teachings and the salvation he accomplished as found in the New Testament's four Gospels. But the Qur'an does not use al-injil to refer to any of these things, leaving the question of what it does mean wide open. Since we have no evidence that Arab Christians used Gospel to refer to the entire New Testament, it seems that the qur'anic author exercised his characteristic originality in his use of the word.

Most Muslims now resolve the discrepancy between the qur'anic presentation of the Injil and a New Testament that bears almost no formal resemblance to the Qur'an by alleging that Christians have falsified their scriptures. Some even posit that the Qur'an uses *al-injil* to refer to an "original Gospel" Jesus allegedly received from God, a scripture no longer extant. Muslims have enthusiastically embraced such theories as the fix needed "to rebuff any arguments based by Christians on the Bible."[7] In fact the doctrine that Jews and Christians have falsified their scriptures[8] has proven so comprehensive a solution that it has become the "central point of Muslim polemic."[9] Some Western scholars also seem to accept the popular Muslim interpretation of *al-injil* whether or not they believe an "original Gospel" ever actually existed.[10]

In fact, the real problem in reconciling the Injil to the New Testament is doubtless far more theological than formal, related to the biblical scripture's radically different contents. As we have seen, it is impossible to harmonize many of the Qur'an's teachings with those of the New Testament, for so central are Christ's deity and redemptive death to the New Testament that to excise them is to eviscerate it. Hence most Muslims conclude that the New Testament cannot possibly be the Injil the Qur'an calls them to believe and reject the Christian scripture as a forgery.

But the theory of biblical corruption did not grow up overnight. It developed after Muhammad's death, when Muslims realized the extent to which the Bible contradicted the Qur'an. And it took the better part of a millennium to attain the status of established "fact."[11] For although the justifications for this popular

---

[7]W. Montgomery Watt, *Muslim-Christian Encounters: Perceptions and Misperceptions* (London: Routledge, 1991), 30.

[8]This doctrine goes by the name of *tahrif*, meaning "corruption" or "alteration."

[9]Ignàc Goldziher, quoted by Gordon Nickel, *Narratives of Tampering in the Earliest Commentaries on the Qur'an* (Leiden: Brill, 2011), 2.

[10]Sidney H. Griffith, s.v. "Gospel," in *EQ*. This acceptance of the Muslim understanding may be due to the fact that Western culture has made tolerance issuing in interfaith agreement primary.

[11]Although almost all Muslims today take the theory that the text of the Bible has been corrupted for granted, it was doubtless never in the minds of Muhammad's original hearers. An Andalusian polemicist named Ibn Hazm systematized the theory in the eleventh century. The Gospel of Barnabas, originating no earlier than the fourteenth century in Italy or Spain, lent credence to it by presenting a narrative in which Judas dies in Jesus' stead. An Indian debater in the nineteenth century named al-Kairanawi then married the theory to the views of modern European historical critics to allege that all the best Christian scholars agreed with it. And ever since a Saudi-funded Muslim polemicist named Ahmed Deedat popularized it in the closing decades of the twentieth century, most Muslims now deem proof unnecessary.

theory are no stronger now than when it was first proposed, polemics can easily trump everything else in scriptural interpretation, as we have seen.

This notion that the biblical text itself has been corrupted was seldom taken seriously in Islam's first five centuries.[12] And throughout history a number of leading Muslim scholars have argued against it. But alas, among Muslims today, they are voices crying in the wilderness. One of the best-known Qur'an commentators, Ibn Kathir (d. 1373), explained the phrase, "None can change God's words" (Q 6:115; 18:27), by quoting Wahb ibn Munabbih (d. 731): "The Tawrah and the Injil remain as Allah revealed them, and no letter in them was removed."[13] Ibn Qutayba (d. 885) held a similar view. Great Muslim historian Ibn Khaldun (d. 1406) likewise pointed out how illogical the doctrine of scriptural corruption is, saying that no good scholar could accept it "since custom prevents people who have a (revealed) religion from dealing with their divine scriptures in such a manner."[14]

For Christians to corrupt their actual texts, they would have all had to agree on changing them in the very same way—not just in Palestine, but also in Europe and the Middle East—and the same is true of Jews. It would have been virtually impossible to get either group to agree universally on such changes, and even if Christians or Jews in just one locale had failed to cooperate or "get the memo," their (unchanged) texts would provide indisputable evidence of the corruption that had taken place elsewhere. But no such evidence exists. More impossible still would be getting Jews and Christians—bitter enemies from early on—to change their Hebrew Bible (Old Testament) texts identically. Hence Ayoub wisely writes, "Contrary to the general Islamic view, the Qur'an does not accuse Jews and Christians of altering the text of their scriptures, but rather of altering the truth which those scriptures contain."[15]

---

[12]Martin Accad, "The Gospels in the Muslim Discourse of the Ninth to the Fourteenth Centuries," in *A Common Word: Muslims and Christians on Loving God and Neighbor*, ed. Miroslav Volf, Ghazi bin Muhammad and Melissa Yarrington (Grand Rapids: Eerdmans, 2010), 59.

[13]Ibn Kathir, quoted in Abdu H. Murray, *Grand Central Question: Answering the Critical Concerns of the Major Worldviews* (Downers Grove, IL: InterVarsity Press, 2014), 184.

[14]Nickel, *Narratives of Tampering*, 22.

[15]Ayoub continues, saying that this is more a matter of "interpretation than . . . actual addition or deletion of words from the sacred books." Ayoub, "Uzayr in the Qur'an and Muslim Tradition," in *Studies in Islamic and Judaic Traditions*, ed. W. M. Brinner and S. D. Ricks (Atlanta: Scholars Press, 1986), 5. See also Abdullah Saeed, "The Charge of Distortion of Jewish and Christian Scriptures," *Muslim World* 92 (2002): 419-36.

The Contents of the Injil

We should also note that the theory of biblical corruption could never have arisen if the Qur'an had given more attention to the actual contents of either the Torah or Injil. Regarding the latter, the Qur'an says it contains guidance, admonition and light. Qur'anically, Jesus' teachings were given to him by revelation and so seem to have made up the contents of the Injil. Hence, according to Q 3:49-51, the Injil tells Jesus' followers what they can eat and store in their houses and confirms the previous scripture, the Torah. It also makes some things previously forbidden lawful and urges obedience to God on the straight path it marks out for believers (Q 3:49-51). But its mention of Jesus' regulation of food and possessions and his relaxation of the previous law are very general. Hence, if we add the Injil to the scriptures confirmed, the passage could be talking about Muhammad. Q 7:157 similarly depicts the Injil as a book that commands good, forbids evil and releases people from their burdens. But again, so general is the description that it could apply to almost any scripture.

In fact, the Qur'an makes only three types of specific statements about the Injil's contents:

1. It predicts Muhammad's coming (Q 7:157; 26:196; 61:6), but as we have seen, this does not connect with any specific New Testament passage.

2. Together with the Qur'an and Torah, it promises paradise to those who die fighting for God's Cause (Q 9:111).

3. Together with the Torah, it describes faith in terms of a growing plant (Q 48:29).

Ironically, none of these descriptions is specific enough to determine the text to which the Qur'an refers.[16] So general is its statement concerning the Injil's prediction of Muhammad's coming that it seems almost to put the onus on its hearers to locate all possible predictions and prove them otherwise. The Qur'an apparently has no specific passages in mind when it claims that the Torah and Injil promise paradise to martyrs for God's Cause. In the third case, it gives us only a general biblical motif.[17] Interestingly, all three points

---

[16]With respect to the Hebrew Bible, however, Q 5:45 refers clearly to the Mosaic *lex talionis*.
[17]Ps 1; Is 61:3; Hos 14:6; Mt 13:31-32; Jn 15:1-5 have all been suggested as intended by Q 48:29. But that in itself tells us the qur'anic data is insufficient to identify the texts.

are made with respect to the Torah also, which points again to the Qur'an's "homogenization" of all the preceding scriptures.

In terms of the promise of paradise for those killed in battle, this clearly shows that the qur'anic author views the Christian community as a geopolitical entity, like the Medinan *umma* and the Israelites under Moses. It is easy to see why he would draw this conclusion, given that Heraclius had so recently promised his troops that anyone killed under the banner of the cross would go directly to heaven. But during its first three centuries Christianity had no geopolitical aspect whatsoever, being officially outlawed and persecuted.[18]

From all this one gets no sense of the qur'anic author's familiarity with the Injil. In fact, nothing suggests that he has any real interest in the Injil beyond its use as an endorsement of Muhammad and God's Cause. That being so, later Muslims were free to make the Injil into whatever their polemics required. And the Qur'an's unique use of the name *injil* combined with its total lack of clarity on that scripture's contents enabled them to do so.

The Identity of al-Injil *in the Qur'an*

Despite its current popularity among Muslims, the theory that Jesus received a book of scripture from God that Christians later corrupted founders on a series of immovable rocks both internal and external to the Qur'an. All of the following point to the Qur'an's identification of *al-injil* with the scripture possessed by Muhammad's Christian hearers—that is, the New Testament:

- the qur'anic data on *al-injil*
- early Muslim understandings of the term
- theological problems with the popular Muslim theory
- textual evidence for the New Testament's authenticity

To begin, we are told that Muhammad's revelations confirm what the Christians in his audience "already have in their scripture" (Q 4:47; 35:31; cf. Q 46:12). Q 7:157 similarly claims that Muhammad is the prophet Jews and Christians "find described in the Torah and Injil in their possession." Also, as Madigan has

---

[18]Hence one of the few specific teachings with which the Qur'an credits the Injil represents a clear anachronism. The claim is anachronistic of the Hebrew Bible also, but for different reasons.

shown, the expression *ma bayna yadayhi* in Q 5:46 and 5:48 (literally, "what is between his hands") should be translated as "what is already present," since it refers to scriptures not just chronologically but also physically before Jesus and Muhammad. Thus Muhammad confirms the scriptures existing in his day just as Jesus had done in his.[19]

Clearly, both the Jewish and Christian scriptures were still extant in Muhammad's day, which is why the Qur'an calls Muslims to believe them (Q 3:84; 4:136). The Qur'an never cautions them to believe in only what the biblical scriptures *originally were*, not what they had since become. And what point would there be in the qur'anic call if the Injil were not the Christian scripture but rather some already extinct book? So naturally, Muhammad's first hearers understood *al-tawrat* and *al-injil* to refer to the Hebrew Bible and New Testament. The qur'anic descriptions of the Torah and Injil would not be so "uniformly positive and respectful" if these scriptures were actually corrupted and existed only as shadows of their originals.[20] All of the other qur'anic references to the Injil confirm this.[21] The Qur'an faults Jews and Christians not because they follow corrupted scriptures but rather because they refuse to submit to their scriptures and embrace Muhammad's recitations. It "never gives a hint of a distinction" between its Injil and the scripture Christians then revered.[22]

---

[19]Daniel A. Madigan, *The Qur'ân's Self-Image: Writing and Authority in Islam's Scripture* (Princeton, NJ: Princeton University Press, 2001), 137.

[20]The accusation in Q 2:140 that Christians and Jews are hiding what they received from God also implies that they still possess it—otherwise, how could they hide it? Q 5:46-47 specifically commands the followers of the Injil to "judge according to what God sent down in it" lest they defy God in their disobedience. Again, they could only obey the command if they possessed the scripture by which they were to judge. Q 2:213 views the Jews and Christians' recitation of their scriptures positively, implying that its text still represents what their prophets received. The Qur'an would not have approved of their reciting a grossly distorted text. Q 5:68 tells Christians (and Jews) they have nothing to stand on unless they stand firmly on their scriptures, the Torah and Injil. While the qur'anic author criticizes Christians for various things (e.g., Q 5:116-18; 57:27), he never faults them for falsifying scripture; Nickel, *Narratives of Tampering*, 224.

[21]If anyone is said to fabricate scripture—which seems unlikely—it is the Jews. They are repeatedly faulted for substituting human words for God's words, twisting them or distorting them. Each of the following passages either specifically names Jews as the subjects or else the context indicates it: Q 2:75-79; 3:78; 4:46; 5:12-19; and such charges relate mainly to misinterpretation. For a thorough treatment of this, see Gordon Nickel, *The Gentle Answer to the Muslim Accusation of Biblical Falsification* (Calgary: Bruton Gate, 2014), 17-45, 61-90; cf. Gabriel Said Reynolds, "On the Qur'anic Accusation of Scriptural Falsification (*taḥrīf*) and Christian Anti-Jewish Polemic," *Journal of the American Oriental Society* 130, no. 2 (2010): 194-95.

[22]Gordon Nickel, personal correspondence, July 1, 2014.

The popular Muslim theory also contradicts numerous early witnesses. As Nickel has shown, the early commentators, the hadith, the *sira*,[23] al-Tabari's *History of the Messengers and Kings* (*Ta'rikh al-rusul wi 'l-muluk*) and the "occasions of the revelation" (*asbab al-nuzul*) all attest to the fact that the early Muslim community accepted the textual integrity of the biblical scriptures.[24] We also have positive evidence that early Muslims used *al-injil* "to indicate the whole New Testament, in the same way that 'Torah' was used not only for the Pentateuch, but for the entire collection of Jewish scriptures."[25] Hence, when the Qur'an advises Muhammad to consult those who have been reciting scripture before him, the commentators took it to mean the Jewish and Christian scriptures (Q 10:94; 21:7). They likewise understood his specific references to passages in the Injil to refer to the New Testament (Q 7:157; 48:29). The scripture "sent down to Jesus," which Muslims claim to believe, is quite clearly the same one Christians believe.[26]

The falsification theory is theologically untenable also, for the Qur'an teaches that God chose to bless and favor Jesus' disciples over their enemies until the end of time (Q 3:55; 61:14). Yet according to the popular theory, Jesus' disciples were the very ones who turned the Injil into a travesty of the original. Why would God bless them, knowing they would do that? Also, why would he protect the Qur'an (Q 15:9) but not the Injil or Torah, when the Qur'an is emphatic that God's word cannot be changed (Q 6:34; 10:64; 18:27; 50:29)?[27]

Finally, the Muslim theory contradicts the textual evidence for the New Testament. A religious community as widely dispersed as the Christian

---

[23]Including that of ibn Ishaq and *Kitab al-tabaqat al-kubra* of Muhammad ibn Sa'd (d. 845).

[24]Nickel, *The Gentle Answer*, 47-60.

[25]Griffith, "Gospel."

[26]No early commentator suggests that what was "sent down" to Jesus was different from what was accessible to Muhammad (Q 2:136, 285; 5:48; 29:46).

[27]Some Muslims explain the extent of the divergence between the New Testament and the Qur'an by claiming—with David Strauss, A. N. Wilson and others—that Paul was Christianity's real founder and that he effectively hijacked Jesus' gospel. But this fails to solve the problem for three reasons: (1) even disregarding Paul's writings, we still have four Gospels, not one; (2) no New Testament writer evidences knowledge of an "original Gospel" given to Jesus; and (3) though their approaches differ, each New Testament writer presents Jesus as the God who loved us enough to come to earth and die for us. As N. T. Wright puts it, "Paul was one true voice in a rich harmony of true voices in the New Testament, but the writer of the song was Jesus"; quoted by Murray, *Grand Central Question*, 186. For a basic comparison of Paul and Jesus' teachings in the Gospels, see Murray, *Grand Central Question*, 186. See also David Wenham, *Paul: Follower of Jesus or Founder of Christianity?* (Grand Rapids: Eerdmans, 1995); and N. T. Wright, *What Saint Paul Really Said: Was Paul of Tarsus the Real Founder of Christianity?* (Grand Rapids: Eerdmans, 1997).

community does not simply discover one day that its sacred scripture has been replaced and take it in stride. The Qur'an says Jesus received a scripture, the Injil, from God. Yet Jesus never once mentions the book he allegedly received. This means the early Christians would have had to erase all trace of it deliberately and to an unimaginable degree. But all the evidence points to the fact that the Christian scripture has only ever existed as a collection of writings produced by a multiplicity of authors after Jesus' death.[28] And the fact that there is no evidence for the Muslim theory is all the more irrefutable because the authenticity of the New Testament's text is so well attested— better attested, in fact, than any other ancient book on earth.[29] The Christians in Muhammad's day had the selfsame scripture we have today.[30] Hence, despite its being taken as fact by nearly all Muslims today, the theory is both illogical and without merit.

It may already have occurred to the reader that the Qur'an most likely uses *al-injil* to refer to the New Testament for the same reasons it uses *ʿIsa* to refer to Jesus, *Yahya* to John and *al-nasara* to regular, mainstream Christians. Muhammad's need of Jewish support, besides the qur'anic author's need to Islamicize his Christian inclusions, is why he chooses *al-injil* over the "New Testament" (*al-ʿahd al-jadid*), which implies supersession and the Jews' possession of only the "Old" Testament.[31] As with *al-nasara*, Muhammad did not use *al-injil* until after the *hijra* (Q 7:157), by which point his prospects had brightened and his need of Jewish support abated. Even so, the unusual terms were chosen seemingly to avoid being perceived as anti-Jewish. In any case, it bears repeating that a word's usage, not its derivation, determines its meaning. Hence we only confuse the matter by translating *al-injil* as the "Gospel."[32]

---

[28]Abdullah Saeed, "How Muslims View the Scriptures of the People of the Book: Towards a Reassessment?," in *Religion and Ethics in a Globalizing World: Conflict, Dialogue and Transformation*, ed. Luca Anceschi et al. (New York: Palgrave Macmillan, 2011), 191-210.

[29]On the reliability of the text of the Gospels, see Paul Rhodes Eddy and Gregory Boyd, *The Jesus Legend: A Case for the Historical Reliability of the Synoptic Jesus Tradition* (Grand Rapids: Baker Academic, 2008). On the New Testament documents generally, see F. F. Bruce, *The New Testament Documents* (London: Inter-Varsity Fellowship, 1960). The same is true of the Hebrew Bible since the discovery of the Dead Sea Scrolls: we have an abundance of Old Testament texts predating Muhammad by centuries. None of them mention Muhammad, and none give any indication of falsification; Nickel, *The Gentle Answer*, 75-89, cf. 156-74.

[30]Saeed, "Charge of Distortion of Jewish and Christian Scriptures," 419-36.

[31]Also, the novelty of this use of *al-injil* is not an issue when the Qur'an defines it on its own terms.

[32]If we are to translate *al-injil*, "New Testament" is the best choice; cf. 260n6 above.

The Charge of Biblical "Corruption"

While the Qur'an attests to the biblical text's general reliability, it also criticizes the People of the Book—or at least some of them—for their the mishandling of it.[33] Based on a detailed examination of the related semantic field, Gordon Nickel sees no reason to view the Qur'an as accusing Jews or Christians of fabricating or corrupting biblical texts.[34] Reynolds, likewise, concludes that the scriptural falsification the Qur'an intends "involves reading or explaining scripture out of context, not erasing words and rewriting them."[35] The basic idea to be drawn from the qur'anic data is that the Jews and Christians are unfaithful custodians of the scriptures entrusted to them since they refuse to admit that their scriptures predict Muhammad's coming. This alleged failure prompts the Qur'an to accuse them of misusing the scripture God has given them, not of counterfeiting it. They only suppress the truth in it that the Qur'an now reveals.

Nickel also carefully studies two of the earliest Muslim commentators on texts used to support the doctrine of scriptural corruption, Muqatil ibn Sulayman (d. 767) and al-Tabari (d. 923), and concludes that they only rarely and tentatively saw those texts as accusing the Jews of scriptural falsification.[36] Instead, the Jews and Christians may have distorted their text's meaning or heeded merely human words—for example, from the Talmud—instead of God's words. In the few cases where these commentators took qur'anic verses to mean that Jews or Christians had changed the actual wording of their scriptures, they took it in a very limited sense, as willfully modifying intact texts

---

[33]A variety of words and expressions are used to refer to what later Muslims came to understand as the Jews and Christians' "corruption" (*tahrif*) of the text of their scriptures. The children of Israel are said to conceal (*katama*) and confound or confuse (*labasa*) the truth (Q 2:42, 146; 3:71). They are said to reveal some of what their parchments say but to hide (*akhfa*) much (Q 6:91; cf. Q 2:174; 3:187). They substitute (*baddala*) their own saying for God's saying (Q 2:59). They twist (*lawa*) God's revelation with their tongues (Q 3:78), forget (*nasiya*) his reminder to them and tamper with (*harrafa*) his word to them (Q 2:75). They throw God's revelations behind their backs and sell them for cheap (Q 2:41, 174; 3:78). These charges are most frequently made against the Jews and not once against Christians specifically.

[34]Nickel, *Narratives of Tampering*, 50-66.

[35]Reynolds, "On the Qur'anic Accusation of Scriptural Falsification," 194.

[36]They view the qur'anic data on "tampering" as referring to a variety of actions on the part of Jews and Christians, often concealing prophecies about Muhammad in the Torah and Injil. Muqatil views only Q 2:79 and 3:78 as referring to such falsification. To these verses, Tabari adds only Q 5:13. His amplification of Q 5:14 has Christians changing their religion but not specifically their scripture; Nickel, *Narratives of Tampering*, 100-101, 116, 152-55, 159-64.

only by reciting them incorrectly. Such changes did not affect their scripture's actual text, however. They thus used the relevant qur'anic passages primarily to highlight the Jews and Christians' rejection of Muhammad "despite the clear information about him in the books in their possession."[37]

Christians in the Meccan Suras

Having seen how the Qur'an refers to Christians and the New Testament, we can now examine the remaining qur'anic data on Christians. Here we detect shifts in both content and tone relative to the point in Muhammad's prophetic career at which each recitation was given. In fact, as David Marshall has shown, we find four somewhat distinct periods, moving generally from sympathy to censure toward Jews and Christians, though on different time scales for the two groups.[38]

During Muhammad's later years in Mecca, the Qur'an characterizes Jews and Christians by commendation on the one hand and criticism on the other. It describes the children of Israel under Moses in generally positive terms (e.g., Q 6:154; 10:90-93). It assures the Meccans the following:

• The God of Jews and Christians is also the God of Muslims, who believe in the biblical scriptures also (Q 29:46).

• The recipients of the earlier scriptures recognize the Qur'an "as they recognize their own sons" (Q 6:20 Jones; cf. Q 6:114; 28:52-53; 29:47).

• There is no argument between Muslims and Christians, and God will ultimately heal the breach between them (Q 42:15).

It tells Muhammad to consult the children of Israel on a matter of truth, mentions a Byzantine defeat and predicts the Byzantines' victory over their enemies—doubtless the Sasanians—with God's help (Q 17:101; 30:2-5).

But between the lines, one discerns that not everything is right between the Muslims and the People of the Book. The Qur'an warns repeatedly about

---

[37]Nickel, *Narratives of Tampering*, 222. But the early commentators' discussion implicitly attests to the fact that there was understandable confusion over the state of the biblical texts, and at least one hadith claims that biblical texts had been changed; Reynolds, "On the Qur'anic Accusation of Scriptural Falsification," 189. But most of the early evidence points in the opposite direction, confirming that Muhammad's followers interpreted the data on Jewish and Christian obstinacy with regard to their scriptures like Muqatil and Tabari, seminal commentators from Islam's early centuries.

[38]David Marshall, "Christianity in the Qur'ān," in *Islamic Interpretations of Christianity*, ed. Lloyd Ridgeon (Richmond, UK: Curzon, 2001), 24-25.

the rivalry and divisions of the People of the Book, which await God's judgment, and cautions against following their whims (e.g., Q 23:52-53; 42:13-19; 45:17-18). Its directive that Muhammad and his followers argue with them in a constructive manner betrays an element of resistance on their part, though perhaps hope of agreement also (Q 29:46). There is also an acknowledgment that some of them may now reject Muhammad's prophecies, like those of their ancestors who unjustly refused God's prophets, Muhammad's predecessors (Q 35:25-26). Even more telling is the warning that hell awaits any Jews or Christians who refuse to stop arguing—when everything has been said (Q 42:16). Most importantly, one late Meccan sura speaks of God's entrusting his revelations to those who believe—i.e., the Muslims—in case those previously favored with them do not believe (Q 6:89). In other words, the Jews and Christians' lease on divine revelation is up for renewal, and its renewal depends on their embracing the Qur'an. The Meccan suras also criticize belief in divine sonship, likely intending that of both polytheists and Christians.[39] But it is almost as if Jews and Christians are themselves outside the room: the Meccan suras address them far less frequently than the Medinan suras.

The Meccan suras also seem reluctant to differentiate between Jews and Christians. As we have seen, they call Christians only scriptuaries, the People of the Book and Children of Israel, which refers to either or both Jews and Christians.[40] Furthermore, three Meccan suras use Christian stories, but de-Christianized, presenting each story's heroes as generic believers.[41] Again, this enables the Qur'an simultaneously to avoid offending Jews in a position to offer Muhammad refuge and to Islamicize the stories, for these pericopes are recited when he and his fledgling *umma* are in their direst need.

---

[39]Apparently Jews too, as Q 9:30 later reveals.

[40]That is, apart from one reference to the Romans (Byzantines), as previously mentioned.

[41]Q 85:4-8 alludes to the story of "the Men of the Pit," which the Muslim tradition identifies with the Christian martyrs of Najran. Not only does the Qur'an omit the Christian identity of the story's heroes, it leaves their Jewish persecutors equally mysterious. The earliest versions of the Syriac legend of the Seven Sleepers, referred to in Q 18:9-26 as "the Men of the Cave," present its heroes as young Christian martyrs who refused to embrace Roman idolatry. But the Qur'an presents them simply as youths and believers. Likewise, Q 36:13-32 recounts the story of three Christian evangelists preaching in Antioch but presents them simply as witnesses to God's truth to a nameless city; Marshall, "Christianity in the Qur'an," 8-9. That these suras echo these three stories, stripped of their characters' religious affiliation, strongly implies that Muhammad was from neither a Jewish nor a Christian background.

Christians in the Early and Middle Medinan Suras

We observe gradual development in the Medinan suras' approach to Christians. The first Medinan phase, represented by Sura 2, runs from the *hijra* to the Battle of Badr. During this period the *qibla* is changed to Mecca, signaling the souring of Muhammad's relationship with Medina's Jews. Accordingly, this phase is marked by an increasingly strident polemic against the Jews.

Another difference between the Meccan suras and Sura 2 is that the latter's criticism, commendation and appeals are much more direct, since Muhammad now has many Jews in his audience. What Sura 2 says to them is usually sharper also, the stakes being higher for both, given that he is at war with Mecca and the Jews support—or at least side with—his enemies. Here the Qur'an distinguishes Jews and Christians by name, focusing much more on the former, though some of what it says to Jews may apply to Christians too. Claiming that it is continuous with their scriptures, the Qur'an demands their equal faith, asks whether they believe in only parts of God's revelation and warns that doing so will lead them to hell (v. 85). Claiming to follow Abraham's religion, it rhetorically asks whether they think Abraham, Isaac, Ishmael and the Tribes were Jews or Christians. That is, it claims to represent the pristine "original religion," untainted by either group. And it asks who could possibly commit a greater sin than hiding testimony received from God, pointing to their evil of withholding their scriptures' witness to Muhammad's prophethood as well as his need to proclaim the messages he receives (vv. 139-40).

Positively, the Qur'an promises that Jews, Christians and Sabians (*al-sabi'un*) who act righteously will be rewarded with paradise. But such righteousness doubtless includes acceptance of Muhammad's prophethood (v. 62; cf. Q 5:69).[42] It also says that recipients of the biblical scriptures who recite it correctly believe in it too and asks how they can argue with Muslims about God when he is Lord of both and they must both answer to him for their deeds (vv. 121, 139). It also reassuringly disallows any forced conversion of Jews and Christians (Q 2:256).

Negatively, Sura 2 warns Muslims against Christians and Jews who seek to make them unbelievers (vv. 109-11). For the Qur'an has two serious problems with Jews and Christians: they are exclusive, and they ascribe associate deities

---

[42]A more nebulous statement in Q 22:17 includes the Mazdeans (*al-majus*).

to God. Each claims the other is wrong and insists that they alone will enter paradise (vv. 111-13), which is why they won't be satisfied till the Muslims become Jews or Christians (v. 135).[43] With this, the Qur'an contrasts the "religion of Abraham," who was pure and worshiped no god beside God (v. 135). The Qur'an thus lumps Jews and Christians together with pagans, since they all say God has fathered a son (v. 116).[44] Christian belief in Jesus' divine Sonship is thus equated with paganism. Hence, anyone following the Christians or Jews will incur God's judgment. For, they are warned, his covenant does not apply to evildoers, even if they are Abraham's descendants (vv. 120-22).

The second Medinan phase includes the total breakdown of Muhammad's relationship with the Jews, culminating in his destruction of Medina's last Jewish tribe, the Qurayza. Accordingly, these suras are dominated by his heightened polemic against the Jews and declare that God granted Jesus' followers victory over their enemies, the Jews, and that their dominance would continue till the resurrection day (Q 3:55; 61:14). The Qur'an also allows that some People of the Book are believers and entirely trustworthy, although such positive acknowledgments are typically qualified in some way (Q 3:64, 75, 110). For example, it says God put mercy and compassion in the hearts of Christians but never intended their monasticism (Q 57:27).[45]

In this phase far more criticism is leveled at the People of the Book than commendation, but most of it targets the Jews, and it is difficult to know what relevance it has to Christians. For example, the Qur'an urges Muslims to beware the People of the Book, who are full of rage toward them and want to lead them astray (Q 3:69, 100, 113). It asks why they turn believers away from God's path and try to make it crooked when they ought to witness to the truth about Muhammad (Q 3:99). For these reasons unbelievers among the People of the Book are grouped with idolaters as the worst of people (Q 98:6). The Qur'an argues with them over Abraham's religion, which cannot be improved on and which it seeks to restore (Q 3:65; 4:125; cf. Q 2:139). It says even Abraham's descendants will be sent to hell if they reject Muhammad's revelations

---

[43]Ironically, the qur'anic author faults them for doing the very thing he does.

[44]Jews, too, are accused of such a belief during Muhammad's final years (Q 9:30).

[45]It may refer to Christian monks when it says God will reward the upright, who recite divine writ in the night and are quick to do good deeds (Q 3:113-15; cf. Q 24:36-37). It seems also to say Christians inherited revelation from the Jews, though it implies that they too have squandered the trust God gave them (Q 7:168-70).

(Q 4:54). It seemingly disqualifies Christians as custodians of God's revelation because they care more about this passing world than the world to come. And it categorically condemns their belief in Jesus' divine Sonship (Q 4:168-73).

Christians in the Late Medinan Suras

The final Medinan phase, represented by Suras 9 and 5, is marked by a shift in Muhammad's general policy toward Jews and Christians. That change follows three key events: Muhammad deals decisively with Medina's last Jewish tribe, he secures a peace treaty with the Meccans, and he finally triumphs over them. Soon afterward the Qur'an changes its policy toward Christians and Jews, prompting Muhammad to demand the submission of the tribes in both Yemen and the northern Hijaz. That change is found in the command to "Fight those from among the People of the Book who do not believe in God and the Last Day, who do not forbid what God and his messenger have forbidden and who do not follow the true religion, until they pay the *jizya* promptly, having been humbled" (Q 9:29). Without submission to Muhammad, belief in God and the Last Day is insufficient and warrants military attack. The temporal clause here underscores this, for the *jizya* was a poll tax that served as material proof of submission to Muhammad's rule. The People of the Book, who must pay this tax "promptly, having been humbled," are now under Muhammad's domination.

This marks a radical shift in the Muslim prophet's approach to Jews and Christians. Previously he had physically attacked the People of the Book only as necessary to maintain his hegemony and defeat the Meccans. Now that he has won that war and secured his hold on the central Hijaz, however, the Qur'an expands the Muslims' strategic objectives to include Christian and Jewish territories, with no limits on their location.[46] But having already ruled out their forced conversion (Q 2:256), it does demand only their submission to Muhammad's rule.

What justifies this expansion of violence? The verses immediately following say Christians and Jews are guilty of polytheism (*shirk*), the Qur'an's unforgivable sin, twice over (Q 9:30-31).[47] And equally damning is their attempting to extinguish God's light—in the Qur'an—with their words, which light God

---

[46]While this was not strategically viable until Muhammad had dealt decisively with Medina's Jews and subdued Mecca, it may well have been the plan from the first.

[47]They have respectively called Jesus and Ezra the "son of God" and taken their monks and rabbis as "Lords" beside God.

has determined to bring to its zenith no matter how much the unbelievers (*al-kafirun*) hate it (Q 9:32). This should not surprise us, for, as the *sira* attests, Muhammad even resorted to assassination to silence those who ridiculed him or otherwise tried verbally to contest his preaching. So when Q 9:33 says God has sent Muhammad "with Guidance and the true religion that he may make it prevail over all other religions," it envisions a triumph dependent on the physical subjugation of everyone it deems unbelievers. In qur'anic thinking, truth and right prevail in the world by force of arms. When Christian and Jewish tribes are ordered to submit to Muhammad's rule, the wise do so. But the Muslims are told to attack all who resist God's rule through his prophet. In fact, the Qur'an says they deserve death, brutal and grotesque punishment[48] or banishment, not to mention the torments of hell (Q 5:33; cf. Q 9:34).

The qur'anic hope for the People of the Book involves more than just their political submission, however. Christians and Jews are called to embrace Muhammad's religion also, for, as Q 5:15 says, in Muhammad a light has come and a scripture been given to end their confusion, bring them out of their darkness and guide them to the straight path. Christian belief in the Trinity is considered an appalling denial of God's truth as is the Christian's alleged smugness (Q 5:17-19, 72-75, 116-18). As previously noted, Christians must judge by what God has given them in the Injil, apart from which they are lawbreakers (Q 5:47). They must also obey the Injil and stand on it (Q 5:66-68). We will momentarily return to the tension such statements create. But for now we must try to appreciate the qur'anic viewpoint, that the Injil basically agrees with the Qur'an (Q 5:65-66) while Christians have forgotten what their scriptures say, have a distorted understanding of them and have thus been led astray (Q 5:12-14, 66, 77). If they do not accept the Qur'an and renounce belief in Jesus' deity, they face damnation (Q 5:72, 86). Jesus himself implicates his followers as guilty of distorting his message and disassociates himself from them (Q 5:116-18). In a moment of angst over the Christians' belief in the Messiah as the Son of God, the Qur'an even exclaims, "May God destroy them! How deluded they are!" (Q 9:30).

Alternately, the Qur'an describes Christians as friendly to Muslims—or less hostile than Jews—and not arrogant, due to their having priests and monks

---

[48]As if it were entirely normal, Q 5:33 actually specifies the amputation of alternate limbs.

among them (Q 5:51, 82). It also promises paradise to those who believe and act righteously (Q 5:69). But again, true belief and righteousness intrinsically involve submitting to Muhammad's prophethood. On the other hand, it cautions Muslim believers against befriending Christians and labels those who oppose Muhammad, whether physically or verbally, dangerous reprobates. Thus only those Christians who respect Muhammad and convert on hearing the Qur'an are "closest" to the believers (Q 5:59, 66, 83-84). But the Qur'an does not require Christians to convert, as it does pagans. This shows that it does make some distinction between pagan and Christian "polytheism."[49]

How Then Should We Understand the Qur'anic Claims?

Among the many claims the Qur'an makes, two are of critical importance. It declares that

- its exclusive source is the God of the Bible (e.g., Q 3:3); and
- both Old and New Testament predict Muhammad's coming (Q 7:157; 61:6).

In a very real sense these claims stand or fall together, for biblical predictions of Muhammad's coming could only mean the Bible and Qur'an have the same source, and it is unthinkable that the Bible would not foretell the "Seal" of God's prophets if both scriptures are divine in origin.

Hence these claims must be judged in terms of the full content of the biblical and qur'anic understandings of God, the life to which he calls us and his actions on our behalf. In other words, we must judge them by everything else the Qur'an and Bible say, and we do not look far without encountering major contradictions. The claim that the Bible predicts Muhammad's coming is especially problematic because it means not just that the Bible predicted that one more prophet would come but rather that God's definitive revelation to humankind did not in fact come in Jesus.[50] And the New Testament writers

---

[49] Ahmad von Denffer distinguishes between different aspects of the Muslim view of Christians: they are classed as unbelievers, theologically speaking, but not in legal or social terms; Ahmad von Denffer, *Christians in the Qur'an and Sunna* (Leicester, UK: Islamic Foundation, 1971), 32-41. The Qur'an thus affirmed their social inclusion as "believers" until Muhammad's political power was sufficient for him to stress their theological exclusion.

[50] The New Testament does allow for additional prophets after Jesus (Acts 11:27; 13:1; Eph 4:11), but not for any definitive prophet who would replace him, as Muhammad seeks to do.

clearly present Jesus as God's ultimate revelation.[51] These and many other teachings make it impossible to reconcile the Qur'an with the Bible.

Given that disparity, one wonders how best to understand the qur'anic author here. From the number of times he refers to arguments between Muslims and Christians or Jews, it is clear that Muhammad's claims about the Bible did not go uncontested. The same Bible we have today was available then.[52] In their predominantly oral, polyglot culture, Arab Christians would have memorized any biblical passages needed for church liturgy as well as many Gospel stories and sayings. But since the Qur'an says so little of the Bible, that may not have helped them to contest Muhammad's claims. Naturally, priests and monks would likely have known their scriptures better than most Christians, who would have had to rely on them to mount a defense of their primarily foreign-language scripture.

If most Arab Christians were unfamiliar with the biblical text, this would have been truer still of Muhammad's pagan tribesmen. Even if they had wanted to navigate it, they could not have done so. This is why bold qur'anic claims contested by Jews and Christians were nevertheless believed by Mecca's pagans, who could not hold them up to scrutiny without relying on the former, who in turn relied on their professionals to interpret their scriptures. Though most pagans had some awareness of the broad outlines of Jewish and Christian belief, they would have had little knowledge of the Bible's actual contents. And this proved a winning combination for Muhammad, especially when the Qur'an excelled at making broad claims about the Bible while providing almost no content to back them up. This made it relatively easy for the qur'anic author to claim continuity with a biblical text that many of his teachings subverted. In Mecca he declares that the learned of the Children of Israel had accepted the Qur'an (Q 26:197), while in Medina he challenges the Jews to bring out the Torah to prove their point and charges monks and priests with selfish motives, implying that they are untrustworthy guides (Q 3:93; 9:34).

---

[51]Muslims often view Deuteronomy 18:15 as a biblical prediction of Muhammad, but the New Testament clearly says that it was fulfilled in Jesus (Acts 3:22-24; cf. Acts 7:37).

[52]That is, it was available in Syriac and Aramaic, with much, if not all, of it available in Arabic at least in oral form. The earliest evidence we have of written Arabic texts of the Bible are from the late seventh century or later; Sidney H. Griffith, *The Bible in Arabic: The Scriptures of the "People of the Book" in the Language of Islam* (Princeton, NJ: Princeton University Press, 2013), 97-126; cf. Brown, "Who Was 'Allah' Before Islam?" 158-61.

Hence the Meccans' general awareness of the monotheistic faiths combined with their biblical vacuum to make Mecca the perfect situation for Muhammad to make the claims he made.

Furthermore, that the Qur'an asserted that the Injil prophesies Muhammad's coming without ever quoting specific biblical predictions would have made it impossible for his Christian interlocutors to counter effectively. Later Muslims did designate various biblical texts as those predictions. But again, it is not simply a question of whether such verses can be adequately linked with Muhammad. Rather, two larger questions need answering, questions we will take in turn in chapters eighteen and nineteen. First, what sort of reinterpretation of biblical theology does the Qur'an represent? The short answer to that, I would argue, is that it views biblical theology through a distinctively Arab and tribal lens. And second, does the Bible really prepare us for the God of the Qur'an, its prophet Muhammad and the life to which it calls us? Or put differently, is it reasonable for us to accept that the Qur'an is the Bible's true sequel?

Part IV

Christian
Response

Eighteen

An Arabic Qur'an *for the* Arab People

The Qur'an was given to the Arabs in Arabic since, it says, God always speaks to a people in their own language. It combined exalted Arabic with familiar folklorist oral transmission techniques, implicitly elevating both to the level of the divine in Arab thinking. But it was not only its language that made the Qur'an appeal to the Arabs. It also used standard religious and social categories, even though it challenged them in some respects. For while it refused any lesser gods, it essentially advocated a God resembling the noble Arab of pre-Islamic times, haughty in his refusal to submit or humble himself. This manifested itself in the scripture's heavy emphasis on divine transcendence and its intended avoidance of divine-human analogy, human intimacy with God and divine grace seeking the unrepentant, all core features in biblical monotheism. The Qur'an also reflected Arab tribal thinking in its view of the contest between faith and unbelief, and presented an Arabized Abraham—who, it claimed, founded the Kaʿba—effectively making Mecca the world's spiritual center. It centered its spirituality on a concept of appeasing God primarily by means of religious practices familiar to pagan Arabs. Dehistoricizing Jesus, it made its own Arab prophet supreme in the divine economy. It validated and entrenched Arab patriarchy in many respects, along with the geopolitical view of religion so familiar to seventh-century Arabs. And last, it offered the Arabs a vision of their own greatness, legitimized their expansionist goals and sacralized the violence necessary to attain them.

The Qur'an emphatically states that it is an "Arabic Recitation," or Qur'an (Q 12:2; 42:7), its point being to assure Muhammad's audience that God always speaks to a people in their native tongue.[1] The early Meccan suras also used the accent poetry (*saj'*) of the pre-Islamic soothsayers.[2] Clearly these things gave it appeal to many Arabs. And its exalted Arabic in the Meccan suras spoke powerfully to them in a culture that prized the spoken word above almost everything else. The Qur'an also made extensive use of familiar folklorist oral transmission techniques. It thus took aspects of Arabic literature and effectively elevated them to the level of the divine or eternal in Arab thinking. But it appealed to pagan Arabs for other reasons too. To begin, its injunctions were highly demanding yet very doable, that combination being the essence of pagan religion and making Islam very competitive in the Hijazi marketplace of religions.

Qur'anic Theology

The Qur'an also used categories familiar to the Arabs, as is most evident in its theology, its corrective task being to insist on its own version of "unadulterated" monotheism—against a pagan view of God, on the one hand, and Jewish and Christian conceptions of him, on the other. Muhammad preached this message, declaring himself a prophet commissioned by the God of the Bible. On close inspection, however, the Qur'an's theology is not at all close to that of the Bible. Rather, in calling its hearers to the exclusive worship of *Allah*— the Arabic name simultaneously used by Jews and Christians for God and by pagans for the High God—it both commingles biblical and pagan categories of thought and challenges them in other respects.

Starting with polytheism's remote and terrifying High God, the qur'anic author makes two very dramatic changes. First, he insists that, unlike the *jahili* conception, God is both immanent and the Lord of human history. For the claim that Muhammad is God's prophet does not stand alone: it is part of a whole complex of ideas that must be taken together. In accord with biblical

---

[1]Ironically, this pertains only to its original recipients, the Arabs, since the Qur'an is said to be given "in clear Arabic" (*bilisanin 'arabiyyin mubinin*, Q 26:195). And while they viewed it as having universal applicability, the Qur'an was bound to both the Arabs' language and categories of thought, meaning that for non-Arabs, Islam demands a significant degree of Arabization.

[2]Devin J. Stewart, s.v. "Rhymed Prose," in *EQ*.

teaching, qur'anic theology presents God as creating and controlling every-thing, providing bountifully for humankind, protecting his people from evil, demanding moral living, seeing all we do and ultimately judging us on that basis. That is why he sends prophets to call humankind back to his path. None of this was native to *jahili* paganism. Second, the Qur'an strongly rejects poly-theism's humanization of God by completely clearing off its "lower shelves" of companion gods and forbidding any talk of divine "begetting." But the qur'anic author's single-mindedness relative to what he saw as humanizing God led him also to reject as polytheistic what he deemed Christianity and Judaism's corruptions (while leaving utterly unchallenged the animism inherent in the Meccan pilgrimage—i.e., ritual circumambulation around a sacred stone).

Rejecting any notion of God's seeking humankind himself, God's inti-mately revealing himself to us and especially God's humbling himself—all concepts vital to biblical monotheism[3]—the qur'anic author attempts to "out-monotheize" the monotheists. But he avoids only those aspects of biblical theology that challenge the *jahili* concept of nobility, making his portrayal of God closer to the pagan High God. Hence, the qur'anic author does not ulti-mately escape from humanizing God: he simply humanizes God on his own *jahili* terms. That is why, at its core, qur'anic theology

- considers God to be distant, haughty, unwilling to bow;

- presents him most basically as our master and divine-human intimacy as one-sided;

- is acutely sensitive to anything it deems an infringement of God's tran-scendence;

- does not center God's ethical attributes in his essential holiness or love; and

- virtually omits the core biblical concepts of love for and friendship with God.

Because it is paganism's High God whom the Qur'an brings near, he is terrifying in his nearness. The frequent mention of his mercy may mitigate that terror slightly, but since this immanent God refuses to reveal himself to us, it is difficult to know how much his mercy in forgiving sins really amounts to and how it re-lates to his justice. Here the Qur'an simply takes refuge in God's unknowability: he does as he pleases and is himself answerable to no one for anything.

---

[3]We will examine these topics in chapter nineteen.

Qur'anic Anthropology and Soteriology

Regarding the creation and fall narratives, the Qur'an exhibits many clear similarities to the Bible. But they are overshadowed by three major differences needed to make the narratives fit the qur'anic framework, with its acute stress on divine transcendence. The Qur'an

- locates humankind's creation in an extraterrestrial garden;

- avoids framing humankind's creation in God's image; and

- makes God's reaching out to the fallen Adam contingent on the latter's repentance.

First, God's intimate involvement in Adam's creation may be explained by the fact that it is not on earth but rather in an otherworldly setting. Second, it is not by chance that the qur'anic accounts of Adam's creation avoid any notion of the image of God, the central feature in the biblical narrative. Rather, its absence is vital for the story to fit the Qur'an's unique brand of monotheism, with its heavy emphasis on God's being unlike us, an emphasis that fits with its clear avoidance of the central biblical notion of our need to be like God ethically. That notion also runs completely counter to paganism, which makes the gods unsubmissive and their moral character nothing for us to imitate. By contrast, the Bible presents God as humble in his exercise of authority and calls us to be the same. The last major difference here is in the divine response to Adam and Eve's transgression. In the biblical narrative, God condescends by seeking his unrepentant vicegerents simply because he loves them. But in the Qur'an, God extends his mercy only after they have repented.

The Qur'an also presents another picture of humankind, one reflecting Arab tribalism in its

- converse idealization of both the supertribes of faith and unbelief;

- making loyalty to God, his prophet and his supertribal Cause, humankind's supreme moral requirement; and

- making salvation synergistic, based on God's mercy plus loyalty, valor and good deeds in the service of the supertribal Cause.

Like early Arabic poetry, the Qur'an idealizes insiders and vilifies outsiders, in this case the supertribes of faith and unbelief. This bifurcation of the race and the exigencies of the *umma* in both Mecca and Medina result in the Qur'an's making loyalty its ethical essential. That is, submission, faith and loyalty all meld together into one, since Muhammad's ongoing qur'anic messages protect him from nearly all criticism. Given that there are two great warring super-tribes, humanity's primary need is for guidance to join God's side and exhortation to remain loyal to it. And as with Arab intertribal relations, the Qur'an's relationship to non-Muslims is very pragmatic, ranging from invitation and patient endurance to violent attack.

While the Qur'an claims the heritage of the biblical prophets, it singles out the Arab Ishmael and especially his father, its Arabized Abraham, as the progenitors of the true faith, linking them with the Ka'ba. It then makes Muhammad the fulfillment of Abraham and Ishmael's prayer for a messenger from among the Arabs to guide and purify them. Like the Bible, the Qur'an presents its prophets as able to commit sins, but it minimizes their sins in accord with its idealization of the supertribe of faith. The Qur'an highlights itself as the last in the series of God's revealed scriptures, its major precursors being those of Moses, David and Jesus. But its concept of revelation differs markedly from that of the Bible, which allows that the prophet's individuality shapes the Word he delivers. Instead, the Qur'an portrays its prophets as mere mouthpieces of God, a notion akin to the pagan poets' inspiration, attributed to controlling *jinn*. Furthermore, just as that poetry spoke about not the *jinn* but rather the Arabs' way of life, so also the Qur'an, uneasy with any idea of divine intimacy, purports to reveal the path of salvation but not the God who speaks, as is emphatically the case with the Bible.

Qur'anic Spirituality

Qur'anic spirituality's devotional dimension also relates closely to pre-Islamic Arab religion in a number of respects. To begin, both are fear driven, not love driven. Circumambulation of sacred stones was part of Arabia's pagan pilgrimage rites, as was the practice of animal sacrifice and the observation of sacred months. Pagan prayer rites also involved recitation of prescribed formulas rather than genuine communication with the deity. Initially the Muslim prophet needed to appeal to Jews, and so the direction of prayer for the *umma* was toward Jerusalem. Within two years of the *hijra*, however, the direction was changed to Mecca, signaling the faith's further Arabization.

In terms of the social aspect of its spirituality, the Qur'an resembled Hijazi customary law in many respects and guaranteed the continuation of Arab patriarchy by (1) permitting men multiple wives, concubines and slaves, (2) licensing a husband's corporal punishment of his wives, (3) decreeing that a marriage's children belong always to the father, and (4) marginalizing women in communal prayers. While challenging Arab society on the place of women in some respects, it largely supported existing Arab social structures—to the great relief of the men in Muhammad's audience.

Qur'anic spirituality's political dimension was to prove the greatest single factor in the early spread of the nascent faith. And essential to that is its viewing religion through the geopolitical lens so familiar to the Arabs influenced by the Byzantine and Ethiopian Christian and Himyarite Jewish views of religion. It also took full advantage of the Arabs' tribal dynamics and warring instincts. And that was one reason military jihad, the faith community's struggle against all comers, pagan or monotheistic, came to define the *umma* for more than a century as its hegemony expanded from Medina to Spain and India. During that formative period, military jihad made death-defying loyalty to God's Cause

- the essence of Muslim virtue and potentially the believer's direct ticket to paradise;

- a valid way to increase one's wealth in real estate, women and other booty; and

- the expression of a universalized and sanctified version of Arab tribalism.

All these things made military jihad very popular among Arab men in the early period. The Muslims' toleration of those Christians and Jews who surrendered to them was also the essence of practicality. It made no sense to slaughter non-converts when in the short run they could still benefit their Arab rulers in numerous respects. And in the long run, their communities' gradual slide toward extinction was virtually guaranteed by subtler forms of coercion and by the law of apostasy, which combined to make the empire's Islamization move forward, ratchet-like, in gains that could not be lost to anything so insignificant as a convert's second thoughts. Those monotheists who resisted the Muslims' advance were typically dealt with harshly: the men put to death, the women and children enslaved or forced to convert. This combination of Muslim tolerance and brutality made submission the prudent choice for most of the monotheists they targeted. And like jihad, the toleration of treaty-protected monotheists, and the law of apostasy, every other aspect of the Qur'an's political spirituality fit very well with the Arabs' shame- and honor-based, success-oriented culture.

Qur'anic Jesus

Pagan Arabs in Muhammad's audience were familiar with Jesus and would have found everything in the qur'anic portrayal of him agreeable except his foreignness (Q 43:58). Most importantly, the Qur'an subordinates Jesus to the "Seal of the Prophets," whom the Arabs could call their very own. This requires the qur'anic author to extract Jesus from his historical context and recast him in the Qur'an's own framework, facilitating his only slight agreement with the Bible. But that posed no problem to the pagans in Muhammad's audience, especially when the Qur'an implicitly gave them—as Abraham's *true* followers—a stronger claim on Christ than the Christians had. To the Arabs in a world increasingly dominated by Christian ideology, that must have been a powerful tonic indeed.

The Genius of the Qur'an

The Qur'an exerted its power to warn, teach, inspire and unite the Arabs in "God's Cause" by effectively combining elements vital to them in their seventh-century Arab context:

- pagan Arab categories of thought and practice adjusted to fit monotheistic prophecy
- Arabic literature exalted to a position of eternal worth and power
- a vision of Arab greatness, both religious and geopolitical, sacred and imperial
- a divine mandate for Arabs to pursue that vision with all the zeal they possessed

Muhammad's Arab tribesmen doubtless appreciated seeing familiar categories of thought reflected in the Qur'an. They also enjoyed the Qur'an's literary artistry and were inspired by a religio-political offensive yielding rewards both now and in the hereafter. For besides giving them a vision of Arab greatness, the Qur'an legitimized their expansionism and sacralized the violence needed to power it. Combined with key political and socioeconomic factors, all these things enabled the Arabs to change the course of the seventh century and, with it, the face of the world.

But contrary to Muslim belief, the critical issue relative to the Qur'an's truth claims is not ultimately how effective the Arabs were in their conquest.[4] It is rather whether we can reasonably consider the Qur'an a true sequel to the Bible. And to that question we now turn.

---

[4]Most Muslims believe the effectiveness of the conquest demonstrably proves the truth of the Qur'an. For a balanced historical treatment of the many factors that contributed to the success of the Arab conquest, see Robert G. Hoyland, *In God's Path: The Arab Conquests and the Creation of an Islamic Empire* (New York: Oxford University Press, 2015).

Nineteen

Could *the* Qur'an Be *the* Bible's Sequel?

The Qur'an claims to be the biblical Scriptures' sequel. Since continuity and organic development are the chief marks of a satisfying sequel, we can very reasonably look for central biblical motifs to be developed in the Qur'an. Hence this chapter surveys diachronically in the Hebrew Bible, the New Testament and the Qur'an three closely related core biblical themes: namely, friendship with God, the free grace of God and divine humility. Biblically, human friendship with God begins in Eden and takes on deeper meaning in the stories of Abraham, Moses, David, Jesus and the Holy Spirit, as well as teachings concerning the consummation. The Qur'an affords us only one remnant of this and no development whatsoever. Likewise, the free grace of God is evident from Eden on, especially in its ultimate expression in Jesus' self-sacrifice for the world. But while the Qur'an presents some residue of divine mercy in advance of repentance, it radically reduces it. Finally, divine humility is evident from Genesis to Revelation as God seeks intimacy and oneness with humankind and through Jesus Christ fully realizes his desire in the consummation. By contrast, the Qur'an gives us only unconscious traces of this, virtually imperceptible in a context so acutely sensitized to divine transcendence. Hence it is impossible to see how the Qur'an's minimization of these three motifs to the point of subversion does not undermine the qur'anic claim to be the Bible's sequel.

As we have just seen, the theory of biblical corruption does not actually fit the evidence: the massive falsification of the biblical text most Muslims believe happened has no factual basis whatsoever. Hence it is very reasonable to compare the Qur'an with the Bible, especially since the Qur'an claims to be the concluding sequel to the biblical Torah, Psalms and Injil.

Both the New Testament and the Qur'an claim to be the previous scriptures' sequel. The question is, Do both alleged sequels meet the reader's reasonable expectation of continuity with the preceding scriptures? Granted, they join the Old Testament in detailing divine interventions to save humankind. But how and why does God do what he does, and to what extent do the later scriptures develop the earlier scriptures' numerous subthemes? That is, does each scripture tell the same sacred story? For a sequel requires more than just broad surface similarities: belief in God, the need for moral living and some sort of prayer. It demands organic unity, as what first appears in bud opens full flower and ultimately produces the long-awaited fruit. So as with the New Testament, it is only reasonable that we look for key themes and distinctives from the earlier scriptures in the Qur'an. Just as these features develop within the Hebrew Bible, they should develop further in any subsequent scriptures.

In order to assess whether this is true of the Qur'an, then, we will diachronically survey the following three integrally related biblical motifs in the Hebrew, Christian and Muslim scriptures:

- friendship with God

- the free grace of God

- the humility of God

Since all three motifs are evident from Genesis to Revelation, it is only right that we assess to what extent the Qur'an further develops them. I have chosen these particular motifs because they are integral to biblical monotheism and cast into bold relief how radically different the Bible and Qur'an are.

Friendship with God

We already see friendship with God in the very beginning, when God invites Adam and Eve to live in his royal residence and comes to enjoy their company as evening cools (Gen 2:8-9; 3:8). Disregarding their intimacy with him, they choose to desert their divine lover and seek their own independent greatness, but he purposes to restore them to friendship, as is evident from his

- tempering his judgment of their sin with grace;
- continuing to bless and guide them and their children (e.g., Gen. 4:6-7); and
- taking Enoch into such intimacy that he eventually translates him to be with him (Gen 5:21-24).

However, where God means to take his friendship with humankind becomes clear only when he calls Abraham. For he commits to being on Abraham's side and to partnering with him and his family to accomplish his redemptive purposes for the world. As Abraham soon discovers, this does not mean he has God on a tow rope, for God's love is impermeable to all our attempts to domesticate, manipulate or manage it. Nevertheless, friendship is definitive of God's relationship[1] to Abraham and his family:

- Scripture designates Abraham the "friend of God" (2 Chron 20:7; Is 41:8; Jas 2:23).
- Despite Abraham's limited understanding, God informs him of his plans and permits him to question them (Gen 18).
- God engages with Sarah also, allowing her to dispute what he says (Gen 18:9-15).
- God pursues Abraham's egocentric grandson Jacob, inviting him into personal relationship and promising to bless him (Gen 28:10-17).
- God even allows a desperate Jacob to wrestle with him physically (Gen 32:22-32).
- God invites Moses into close friendship, one in which Moses sometimes argues with God (Ex 32:7-14; 33:11).
- God comes to live among his people at Sinai despite their frequent complaints and unfaithfulness (Ex 25:8; 13:21; Num 2:1-34; cf. Ex 33:12-17; 40:34-35).[2]

---

[1]Many of these encounters involve theophany; see 299-300 below.
[2]God's tent is pitched in the center of the camp, with the Israelite tribes surrounding it.

- Accompanying his people on the journey to Canaan, God protects and guides them, provides for them and disciplines them in love (Deut 32:8-14).

In numerous stories, we see that God longs for our friendship even when we do not seek him, that he patiently waits for us to turn to him and is not at all affronted by our honesty.

This theme of divine-human friendship continues right through the Old Testament. God calls David a "man after his own heart" because of the way his friendship with God shapes his inner life (1 Sam 13:14). That intimacy is nowhere more evident than in the Bible's prayer book, the book of Psalms (*zabur*), given to stamp the nation's entire relationship with God.[3] There we find prayers personal and honest to the point of often taking God to task. We also find the psalmist celebrating the day when Egyptians and Canaanites,[4] no less than Israelites, are full citizens of Zion and delight in God (Ps 42:1-2; 87:3-7). Jeremiah predicts the day when God will make a new covenant with his people, writing his law on their hearts so that each of them knows him personally. Through Jeremiah, God says, "I will be their God, and they shall be my people. No longer shall they teach one another, or say to each other, 'Know the LORD,' for they shall all know me, from the least of them to the greatest" (Jer 31:33-34). Isaiah and Habakkuk also predict the day when "the earth will be filled with the knowledge of the glory of the Lord, as the waters cover the sea," and Isaiah assures us that only in that knowledge will humankind find the peace that so eludes our troubled world (Is 11:6-9; Hab 2:14).

This clear Old Testament motif of divine-human friendship gives us the basis for understanding the incarnation, God's coming to live and walk among us in the person of his Son. The Gospel writers show him coming to us in our pain, doubt, anger and rebellion, offering friendship to all who accept his open invitation. In that regard, he quickly earns a reputation for befriending all the wrong kind of people: prostitutes, tax collectors, society's moral riffraff (Mt 11:19). Jesus is clearly intent on inviting not just the pious to become his friends but rather everyone without exception (Lk 5:30-32; 14:15-24).

Jesus is accompanied by twelve disciples, or apprentices. Near the end of his time with them, Jesus—God in human form—tells them he no longer calls

---

[3]Equally personal and intimate, for example, are the prayers voiced by Hannah and Mary (1 Sam 1:11-13; 2:1-10; 2 Chron 6:1-42; cf. Lk 1:46-55). On the Psalms, see 171 above.
[4]In modern terms, "Palestinians."

them servants but friends, since he has withheld nothing from them (Jn 15:15).[5] And though they are not yet ready, he has ultimately chosen to partner with them in the great work of reconciling the world to God (2 Cor 5:20; 6:1). He says that eternal life consists in personally knowing God and Jesus Christ, whom he has sent (Jn 17:3). After he ascends to his Father, Jesus sends the Holy Spirit to live within his followers and be their constant companion and guide (Jn 14:15-27). So the Spirit takes up residence in every believer in a friendship that becomes the defining feature of their lives (Jn 14:15–15:17; Gal 5:13-25). Gradually transforming them into Christ's likeness, the Spirit rewrites their internal moral code and empowers them to represent Christ's lordship to a world that rejects him (Acts 1:8; 4:8-13, 23-31). The believer's life then revolves around an intimate personal relationship with God, one characterized by the immediate knowledge of God (Jn 17:3; Phil 3:7-11), and thus Jeremiah's prophecy is fulfilled (Jer 31:33).

The book of Revelation brings this motif to its climax in three powerful images:

- Excluded by a local church, Jesus seeks entrance that its members might share the simple joys of friendship with him (Rev 3:20).

- God's eternal union with his people is called the "marriage of the Lamb," with all the intimacy and ecstasy that marriage is meant to signify (Rev 19:6-9).

- The heavenly city—of which Christ is both the light and the temple— descends to earth. As it does the proclamation is made that God's home is now among his people: "He will live with them, and they will be his people. God himself will be with them. He will wipe every tear from their eyes, and there will be no more death or sorrow or crying or pain. All these things are gone forever" (Rev 21:3-4 NLT; cf. Rev 22:3-5; Is 60:19-20).

We thus see organic development in this motif, leading to full fruition. God always intended to live among humankind as one of them. He remained undaunted by the fall, promising to extend his blessing to the whole world through Abraham and Isaac's family. Coming to earth in the person of his Son, he offered his people total restoration. Though they refused his friendship in

---

[5]Most incredible here is the fact that this divine friendship permits intimacy with God, but not at the cost of reverence. For God establishes intimacy by his supremely awe-inspiring act of devotion to us as the friend who lays down his life for us (Jn 15:13).

Gethsemane just as resolutely as they had in Eden, their rejection did not thwart God's plan there either (Jn 18:1-11).[6] Instead, he used it to win the right to bring the entire creation back into joyful relationship with himself. At Pentecost, Jesus poured out his Spirit on his followers, so that he might live in them, and soon after extended the blessing to all who received Jesus—Jews and Gentiles together. And when God makes all things new in the consummation, his original intention to live among his people in a relationship of intimate friendship, harmony and joy will be fully realized.

Turning to the Qur'an, we find very little of this. God is spoken of as the believer's ally (*wali*) and is the *umma*'s God since believers are on his side (Q 5:54-55; 30:6). But ultimately, the Qur'an refuses to "obligate" God to anyone or allow for any familiarity with him. The Jews are specifically faulted for considering themselves exclusively God's allies (Q 62:6). God is nowhere presented as longing for deep friendship with his people or they for deep friendship with him. The metaphor of his being humankind's master so dominates that it precludes any idea of divine-human friendship. The only exception to this rule is the prophet the Qur'an makes second only to Muhammad, for it does call Abraham the "friend" (*khalil*) of God, but without ever stating why (Q 4:125). If the Qur'an actually refers to an intimate relationship between God and Abraham, it gives us no picture of it. For Abraham does not know whether he will be forgiven on the Last Day (Q 26:82; cf. Q 19:66-72). So whatever the friendship signifies, it seems very distant.

Beyond friendship, the idea of God's living among his people—let alone *within* them—is entirely out of place in the Qur'an. The biblical metaphors of God's being "father" or "husband" to his people, with all the intimacy they suggest, are still more jarring to the qur'anic ear. In a few passages, believers are encouraged to seek God's face, but this refers only to seeking his approval, not intimate relationship, and the qur'anic paradise confirms this, picturing God as hosting a great feast, with only the best of believers near enough to see his face (Q 56:11; 83:24, 28). So while there is some brief mention of nearness to God, it in no way compares with the biblical emphasis. Instead of developing the biblical motif of divine-human friendship, the qur'anic author appears to have totally recoiled from it. He mentions it only once in connection

---

[6]The Jews' rejection of Jesus was coupled with that of the Romans, who were responsible for the crucifixion itself. So the nations conspired against God and his Messiah (Ps 2:1-3).

with Abraham, but with no explanation or thought of friendship with God as being possible for everyone who believes as Abraham does. And the Qur'an does not encourage ordinary believers to think they can influence God's actions, a vital aspect of the biblical concept of prayer. Instead the Qur'an invites us to a far more distant relationship with God.

The Free Grace of God

Another central biblical motif is that of God's free grace, by which he gives sinners the very opposite of what they deserve. This motif is all about reversal, God's taking our curse to give us the blessing we do not deserve. Thus it is that the high and holy God bends low to save sinners.

We first see free grace when Adam and Eve have committed high treason against God—thus making themselves deserving of death—and are magnanimously granted a reprieve instead. God does not require them to accept their blame, let alone cry for mercy, in order to defer their sentence. Instead, while they are still unrepentant—seeking to evade him—he searches them out and liberally mingles mercy with judgment by

- instituting sacrifice to deal with their shame brought on by their sin;

- denying them access to the tree of life lest they make their lostness eternal; and

- promising a champion who will ultimately release their race from Satan's tyranny.

So though they deserve only judgment, God does not cut them off. Instead, refusing to be overcome by their rejection, their king graciously offers them a way to regain what they have lost (Gen 3:21-24). Later, when human evil reaches an intolerable level, he cleanses the earth by flood, graciously safeguarding the earth's future (Gen 6:1–9:17). When arrogant men attempt to "storm" heaven itself, God graciously saves them from themselves by halting their insolent project midcourse (Gen 11:1-9). In each case God minimizes punishment to safeguard humankind's opportunity to respond to his grace.

Animal sacrifice appears in large writ across the entire Hebrew Bible—in the stories of Cain and Abel, Noah and the patriarchs, as well as those of the exodus and conquest. Sacrifice holds a central place in Israel's worship, in both tabernacle and temple (e.g., Lev 1; 3–7; 17:10-16). It functions as an illustration of reversal, of the believer's desperate need of grace to atone for her sins and enable her to please God. A meal was typical of the sacrificial ritual, that meal depicting the sacrificial victim's literally giving its life to the believer. In the supreme test of his faith, Abraham is asked to sacrifice his long-promised son. But God executes a dramatic reversal—as Abraham knew he would—by graciously providing a ram to die in Isaac's place.[7]

The Old Testament portrays the reversal inherent in God's grace in many other stories, such as those of Jacob, Joseph and the exodus. Though Jacob is a first-rate scoundrel, God does not wait for him to clean up his act or even seek him. Instead, God takes the initiative to seek Jacob while he is still unrepentant, fleeing the effects of his sin (Gen 28:10-22). Later, when Jacob—running from one enemy to another—finally seeks God's help, God grants him the blessing he does not deserve and transforms him in the process (Gen 32:22-32). In Joseph's story, like that of Jacob, God graciously renovates his life through suffering. In God's larger purposes, he uses both the evil of Joseph's brothers and Joseph's forgiveness of them to save Jacob's entire family from starvation. And in so doing, God again depicts the reversal inherent in his grace, which bears the undeserved curse in order to bless the guilty (Gen 50:20). Finally, in the classic case of Old Testament reversal, God releases the Hebrew nation from slavery in Egypt, despite their spiritual blindness and rebellion. Though they do not really want him as king, he embarks on a long journey with them, bearing their rejection and refusing to abandon them, repeatedly returning blessing for cursing.[8] While God does discipline his people, he does so within the context of an ongoing relationship of parent to child. And we repeatedly find echoes of the exodus—for example, when God sees the suffering of his people in Babylon and "gathers the outcasts of Israel," restoring them to their land (Is 56:8). Thus the Hebrew Bible consistently presents human brokenness and faith as overlapping categories and God's work of grace as occurring within that overlap.

With all of that as New Testament background, God sends Christ into the world. As John Goldingay says, "The fact that God had been acting in this way

---

[7]By now Abraham knows that God is committed to fulfilling his promises to him through Isaac and no one else. That gives the divine command an air of impossibility, prompting Abraham's audacious faith and the reader's hope for a surprise ending (Gen 22:1-19). Abraham obeys God because he truly believes God will provide the sacrifice (Gen 22:8; cf. Heb 11:17-19).

[8]John Goldingay, *Do We Need the New Testament? Letting the Old Testament Speak for Itself* (Downers Grove, IL: IVP Academic, 2015), 12.

through Israel's story didn't make it redundant for God to bring his self-sacrifice to a climax in Jesus. This last self-sacrifice was the logical and inevitable culmination of that earlier way of acting and letting himself be acted on, the final expression of it." In other words, the Old Testament prepares us for just such a story as we find in the Gospels.[9]

Jesus has every right to call the nation of Israel to account as he does. However, he comes not to destroy his people but to reveal God's heart of love for them, and in that we see astonishing grace (Jn 3:16-17). Jesus repeatedly demonstrates grace, for example, by

- enduring his disciples' egotism, spiritual blindness and immaturity (Mk 10:35-45);

- proclaiming the Jubilee, the year of nationwide reversal (Lk 4:19);

- calling us to love our enemies and forgive without limit (Mt 5:44; 18:21-22);

- releasing an immoral woman from condemnation to a changed life (Jn 8:1-11); and

- honoring and caring for a Samaritan outcast (Jn 4:1-42).

Jesus illustrates the reversal of grace most scandalously in his story of the father whose deep love for his wayward son enables him to forgive his boy for rejecting him and squandering his inheritance and to reinstate him as his son before he even repents (Lk 15:11-32).

Forgoing his use of unlimited force against those who are leading the nation to its ruin, Jesus' sharpest words to them and his sole act of coercive judgment display impressive restraint (Mt 21:12-17; 26:53).[10] Fully aware that his disciples will abandon him in his Passion, he devotes his last days with them to graciously preparing them for the trauma they are about to undergo (Jn 13–17). During their last meal together, the Passover, he speaks of his self-sacrifice and institutes the observance of the Communion meal, teaching that the Old Testament's sacrificial imagery expressed that he would die "without sin in substitution for our sins" (Mt 26:28; Lk 24:26-27; 1 Cor 11:23-25; cf. Jer 31:31-34).[11] Even when the nation's leaders falsely condemn and crucify him, he uses his failing

---

[9]Ibid., 12.

[10]See 193n29 above.

[11]Joachim Jeremias, *The Central Message of the New Testament* (New York: Charles Scribner's Sons, 1965), 36.

breath on the cross to forgive them. Then, after his resurrection, he restores his disciples, who had deserted him (Lk 23:34; Jn 21:15-17).

After his ascension, Christ sends his Spirit to lead and empower his people, and the Spirit opens the door to the nations, breaking down the Jew-Gentile division. God does this not because Gentiles deserve his mercy any more than Jews, but simply because he is gracious and had intended from the very first to grant the blessing of salvation to every people under heaven (Gen 12:1-3; Acts 10:1-48; Rom 11:11-24). Thus the story of God's alternately enduring his people's rejection of him and disciplining them as their loving Father continues on in the story of the church, called to extend the same grace to outsiders that Jesus gave us when we were outsiders (Lk 22:20; Col 4:6).

Finally, the central image of Christ in the book of Revelation is that of a Lamb, slaughtered but resurrected, undefeated (Rev 5:6). This Lamb is also the "Lion of the tribe of Judah" and the "Root of David," images referring to his regal power and Davidic descent as Messiah (Rev 5:5). To this slain and resurrected Lamb is given earth's destiny, including the power to renew the entire cosmos, putting everything to rights and forever banishing evil, violence and death in the consummation's great reversal (Rev 5:1-14; 21:4-5).

Turning now to the Qur'an, we do find a significant emphasis on God's mercy and forgiveness there. In fact, nearly every qur'anic sura begins with the words, "In the name of God, the Merciful and Compassionate." God is merciful to all his subjects in two important respects:

1. He gives life and breath, sunshine and rain for their crops, and help in times of trouble.

2. He sends prophets to guide humankind to the path of obedience, warn of judgment and promise reward.

But despite these similarities, the Qur'an also presents God's mercy very differently from the Bible. It has no issue with God's offering repentant sinners forgiveness provided they do not seriously reoffend. It also portrays him as forgiving certain believers—among them, Adam, David, Solomon and Muhammad. But by markedly obscuring their sins, the Qur'an inevitably trivializes their forgiveness.[12] And the Qur'an implicitly denies that God chooses

---

[12]As previously noted, classical Muslim commentators minimized them further still. On the qur'anic author's treatment of the prophets' sins, see 149-51 above.

to be merciful to unworthy, unrepentant sinners. It does this by either radically revising or totally omitting any biblical stories emphasizing that theme. Only in God's sending prophets to sinners and exercising patience while they resist his Word does the Qur'an present his saving mercy as offered to those not seeking it. But having once received his mercy, the believer is responsible from that point on to save herself. And in sharp contrast to the Bible, the Qur'an has no mercy for those who defame or kill God's prophets.

Humankind's need of God's mercy is clearly evident in our need of prophets who call us to seek God's forgiveness. But missing is the idea that, apart from God's radical free grace, no one chooses God, all of us being so spiritually blind that, on our own, we do not even know we do not see. The Qur'an plainly omits that biblical emphasis and with it the magnitude of God's grace dispensed in Christ, doubtless out of fear that it will diminish human responsibility and encourage careless living. Likewise, all thought of substitutionary atonement for sinners is replaced by the Qur'an's strong emphasis on salvation through self-reliant self-effort.

The Humility of God

We see divine humility in the Hebrew Bible in numerous respects. To begin, humankind's creation in God's image signifies his intention to relate closely to us and to make humans his perfect means of self-expression in his world.[13] On Adam's creation, God speaks to him, and, as noted earlier, all of God's communication with humankind is akin to his using "baby talk."[14]

The concept of God's creating humankind in his likeness prepares us for Old Testament theophany, the phenomenon in which God appears in human form.[15] In Genesis 18, for example, Abraham extends hospitality to a stranger and converses with him, only gradually realizing that the "stranger" is God. In doubtless the strangest case of biblical theophany, God physically wrestles with Jacob (Gen 32:22-32). So while the Old Testament presents the Creator as altogether distinct from his creation, he sometimes exercises his freedom

---

[13]See the quotations of N. T. Wright on 92 above.

[14]Rather than requiring any particular adaptation or exaltation on the part of the humans involved, all such communication represents a case of God's stooping to our weakness, using language so we can understand everything he says revealing himself, which also implies humility.

[15]And, as will become evident, the theophanies in turn were foreshadowings of the incarnation of God the Son.

to take on human form in his interactions with us. Also evidencing its full acceptance of divine-human analogy, the Old Testament uses a wide range of metaphors to describe God's relationship to his people, including father, husband, friend, lover, shepherd, redeemer and savior, all clearly implying humility (Ex 14:13-14; Pss 3:8; 18:2; Is 43:11; 45:21-22; 47:4).

This God also repeatedly commits to being Israel's God: "I will be their God, and they shall be my people," something all the more remarkable when we recall Israel's slave origins (Jer 31:33; cf. Gen 12:3; Ezek 37:27; Hos 2:23; Zech 8:8). And Isaiah quotes God as saying,

> I dwell in the high and holy place,
>   and also with those who are contrite and humble in spirit,
> to revive the spirit of the humble,
>   and to revive the heart of the contrite. (Is 57:15)

Despite their many failings, God is on his people's side and loves them deeply (Gen 12:1-3; Deut 10:15). And love inevitably involves vulnerability—that is, humility—since there is no guarantee that one's love will be returned.[16] Humility is also inherent in God's making promises in covenant relationship with his people and doing so for the very purpose that they should hold him to his word. Only a humble God would so engage his most marginalized subjects,[17] reach down to them in their weakness and lovingly lift them up (Ps 22:24; 147:2-3).

Against this Old Testament background, the New Testament further reveals God's humility when he comes to live among his people in the person of his Son, as one of them. Everything about his incarnation, from his birth onward, points to his voluntary abasement. For example,

- Jesus is conceived out of wedlock, making his legitimacy suspect (Mt 1:18-24);

- besides Jesus hailing from a backwater town under the heel of imperial Rome, his parents are poor (Mt 2:19-23; cf. Lk 2:22-24); and

---

[16]God's commitment to his people moves him to endure their ignorance, questions, complaints and even angry accusations as a father endures his child or a friend her friend (e.g., Gen 18:22-33; Job 16:7-22; Ps 10). God makes himself vulnerable also in his deferral of justice, as our sin offends him and provokes his anger (Gen 39:9; Ex 32:13-14, 22; Neh 1:7). Jeremiah speaks of God's being hurt by his people and weeping for them (Jer 8:21–9:1). Hosea 11:1-8 likewise presents him as sovereignly choosing to endure their sins because of his deep love for them.

[17]Given ancient Semitic culture's pronounced male chauvinism, it is remarkable that Genesis presents God as conversing with Sarah and even her slave girl Hagar, caring about their needs and promising them blessing (Gen 16:7-14; 18:9-15).

- when the king seeks to kill the infant Jesus, his parents are forced to flee with him as refugees (Mt 2:13-18).

This marginalization is followed by his rejection by society's powerbrokers, all being according to divine design, for he offers hope especially to the poor and the weak. Jesus touches lepers, welcomes reprobates and lifts up the fallen (Mt 8:3; Jn 8:2-11). While the nation's religious leaders have no truck with such "riffraff," Jesus likens his whole mission to someone inviting society's outcasts to a feast, since none of the "respectable" people will come (Lk 14:15-24).

Jesus lives a simple life and chooses twelve disciples, who are ordinary and unschooled—even unpromising, humanly speaking. Obsessed with their own status, they do not grasp his counterintuitive message (e.g., Mk 10:35-45). Centering his ethic in love, he calls his followers to love their neighbors—enemies included—as themselves, all of which involves costly humility (Lk 6:27-35). He insists on washing his disciples' feet, subverting their thinking on lordship, status and rights. For in the economy of his kingdom, whoever wants to be first must make himself the servant of all (Jn 13:1-17).

Then, in his boldest act of servanthood, Jesus gives his life a ransom for many (Mt 20:28; Mk 10:42-45). He endures the humiliation of betrayal by a disciple and then desertion by the rest, not to mention his lead disciple's denial (Mt 26:14-75). He is tried by an impious religious court, dragged before a weak-willed but imperious governor and judged according to the whim of the fickle mob. In his crucifixion, the very people he came to save utterly reject and physically violate him, making him an object of pity and scorn (Mt 26:57–27:44). But in all this, God not only condemns evil and the arrogance and injustice it spawns—he also undoes them. When God allows evil to do its very worst to Jesus, it is no match for his love. Hence "the crucifixion is God's exclamation point to turning the world upside down. The last becomes first; the least is greatest; the crucified becomes King."[18] It is his humility that ultimately qualifies this king to judge the nations, and so fully does he identify with the weak and poor that he reckons our treatment of them our treatment of him and judges accordingly (Mt 25:31-46). And the humility so beautifully modeled by Jesus is, in one sense, what binds Father, Son and Spirit

---

[18]David Capes, Rodney Reeves and E. Randolph Richards, *Rediscovering Jesus: An Introduction to Biblical, Religious and Cultural Perspectives on Christ* (Downers Grove, IL: IVP Academic, 2015), 186.

together in the one eternal God. So it is no exaggeration to say that the Bible puts divine humility at the heart of both its soteriology and its theology.

Turning to the Qur'an, we find that instead of developing the theme of God's humility further, the Qur'an rather appears to abhor anything even bordering on it. In fact, we find only unconscious traces of it in the Qur'an's use of theomorphic and theopathic terms. As in the Bible, God is intimately involved in Adam and Eve's creation and speaks to human beings through his prophets. He relates to them as a person and compares himself to humans in many regards. But all such traces go unnoticed in a context so acutely sensitized to divine transcendence. The idea of humankind's imaging God is noticeably absent in the Qur'an's creation myth. Many other aspects of qur'anic theology confirm that the omission is deliberate. God is never said to reveal himself, as we repeatedly find in the Bible. Rather, he is only ever said to be unlike anything in creation. The range of metaphors referring to him is much narrower in the Qur'an than the Bible, and that reduction has largely to do with the Qur'an's aversion to any notion of reciprocal divine-human intimacy. The Qur'an never refers to God as his people's father or husband and only very occasionally as their savior and friend. Qur'anically, it is inconceivable that God would become a man and live among us, and the very idea that he would die a humiliating death is utterly abhorrent. The absoluteness of this disjunction makes it impossible to reconcile the Bible with the Qur'an.

Organic Unity and the Falsification Theory

As previously noted, most Muslims today use the theory of biblical corruption to explain all the theological discrepancies between the Bible and the Qur'an. This enables them to view the Qur'an as the restoration of what the Bible "originally contained." Indeed, given the extent of the theological discrepancies between the two scriptures, no other Muslim explanation reasonably works. But as we saw above, this theory was not held by Muslims at the start but rather developed over time, and, despite its immense popularity, all the evidence contradicts it.[19]

---

[19]There is no corruption of biblical manuscripts beyond the sort of textual variants that exist in all ancient texts, the Qur'an included—such things as unintentional scribal omissions or repetitions of a word or the occasional inclusion of an interpretive gloss. But with so many early biblical manuscripts against which to check the text, all such corruptions are quite easily corrected. See 266-67 above.

The organic development of the three biblical motifs just surveyed further undermines the corruption theory, for these motifs are not just foreign to the Qur'an: it consistently subverts them. Its portrayal of the divine-human relationship excludes the believer from any real friendship with God, which involves intimate knowledge of God. Its treatment of sin never once questions humankind's ability to save themselves by following the divinely revealed path. And its presentation of divine transcendence leaves no room for an explicit acceptance of divine humility. So if the corruption theory were true, all we have seen of these motifs would represent falsification. Not only that, these three motifs are merely representative of many more like them: certainty versus doubt, love for God and neighbor, holiness, prophethood, revelation and prayer as real communication, for example. This means the alleged falsification would have to have been truly massive in both scale and depth. And if the Jews had actually falsified their scriptures, why would Jesus and the New Testament writers not have attacked them for doing so? Given that Christians and Jews were so sharply at odds right from the first, it might make sense if the Jews had falsified their scripture in one direction and the Christians in another. But it makes no sense that the early Christians fabricated these three motifs in their scripture in the very same direction as their persecutors did.

When one observes how ubiquitous and how deeply interwoven into the fabric of the biblical text these motifs are, it is impossible to think of anyone adding them later. Given the Bible's organic unity and development in the motifs we have considered, we can only view them as being original and authentic features of the biblical text. Thus the Qur'an's minimization of them to the point of subversion makes its claim to be the Bible's sequel appear highly illogical.

It also raises the question of why the qur'anic author chose never openly to challenge the Bible on any of these three points. That leads to an even larger question: why he chose not to challenge the Bible on anything at all—even its affirmation of Jesus' divinity.[20] If the answer to that question lies in the

---

[20]While the New Testament never uses the word *Trinity* to describe its doctrine of God, it often presents Jesus as worthy of the worship that belongs to God alone (Rev 5:11-14; cf. Mt 14:33). God the Father says to Jesus, "Your throne, O God, is forever and ever" (Heb 1:8). Paul calls Jesus "our great God and Savior" and says that Jesus existed as God prior to his incarnation (Tit 2:13; cf. Phil 2:5-8). Hence Jesus is described as the Creator himself (Jn 1:3; Col 1:16-17). The qur'anic author certainly attacks Christians for this belief, but never the Bible, its source.

qur'anic author's insistence that Muhammad had been sent by the God of the Bible, it raises ethical questions and seriously complicates the task of Christians seeking to respond to the Qur'an with grace and truth.

Twenty

The Bible *and the* Qur'an: So Close, Yet So Far

To understand and respond Christianly to the Qur'an, we must grasp its early seventh-century Hijazi milieu and its Muhammadan narrative. Although Muhammad's people were pagan, they were in a sense "besieged" by the biblical religions, and it is their scriptures that the Qur'an claims endorse him. The worldview of the Qur'an evidences its author's transposition of biblical teaching into the pagan register, thus reflecting the biblical worldview in many respects while implicitly subverting it in many others. For example, it presents God as ultimately unknowable and humankind as able to save themselves in response to his revelation—that is, without any deep work of grace. It entirely omits the Bible's cosmic drama of redemption and makes salvation primarily a matter of human discipline in response to divine guidance. It also constitutes the community of faith as a geopolitical entity with a violently coercive mandate. It is in the light of such qur'anic teachings on God, humankind, sin, salvation and spirituality that we truly understand its treatment of Jesus. It is not surprising, then, that the Qur'an repeatedly subverts Jesus' teachings, especially on humility as the path to true power. While the Qur'an calls Jesus the Messiah and honors him in other ways, he is merely a prophet, emphatically not the eternal Son of God. By its mix of flattering and unflattering attention to Jesus, the qur'anic author deftly marginalizes him while seeming to revere him. Hence we must question the Qur'an's implicit claim to honor Jesus. Two other issues on which we must dialogue with our Muslim friends are the Qur'an's (re)sacralization of violence and its apparent criticism that the biblical text has been seriously corrupted. But in all our dialogue, we must ensure that our response to the Qur'an is characterized by those two qualities that constitute it as truly Christian—grace and truth.

*T*o respond Christianly to the Qur'an, we must read it in a manner that is faithful to its historical and narrative context and view its presentation of Jesus within its larger worldview. But as we do so, we must never forget that this scripture is treasured by Muslims the world over, women and men who believe their eternal destiny hangs on their response to God's word. This means we must be as gracious as we are truthful in addressing our concerns about the Qur'an.[1] Though that endeavor is today fraught with many perils, it is nevertheless eminently worthwhile. Indeed, I believe it is the very least we can offer our Muslim brothers and sisters.

Qur'anic Context

To make sense of the Qur'an, we must approach it with some grasp of its context—its cultural background, its milieu and its narrative. Even though this is highly disputed today, everyone approaches the Qur'an with a working hypothesis about its origins. Two common approaches are fully to accept or reject the traditional story. While Muslims are taught to accept it unquestioningly, Westerners can be equally unthinking in rejecting tradition, since the historical method prejudices us against tradition. That the hadith literature is of such uncertain value fits hand-in-glove with that false assumption, prompting some to trash the hadith in toto. But since some of their historical data is clearly verifiable by early non-Muslim sources, we are wrong to dismiss all the hadith out of hand.

Another factor critical to our approach here—a factor we scholars rarely talk about—is our own personal agenda relative to the Muslim scripture. If we deeply desire peace, we may be tempted to view the Qur'an as a now tragically misunderstood call to "ecumenism," for example, and easily "find" that call simply by overhauling the narrative behind the Qur'an and the milieu in which it played out. Likewise, a fervent desire to see Muslims evangelized can skew a Christian's reading of the Qur'an. For us to hold honesty as the highest of scholarly virtues means that we must sift our motivations.

While every scholar approaches the Qur'an with assumptions, some assumptions are more misleading than others. One signally unhelpful assumption is that

---

[1] While no serious consideration of the Qur'an can be complete if it sidesteps the Qur'an's truth claims, I believe we are far wiser to ask good questions here than make definitive "rulings." Even our questions may be hard for Muslims to hear. We can only hope that they will show the same generosity to us, asking us hard questions about the truth of our beliefs.

the later Muslim community somehow pressed the Qur'an into a far different service than its author intended, meaning that Islam's origins were radically different from those presented by tradition. Another is that the Qur'an addresses biblical topics as part of an extended dialogue with Christians and should be viewed through a biblically shaped lens. On the other hand, Arabia was not an island, insulated from the rest of the region: stories were typically "traded" along with goods, religion was one of Arabia's hottest topics, and the biblical traditions offered the only real counterstories to paganism. Hence we can assume that Mecca's pagans would have been familiar with some biblical narratives. As for the elliptical style of the Qur'an's prophetic narratives, it says as much about Muhammad's style of messianic leadership as about his milieu.

We should not accept the traditional origins narrative and qur'anic interpretation uncritically any more than we should reject it uncritically. The Qur'an originated within the flow of a Middle Eastern religious discourse rich with Jewish and Christian texts near the start of the seventh century. The Qur'an clearly echoes this rich and varied, mainly noncanonical Judeo-Christian literature, demonstrating that Muhammad was strongly inclined toward an eclectic spirituality. The Qur'an provides ample internal evidence that its milieu was pagan, though pagan Arabia was in a sense "besieged" by the biblical faiths. But taking an approach of critical realism means that we do not dismiss tradition where early non-Muslim historical witnesses corroborate it. And that leads us at least to accept the following statements:

- Muhammad, a seventh-century trader, presented himself to his fellow Meccans as God's prophet.

- According to him, God was calling pagans, Christians and Jews alike to abandon their perversions of truth.

- He assumed theocratic rule in Yathrib and led his followers to conquer in God's name.

All of this background profoundly affects the way we interpret the Qur'an.

Qur'anic Worldview

A gracious response to the Qur'an begins with the recognition that Muslims and Christians share a common pursuit as fellow seekers after truth. We interpret the Qur'an in the light of its historical context and strive to avoid imposing external categories on it. We acknowledge both where the Qur'an converges with and where it diverges from biblical teaching. And we assess its truth claims on that basis.

The qur'anic worldview is undeniably similar to the biblical worldview in many respects. But despite the similarities, the two scriptures embody "quite different outlines, characters and structures,"[2] and we must understand the qur'anic Jesus against the backdrop of the qur'anic worldview—that is, against the Qur'an's primary teachings on God, humankind, salvation and spirituality, viewed in terms of how they both agree with and challenge their biblical equivalents.

Theology Compared and Contrasted

Asserting that there is only one God, peerless in the universe, the Qur'an claims that its source is the very God who authored the biblical scriptures. It portrays him as

- the creator and sustainer of all things;

- the Lord of worlds and Master of the Day of Doom; and

- unapproachably transcendent.

Being aware of every human being's thoughts and deeds, he stands ready to judge all. He tests humankind through life's circumstances and counts our moral choices of great import. We also find him presented as a deliverer, since he sends prophets to guide all who will heed them into the true path. But the one qur'anic metaphor for the divine-human relationship more basic than any other is that of master-servant, a central biblical metaphor also.

In both scriptures, morality is rooted in God's nature, since both mercy and justice characterize him. The Qur'an similarly asserts that God never wrongs anyone, always stands for righteousness and opposes evil, and will reward and punish accordingly. All of this points to a paradigm of reciprocity whereby God rewards in kind—blessing for good, cursing for evil. We see this also in the Qur'an's commitment to the general fixity of moral standards. But both the Qur'an and Bible point to the operation of another paradigm also, that of reversal, by which God permits good people to suffer and returns blessing for

---

[2]Charles J. Adams, "Islam and Christianity: The Opposition of Similarities," in *Logos Islamikos: Studia Islamica in Honorem Georgii Michaelis Wickens*, ed. Roger H. Savory and Dionisius A. Agius (Toronto: Pontifical Institute of Mediaeval Studies, 1984), 287.

evil. Reversal is what allows for God's providential care for all, his sending prophets with guidance and his willingness to forgive the guilty. It also explains the great contest that rages between believers and unbelievers.

In terms of theological contrasts, the Qur'an stresses divine transcendence far more than immanence, whereas the biblical writers do not allow either one to limit the other. The Bible balances God's sovereignty not just with human responsibility, as in the Qur'an, but also with God's faithful self-revelation and ethical holiness. Lacking the tension inherent in that, the Qur'an never raises the question of how a just God could allow evil or suffering. Neither does it lessen the tension by asserting with the Bible that, in Christ's crucifixion, God makes the very evil that causes suffering party to his decisive overthrow of evil. Nothing in the Qur'an correlates to this. Integral to the biblical emphasis on God's immanence is its use of four metaphors for divine-human intimacy that are either entirely absent from the Qur'an or greatly diminished: God as father, husband (or lover), friend and deliverer. But the most striking dissimilarity between the two scriptures' theology is that, biblically, God is not only master but eternally servant also, with each member of the Trinity serving the others. Hence in Christ's incarnation, God comes to earth himself to serve and to save his creatures, an idea unthinkable in the Qur'an. So while the qur'anic author would agree with the biblical writers that God is awesome in his majesty, that majesty has nothing to do with humility or his seeking the lost. Also in contrast to the Bible, the Qur'an views divine-human intimacy as one-sided, with only God knowing us truly. This means that, despite its pronounced theocentricity, the Qur'an keeps God always slightly "out of focus," while the Bible presents him in high definition, despite his being infinite mystery.

Further in contrast to biblical theology, the Qur'an presents God as

- loving only those who deserve his love;
- implicitly not choosing to reveal himself to us;
- not sacrificing himself to save his people; and
- not binding himself to show mercy to anyone.

Thus biblical theology's central ethical attribute, that of unconditional love, is virtually absent from the Qur'an—and with it the divine vulnerability of

God's longing for the return of rebel sinners. Neither does the Qur'an root God's ethical attributes in his essential moral holiness, as the ground of moral obligation. Nor is the anomaly of a just God's forgiving sinners even an issue in the Qur'an. Biblically, that anomaly is resolved by Jesus' redemption, in which God's holiness prompts him to bear the punishment we deserve. The most radical theological disjunction between the two scriptures relates to the concept of divine humility. Though that concept is inherent in all monotheism, the Qur'an never even comes close to acknowledging it out of deference to its pre-Islamic Arab concept of nobility. By contrast, the Bible tells us that God's majesty and nobility are most fully revealed in his humility—especially in Jesus' death for us.

Essentially, the New Testament and Qur'an both present new conceptions of the God of Abraham. In the case of the New Testament, God is freshly conceived around Messiah and Spirit,[3] while the Qur'an rejects that conception, presenting him as a divine master whose transcendence admits no intimacy at all on his people's part. The New Testament writers thus effectively say that the God of the Hebrews has spoken afresh, revealing himself in a fuller, three-personed way, while being no less exclusively one God. The qur'anic author likewise claims to bring a new revelation but rejects both the New Testament's conception of a triune God and also implicitly much of the Hebrew Bible's conception of him. Hence the Qur'an claims to be from the selfsame God as the Bible, which it in many respects denies, and that is clearly problematic.

Anthropology Compared and Contrasted

The Qur'an's story of our race begins with a creation myth echoing that of the Bible. In it God

- creates Adam out of clay, breathes life into him and creates his wife out of him;

- appoints him vicegerent and gives him knowledge no other creature has;

- establishes a covenant with humankind, promising his care and requiring submission; and

- grants humankind free access to all but one tree in the garden.

---

[3]N. T. Wright, "Israel in Pauline Theology" (lecture, Houston Baptist University, March 20, 2014), www.youtube.com/watch?v=W-EOnKJEZRg.

But there are major differences between the two scriptures' creation accounts too. The Qur'an gives humankind's creation extraterrestrial location and frames Adam's fall with the fall of Satan, implicitly making human history an extended postlude to the latter. This means we find creation plagued with evil from the start. Implicit in all of the Qur'an's positive theology, especially its covenant reciprocity, is the concept of divine-human likeness. But the Qur'an never refers to such analogy, and that can hardly be mere oversight given its discomfort with God's being likened to anything in creation. The Qur'an never details Adam's responsibilities as vicegerent and omits elements from the Genesis account pointing to humankind's intimacy with God. It also presents another, much darker story in which God blames Adam for arrogantly accepting the vicegerency, thus casting a pall of negativity over the entire human enterprise.

We find many similarities between the biblical and qur'anic accounts of humankind's fall:

- Satan determines to lead the human race astray.
- God warns Adam that violating his prohibition will result in punishment.
- Adam and Eve choose to follow Satan and deliberately disobey God.
- God expels them from the garden, but not without showing mercy.
- Adam and Eve's progeny share in their expulsion from the garden.
- The earth is turned into a war zone between the followers of God and Satan.

But the qur'anic and biblical stories of humankind's fall differ markedly also. In the qur'anic fall,

- Adam and Eve's choice is not specifically related to knowledge, nor its penalty to death;
- God's covering their nakedness involves no animal sacrifice;
- the earth is not said to be cursed due to Adam's sin;
- God grants Adam and Eve mercy only after they have repented; and
- Satan's historic defeat by a human champion is not predicted.

Both scriptures give abundant evidence of God's responding to human sin in terms of both covenant reciprocity and reversal. But while reversal is inherent in the deferral of judgment necessary for salvation, it allows a great deal of suffering and injustice in the interim. Because God is just, these two paradigms operate together, creating tension between his covenantal justice and his deferral of rewards, a tension that calls for resolution. Thus both scriptures evidence a similar dynamic in which human faith and obedience operate in a hostile environment.

But while the Bible presents humankind as hopelessly lost unless God opens our eyes to his truth, the Qur'an says we need only be shown the true path in order to follow it. This derives from the Qur'an's second, nonmythological picture of humankind, which

- views the tension between good and evil as primarily communal;

- roots good and evil in the supertribes of faith and unbelief;

- presents believers as seemingly naturally obedient although still needing to be exhorted; and

- portrays unbelievers as either needing only to hear to convert or else diabolical in their perversity.

The Qur'an then puts relatively little emphasis on the believer's having to struggle hard to overcome evil within himself. Rather, it mainly focuses on sins that mark the boundary between the *umma* and its enemies—adherents of false belief systems and pretenders to faith. By contrast, the Bible moves in the opposite direction, judging insiders more severely than outsiders on the basis of the former's increased light. It also views believers as no less inherently inclined to sin—or hopeless apart from Christ's redemption and the Spirit's application of it to their lives—than unbelievers. And this represents a major divergence between qur'anic and biblical anthropology.

Soteriology Compared and Contrasted

There are a number of important soteriological similarities between the two scriptures:

- The human problem and its solution are spiritual and moral.

- Divine mercy stands at the heart of soteriology, opening heaven's gate.

- God graciously extends his offer of salvation to humankind through his prophets.

- Humankind must repent of their sins, believe and live out their faith.

- Sins must be atoned for in some respect.

- Some suffering and some deaths play salvific roles.

- The path of salvation is laid out for individuals to follow within a community of faith.

- Salvation lies at the confluence of revelation, spirituality, community and the divine will.

On some of these points, however, the convergence is only slight, but this can result in major differences between biblical and qur'anic teaching. The most striking difference is that, while the Qur'an seems somewhat reserved about presenting God as the believer's deliverer, the Bible stresses God's saving activity, without which we are all hopelessly lost. So what is at the very heart of biblical theology is seriously marginalized in the Qur'an.

In contrast to the Bible, this leads the Qur'an to

- depict God's part in salvation as simply sending guidance and granting forgiveness;

- present salvation as synergistic, the combined work of God and the believer;

- give believers no real indication of salvation's modus operandi;

- say nothing of the believer's need of the Spirit to unite her with God; and

- make the believer's acceptance by God unknowable until the Last Day.

Salvation—atonement included—is something the believer accomplishes for herself by giving herself to "God's Cause" and doing good deeds prescribed by God through his prophet. Conversely, the biblical writers put it the other way around, with both spirituality and community flowing out of God's gracious work of salvation. Biblically, everything begins with God, whose redemptive work is also his greatest self-revelatory act. By embracing the biblical Christ, we are united with him and made right with God. By contrast, the Qur'an does not indicate why God grants or withholds forgiveness. Further, biblically believers please God solely on the basis of their present-tense salvation, united with Christ in his death, resurrection and ascension and adopted into God's family. Qur'anically, to claim such a relationship with God is deemed preposterous, since Jesus is only a prophet and believers can neither know God intimately nor have any assurance concerning their fate on the Last Day.

Hence qur'anic soteriology features nothing remotely like Christ's re-demptive sacrifice on behalf of sinners or union with him. It considers no work of God necessary to fully remedy Adam's fall by undoing evil on a struc-tural level. So just as the Qur'an implicitly subverts the biblical notion that human beings cannot save themselves, it also implicitly denies the biblical teaching that our salvation is found in God's revelation of himself in Jesus. Instead, it substitutes itself as God's perfect revelation for humanity.

Though the Bible and the Qur'an both speak of salvific suffering, they are very much at odds over its place, the Bible making it central—in Christ's Passion—the Qur'an making it peripheral, related primarily to believers' struggle in God's Cause. Paradoxically, the Bible brings the paradigms of reversal and reciprocity to their full realization and reconciliation in Christ's redemptive death. There good and evil find their fullest expression, as cursing and blessing were never more undeserved. In his death, Jesus shone the light of justice, mercy and hu-mility perfectly to the end and so vanquished the darkness of evil forever. Hence his victory was a case of the eschaton's breaking into the present as God trans-formed the paradigm of reversal from something provisional, *permitting* human salvation—and human evil too—into something perfect, *securing* salvation in evil's eternal undoing. Thus God began his work of putting our world to rights, and everyone united with Jesus has a share in that work.

The Qur'an, by contrast, has no place at all for such cosmic drama, viewing God's work of salvation in two stages: his sending prophets to convey his rev-elations and then, on the Last Day, his destroying all evildoers and saving deserving believers. So while the Qur'an never actually challenges the biblical view of salvation, it does so implicitly by saying nothing of a redeemer who bears humankind's sins or reveals the depths of God's love.

Spirituality Compared and Contrasted

Both the Bible and the Qur'an view human history as an age-long conflict pitting God against Satan. While individuals are responsible to God for their moral choices, believers are viewed not as isolated individuals but rather as part of a faith community with a God-given ethic and vision pertaining to the community's role in the great contest between faith and unbelief. Both scrip-tures view their message as universally applicable, with the community's ex-clusivity geared to its divine mandate to rule the whole earth.

The two scriptures differ sharply, however, in how that mandate works, given the nature of the faith community and the believer-unbeliever divide. Unlike the Bible, the Qur'an views the community of faith in supertribal terms as a geopolitical entity with a military force. It further views the confrontation between faith and unbelief as territorial and to a degree cultural also. By contrast, the New Testament views its community of faith, the church, as a voluntary association commissioned to proclaim its countercultural message in word and deed.[4] The good news of Jesus' kingdom rule produces a confrontation, even though that rule is spiritual, not geopolitical, in nature. For the church is thoroughly to permeate the world's nations and cultures with the gospel's goodness, love and truth.

Both the Qur'an and Bible take a holistic approach to spirituality since God's truth relates to all of life. Spirituality in both the Qur'an and Bible is expressed in

- belief, prayer, fasting, charity, etc., and devotion to God's cause in the world;

- virtues like honesty, generosity, faithfulness and self-discipline; and

- principles and rules governing marriage, business, politics, care for the poor, etc.

But despite the common ground between them, the two scriptures diverge widely on spirituality also. For example, while the Qur'an views prayer as a largely ritual act involving little real communication, the essence of the Bible's concept of prayer is real communication with God, who has made believers his friends in Christ. Qur'anically, the believer's primary motivation is fear of God and his punishment. Biblically, by contrast, since the believer is created to know God intimately, her life is an expression of her love for God and neighbor. Thus the believer's fear of God is evenly balanced by love for him.

Qur'anic spirituality's social dimension reflects Arab norms, though somewhat reformed. For example, the Qur'an forbids adoption, limits polygyny, advises men on how to discipline their wives and allows for easy divorce. By contrast, the New Testament permits adoption and holds to monogamy, mutual submission in marriage and a much more restricted approach to divorce. While qur'anic ethics tend strongly toward culture

---

[4]While the New Testament constitutes the church with qualified, ordained leadership, the Qur'an does not specify what the *umma*'s organization or leadership should be after Muhammad is gone.

specificity,[5] biblical ethics are centered in the universal rule of loving one's neighbor as oneself. Where the Bible makes that principle specific to culture, Christians generally accept the need to contextualize its applications, that process being guided by the ethical trajectories found in the Bible's millennia-long salvation history.

Finally, both the Bible and Qur'an seek to honor God in the political sphere, but they approach politics very differently. The Qur'an sanctions the *umma*'s use of military force to extend its hegemony and achieve its vision. By contrast, since the New Testament does not view the church in geopolitical terms, its vision involves participating in and renewing existing cultures and institutions rather than vying with empires for world domination. Believers are rather to triumph over evil in the world not by force of arms but by sacrificial love and their declaration and embodiment of truth. Being geopolitical in nature, the Muslim *umma*'s approach to religious pluralism is defined by the need to convert pagans and to subjugate other monotheistic communities, imposing sufficient legal strictures to ensure their ultimate demise. It also allows religious conversion only *into* but never *out of* the Muslim *umma*. By contrast, New Testament evangelism is completely noncoercive, marked by tolerance of other worldviews and openness to truth outside itself.

Qur'anic Jesus

In a word, the Qur'an presents Jesus as an exalted prophet, but no more. Both the Bible and Qur'an present God as addressing humankind through his prophets, some of their messages being preserved in authoritative scriptures. But while the biblical concept of revelation points to dual authorship, with God using the prophet's personality to express the prophet and himself (i.e., God) equally, the Qur'an sees verbal revelation exclusively in terms of dictation. Hence, when it says God taught Jesus the Injil, it means something radically different from the biblical idea that Jesus' teachings originated from his Father.

Like the Bible, the Qur'an honors Jesus in many respects:

- honoring his mother for her purity and faith and presenting him as virgin-born

- attributing sinlessness to him and associating him with John the Baptist, who honors him

[5]The sharia reflects this in its effort to establish specific moral norms for all of life and for all time.

- presenting him as God's devoted servant, a miracle worker and the Messiah

- describing him as a blessing, a mercy, near to God

- affirming that he will be highly honored in the hereafter

Furthermore, both scriptures clearly refer to Jesus' death and resurrection and affirm that God did not abandon him to his Jewish crucifiers: rather, his crucifiers merely fulfilled God's sovereign plan, though they were culpable for their evil.[6] In saying that Jesus ascended or was translated to heaven, the Qur'an must also imply his resurrection by God's power.

However, the Qur'an radically diverges from the Bible on Jesus in two basic ways: it both dehistoricizes and marginalizes him. In terms of the former, the Qur'an is far more interested in extrabiblical than biblical accounts of Jesus' life—for example, presenting him as a child miracle worker. Of Jesus' story as found in the Gospels, the Qur'an actually gives only two brief, barely recognizable snippets—in other words, nothing that would give its readers any clear sense of who he was or how his ministry played out. In keeping with that, the Qur'an calls Jesus the Messiah but gives the term no meaning whatsoever.

As already noted, the Qur'an presents Jesus as only God's messenger and emphatically not the Son of God, belief in which it repeatedly attacks as a form of polytheism. Since the Qur'an views the Creator-creature distinction as inviolable even by God, the mere fact that Jesus had a physical body means he cannot possibly be divine. Thus it leaves no room for either the New Testament's incarnation or the doctrine of the Trinity behind it. In keeping with that, the Qur'an stresses that Jesus had no power in himself to do miracles. While the Qur'an portrays him as being near to God, Jesus is clearly not the one in whose coming God has come near to us. So while the Qur'an honors him, it honors only its dehistoricized version of Jesus, a version radically reduced from that of the Bible. And even then, it honors him uneasily, stripping his story of virtually all the biblical narratives and teachings that convey his greatness and glory. Despite his honorifics, in fact, it often makes him look weak and unappealing, even freakish, and this seriously marginalizes him.

Further, the Qur'an does not view Jesus' death and resurrection as redemptive in the sense that Jesus died to bear the sins of the world and was

---

[6]Again, this is what the Qur'an says, despite the fact that Muslims took the Qur'an's dehistoricized Jesus and further dehistoricized him by making Q 4:157-58 a denial of his death.

raised to life as the beginning of God's new creation. In the Qur'an, Jesus' death is no more than that of a noble martyr for God's Cause.[7] Instead of viewing Jesus as God's definitive Word to humanity, the Qur'an reserves that honor for itself. Finally, it makes no mention of Jesus' second coming and would emphatically reject the notion that Jesus has been made the Lord of all creation by triumphing over evil on the cross. Instead, the Qur'an shows him summoned by God to defend himself against a truly damnable charge.

The Qur'an's ultimate purpose relative to Jesus is clearly to establish his unqualified endorsement of Muhammad as God's ultimate prophet. It thus includes very little biblical content on Jesus, and what it does include is adjusted to deny Jesus' centrality. Flatly rejecting Jesus' deity and obscuring his death and resurrection, it makes Abraham more central to God's plan of salvation for the world than Jesus and presents Muhammad and his scripture as the fulfillment of that plan. The Qur'an also entirely omits the redemptive narratives of Israel and the church, so integral to the biblical vision of God's restoration of his rule on earth.[8] In place of them, it substitutes a collage of quasi-biblical stories that allows it to claim the biblical heritage and identify itself, its prophet and its sacred shrine with the biblical God. Presenting Muhammad as God's ultimate prophet to whom all of creation must defer, the Qur'an boldly gives him the place the New Testament writers reserve for Jesus. By claiming to return to the purity of Abraham's piety, the Qur'an effectively sidelines Jesus and the Bible even while claiming their endorsement of Muhammad. And that is how it subverts the message of the Bible.

Issues Calling for Further Discussion

In view of all this, three matters call for our concerted attention in dialogue with Muslims. But dialogue is counterproductive if we do not engage in it in the right spirit, for its participants benefit from such joint exploration only to the degree that they engage in a healthy manner, their approach characterized by

---

[7]Except in Q 19:33, Jesus' resurrection is only implied. This is because it has no place in either the Qur'an's anti-Jewish polemic or its soteriology.

[8]As we have seen, the Qur'an makes free use of many biblical stories to assert the normativity of both Muhammad's revelations and prophetic experience. But to do so, it presents those stories apart from the metanarrative in which the biblical writers embedded them, such that God has no overarching plan for Israel and the church is utterly unremarked.

- a concern for truth and winning a friend more than "winning the argument";

- kindness of speech and a gentleness that listens well and is open to correction; and

- an honest acknowledgment of our differences, including underlying presuppositions.

We must not mistakenly equate surface similarities with actual agreement or mere positivity with assent. And we must not allow our desire to be gracious in dialogue to keep us from being honest in our shared pursuit of truth. With all that in mind, the three areas most urgently calling for further consideration are

- the Qur'an's implicit claim to honor Jesus highly;

- its remarriage of monotheism to geopolitical violence; and

- its seeming charge that the biblical text has been corrupted.

For the Christian, the primary issue must be the Qur'an's treatment of Jesus. I am not even thinking of its rejection of Jesus' deity, which is admittedly highly problematic from a biblical point of view. For argument's sake, let us suppose—as Muslims do—that Jesus is neither the Son of God nor the Savior of the world and is to be honored only as God's messenger. Apart from that, how much does the Qur'an truly honor Jesus? It devotes fewer than twenty-five verses to his adult ministry, teachings and death, in contrast to many times more that number to Moses.[9] In fact, it says so little about Jesus' adult ministry that Muslims get a picture of who he is only by generously supplementing it with data from the hadith. Further, the only qur'anic stories highlighting Jesus' greatness are from his childhood, and these undercut the honor they appear to give him by making him look strange, freakish even. The Qur'an includes just two narratives from Jesus' adult ministry and tells both in a way that makes Jesus appear weak in the presence of his disciples, who effectively lead their leader (Q 3:49-53; 5:111-15).[10] Finally, how much does the Qur'an truly honor Jesus by giving him empty honorifics—for example, calling him

---

[9]The contrast between the Qur'an and the New Testament is greater still, the latter devoting over 3,500 verses to Jesus' adult ministry, teaching, death, resurrection, ascension and return in power.

[10]Those stories reverse the picture all four Gospels give us: there Jesus' disciples need him and understand little without him, while in the Qur'an he needs them and is more ignorant than they.

Messiah but divesting the term of all its redemptive meanings and investing it with no other meanings? There is also the issue of the Qur'an's clear, albeit implicit, rejection of Jesus' approach to power.[11]

The world has never lacked for leaders who began in relative obscurity and weakness but nevertheless found a way to wrest power from the rich and mighty. So successful are some such men and women that they have played leading roles on the world stage. But regardless of the heights of power they have attained, they have all reached that place by the very same route—one that involves using whatever physical, spiritual, social and political means they can while engaging in relentless, though often hidden, self-promotion. As presented in the Bible, Jesus' humility utterly exposes such an egocentric approach. Jesus could easily have taken that far easier, self-promoting route.[12] But instead of finding ways to bend others' will to his own, he passionately invited his hearers to choose freedom while he remained true only to the will and character of his heavenly Father, even to the point of willingly dying a painful, humiliating death (Jn 4:34; 8:54-55). This revealed the glory of God's perfect humility and thus shined his light into the darkness of our world.

Biblically, that is why Jesus chose the lonely path he did. He knew he would never change the world by joining the myriad of others who do no better than to offer egocentric solutions to the egocentrism that wreaks such havoc in our world. But like no one before or since, Jesus exercised supreme authority with perfect humility. He is thus the only one to whom everyone everywhere must submit (Deut 18:18-19; Jn 6:14; Acts 3:22-23; 7:37-38).[13]

The Qur'an essentially gives that same role to Muhammad (e.g., Q 3:81), but detached from the nonviolence and humility essential to it, biblically

---

[11]That is, Jesus' approach as presented by the biblical Evangelists. Essentially, there exist in the world only four substantial early accounts of Jesus' life and teachings, all four being included in the New Testament. To substitute in place of their combined witness a disparate account of Jesus' life would require more early reliable sources or else a divine source, which is precisely what the Qur'an claims to be. But the manner in which it portrays Jesus—neither freely honoring him nor openly challenging the biblical witness to him—raises serious questions about its intentions. The Qur'an does this in its effort to sideline Jesus as being far less important than Muhammad while at the same time presenting him as one of Muhammad's chief backers.

[12]Jesus had another chance to take the broad path besides Satan's offer of this world's kingdoms. But when ecstatic crowds tried to force Jesus into being king, he evaded them till their fervor had abated: he knew their plans necessitated "sacred" violence he would have no part in (Jn 6:15).

[13]Numbers 12:3 says Moses was humbler than anyone else on the face of the earth. Jesus was also like Moses in that God spoke to him directly, with no intermediary (Deut 34:10-12; Jn 8:38).

understood. In so doing, the Qur'an implicitly rejects Jesus' approach to power as presented by the Bible. Even supposing the qur'anic author was right to do so, we are still left wondering why he does so without ever explicitly challenging either the Bible or Christians on that point.[14] When one considers how little of substance the Qur'an says about Jesus, how unflatteringly it sometimes presents him and how decisively it rejects his humble, nonviolent approach, it is difficult to understand the Muslim claim that the Qur'an highly honors Jesus.

The second issue, the Qur'an's marriage—or from a biblical standpoint, its remarriage—of monotheism to violence, flows directly from the first. Ignoring as irrelevant Jesus' humble disavowal of coercion, the Qur'an sanctions war in God's name. And the founder's modus operandi sets the course for his community in how it should fulfill its mission.[15] The Old Testament similarly presents God's people as a theocracy under Moses. But while most Jews in Jesus' day expected the Messiah to fulfill Israel's geopolitical dream by violently overthrowing its foes, Jesus took the concept of God's reign on earth in a radically different direction, one that altogether excluded sacred violence. Hence the Qur'an's Medinan suras essentially rejoin what Jesus had deliberately sundered. They also repurpose the Jews' national dream in its universal *umma*. Further, they constitute the life of faith as something governed by revealed laws and apostasy incurring capital punishment. But despite its geopolitical vision and militarism, the Old Testament, like the New Testament, makes love for God, not mere submission to him, the believer's primary obligation. And likewise the biblical Testaments' social ethics are driven by love for neighbor. But if the importance the Bible ascribes to love is greatly diminished by the Qur'an, it utterly omits the biblical motivation for that love, which, again, both biblical Testaments root in moral conformity to God's character, a notion quite alien to the Qur'an.

This recasting of biblical spirituality and revisioning of the New Testament concept of an apolitical, nonaggressive and tolerant faith community with its militant geopolitical *umma* raises a very important question. How can the Qur'an's claim to confirm the biblical scriptures be taken seriously when it

---

[14]Cf. 303-34 above.

[15]Such a union of religion and violence was clearly normative among both Jews and Christians during Muhammad's lifetime. But that was because Christianity had lost its way, authorizing Roman coercion and violence in Christ's name in exchange for Roman legitimacy and honor. It is thus very natural that the qur'anic author would make armed warfare central to his vision.

rejects much of their spirituality, authorizing violent aggression in coercing non-Muslims to submit to Muslim rule?

The Bible overwhelmingly promotes a politics of moral engagement consistent with God's approach to humankind in the Garden of Eden. There he gave them freedom of choice and granted them their choice, though completely contrary to his plan. While Israel's theocracy involved a politics of authority, that theocracy was relatively short-lived[16] and so cannot be said to define God's approach. Most importantly, biblically God upheld humankind's freedom of choice when he refused to impose his will on humankind in the Garden of Gethsemane. I refer to the decision on the part of the Son of God incarnate to accept his people's rejection of him, though it cost him his life (cf. Mt 26:53). Biblically, then, God's mission has never been to enforce submission on the world. Rather, it is to win our love and infuse his love into the world as believers graciously engage with its cultures morally, politically and in every other respect. That is what Jesus' kingdom is about. While the Qur'an does not openly reject this, it certainly does so implicitly.

When faced with so major a divergence between the approaches of the Bible and Qur'an, most Muslims argue that biblical falsification explains it all. Indeed, we might say that nearly all Muslim belief currently rests on that theory, almost universally accepted by Muslims. Thus it is only fair that we examine it, asking the following questions:

- How could the People of the Book have let their scripture become so thoroughly debased?

- What textual evidence supports this accusation?

- How does the Qur'an confirm the Bible when it clearly subverts so many of its teachings?

These questions are simply unavoidable. But having said that, we must not forget how difficult they are for Muslims. Accordingly, asking them demands real sensitivity on our part.

Like so many things, interfaith dialogue is fruitful only to the degree that we do it well. It is about engaging with others with whom we disagree on many points but in a manner that is constructive, respectful and, hopefully, mutually

---

[16]It lasted about three hundred years.

enriching. Only grace and humility can lead us to Rumi's judgment-free field where we truly listen well. But that does not mean ceasing to be who we are or forsaking truth. We must speak the truth even when it "seems most unsuitable to actual circumstances." For it is then that dialogue bears its sweetest fruit, however the conversation plays out. Responding with grace and truth sometimes means raising hard questions like those posed here. We cannot control the outcome of such dialogue, but justice and peace embrace only in the union of grace and truth (Ps 85:10). Our dialogue will be robust, passionate even, for the simple reason that truth's hour is always now. And biblically, all these things root it in the very character of God and make it a fitting expression of the kingdom Jesus established on earth.

Glossary

Ahmadi—a member of an apocalyptic Muslim sect that originated in nineteenth-century India; used as an adjective also

Allah—the Arabic word for God; used in pre-Islamic times by pagans of the High God as well as by Arabic speaking Jews and Christians from pre-Islamic times down to the present

dhimma—a treaty between a subjugated non-Muslim community and their Muslim conquerors

dhimmi—a non-Muslim (whose legal status depends on her *dhimma*) in the Muslim state

hadith—a report (originally transmitted by word of mouth) about the words and deeds of Muhammad and his Companions; plural also hadith; cf. *isnad*

hajj—pilgrimage to the holy sites in Mecca and its vicinity

henotheism—the worship of only one of a plurality of gods

Hijaz—the western Arabian region in which Mecca and Yathrib/Medina are located; as now, it was infertile land in the seventh century except for occasional oases

Hijazi—adjective form of Hijaz (see above)

hijra—the emigration from Mecca to Yathrib of Muhammad and his followers, marking the point at which his community attained sovereignty and thus the start of the Muslim calendar

Himyar—Late Antique kingdom in southwestern Arabia (Yemen) whose rulers adopted Judaism in the late fourth century; adjective form, Himyarite

Iblis—the devil, understood to mean "the Satan" (*al-shaytan*), whom the Qur'an depicts as refusing to bow before Adam and leading unbelievers in their opposition to God

Injil (*al-injil*)—the Christian scripture, which God gave to Jesus according to the Qur'an

Islam—literally, "submission"—qur'anically, submission to God, modeled primarily by Abraham—the word came to refer to the entire lifeway deriving from the Qur'an and practice of the prophet Muhammad

Islamic—the adjective of Islam (see above)

Islamist—member of a radical Muslim group (e.g., the Islamic State, Muslim Brotherhood) which seeks to establish sharia-based government and opposes Western secularism, often by violent means; used as an adjective also

Isma'ili—a member of a branch of Shi'ite Islam that was powerful in the tenth to twelfth centuries; used as an adjective also

isnad—a chain of authorities who transmitted a hadith or other early account (e.g., *D* heard from *C,* who heard from *B,* who heard from *A,* that Muhammad said or did *x*)

jahili—adjective form of *jahiliyya*

jahiliyya—the pre-Islamic period in Arabia that early Muslims characterized as barbaric or hedonistic; later Muslims interpreted it to mean "ignorant"; see also *jahili*

jihad—struggle in the cause of God, including military combat in God's name

jinn—supernatural beings (somewhere between angels and demons) who pre-Islamic Arabs believed inspired poets; the Qur'an generally associates them with evil

jizya—a head tax or poll tax levied on non-Muslims to signify their subjection to Muslim rule

Ka'ba—the cube-like pre-Islamic building in the center of the Meccan shrine that is the focal point in Muslim prayers and pilgrimage and that the Qur'an claims Abraham founded; see *qibla*

Late Antiquity—the period of transition in Europe and the Middle East from Classical Antiquity to the Middle Ages; it runs from the third century CE to the Muslim conquest; adjective form, Late Antique

Mazdaism—founded by Zarathustra (also called Zoroaster), this dualistic religious tradition (also called Zoroastrianism) was the official religion of the Sasanian Empire; adherents are called Mazdeans.

Mecca—(*Makka*) the Hijazi town in which the Kaʿba is located and Muhammad spent the early part of his prophetic career; adjective form, Meccan

Medina—(*Madina*, from *madinat al-nabi*, City of the Prophet) the Hijazi town, also called Yathrib, in which Muhammad spent the final decade of his prophetic career; adjective form, Medinan

Muhammadan—what specifically derives from or is specifically related to Muhammad; note that Muslims are offended when Muhammadan is used as a synonym of "Muslim" or "Islamic"

Muslim—a person who submits to God according to the Qur'an; hence an adherent of Islam; also used as an adjective equivalent to Islamic

myth—a narrative that tells us fundamental truths about the world and our place in it

qibla—the direction Muslims face in prayer; originally the Jerusalem temple site, but changed to the Kaʿba early in the Medinan period

Quraysh—Muhammad's tribe, which controlled Mecca and its Kaʿba

Ramadan—the month in which the Qur'an prescribes dawn-to-dusk, communal fasting

Sabians—the qur'anic term designating a religious community grouped with Jews and Christians and most likely to be identified with Manichaeans

salat—the prescribed five-times-daily Muslim prayer rite

Saracen—a medieval term for Arab

sawm—the Muslim practice of fasting, especially as required of Muslims during Ramadan *shahada*—the brief confession of faith or creed, profession of which effectively makes one a Muslim

sharia—the Muslim community's sacred law

Shiʿism—the smaller of Islam's two main branches, named after the "party" of Ali's supporters, who believed the Muslim community's leadership should have passed from Muhammad directly to Ali and his descendants (cf. Sunnism); adherent and adjective form, Shiʿite

shirk—literally, associating anyone or anything created with God in the sense of putting him/her/it on God's level; polytheism, any belief or practice implying a plurality of gods

sira—the biography of Muhammad

sunna—the normative practice of Muhammad and his Companions

Sunnism—the larger of Islam's two main branches, which accepts the legitimacy of the historic caliphate, beginning with Abu Bakr (cf. Shiʿism); named after the *sunna* of Islam's prophet; adherent and adjective form, Sunni

sura—a chapter of the Qur'an

tanzil—the "sending down" of the qur'anic (and other scriptural) messages to Muhammad from heaven

al-tawrat—the Torah, which God gave to Moses according to the Qur'an

umma—the (worldwide) community of Muslims

Yathrib—also called Medina, the town in which Muhammad implemented the qur'anic vision and from which he triumphed over the Meccans

al-zabur—the Psalms, which God gave to David according to the Qur'an

zakat—the practice of almsgiving as prescribed by the Qur'an and regulated by the sharia

Author Index

Abdel Haleem, M. A. S., 86, 98, 146-49, 192
Abou El-Fadl, Khaled M., 184, 190-91
Abraham, Binyamin, 155
Accad, Martin, 186, 262
ACW (A Common Word) Letter, 56, 180-82, 237
Adams, Charles J., 7, 308
Akhtar, Shabbir, 191-92, 234
Azad, Abul Kalam, 74
Al-Azmeh, Aziz, 19, 21, 34, 57
Ali, Muhammad, 218
Ali, Yusuf A., 74, 98
Alkier, Stefan, 6-7
Andrae, Tor, 123
Arberry, A. J., 75, 95, 98, 218, 240
Ayoub, Mahmoud, 111, 116, 134, 243-45, 248, 262
Azad, Abul Kalam, 74
Bakhtiar, Laleh, 248
Bakker, Dirk, 123
Baljon, J. M. S., 74
Bannister, Andrew G., 25, 84, 158
Basetti-Sani, Giulio, 19
al-Baydawi, Abd Allah, 244
Bell, Richard, 73, 153
Bellamy, James A., 143
Berkouwer, G. C., 92
Block, C. Jonn, 23, 36, 45-46, 48-49
de Blois, François, 45
Bodman, Whitney S., 84, 91, 123
Bonner, Michael, 186
Bottéro, Jean, 64, 80, 180
Boulatta, Issa J., 149
Boyd, Gregory, 267
Brodeur, Patrice C., 146
Brown, Rick, 43, 54, 276

Bruce, F. F., 267
Brueggemann, Walter, 179
Buber, Martin, 10
Burton, John, 160
Caird, G. B., 62
Calvert, John, 190
Cameron, Averil, 45, 217
Capes, David, 182, 301
Cassuto, Umberto, 89
Chelhod, J., 126
Chirri, Mohamad, 133
Coleson, Joseph, 89
Conn, Harvie, 89, 173
Cook, Michael, 2
Corduan, Winfried, 65
Cragg, Kenneth, 66, 75, 102, 167-68, 208
Crone, Patricia, 3, 5, 21
Crouch, Andy, 90, 195
Cumming, Joseph L., 244
Cuypers, Michel, 233
Donner, Fred M., 25, 48-49, 122-23, 131
Douthat, Ross, 238
Dundes, Alan, 25
Eco, Umberto, 6
Eddy, Paul Rhodes, 267
Eliade, Mircea, 112
Eriugena, John Scotus, 131
al-Faruqi, Ismail Ragi, 63, 69, 128
Ferguson, Sinclair B., 129
Finster, Barbara, 28
Firestone, Reuven, 38, 189, 191
Fisher, Greg, 30
Forsyth, P. T., 76
Fowden, Garth, 29
Frame, John M., 55
Friedmann, Yohanan, 188, 197, 199-200
Geiger, Abraham, 86
al-Ghazali, Abu Hamid, 127, 244

Ghazi bin Muhammad, Prince of Jordan, 180
Geiger, Abraham, 86
Gilliot, Claude, 150
Goldingay, John, 296-97
Goldziher, Ignác, 33, 48, 261
Graham, William A., 26, 157
Griffith, Sidney H., 38, 41-42, 45, 153, 258, 261, 266, 276
von Grunebaum, Gustave E., 99, 108, 130
Guillaume, Alfred, 16, 54
Haddad, Yvonne Y., 209
Hamilton, Victor P., 89
Hawting, G. R., 20, 24
Hengel, Martin, 242
Herodotus, 22
Horovitz, Josef, 153
Hourani, G. F., 156
Howard-Johnston, J. D., 30
Hoyland, Robert G., 21-23, 30-32, 36, 46, 48-49, 190, 288
Ibn Hisham, Abd al-Malik, 16, 230
Ibn Ishaq, Muhammad, 16, 230
Ibn Kathir, 243, 262
Ikhwan al-Safa, 244
Ishoʿyahb III of Adiabene, 22, 48-49
Izutsu, Toshihiko, 31, 33, 59-60, 67-68, 80, 87, 94, 102, 124, 126, 156-57, 242, 244
Jacob, Bishop of Edessa, 23
Jeffery, Arthur, 42, 208, 252
Jeremias, Joachim, 297
John of Damascus, 48
Jones, Alan, 10, 98, 218-19, 241
Kaltner, John, 59, 144, 146, 214, 219, 226
Karl-Heinz, Ohlig, 19
Kateregga, Badru, 128
Keller, Tim, 137

Kelly, Thomas R., 138
Kennedy, Hugh, 190
Kermani, Navid, 30
Khalidi, Tarif, 247-48
Khan, Mohsin, 86
Kirby, Peter E., 232
al-Kirmani, Hamid al-Din, 68
Kline, Meredith G., 89-90, 115
Kropp, Manfred, 42
Lawson, Todd, 241-42, 244
Leeming, David Adams, 54
Lodahl, Michael E., 38, 159
Long, V. Philips, 20
Longman, Tremper, III, 20, 193
Luxenberg, Christoph, 19
MacDonald, D. B., 105
MacLean, W. Paul, 4
Madelung, W., 150
Madigan, Daniel A., 155, 157, 168-69, 265
Marshall, David, 9, 74-75, 153, 190, 269-70
Mawdudi, Abul A'la, 174, 190
McAuliffe, Jane Dammen, 138, 258
McCabe, Herbert, 255
McKnight, Scot, 178
Montgomery, James, 172
Moore, Sebastian, 171
Morey, Robert, 54
Mourad, Suleiman E., 248
Movsesian, Mark, 197-200
Moyise, Steve, 160
Murray, Abdu H., 262, 266
Murray, John, 130
Nasr, Seyyed Hossein, 180
Nebes, Norbert, 47
Neuwirth, Angelika, 1-3, 40-42, 84, 91, 99
Nickel, Gordon, 186, 188-89, 262, 265-69
Nolan, Kenneth, 245
O'Shaughnessy, Thomas, 86
Paret, Rudi, 153

Parrinder, Geoffrey, 19, 45, 208, 211, 213, 217, 230, 241, 248
Peirce, Charles Sanders, 7
Peterson, Eugene, 171
Pickthall, Mohammed Marmaduke, 98
Piper, John, 56
Popp, Volker, 19
Porter, James, 30
Powers, David S., 150
Provan, Iain, 20, 63-64, 91, 127, 151
Qaribullah, Hasan, 249
al-Qurtubi, Abu Abdullah, 244
Qutb, Sayyid, 240, 245
Rahbar, Daud, 60, 74-75
Rahman, Fazlur, 60, 74, 93-94, 127
al-Rassi, al-Qasim ibn Ibrahim, 244
Razi, Muhammad ibn Zakariyya, 149, 213, 244
Reeves, John C., 86
Reeves, Rodney, 182, 301
Renard, John, 165, 167, 169
Reynolds, Gabriel Said, 41, 243, 245, 265, 268-69
Richards, E. Randolph, 182, 301
Ricoeur, Paul, 3, 98
Ridda, Rashid, 245
Rippin, Andrew, 21, 47-48, 196
Robertson, Pat, 54
Robinson, Neal, 22, 246, 250-52
Rodinson, Maxime, 21
Rumi, Jalal al-Din, vii, xiii, 323
Saeed, Abdullah, 200, 262, 267
Saeed, Hassan, 200
Sanneh, Lamin O., 137, 139-40
Satinover, Jeffrey, 192
Schippers, Arie, 155
Schirrmacher, Christine, 78
Schoeler, Gregor, 21-22
Schweitzer, Albert, vii, xii

Shaban, M. A., 190
Shah-Kazemi, Reza, 139
Sharon, Moshe, 44
Shenk, David W., 128
Sibbes, Richard, 130
Sinai, Nicolai, 155
Small, Keith E., 24-25
Smith, Jane I., 209
Smith, Wilfred Cantwell, 4, 168, 186
Sophronious, Patriarch of Jerusalem, 22
Stackhouse, John G., Jr., 195
Stewart, Devin J., 282
Stott, John, 76
Stowasser, Barbara Freyer, 209
Swanson, Mark N., 241
al-Tabari, Muhammad ibn Jarir, 23, 244, 250
Totolli, Roberto, 143
Van Bladel, Kevin, 41
Van Til, Cornelius, 68
Vanier, Jean, 137
Vasalou, Sophia, 149
Volf, Miroslav, 74, 237
Von Denffer, Ahmad, 275
Walker, Paul E., 150
Waltke, Bruce, 112
Wansbrough, John, 19-20
Watt, W. Montgomery, 73, 126, 230, 261
Webb, William J., 173
Wenham, David, 266
Wensinck, A. J., 150
Wheeler, Brandon M., 145
Wild, Stefan, 155-56
Wilde, Claire, 138
Wilson, R. McL., 209-10, 232
Witzum, Joseph, 159
Wright, N. T., 5, 8, 92, 236, 238, 266, 299, 310
Zahniser, A. H. Mathias, 241, 243, 246-48, 255

Subject Index

Abraham (*Ibrahim*)
  qur'anic, 126, 141-47, 149, 155, 159, 253
  biblical, 151
abrogation in Muslim theology, 159-60
ACW Letter. *See* Common Word initiative
Adam, biblical
  creation of, 89-93
  fall of, 108-12
  image of God in, 91-93
  vicegeral mandate of, 89
  See also Adam, qur'anic
Adam, qur'anic
  as vicegerent, 67, 83, 86-91, 93-95, 99-100, 107, 109-10, 114, 250, 284, 310-11
  creation of, 83-86
  fall of, 97-111
  minority position on, 93-95
  missing image of God in, 91-92
  mythological stature of, 98-108
  See also Adam, biblical
adoption in Qur'an, 18, 176, 315
angel, 31, 85-87, 106, 114, 153, 157, 166, 209, 211-14, 216, 229, 238, 250-51
animism, 31, 283
anthropology
  qur'anic, 120-21, 126-28
  biblical, 91-93, 128-30, 135-37
apocalypticism, jahili, 33-34, 38
apostasy, law of, 198-200
  biblical approach to, 200-201
assassination. *See* blasphemy
atonement
  in Bible, 76-78

in Qur'an, 71, 77-78, 126, 299, 313
Bible. *See* Abraham; Adam; apostasy; blasphemy; covenant; creeds; David; divorce; ethics, biblical; friendship with God; Holy Spirit; Ishmael; Jesus; John the Baptist; Joseph; marriage; Moses; pluralism; prayer; prophets; revelation; salvation; text, biblical *and* vicegerency
blasphemy
  in Bible, 201
  in Islam, 197, 200, 203, 274
booty, 2, 17, 23, 174-75, 286
breath (*ruh*), 86, 214
Brotherhood, Muslim, 190, 240, 245
Byzantines, 28-30, 43, 47, 190, 193, 236, 258-59, 269-70, 286, 32
  martyrs promised paradise, 29-30, 264
  warfare, 29-30, 264, 321
  See also War of 602–628
Cause of God (*sabil Allah*), 1, 17, 115, 121-22, 124-27, 133, 135, 139, 153, 165, 185, 187-88, 190-92, 226, 234, 245, 254, 263, 265, 286-87, 313-15, 318
  sacralized violence in, 154, 185, 187-91, 287
  warfare for, 2, 17, 188-91
Christianity
  in Arabia, 16, 22, 25, 28-29, 31, 33-34, 81, 227-28
  during or after the conquest, 22, 24-25, 196, 198, 231, 256
  in hadith, 24

in Palestine-Syria, 41
  in Qur'an, 3, 37-39, 43-49, 77, 81, 134-35, 134, 139, 243, 254, 282-83, 321
  See also Byzantines *and* Christians
Christians, 2-3, 23, 45, 127, 184, 216-22, 267, 272, 274, 303, 307
  in early and middle Medinan suras, 271-73
  identity of *nasara* in Qur'an, 258-60
  in late Medinan suras, 273-75
  in Meccan suras, 269-70
  See also Byzantines *and* Christianity
chronology, *see* Qur'an *and* Muhammad
coercion in Islam, 136, 181, 184, 190, 195-97, 199, 286, 305
  See also Jesus, biblical, on wordly power and coercion
Common Word initiative, 56, 180-82, 237
community
  Christian (church), 78, 131, 135-38, 145, 152, 154, 159, 200-1, 236, 293, 298, 315-16
  Muslim (umma), 2, 17, 21, 37, 46, 61, 76, 98, 119, 121-25, 127-28, 132-36, 139, 143, 146, 154, 170, 174, 187-91, 203, 244, 264, 270, 286, 315-16, 321
concubinage, 174-75
  See also marriage
conquest, Muslim, 18, 22-24, 34, 36-37, 121, 131, 154, 184-85,

187, 189-91, 196, 256, 286-88, 307
  in Old Testament, 295, 322
covenant, in Bible, 65, 68, 78, 80, 110-11, 117, 125, 130, 134, 143-45, 161, 214, 292, 300, 312
covenant, in Qur'an, 8, 58, 67, 72, 85-88, 91, 93-95, 98, 100-101, 107, 117, 125, 128, 144, 243, 272, 310-12
  Abrahamic covenant omitted by Qur'an, 144-45
  of ʿUmar, 196
creeds
  biblical, 165, 170
  qur'anic, 165-66
David (Dawud)
  biblical, 151, 201, 221, 292, 292
  qur'anic, 149, 155, 159, 229, 285
dhimmi. See treaty-protected monotheists
dialogue, Muslim-Christian, xii-xiii, 6, 9
  grace and truth in, 4, 9-11
  Muslim protectionism and, 10-11
  the need to address core difference in, 9
  peace and, 10
  truth claims and, 8
divine attributes, biblical
  holiness, 76-77
  humility, 79-80, 299-302
  love, 65, 68, 75, 291-92, 300, 309, 314
  scandalous grace, 235, 284, 295-98
  unity, 65-66, 77, 221
  See also divine attributes, qur'anic; God; Jesus, biblical *and* Trinity
divine attributes, qur'anic
  justice, 72
  love, 55, 72, 74-75, 179-82
  mercy, 74, 298-99
  nobility (related to arrogance), 62, 80-81, 283, 310
  sovereignty in Qur'an, 60

  See also divine attributes, biblical *and* God
divorce
  in Bible, 177
  in Qur'an, 18, 175-77, 236, 315
early testimony on Islam, 22-24
  Christian, 48-49
ethics, biblical
  of Decalogue, 92, 161, 173, 178-79, 181
  diachronic trajectories in, 173
  loving enemies, 235, 297
  loving God, 178-80, 321
  loving neighbor, 178, 181-82, 194, 201, 203, 234, 316
  See also apostasy; blasphemy; divorce; ethics, qur'anic; Jesus, biblical; marriage; pluralism; spirituality *and* warfare
ethics, qur'anic, chapters 12-13
  defense of *umma*'s political power, 203
  external emphasis, 202
  fear-motivated, 285, 315
  on forgiving others, 182
  love for enemies not commanded, 181
  loving God in, 179-81, 285
  loving others in, 181-82
  loyalty, as supreme requirement, 124-25, 179-80, 284-86
  as reflected in theology, 71-81
  rejection of pagan values, 202
  timelessness of, 3, 173
  "watershed sins" in Qur'an, 121-24, 202, 312
  See also abrogation; ethics, biblical; Qur'an *and* spirituality
Ethiopia, 16, 28-29, 31, 36, 43, 45-47, 286
fast, *see* Ramadan
Fate, *see jahili*
Fire, hell, 61, 248

friendship with God
  in Bible, 290-94
  in Qur'an, 294-95
Gabriel (*Jibril*), 15, 86, 153, 157, 209, 210-11, 214
  holy spirit, 214, 233
Garden
  of creation, 83, 85-87, 91, 95, 97, 99-100, 104-7, 120, 125, 248, 310-11
  in Genesis, 89-90, 101, 322
  of hereafter, 112, 117
God
  biblical metaphors for, 62-63, 300
  identity of Allah, 54
  jahili God, 32, 57, 62, 64, 80-81, 282-83
  qur'anic in relation to biblical God, 54-57
  qur'anic metaphors for, 57-63
  See also Cause of God; divine attributes; Jesus, biblical *and* Trinity
Gospel of Barnabas, 261
hadith, 5, 18-21, 23-25, 42, 46-49, 86, 105, 149, 157, 172, 176, 180-81, 184-85, 191, 199-200, 203, 237
  and Arab norms, 18
  basic agreement of, 21-22
  on the biblical text, 266, 269
  historical value of, 24-25
  on Jesus' death, 244, 247, 249-53
  on Jews and Christians, 46
  oral origins of, 19, 21
  presence of Christian materials in, 47-48
  revisionist rejection of, 18-20, 306
hanif, 47-48, 145
Heraclius, 29-30, 135, 264
Hijaz, the
  as qur'anic context, 21-22, tribalism of, 28, 30-32, 124-26
  view of Jesus in Hijazi milieu, 32, 37-49, 207-8,

240-41, 254, 276
  See also jahili *and* jahiliyya
Himyar. *See* Yemen
historical knowledge, 20-21
Holy Spirit
  biblical, 65, 137, 221, 231,
    293
  qur'anic. *See* breath *and*
    Gabriel (*ruh*)
Hubal, 32, 54
Hypocrisy. *See* hypocrites *and*
  Jesus, biblical
hypocrites, in Qur'an, 17, 37, 93,
  121-22, 185, 188, 193, 203,
  234
  See also Jesus, biblical
Iblis, Satan, 84-87, 89-91, 95-96,
  98-107, 109-13, 116-17, 122-23,
  131, 188, 192, 209, 295, 311,
  314, 320
  biblical, 98, 110
idolatry. *See* Mecca, paganism
incarnation of Christ
  biblical, 65-66, 78-79, 92,
    118, 152, 154, 161, 219-20,
    292, 299, 300, 303, 309,
    322
  qur'anic omission of, 55, 81,
    141, 220, 317
Injil
  book allegedly given to
    Jesus, 260
  contents of, 263
  identity of, 264-67
  of Muslim polemics,
    260-62
  translation of the term, 267
interpretation of the Qur'an, 3-7
  critical realism in, 8
  ecumenical, 19, 23, 48-49,
    139, 306
  evangelical, 9, 20
  Muslim, 3-4, 8
  presuppositions in, 9
  See also Qur'an
Ishmael (*Isma'il*)
  biblical, 143-47
  qur'anic, 23, 126, 143-47,
    149, 159, 285
islam, meaning of, 83-84, 92,
  95-96, 167-68
Islam, my use of term, 3, 16

Islamic origins narrative, *see*
  origins
jahili, 53, 57-58, 60, 62-64, 71,
  77, 80-81, 94, 125
  concept of Fate, 32
  concept of morality, 124-25
  concept of nobility, 53, 62,
    71, 80, 94-95, 281, 283, 310
  hedonism, 31, 33, 58, 202,
    282
  High God, 60, 282-83
  perception of biblical
    religion, 32, 142
  polytheism, 32, 282-83, 285
  See also apocalypticism;
    Fate; God; *jahiliyya; and*
    poetry
jahiliyya, 33, 84, 88, 94
  See also jahili
Jerusalem, 17, 22-23, 77, 145,
  250, 285
Jesus, biblical
  on adultery, 234
  death and resurrection of,
    254-55
  on hypocrisy, 193, 203
  his love, 254-55, 266
  miracles of, 232-33, 237
  origins of, 211-12
  person, 220-22
  role as Messiah, 212-14,
    220-21
  second coming of, 255
  Son of God, 92, 220-21
  teachings of, 57, 224, 233-37
  wisdom of, 57, 180, 224, 237
  on worldly power and
    coercion, 135, 192-93,
    201, 297, 316, 321-22
  See also apostasy;
    blasphemy; divorce; God,
    Jesus (qur'anic);
    marriage; pluralism;
    Trinity *and* warfare
Jesus, qur'anic (*'Isa*), 7
  death, as martyr, 240-56
  denial of divine Sonship,
    44-46, 212, 216-19,
    272-74, 317, 319
  honorifics, 214-15
  marginalization of, 210-11,
    225-29

miracles of, 222, 232-33
  nobility of, 211, 215, 283
  omission of second coming,
    249-53, 255-56
  origins of, 208-10
  portrayed as weak, 225-28,
    232
  prediction of Muhammad,
    226, 230-32
  sinlessness of, 219, 222
  son of Mary, 211-13, 216,
    241, 247-48, 250, 259
  teachings of, 146, 229,
    230-32
  title of Messiah, 213-16, 221
  virgin birth, 208-9, 211, 215,
    217, 219, 222, 259, 316
  See also Hijaz *and* Jesus,
    biblical
Jews
  of Medina, 17-18, 24, 28-29,
    37, 42, 44, 47, 271
  See also Judaism *and* Yemen
jihad, ix, 111, 115, 120-21,
  183-92, 195-96, 203, 286
  jahada and *qatala*, 187-90
  massacre said to be in Injil,
    263
  militarization of *jihada*, 187
  Muslim resistance to
    qur'anic militarism, 191
jinn (spirit beings), 31, 85-86,
  142, 157, 285
John the Baptist (*Yahya*)
  biblical, 193
  qur'anic, 208-11
Joseph (biblical father of Jesus),
  omitted in Qur'an, 211
Joseph (*Yusuf*)
  biblical, 296
  qur'anic, 121, 153, 224
Judaism
  in Arabia, 25, 28-29, 31-34,
    38, 41, 43-44, 47, 81
  in Qur'an, 3, 43-46
Judeo-Christian lore in the
  Qur'an, 38, 41, 224, 307
  Alexander legend, 38, 41
  apocryphal literature, 210,
    232, 238
  "interpreted Bible," 38, 91, 159
  Seven sleepers legend, 38, 41

Ka'ba, 16, 18, 23, 32, 67, 136, 186-87, 259
    Abrahamic founding of, 144, 285
    purification of, 145
    See also Mecca
Manichaeans, 24, 139. See also Sabians
marriage
    in Bible, 176-77
    in Qur'an, 174-77
    qur'anic authorization of wife beating, 175-76
martyr
    immediate entrance to paradise, 30
    in military campaigns, 117, 191-92
    prophet as, 151
    qur'anic Jesus as, 245-46, 254, 318
Mary
    biblical, 111-12
    qur'anic (Maryam), 32, 45, 89, 208-17, 219-21, 228, 241, 243, 247-48, 250-51, 259
Mazdeans, 24, 29, 184, 197, 271
Mecca, 16-18, 22, 24, 31-32, 37, 43, 46, 121, 145-46, 165-67, 186-87, 196-97, 199, 203, 207, 217, 240, 259, 271, 273, 276-77, 283, 285, 307
    location of, 16, 22-23, 135
    paganism, idolatry, 16, 18, 20, 24, 143
    victory over, 17-18
    war against, 17-18
    See also apocalypticism; Hijaz; jahili; jahiliyya; Ka'ba and Muhammad
Medina (Yathrib), 3, 17-18, 22, 42-43, 46, 49, 61, 86, 123, 135, 139, 154, 166, 187, 191, 203, 225, 240, 273, 283, 285
    constitution of, 17
    See also Christians; Hijaz; Jews; Judaism and Muhammad
moderate Muslims, 36, 183-86, 190-91

monotheism
    biblical, 63, 283, 310
    divine-human analogy in, 66-68
    qur'anic, 3, 24, 26, 34, 63-64, 80-82, 172, 180, 221, 282-84, 310, 319, 321
monotheists, treaty-protected monotheists (dhimmi), 183, 197, 203
Moses (Musa)
    biblical, 110, 149, 151, 153, 161, 177, 201, 320-21
    qur'anic, 41, 144, 146, 155, 159, 224, 245, 253, 269, 285, 319
mosque, in communal life, 169
Muhammad,
    and 'Aisha, 17
    and Khadija, 16-17
    chronology of prophetic career, 20-21
    execution (or assassination) of enemies, 18, 197, 203, 274
    life of, 16-18, 154
    messianic leader, 40-41, 49, 158, 307
    moral character of, 16
    as moral example, 18, 175
    Night Journey of, 16, 24, 249
    prophetic call, 16, 191
    prophetic supremacy of, 143, 147-48, 222
    theocratic ruler in Medina, 17, 24, 34, 154, 307, 321
    See also hadith and Zayd
Muslim divisions and sects,
    Ahmadi, 241-42
    Isma'ili, 241-42
    Mu'tzila, 60, 150
    Shi'a, 93, 111, 150, 173, 244
    Sufi, 59, 68, 105, 154, 164, 180
    Sunni, 60, 105-6, 108, 172-73, 244
Muslim, my use of term, 3, 16
orality of Arabic culture, 24, 46, 224, 276
    See also hadith and Qur'an, oral-formulaic composition

origins narrative, Islamic, 5-6, 15-26, 36, 47-49, 307
    evangelical approaches to, 19-20
    and hijra (622 CE), 17
    and interpretation of Qur'an, 6
    Hijazi location of, 5-6
    polemical approach to, 19
    revisionist approaches to, 5, 19-20
    Western approaches to, 18-20
    See also Muhammad
Palestine, 18, 22-23, 29, 41, 44, 262
patriarchy in Qur'an, 163, 174-76, 285, 315
Paul's theology, 238
pilgrimage, 16, 18, 31-32, 145, 165-66, 283, 285
pluralism
    biblical approach to, 200-1
    qur'anic approach to, 195-98
    secular, 8, 11
    See also tolerance
polygyny, 174-75
prayer
    biblical concept of, 171-72
    direction of, 167, 285
    Muslim, 166-70
poetry, pre-Islamic 5, 19, 30, 124-25, 157
    authenticity of, 30
prophetic templates, in Qur'an and Bible, 152-54
prophets, biblical, 151-52, 195, 321-22
    See also prophetic templates and revelation
prophets, qur'anic, 142-44,
    humanness of, 148-51
    martyrdom of, 151
    peccability of, 149-51
    See also Abraham; Adam; David; Ishmael; Jesus; John the Baptist; Joseph; Moses; Muhammad; prophetic templates and revelation
Qur'an

as Arabic scripture, 282
Arabic style of, 282
authorship of, xii, 2
basic theological task of, 3,
    25-26
Christianization of, 4, 47,
    74-75, 180
chronology of, 3, 24
de-Christianization of
    Christian names, 259, 270
as history, 2
interpretation of, *see*
    interpretation
lack of narrative in, 156-59,
    318
milieu of, 3, 5-6, 15, 25, 37,
    39-43, 49, 177, 276,
    306-7
oral-formulaic composition,
    25, 84, 158
orality of, 1, 3, 84, 156-57
pragmatism of, 285
as recitation, 1-2, 16
truth claims of, 6, 8, 10-11,
    275-77, 288, 306
See also ethics, qur'anic;
    revelation; scripture *and*
    text
Ramadan, 165-66
rationalism, 19, 20
religion, qur'anic concept,
    183-84
    Islam's predicted triumph
        over other religions, 170,
        274
religious conversion in Islam, 31,
    125-26, 128, 136, 190, 196-97,
    237, 271, 273, 286, 316
revelation
    biblical concept of, 160-61
    qur'anic and divine
        self-revelation, 77-78
    qur'anic concept of, 156-60
    qur'anic signs of God, 59,
        61, 114-16, 148, 155
    See also scripture
revisionist approaches, *see*
    origins narrative
Sabians, 24, 139, 271

salvation
    in Bible, 128-31, 133-34,
        137-38
    in Qur'an, 124-28, 130-34
Sasanians, 18, 28-31, 36, 269
    See also Mazdeans *and*
        Sasanian-Byzantine War
Satanic verses, 64, 81, 150
scripture
    in Bible. *See* revelation
    homogenization of earlier
        scriptures, 146, 212, 232,
        264
    in Qur'an, 155-60
sharia, 160, 164, 172-73, 175-76,
    178, 184, 196, 198-200, 203,
    316
sin
    biblical concept of, 128-30
    qur'anic concept of, 121-26
slavery, 2, 22-23, 173-75, 179,
    198, 237, 285-86
spirit (*ruh*). *See* breath
spirituality, biblical, 170-71, 173,
    176-82, 192-95, 200-201
    See also ethics, biblical;
        Jesus, biblical *and*
        spirituality, qur'anic
spirituality, qur'anic, chapters
    12-13
    dimensions of, 164-65
    wholeness of, 165
    See also ethics, qur'anic *and*
        spirituality, biblical
text, biblical
    alleged corruption of,
        268-69
    authenticity of, 262, 266-67
    availability in Arabic, 276
    Muslim approach to,
        260-62, 264-69
    qur'anic approach to,
        140-41, 264-65
    See also hadith
text, qur'anic
    authenticity of, 24-25
theocracy
    biblical, 193, 195, 321-22
    qur'anic. *See* Muhammad

tolerance
    in Christianity. *See*
        pluralism
    in Islam, religious, 195-98
traditions. *See* hadith
tribalism, qur'anic, 124-126,
    277, 284, 286
    supertribal division in
        Qur'an, 125, 172, 202,
        235, 284, 315
    See also Hijaz
Trinity, the Christian doctrine
    of, 4, 44-46, 55-56, 64-66, 79,
    165, 217, 219, 221, 274, 303,
    309, 317
    See also Son of God
tritheism, 19, 45, 217
umma. See community, Muslim
usury, prohibition of, 172
vicegerency, 67, 85-91, 93-95,
    99-100, 107, 109, 114, 250,
    284, 310-11
    in Bible, 91, 109-10, 284,
        310-11
War of 602–628, Sasanian-
    Byzantine, 29-30, 32-33, 36,
    264
warfare
    New Testament, 135, 195
    Old Testament, 195
    qur'anic. *See* jihad *and*
        Cause of God
    See also Byzantines
women, in the Qur'an 89, 93,
    168-69, 172, 200, 286
    and dress, 173, 176
    See also apostasy;
        concubinage; divorce;
        marriage; patriarchy *and*
        polygyny
Yemen, 18, 27-31, 34, 41, 43, 44,
    46, 47, 189, 244, 270, 273
    Jewish-Christian conflict in,
        28-29, 34
Zayd, 18, 150, 176-77
Zechariah (*Zakariyya*)
    biblical, 238
    qur'anic, 208-10, 238

Scripture Index

OLD TESTAMENT

Genesis
1–2, 84
1–11, 89
1:9-31, 90
1:26-27, 91
1:26-29, 89
1:28-29, 89
1:31, 103
2:8-9, 101, 291
2:9, 101
2:16-17, 110
2:17, 101
2:19-20, 87, 89, 91
2:20, 89, 90
2:23, 89
2:25, 90, 103
3:7, 100, 101, 103
3:7-10, 104
3:7-11, 103
3:8, 90, 100, 291
3:10-13, 111
3:14-15, 111
3:15, 212
3:17, 110
3:17-19, 99
3:21, 111
3:21-24, 295
3:22, 101
5:1, 91
5:21-24, 90, 291
6:1–9:17, 295
6:5, 109
6:11-12, 109
6:12-21, 110
7:17-23, 110
9:6, 91
9:9-16, 65
11:1-9, 295

12:1-3, 146, 298, 300
12:3, 300
16:1-9, 146
16:7-14, 300
16:11-12, 146
17:18-21, 144
18, 291, 299
18:9-15, 291, 300
18:16-25, 110
18:22-33, 300
21:8-20, 145, 146
21:9-13, 146
21:9-21, 146
21:12, 143
21:12-17, 144
22:1-19, 296
22:8, 296
22:18, 146
28:10-17, 291
28:10-22, 64, 296
32:22-32, 64, 291, 296, 299
39:9, 300
50:20, 296

Exodus
5:2, 55
7:3, 60
13:21, 291
14:13-14, 300
19:3-6, 68
19:17, 38
20:1-6, 92
20:1-11, 179
20:3, 178
20:4-6, 178
20:12-17, 181
21:24, 140
22:18, 201
24:8, 111

25:8, 291
32:7-14, 291
32:13-14, 300
32:22, 300
33:11, 291
33:12-17, 291
40:34-35, 291

Leviticus
1, 295
3–7, 295
5:17, 108
11:44-45, 76, 234
17:10-16, 295
17:11, 77
19:2, 60, 76
19:18, 181
20:26, 76, 128
20:27, 201
24:14-16, 201

Numbers
2:1-34, 291
12:1-15, 201
12:3, 320
26:59, 211

Deuteronomy
5:11, 108
6:4, 41, 92, 178
6:5, 179, 180
7:7-11, 79
7:7-16, 68
7:9, 134
10:12, 179
10:12–11:32, 68
10:13, 72
10:15, 300
13, 201
18:15, 276

18:18-19, 320
20:10-15, 193
30:15-20, 88, 110
32:4, 134
32:8-14, 292
32:43, 87
34:10-12, 320

Joshua
7:10-15, 108

1 Samuel
1:11-13, 292
2:1-10, 292
13:14, 292

2 Samuel
12:1-14, 149
15–18, 201

2 Chronicles
6:1-42, 292
15:2, 72
20:7, 291
24:20, 72
26:5, 88
26:16, 88

Nehemiah
1:7, 300

Job
16:7-22, 300

Psalms
1, 263
2:1-3, 294
2:6-9, 193
8:5, 91
10, 300

18:25-27, 72

22:24, 300

37:11, 194

45:4, 79

50:5, 111

51:3, 108

51:14, 108

85:10, 323

106:7-9, 158

133:1-3, 9

138:6, 79

147:2-3, 300

Proverbs

1:20–9:18, 72

3:3-4, 72

3:33-35, 72

6:16, 179

9:10, 180

11:19, 110

Isaiah

2:1-4, 193

7:14, 212

9:6-7, 193

11:5, 134

11:6-9, 292

11:10, 144

32:3, 160

40:10-11, 193

41:8, 291

42:1-4, 193, 194

42:1-6, 144

42:2-3, 79, 138

42:7, 160

43:11, 300

43:25, 132

44:22, 132

45:21-22, 300

47:4, 300

49:1-6, 144

49:7, 134

52:10, 62

52:13–53:12, 79

53:1-12, 138

53:3, 81

53:3-10, 133

53:5-12, 254

53:7, 193

56:8, 296

57:15, 300

60:19-20, 293

61:3, 263

64:6, 109, 129

Jeremiah

8:21–9:1, 300

17:9, 108

31:31-34, 297

31:33, 293, 300

31:33-34, 78, 292

Ezekiel

18:1-30, 109

18:4, 134

18:4-31, 110

18:14-18, 134

18:23, 75

18:32, 75

28:13-16, 90

33:7-11, 110

37:27, 300

Hosea

2:23, 300

11:1-4, 79

11:1-8, 300

14:6, 263

Amos

1:1, 42

Micah

6:8, 79, 235

Habakkuk

2:14, 292

Zechariah

2:11, 144

8:8, 300

9:9-10, 193

Malachi

1:11, 144

NEW TESTAMENT

Matthew

1:18-24, 300

1:20-22, 220

2:1-12, 211

2:11, 220

2:13-18, 301

2:13-23, 211

2:19-23, 300

3:7-12, 193

4:8-10, 192

5:5, 194, 195

5:17-20, 234

5:21-30, 202, 234

5:27, 39

5:27-30, 234

5:31, 39

5:38-48, 235

5:44, 297

5:45, 73

5:48, 128, 234

6:1-18, 234

6:5-6, 171

6:9-13, 171

6:14-15, 130, 235

6:19-21, 229

7:5, 138

7:12, 10

7:18, 108

8:3, 301

9:1-8, 220

10:16, 138

10:34, 192

11:1-19, 193

11:19, 235, 292

12:36-37, 109

13:31-32, 263

13:31-33, 131

14:13-21, 232

14:22-33, 220

14:33, 303

15:1-20, 234

15:21-28, 237

15:32-39, 232

16:27, 193, 255

18:21-22, 297

18:21-35, 235

18:23-34, 182

19:3-9, 235

19:4-6, 177

19:6-9, 177

20:28, 254, 301

21:12-13, 193

21:12-17, 297

21:22, 171

22:36-38, 181

22:36-40, 179, 236

22:41-46, 221

23:1-36, 234

23:23, 235

25:21-46, 130

25:31-34, 131

25:31-46, 301

25:40, 137

26:14-75, 301

26:27-28, 111

26:28, 129, 297

26:39-46, 192

26:51-54, 192

26:52, 236

26:53, 297, 322

26:57–27:44, 301

28, 220

28:18-20, 131

Mark

1:40-45, 237

2:1-12, 237

3:29, 221

4:35-41, 237

5:6, 220

6:3, 212

6:31-44, 232

7:8-13, 235

8:1-9, 232

8:36, 193

10:20-23, 108

10:35-45, 297, 301

10:42-45, 301

10:46-52, 237

11:12-26, 229

12:29-33, 221

12:30, 180

14:24, 111

14:60-62, 220

Luke

1:30-35, 220

1:32, 212

1:46-55, 292

2:4-12, 220

2:8-38, 211

2:22-24, 300

2:35-38, 220

3:38, 92

4:19, 297

5:30-32, 292

6:27-35, 301

6:31-36, 235

6:35, 137

7:1-10, *237*
7:34, *235*
9:10-17, *232*
10:25-37, *10*
11:5-13, *171*
12:48, *56, 125*
13:34, *75*
14:15-24, *292, 301*
15:11-24, *179*
15:11-32, *57, 235, 297*
16:13, *138*
16:22-26, *134*
17:32, *158*
18:1-7, *171*
18:11-13, *235*
22:20, *129, 298*
22:36, *192*
22:37, *192*
22:37-38, *192*
22:47–23:43, *201*
22:49-51, *192*
23:34, *182, 229, 298*
24, *220*
24:26-27, *297*
24:36-52, *220*
24:45, *160*

John
1:1, *214*
1:1-3, *221*
1:1-18, *134*
1:3, *303*
1:3-4, *214*
1:12, *132*
1:14, *170*
1:17, *4*
1:18, *79*
2:1-11, *237*
2:14-16, *193*
3:16, *129, 133*
3:16-17, *75, 297*
3:36, *129*
4:1-42, *297*
4:14, *129*
4:34, *320*
5:23, *133*
5:24, *129, 132*
6:1-14, *237*
6:5-15, *232*
6:14, *320*
6:15, *320*
6:22-71, *233*
6:25-40, *227*

6:27, *129*
6:40, *129*
6:47, *129*
8:1-11, *297*
8:2-11, *301*
8:7, *108*
8:12, *234*
8:21-24, *110*
8:38, *320*
8:54-55, *320*
8:56-58, *220*
9:38, *220*
10:7-8, *234*
10:9-15, *130*
10:11, *62*
10:17-18, *81*
10:27-29, *130*
10:30-33, *220*
11:25, *234*
12:40, *109*
13–17, *297*
13:1-17, *79, 235, 301*
14, *231*
14:1, *231*
14:6, *134, 234, 255*
14:9, *79*
14:15-27, *293*
14:15–15:17, *293*
14:16-17, *231*
14:18, *231*
14:25, *231*
14:26, *231*
15, *293*
15:1-5, *263*
15:1-8, *130*
15:1-10, *129*
15:13, *134, 293*
15:22, *125*
15:26, *221*
17:3, *78, 221, 293*
17:14-19, *135*
18:1-11, *294*
18:36, *236*
18:36-38, *236*
20:17, *220*
20:28, *221*
21:15-17, *298*

Acts
1:8, *129, 231, 293*
1:11, *255*
2, *137*
2:16-21, *131*

2:23-24, *60*
2:23-26, *81*
2:24, *254*
3:17-19, *81*
3:18, *60*
3:22-23, *320*
3:22-24, *276*
4:8-13, *293*
4:12, *129*
4:23-31, *293*
7:37, *276*
7:37-38, *320*
8:32, *193*
10, *137*
10:1-48, *298*
10:9-16, *233*
11:27, *275*
13:1, *275*
13:27-30, *81*
17:23, *138*
17:23-31, *57*
17:27-28, *138*

Romans
1:18-21, *109*
1:18-23, *105, 160*
1:23, *201*
2:6, *109*
3:9-18, *108*
3:9-20, *109*
3:10-20, *128*
3:21–4:17, *129*
3:23-25, *129*
5–8, *109*
5:1, *129*
5:1-2, *130, 136*
5:1–8:39, *108*
5:6-8, *75, 134*
5:6-11, *130*
5:7-10, *179*
5:12-19, *110*
6:1-14, *129*
6:9, *255*
6:16-23, *110*
6:23, *110*
7, *152*
8:15, *132*
8:20-22, *110*
8:22-23, *131*
8:37, *136*
9:17-18, *60*
10:9, *170*
11:11-24, *298*

11:17-22, *152*
12:2, *135*
12:3-8, *131*
12:9, *129*
12:17-21, *201*
12:18, *9*
12:18-21, *136*
12:21, *131*
14:11-12, *109*
16:20, *112, 131*

1 Corinthians
1:9, *134*
1:26-31, *152*
3:4-14, *201*
3:8, *109*
3:9, *67*
4:4, *160*
4:13, *154*
5:5, *201*
5:7, *201*
5:9, *201*
5:9-13, *135*
5:11, *201*
5:13, *201*
6:19, *221*
6:19-20, *129*
8:4-6, *221*
10:6-11, *152*
10:14, *138*
11:23-25, *297*
12:3, *170*
15:17, *255*
15:20, *255*
15:21-22, *108*
15:24-25, *112, 131*
15:45, *109, 131*

2 Corinthians
4:4, *101, 109*
4:9-11, *154*
5:19, *254*
5:20, *293*
5:21, *255*
6:1, *293*
6:2, *134*
9:7, *179*
10:3-5, *192, 194*
10:4-5, *131*
12:9, *182*

Galatians
1:10, *234*

2:11-16, *152*
2:16, *129*
2:20, *131*
3:6, *39*
3:8, *39*
3:11-13, *39*
3:13, *255*
5:6, *130*
5:13-25, *293*
5:17, *122*
5:19-21, *201*
5:22-23, *130*
6:4-8, *109*
6:10, *10, 137*

Ephesians
1:4-5, *60*
1:7, *255*
1:15-23, *255*
1:17-23, *160*
2:6-7, *154*
2:8-9, *129*
2:11-16, *144*
2:14-22, *136*
4:1-8, *129*
4:4-6, *221*
4:7-16, *131*
4:11, *275*
5:21, *177*
5:21-33, *177*
5:22-33, *177*
6:12, *135*

Philippians
2:1-8, *79*
2:5-8, *221, 303*
2:5-11, *195, 213*
2:6-11, *170*
3:7-11, *293*
3:10, *154*

Colossians
1:15, *78, 92, 255*

1:15-20, *134*
1:16, *221*
1:16-17, *303*
1:21-23, *130*
1:23–2:3, *201*
2:9, *221*
2:15, *131, 254*
3:5, *138*
3:18-20, *177*
4:6, *298*

1 Thessalonians
5:15, *137*
5:17, *172*
5:24, *134*

2 Thessalonians
1:5-10, *193, 201*
2:1-3, *255*
2:8, *255*
3:14-15, *201*

1 Timothy
1:20, *201*
3:16, *170*
6:18, *137*

2 Timothy
4:1, *131*
4:7-8, *192*

Titus
2:13, *303*
3:4-6, *129*
3:10, *201*

Hebrews
1:1-3, *134*
1:6, *86*
1:6-8, *221*
1:8, *303*
2:10, *129*
2:14, *254*

3:11-13, *152*
3:13-14, *134*
4:14-16, *128*
4:15, *128*
7:16, *255*
8:1–10:18, *111*
8:10-12, *129*
9:8, *255*
9:11–10:14, *128*
9:27, *134*
10:10, *129*
10:22, *108*
11:11-12, *146*
11:17-19, *146, 296*
12:2, *129*
12:14, *9*
12:18-29, *88*

James
1:13, *60*
1:19-20, *136*
1:27, *237*
2:18-26, *202*
2:19, *55, 221*
2:23, *291*
4:1, *122*
4:6, *39*

1 Peter
1:3-4, *255*
1:24, *39*
2:17, *180*
2:21, *129, 136,
137*
2:22, *128*
3:15-16, *10*
3:18, *129, 254*
4:17, *56, 125*

2 Peter
3:9, *75*
3:9-13, *193*
3:13, *131*

1 John
1:9, *134*
2:2, *129*
2:15-17, *236*
3:14, *132*
4:2, *170*
4:4–5:5, *136*
4:9-10, *134*
4:19, *138, 180, 236*
5:4, *129*
5:12, *132*

Jude
5, *131*
6, *112*

Revelation
1:7, *221*
1:17, *255*
3:20, *293*
5:1-10, *193*
5:1-14, *221, 298*
5:5, *298*
5:6, *298*
5:11-14, *303*
11:15, *193*
11:17-18, *131*
12:11, *136*
13:8, *81*
19:6-9, *293*
19:11-16, *221, 255*
19:11-21, *193*
20:1-3, *112, 131*
20:7-10, *112, 131*
20:11-15, *110*
21:1-4, *78*
21:3-4, *293*
21:4-5, *298*
21:5, *255*
21:8, *201*
22:3-5, *293*

Finding the Textbook You Need

The IVP Academic Textbook Selector
is an online tool for instantly finding the IVP books
suitable for over 250 courses across 24 disciplines.

www.ivpress.com/academic/